# JOURNEYS IN HOLY LANDS

# JOURNEYS IN HOLY LANDS

## The Evolution of the Abraham-Ishmael Legends in Islamic Exegesis

Reuven Firestone



STATE UNIVERSITY OF NEW YORK PRESS

Published by
State University of New York Press, Albany



Printed in the United States of America



For information, address State University of New York
Press, State University Plaza, Albany, N.Y., 12246

Library of Congress Cataloging-in-Publication Data

Firestone, Reuven, 1952-
Journeys in holy lands : the evolution of the Abraham-Ishmael
legends in Islamic exegesis / Reuven Firestone.
p. cm.
Includes bibliographical references (p.
ISBN 0-7914-0331-9 (alk. paper). — ISBN 0-7914-0332-7 (pbk. :
alk. paper)
1. Abraham (Biblical patriarch) in the Koran. 2. Ishmael
(Biblical figure) in the Koran. 3. Koran—Criticism.
interpretation, etc.—History—Middle Ages, 600-1500. I. Title.
BP133.7.A27F57 1990
297'.12—dc20 90-9661
CIP

10 9 8 7 6 5 4 3 2 1

# Contents


Preface / vii

Introduction / ix

Transliterations / xiii

Abbreviations / xv

*Part One*
*Background* / *1*

1. Biblicists and Arabs / 3

2. The Nature of the Literature / 11

*Part Two*
*The Syrian Prologue* / *23*

3. Abraham's Emigration / 25

4. The Tyrant / 31

5. The Birth of Ishmael / 39

6. Beersheba / 48

7. The Angels Visit / 52

*Part Three*
*The Meccan Sequence / 61*

8. The Transfer to Mecca / 63

9. The Jurhum / 72

10. Abraham's Visits / 76

11. Building the Ka'ba / 80

12. The Pilgrimage / 94

*Part Four*
*The Sacrifice / 105*

13. Prelude to Sacrifice / 107

14. The Sacrificial Act / 116

15. The Redemption / 129

16. Isaac or Ishmael? / 135

Conclusion / 153

*Part Five*
*Appendices / 161*

1. The Exegetes and Their Sources / 163

2. Traditionists Naming Isaac or Ishmael as the Intended Sacrificial Victim / 170

Notes / 179

Selected Bibliography / 245

Index / 259

# Preface

This book would not have been possible without the help and encouragement of friends and colleagues. Professor William Brinner offered early guidance by helping me to wend my way through the maze of problems and issues inherent in the study of *Isrā'īliyyāt*, and continued to offer suggestions and comments throughout. Very helpful comments on parts of all of this work have been offered by Professors Gordon Newby, Marilyn Waldman, Steven Wasserstrom, Jacob Lassner, Robert McChesney, and Ross Brann. They alerted me to a number of errors and stylistic difficulties as well as questions regarding my interpretation of the material, thereby greatly strengthening the book. I am particularly indebted to Professor Bayly Winder, whose passing has been a tremendous loss for the study of the Middle East. And Professor F.E. Peters, who served in many respects as mentor throughout my studies at New York University and beyond, deserves special thanks for his encouragement and willingness to impart some of his tremendous creativity and incisive thinking. This book would have been unthinkable without the patience, support, and encouragement of my wife Ruth, whose own professional and family responsibilities made her support of this enterprise no simple matter.

# Introduction

Pre-Islamic Arabia and the first century or more of Islamicate history remain largely unknown even to specialists. Although fully within the period of recorded history of Late Antiquity and the early Middle Ages, the profound scarcity of contemporary documents renders our knowledge of early Islam extremely tenuous. Information that is available derives almost entirely from literary compilations that were assembled into their present form more than a century after the death of the Prophet, Muḥammad. It is generally accepted by modern scholars that many of these works preserve data that are considerably older, but they also agree that it is extremely difficult to separate the authentic older material from later accretions, insertions, or glosses, which often weave in anachronistic or tendentious information.

This study makes no claim to break the code of historicity in traditional Islamic literature, nor does it claim originality in regard to sources. The primary sources upon which the study is based are all published and available in the Islamic world or in the West. They were chosen as the sample of study partially for this very reason, for their easy availability points to the fact that they continue to be read and studied in today's Islamic world. The fact that the narratives found in sources dating from the early ninth to the fifteenth centuries continue to be published in the modern era shows that they have spoken and continue to speak to the Islamic community, from earliest times to the present.

This is a study of literature which is both oral and written. Although rendered in written form in our sources at least two centuries after the death of the Prophet Muḥammad, the traditions examined exhibit traits of both orality and literacy that suggest their existence in far earlier periods as well. Yet because of the lack of any kind of confirmed chronology, this work makes no claims to represent a strictly historical study. It is, rather, an attempt to put the issue of cross-cultural communication and religious influence in early Islam into perspective, based upon new approaches to intertextuality in the study of traditional religious narrative texts.

The issue of terminology is worthy of discussion in a work such as this, partially because it applies somewhat novel approaches to material or issues that are already familiar, and partially because of the lack of a universally accepted nomenclature. I begin simply with the common term "Bible," which for the purposes of this book refers to the Hebrew Bible (Old Testament). Because a major goal of this study is to seek out the intertextual environments within which Islamic exegetical material about biblical characters evolved, accurate nomenclature must be employed to clarify the nature of those environments. The largely *post*-biblical environment in which extant narratives on biblical themes evolved cannot therefore be accurately termed "biblical"; neither can the narratives themselves located in post-biblical literature, despite the fact that they are associated with biblical themes. The term "biblical" is reserved in this study to refer to material found within the canon of the Bible, and does not include the massive corpus of non-canonical or post-biblical literature based on biblical themes. The familiar term "Judeo-Christian" is also an inappropriate term, despite the fact that this study often refers to an environment of shared scripture between Jewish and Christian groups. Jews and Christians in Late Antiquity developed separate exegetical traditions based upon scripture, though they clearly were familiar with and shared aspects of each others' traditions as well. Despite the commonalities, each community professed differing ideologies, whether Jewish or Christian, and whether eventually determined to be orthodox or heterodox. These distinctions along with differences in self-perception eventuated in their separation into distinct groups that remained religiously separate. "Judeo-Christian" inaccurately implies agreement upon religious concepts derived from a common scripture. In truth, however, Judaism and Christianity have never shared the same view or interpretation of scripture. Even the quite different names employed by both groups, Hebrew Bible by Jews and Old Testament by Christians, points to quite different perspectives which render their readings of scripture to be significantly different. In order to dispel pre-conceived notions of a common exegetical tradition (though in many respects there are indeed real similarities), I refer to the shared scriptural environment of Jews and Christians as a "Biblicist" milieu.[1]

Our terminology for the various forms of prose narratives follows William Bascom.[2] *Legend* refers to prose narratives regarded in their host culture as true and set in an early period, though typically without a preponderance of supernatural phenomena. *Folktale* refers to prose narratives which are generally regarded as fiction, with or without supernatural phenomena. *Tradition* refers to any category of narrative prose that is passed on intergenerationally and usually orally. *Rendition* refers to an individual telling of a narrative, whether a tale, legend, or tradition. It could be unique or could represent one of many renditions of a tradition. *Version* refers to one of at least two different narrative traditions treating a single topic. A version may be composed of a dozen or more renditions, all fitting into the same basic approach to the topic. *Covariant* represents a rendition of a version which differs more from the paradigmatic telling than the average rendition but nevertheless remains similar enough in structure, content, or style to be included as part of the version. The covariant differs always in relation to its related tellings of the same version.

Finally, a word must be said here for scholars of Islam about the accuracy of Islamic traditions based on the reliability of their records of authentication *(asānīd)*, though a more detailed discussion ensues in the following chapters. This study does not analyze the records of authentication attached to traditions, but it does take note of the fact that traditions attributed to specific authorities tend to be quite consistent in content and style. Because of this relation, traditions tend to be organized here according to the earliest members of these records as well as according to topic, and particular versions are identified by their earliest attributed authority. I am less concerned with whether or not the attributed authorities actually related the traditions attributed to them than with the nearly universal recognition among the traditionists that they did. That recognition reflects, in my opinion, a sensitivity to the particulars of content *(matn)* in a tradition as well as its record of authentication *(isnād)*. Generally, therefore, I record the earliest authority listed when providing the sources for narratives examined in this study.

# Transliterations

The transliteration of Arabic words is according to the following alphabetical substitution:

ا –' (omitted at the beginning of a word)

| | | | |
|---|---|---|---|
| ب –b | ذ –dh | ط –ṭ | ل –l |
| ت –t | ر –r | ظ –ẓ | م –m |
| ث –th | ز –z | ع –' | ن –n |
| ج –j | س –s | غ –gh | ه –h |
| ح –ḥ | ش –sh | ف –f | و –w |
| خ –kh | ص –ṣ | ق –q | ي –y |
| د –d | ض –ḍ | ك –k | |

Dipthongs are written *ay* [ بَيْتٌ ] *aw* [ يَوْمٌ ]

The three short vowels are represented by *a* for the *fatḥah*, *i* for the *kasrah*, and *u* for the *ḍammah*.

The long vowels are represented by *ā* for the *alif*, *ū* for the *waw*, and *ī* for the *yā'*.

Final *hā'* is represented by *a* at the end of the word, and by *at* when in construct.

Full declension (*i'rāb*) is not employed in the transliterations.

The following system of annotation has been employed:

a. Qur'ān verses: Q.2:8: SOME PEOPLE SAY: WE BELIEVE IN GOD AND THE LAST DAY, BUT THEY DO NOT [TRULY] BELIEVE.
b. Transliteration (*with italics*).
c. Parenthetical comment or addition or substitution in translation [no italics].

# Abbreviations

| | |
|---|---|
| BR | *Bereshit Rabbah* |
| BT | *Babylonian Talmud* |
| EI1 | *Encyclopaedia of Islam* #1 (Leiden: Brill, 1913-1936) |
| EI2 | *Encyclopaedia of Islam* #2 (Leiden: E.J. Brill, 1960-) |
| EJ | *Encyclopedia Judaica* (Jerusalem: Keter, 1972) |
| Ex | Exodus |
| Deut | Deuteronomy |
| Gen | Genesis |
| IC | *Islamic Culture* |
| IQ | *Islamic Quarterly* |
| JAR | *Journal of the American Academy of Religion* |
| JBL | *Journal of Biblical Literature* |
| Lev | Leviticus |
| MW | *Moslem World/Muslim World* |
| MGWJ | *Monatsschrift fur die Geschichte und Wissenschaft des Judentums.* |
| Nu | Book of Numbers |
| PRE | *Pirkei d'Rabbi Eliezer* (Hebrew text) |
| PRE2 | Friedlander (transl.), *Pirke De Rabbi Eliezer* |
| Q | Qur'ān |
| REJ | *Revue Des Etudes Juives* |
| TJ1 | Targum Jonathan ("full" Palestinian Targum) |
| TJ2 | Fragmentary Palestinian Targum |
| + | Designates the tie between members of an *isnād* (i.e., 'Ikrima + Ibn 'Abbās = 'Ikrima received the tradition from Ibn 'Abbās) |

PART ONE

# Background

# Chapter 1

# BIBLICISTS AND ARABS

The ancient Israelites were keenly aware of their geographic, linguistic, and cultural kinship with Arab peoples, and they set forth a fascinating accounting for that affinity in the genealogical tables of the tenth chapter of Genesis. According to this anthropology, the great grandson of Noah's son Shem had two sons, among whose descendants a great portion of the world was divided. One, Joktan, was the progenitor of thirteen tribes, some with clear Arabic names, whose "... settlements extended from Mesha as far as Sephar, the hill country to the east" (Genesis 10:30). The other son, Peleg, is described in the following chapter as fathering the line that would result in Nahor, Terah, and finally, Abraham, the forefather of the Israelite people.[1].

The striking biblical consciousness of affinity between Israelites and Arabs is tempered, however, by its attempt to maintain a separation. Abraham's son Ishmael, who would father twelve Arabian tribal groupings living to the east of Canaan (Genesis 25:12-18), was forced to leave the patriarchal home in favor of his younger half-brother, Isaac (Genesis 21:9-21). When Abraham took a second wife after Sarah's death and fathered sons with Arabic names, he made certain to send them off eastward as well in order to remove any threat to Isaac's future destiny (Genesis 25:1-6). In the following generation, Esau, who took an Arab wife (Genesis 26:34), also moved to the east of the future Land of Israel. He and his clan dwelt in the land of Edom across the river Jordan (Genesis 31:4, chapter 36).[2]

Peoples with Arabic names or even identified specifically as Arabs in later biblical works such as Isaiah (13:20) and Jeremiah (3:2) continued to interact with the Israelites, although they are inevitably portrayed with little love lost. In the biblical book attributed to Nehemia, for example, an Arab named Geshem (rendered *gashmu* in Nehemia 6:6, with the nominative case ending still found in classical Arabic but lost to Hebrew) joined up with the enemies of Israel to oppose those who returned from Babylon to rebuild the Temple in Jerusalem (Neh. 2:19; 4:1; 6:1-6).

Jewish relations with Arabs continued during the Hellenistic and Roman periods. The Apocrypha refers to the Arab Nabataeans, who were powerful enough to repel two attacks by the Seleucid Syrians on their capital Petra in the late fourth century B.C.E., and whose powerful kingdom just across the Jordan River from Judea survived into the beginning of the second century C.E. The Jewish Hasmonean monarchy had good relations with the Nabataeans for a time, and as neighboring powers, they were in constant communication whether on friendly terms or not. Arabs continue to be mentioned in the Talmud (*Succah* 52b, *Ketubot* 36b, *Baba Metzi'a* 86a, b, *Kiddushin* 49b, etc.), where they are sometimes referred to as Ishmaelites.[3]

As may be inferred from the context of these biblical and post-biblical Jewish references, Arabs mentioned in these texts tended to be those who had moved away from the arid Arabian or Syrian wilderness and into the more settled areas of Canaan or Palestine (or today's Iraq, the Babylon of the Bible and Talmud). The process of migration and settlement from the steppe to the settled areas was an old custom practiced by Arabs from the earliest times.[4] In fact, virtually the entire record of Arab interaction with other peoples prior to the beginning of Islam is found not in Arabic sources, but in sources deriving from the peoples among whom they settled.

These documents account for the movement of Arab groups away from their areas of origin and into the more settled areas of the Fertile Crescent. But interaction between Biblicists[5] and Arabs also took place upon the soil of the Arabian Peninsula. Jewish communities existed in Arabia by the period of the destruction of the Second Temple in 70 C.E.[6] So, too, early Christian communities found a refuge from Roman persecution in the isolation of various Arabian desert regions, and later groups escaped the theological compulsion of the Byzantine Empire in the safety of the Arabian Peninsula.[7] Plenty of documentation exists to support the existence of viable Jewish and Christian communities in Arabia in the sixth century, the period immediately preceding the flowering of Islam.[8]

Jews lived in organized communities in the western central highlands of the Arabian Peninsula known as the Ḥijāz, and populated such settlements as Yathrib (Medina), Khaybar, Fadak, al-'Ulā, Taymā, Tabūk, and Wādī al-Qurrā, as well as various parts of South Arabia.[9] Significant Christian settlements could be found in South Arabia as well as in the northern areas bordering the empires of Byzantium and Persia, although small groups or individual Christian hermits are referred to by pre-Islamic Arabian poets as residing along caravan routes in much of the central Arabian Peninsula as well.[10] Both Jewish and Christian groups spoke the native languages of North or South Arabic and appear to have been deeply integrated into the language and culture if not the religious outlook of the non-Biblicist Arab communities.[11] For all intents and purposes, then, Jews and Christians living in the Arabian Peninsula were culturally and ethnically Arab.[12] The common assumption that all pre-Islamic Arabs were Pagan prior to the lifetime of Muḥammad is simply erroneous.

The various pre-Islamic Arabian tribal and religious populations were not isolated from one another, but enjoyed a great deal of mercantile, social, and cultural interaction. Concern for genealogical purity among the writers of later Islamicate works describing the tribal and social make-up of pre-Islamic Arabia tends to obscure the true heterogeneous nature of that society.[13] The evidence suggests a great deal of social intercourse among Jewish, Christian, and other Arabs in day-to-day activities as well as during the annual fairs.[14]

Non-orthodox Jewish or Christian groups certainly made their home in the Arabian Peninsula as well.[15] Outside the control of Byzantium and Persia, much of Arabia was a logical haven for heterodox groups seeking respite from the pressures and persecutions of either empire.[16] As the various groups living in Arabia interacted with one another over the decades and centuries, it could be safely assumed that in addition to the natural accretion and attrition of membership between groups, new groups or offshoots of established communities formed and developed hybrid ideas and traditions.[17] Certain well-known Arabs living before and during the lifetime of Muḥammad, for example, are considered to have been monotheists in their religious orientation but not clearly adherents of either Judaism or Christianity. Such figures as Zayd b. 'Amr, Umayyah b. Abī al-Ṣalt, Waraqah b. Nawfal, and Maslama (Musaylima) may have represented early syntheses of Jewish and/or Christian and indigenous Arabian religious traditions.[18]

The likelihood of non-Biblicist Arab monotheists living in the peninsula raises the question of exactly what types of religion were practiced by the so-called "pagan" Arabs, the majority population of the Arabian Peninsula. The Qur'ān scorns the practices of unbelievers *(kāfirūn)* and those pagans who assign "partners" to God *(mushrikūn)*, and provides some indirect information about pagan religious practice, which is, of course, given in a wholly negative light.[19] At the same time that it refers to the worship of false deities, however, the Qur'ān also refers to biblical characters as if both its Muslim and pagan audiences were thoroughly familiar with them.[20] In spite of the numerous qur'ānic references to Arab idolaters, any attempts to reconstruct the religious practices of pre-Islamic Arabs from the Qur'ān would be tenuous indeed, and very few early works describing pre-Islamic Arabian society are extant. To add to this difficulty, those sources that have survived tend to have been influenced by norms of historiography that obscure an objective accounting of pre-Islamic life.[21]

To summarize, it is simply not clear exactly what indigenous pre-Islamic Arabian religion(s) consisted of. Some sources stress a pantheon of gods and goddesses, while others describe astral systems.[22] Despite the many references to pre-Islamic Mecca in Islamicate literature, it is still not even clear whether the god known as Allah was considered a pan-Arabian deity or a local god whose worship expanded.[23] What appears most likely is that a variety of religious traditions were practiced by the majority of native Arabians who were not adherents of Biblicist religions. Religious traditions and practices differed between the Yemen, the Ḥijāz, and northern Arabia bordering on Byzantium and Persia. Religious ideologies undoubtedly varied from the fully pantheist to monotheist. When referring to Christian, Jewish, or pagan practice in pre-Islamic Arabia, then, one must take care not to prejudice the discussion with uninformed assumptions about the nature of these religions.

## BIBLICIST LEGENDS IN ARABIA

I have noted how interaction between Arabs and Biblicists in the Arabian Peninsula was not a new phenomenon during and following the lifetime of Muḥammad. At least during the period leading up to the genesis of Islam in the early seventh century if not earlier, Jewish and Christian groups were highly integrated into the fabric of pre-Islamic Arabia. They lived in mixed settlements and, indeed, even in tribes of mixed religious traditions.[24] It would be naive to assume that an orthodox form of Judaism or Christianity was practiced alongside pre-Islamic Arab paganism without one influencing the other.

When people trade with one another in societies where the anonymous department store or shopping mall has not yet overtaken the institution of the private vendor of goods, merchants and customers engage in social intercourse that far transcends the simple transfer of merchandise. This kind of trade involves interaction in which traders swap stories and anecdotes as well as goods. At the annual Arabian trading fairs, where diverse tribal units from broad geographic areas gathered, as well as during other occasions of intercommunal interaction, biblical stories would naturally be traded with local Arabian religious tales. The power or attributes of a universalist God might be described in response to the telling of the power of the local deity. And stories of Arabian heros or jinnis were undoubtedly compared to stories of biblical prophets, holy men, or miracle workers.

As a result, pre-Islamic Arabia contained a wide variety of religious traditions and phenomena, many of which derived from a Biblicist environment. The many references to biblical stories in the Qur'ān are perhaps the most convincing evidence that these or similar stories were known to non-Biblicist Arabs in Mecca and Medina even before the lifetime of Muḥammad.[25] I have previously noted that qur'ānic references to stories or characters found also in the Bible tend to assume that its listeners were already familiar with them. The Qur'ān also provides evidence for the notion that those who opposed Muḥammad in Mecca were familiar with stories of biblical figures before hearing the recitation of the qur'ānic revelations.[26] And a group of Meccan tribal groupings calling themselves *Hums* already associated themselves with Abraham by the year of Muḥammad's birth or before.[27]

As Islam came to dominate the Arabian Peninsula, much of pre-Islamic religious tradition died out or was eliminated. Some of the lore simply lost its inherent power and influence over the people. Divorced from the concrete reinforcement of an active religious cult, for example, legends informing the sanctity of a local religious shrine were soon forgotten. Other material devoted to themes unacceptable to the gradually less compromising Islamic monotheism were purposefully eliminated from the corpus of acceptable tradition.[28]

One result of the great changes brought about by Islamic domination of the Arabian Peninsula was that the once colorful fabric representing the diverse religio-cultural expressions of sixth and seventh century Arabia survived only as disjointed remnants. Some pre-Islamic legends survived through reinterpretation according to the developing religious standards of early Islam. But more often, certain bits and pieces of ancient tales survived as they were reworked into the legends, evolving to serve as foundations for the newly developing religious system. As noted above, one such source containing material bearing strong similarities to Biblicist and indigenous pre-Islamic tradition is the revelation known as the Qur'ān.

## THE BIBLE AND THE QUR'ĀN

The Qur'ān, sacred scripture to hundreds of millions of Muslims throughout the world, is a complex literary work composed of laws, sermons, and theological doctrine. Though unique in its entirety, a great deal of material contained in it is quite reminiscent of material located also in the Bible. This includes a variety of laws, customs, and religious concepts found in similar form in both scriptures. Just as striking, important figures assumed by most Western readers to represent exclusively biblical characters can be found throughout the Qur'ān. Such important figures as Adam, Noah, Abraham, Moses, Solomon, Job, John the Baptist, Jesus, and Mary occur quite commonly, amd major personages such as Abraham and Moses are mentioned hundreds of times in tens of chapters. These "biblical" figures, however, tend to assume somewhat different characters and roles in the Qur'ān, though they would be easily recognizable to anyone familiar with the Bible.

The affinity between the Qur'ān and the Bible was clear to Jews, Christians, and Muslims since the very beginning of the Prophet Muḥammad's religious mission in the early seventh century. Attempts to explain or reconcile the differences have been offered from this period onward and continue to be suggested to this day. Jews and Christians, who consider biblical scripture more ancient and precedential to qur'ānic scripture, have tended to assume an Islamic "borrowing" of biblical material. The supposition of borrowing, of course, denies the viability of true Islamic revelation. Discrepancies between the two texts have therefore been attributed to mistakes on the part of Muslims, who were not able or not willing to borrow or learn the biblical material accurately.[29]

Muslims, on the other hand, and partly in response to Jewish and Christian disdain for the supposed inaccuracy of the Qur'ān, have claimed that qur'ānic and biblical revelation originated from the same heavenly scripture. The existence of parallels can therefore be explained simply by the fact that they both derive from the same original revelation. According to this view, however, it is the Qur'ān, not the Bible, which represents the only truly accurate record of God's will to humanity. Differences between the two scriptures have therefore tended to be explained as resulting from Jewish and Christian distortion of the Bible. One reason for the presumed distortion, known most commonly as *taḥrīf* in Arabic, was to eliminate the once extant prophecies of the coming of the Prophet Muḥammad and the ascendency of Islam, both of which are assumed to have been primary components of the original and true Revelation.[30]

Until recently, the approach of modern Western Orientalist scholarship has not differed significantly from that of medieval European religious disputants. Christian scholars tended to assume a direct borrowing from Christian sources, while Jewish scholars generally assumed a Jewish derivation.[31] A major goal of this type of scholarship was to locate the literary source or "Urtext" of subsequent versions, a scholarly quest which is far less popular in modern approaches to literary research.[32] Modern perspectives on orality-literacy relationships and literary theory have now substantially enhanced our ability to understand the textuality of Islamic religious literature.[33] We are far better equipped today to account for the striking affinity between Biblicist and Islamic texts than the great Orientalist scholars of the nineteenth and early twentieth centuries. But textual analysis of this sort is far more meaningful if conducted with an understanding of the *context*, the historical and cultural environments in which the people referring to the texts interacted.

Social, mercantile, and cultural exchange between the various religious communities of pre-Islamic Arabia has already been discussed. This type of interaction continued throughout the Islamicate world after the Islamic conquests as well. Throughout the first and the beginning of the second Islamic centuries, Muslims were not prevented from seeking out traditions and legends from Jews and Christians.[34] In fact, they were encouraged to learn traditions about the biblical and extra-biblical pre-Islamic prophets, though they were apparently forbidden to study and copy Jewish or Christian scripture or learn their religious practices.[35] One reason for this approach was that early

Muslims seem to have had difficulty making sense of significant portions of their new revelation following the death of Muḥammad.[36] The Qur'ān often makes reference to stories and legends of biblical characters, for example, without actually providing the narratives in the text. It assumes in homiletical fashion that the listener is already familiar with the broad topics being discussed. The details or lessons of the narratives are presumed to have then been provided in discussion subsequent to hearing the recitation of the text. Some of these comments in edited form became the contents of exegetical literature on the Qur'ān, which began to evolve shortly after the death of the Prophet Muḥammad.[37] It is immediately evident from reading samples of qur'ānic exegesis that their contents and style often parallel sources to whom Biblicist lore was familiar. Some are extremely close to known Jewish and Christian extra-biblical legends.

Such prodigious early traditionists as Abū Hurayra (d. 58 A.H./678 C.E.[38] and Ibn 'Abbās (d. 68/687) were known to be familiar with the Hebrew Bible or to collect traditions from Jews and Christians.[39] But Muslims would soon strive to rely only upon what they recognized as their own scholarship and lore. During the period when Muslim rulers attained their status as the mightiest world powers of their day under the great Abbasid Caliphate in Baghdad, religious scholars (*'ulamā'*) began to forbid the transmission of traditions deriving from foreign sources.[40] It was during this period, beginning in the later half of the eighth century C.E., that traditions considered untrustworthy were excluded from the compilations of Islamic lore and legal literature that were being collected at the time. Although this development corresponds chronologically with the period in which the majority population of eastern Islamdom had become Muslim, anti-Jewish or anti-Christian sentiment appears not to have been the driving force behind it.[41] It seems to be connected, rather, with a growing sense of Islamic pride and concern for an integral identity and standardization of practice among what had become an increasingly diverse ethnic Muslim population.

The historical complexities resulting in a greater consolidation of Islam through the institutionalization of Islamic law *(sharī'a)* is a subject that is beyond the scope of this study. I digress briefly nonetheless only in order to comment upon the probable reasons for limiting Biblicist traditions after the end of the eighth century. During the period when the population living under the eastern caliphate had become increasingly Muslim, religious leaders were consolidating and establishing a communal Islamic framework for daily life. Prior to this time greater lenience in practice was the custom, partly because daily practice was based on a looser base of Arabian (as opposed to Islamic) cultural norms, and partly because Islamic religious ideology was still in the process of development. By the late eighth century, caliphal society assumed a more fully Islamic demographic character at the same time that those who had emigrated away from a homogeneous Arabian cultural environment felt less bound by the norms of their Arab cultural heritage. During this time, there grew a greater interest among the religious leadership in re-establishing a homogeneous way of life based on the pristine practice of the young Muslim community of Medina under the leadership of Muḥammad.[42]

In order to promote greater religio-cultural homogeneity among Muslims, huge numbers of whom were converts or were children or grandchildren of converts, the demand grew among the pious to establish a way of life based upon the very acts of the Prophet or those acts approved by him. Because Muḥammad was God's last and greatest prophet, Muḥammad was becoming accepted by this time as having been divinely protected from error.[43] The *sunna* of the Prophet became the norm upon which religious (which included many societal) activities were derived. Its power lay in the fact that its source (God and His Prophet) was purely Islamic; the fact that the actual practice it taught was derived largely from pre-Islamic Arab custom became increasingly irrelevant. Material recognizably distinct from this base, including much of the previously sought-after Biblicist lore, was then considered foreign and unacceptable for inclusion into the corpus of authoritative literature evolving under the tutelage of the religious leadership.[44]

The concern for eliminating foreign religio-cultural lore reflected the growing pride of an empire becoming increasingly Muslim through the voluntary conversion of its subject peoples. Islam came to be seen as first ruling over and then superseding all other religious communities.[45] By the time the issue of foreign lore had become a concern, however, many traditions derived from foreign sources in the pre-Islamic period or collected during the first century and more of Islam had already evolved into a form that would be admissible to the developing canon of tradition. Some material deriving from Biblicist and pre-Islamic pagan environments had become so well integrated into Islamic lore that they were included in the most respected collections and cited freely in authoritative exegesis of the Qur'ān.

# Chapter 2

# THE NATURE OF THE LITERATURE

## ISLAMIC INTERPRETIVE LITERATURE

Islamic exegesis is commonly called *tafsīr*, a word which has taken on the technical definition of external or exoteric exegesis of the Qur'ān.[1] Qur'ānic exegesis represents a vast genre of Islamic religious literature. From the earliest days, pious Muslims sought to establish the actual historical occasions during which Muḥammad received the many bits and pieces of revelation that were assembled into the Qur'ān. These efforts were occasionally collected and committed to writing. These explanations naturally expounded upon why, as well as when and where the revelations were given. Later scholars made compilations of legalistic interpretations of qur'ānic passages. Some composed theological tracts connected to the qur'ānic revelation, and others even wrote grammars and rhetorical works based on the structure and style of qur'ānic discourse. All the major religious movements produced their own specific approaches to qur'ānic exegesis, and no religious scholar was ever considered noteworthy without a thorough knowledge of the Qur'ān and its interpretation.

Other genres of Islamic literature which do not fall into the strict category of exegesis frequently contain qur'ānic interpretations as well. Religious tracts, for example, regularly base their conclusions on premises derived from particular understandings of scripture. And Islamic historiography tends to treat its subject matter with special regard to the qur'ānic world view. The Islamic histories treating the period before Muḥammad's birth, for example, take the qur'ānic view of the pre-Islamic world carefully into account. But since the Qur'ān's own statements concerning pre-Islamic history are not always consistent, the various historical works have had to engage in qur'ānic interpretation through their own account of the unfolding of history.

Several different categories of Islamic interpretive literature take up the account of Abraham and Ishmael. One type is indeed the *tafsīr* or formal exegesis of the Qur'ān, which usually provides comments in a linear fashion according to the order of scriptural chapter and verse. Formal qur'ānic exegesis tends to treat Abraham and Ishmael wherever they appear within the context of the Qur'ān. A second category of exegetical literature treating these characters consists of the Islamic historiographical works *(ta'rīkh)*, which treat the ancient pre-Islamic prophets among whom Islam has numbered Abraham and Ishmael. A third is the collections of popular hagiographic literature known as *Qiṣaṣ al-anbiyā'*, the "Tales of the Prophets." These are compendia of stories and legends that shed light on the lives and activities of figures from a variety of ancient traditions who came to be known as prophets in Islam. A fourth type of literature in which interpretive material treating Abraham and Ishmael can be found is the *Ḥadīth* or Prophetic tradition, the most authoritative category of religious literature aside from the Qur'ān itself.

The Prophetic tradition refers to collections of eyewitness reports relating actions of the Prophet Muḥammad or statements attributed to him. Each individual unit of narrated information collected into these compendia is referred to as a *ḥadīth* (report), the same name used for the genre as a whole. The term *ḥadīth*, which will henceforth be refered to as "report" or "tradition," is used to designate any primary unit of Islamic tradition-literature, whether or not Muḥammad is the subject of the unit of information.[2] Most authoritative histories and Qur'ān commentaries are composed of units of information in the form of these reports as well. Even the collections of popular literature (the Stories of the Prophets) tend to be organized according to the classic form of *ḥadīth* reports or by strings of reports linked together to form a longer narrative unit. A report might consist of an anecdote or story, or may simply represent a comment or statement, the most valued of which can be traced to the Prophet Muḥammad himself.

Every proper *ḥadīth* report is made up of two parts: the story or message *(matn)* and its record of authentication *(isnād)*. The actual content of a report is without value unless a record of those who relayed it from its origin to its final telling is attached to it. A "sound" report, one that is universally respected by Islamic tradition, has a record of authentication that can be traced back uninterruptedly to its source by respected transmitters of tradition who lived in proper geographical and chronological proximity such that they could have passed the information to one another.[3] Because a *ḥadīth* report is a narration that has been passed on through the generations, it functions as a specifically Islamic type of the general phenomenon known as a "tradition," a generic term referring to the oral transmission of knowledge. While a tradition is generally considered to be a unit of knowledge, information, opinion or custom which is passed down by word of mouth, it also refers to units of information which were eventually reduced to writing, and even includes material composed in written form but located within a collection considered to be a work of tradition. The Islamic interpretive literature examined in this study is made up almost entirely of *ḥadīth* reports, most of which are assumed to have been transmitted orally but eventually reduced to writing. The status accorded to each unit by Islamic tradition varies widely.[4]

## NARRATIVE TRADITIONS AND ISRAELITE TALES

Muslim writers occasionally refer to certain narrative traditions treating pre-Islamic biblical and extra-biblical characters as Israelite Tales *(Isrā'īliyyāt)*. This term is best defined as "of Israelite origin," and refers to narrative comments or stories considered by Muslim authorities to be of Jewish origin, brought into the corpus of Islamic literature by Jewish converts or Muslims who heard the stories directly from Jews.[5] As mentioned in the previous chapter, early Muslims were not discouraged from turning to Jewish (and Christian) sources in order to learn their traditions and legends about the biblical motifs and stories found in the Qur'ān.[6]

In fact, however, the stories or legends that are specifically designated by medieval Muslim scholars as Israelite Tales cannot be found in Jewish literature—at least not as they are found in Islamic sources. Certain motifs and concepts parallel those in Jewish sources, but a story deemed by Islam as an Israelite Tale is actually, as we shall see, a unique and authentically Islamic tale. It may have originated among Jews, or may have come from Christians who also used legends based on biblical narratives. Although the motifs or plot of the Israelite Tales may parallel Jewish or Christian legends in many respects, they do not generally typify them. We shall discuss below the process of change many appear to have undergone during their evolution into the realm of the Islamic tale.

By the ninth century C.E., Muslim scholars had come to distrust and eventually reject the Israelite Tales.[7] They were rejected ostensibly because they were not considered to be sound traditions, but the term eventually came to be used to condemn narrative traditions that were not considered authentic or appropriate to Islam by virtue of their content *(matn)* as well as their record of authentication *(isnād)*. Disapproval voiced by the critics was based on the view that the Israelite Tales were traditions that had been distorted by Jews because of their jealousy of the power and political hegemony of the Muslims.[8] Labelling certain traditions as Israelite Tales eventually came to be a simple way of discounting their worth. To claim that a tradition was an Israelite Tale even became a way of disposing of certain kinds of material not in accord with the viewpoint of the author.[9]

Despite the negative label applied to these reports and their rejection from the collections of "sound" traditions, thousands of legends and stories about biblical characters can be found in the most respected medieval religious literature. Many appear to have all the basic qualities of the Israelite Tales without having been excluded from the major works. In point of fact, most of the narrative legends treating Abraham and Ishmael in medieval Islamic literature could properly be considered Israelite Tales on the basis of their form and content, although they are not so labelled because of the derogatory implications of the term. For a legend to be deemed an Israelite Tale necessarily branded it as being unacceptable because un-Islamic. Since according to the Islamic view Abraham was neither a Jew nor a Christian but rather a Muslim,[10] the many important legends providing extra-qur'ānic information about him had to be considered authentic in purely Islamic terms. Eliminating all the legends would have eliminated basic information about Abraham and other qur'ānic figures who served as symbols upon which important religious ideology and practice were based. The power of the stories and their endearment among the people would have rendered the task virtually impossible as well as undesirable. But Islam had to "own" its legends about the legendary religious figures. To posit a foreign origin for its legends would have been tantamount to admitting a foreign origin for Islam itself. Only those stories, therefore, that appeared to contradict Islamic dogma were labelled and outlawed as Israelite Tales.[11] The vast majority, which were in keeping with basic Islamic sensibilities, were not affected.

Condemnation of a tradition as an Israelite Tale, then, was applied only to the obviously inadmissible foreign traditions with roots in Biblicist legends found within the broad category I have defined as narrative exegesis. The more or less acceptable material of this type can still be found throughout Islamic tradition literature. It makes up the bulk of the popular hagiographies and can be found often in histories, Qur'ān commentaries, and even in the canonical Prophetic tradition. Only those traditions that have been considered inappropriate to Islamic doctrine are branded as Israelite Tales. Aside from the issue of dogma, however, there is no consistent difference in structure or content between a narrative labelled as an Israelite Tale and most other Islamic narratives about characters found in the Qur'ān and the Bible. It was not the poor quality of their records of authentication that rendered them inadmissible, but rather their inappropriate content.[12]

The raw material of this study consists of hundreds of examples of exegetical narrative *ḥadīth* reports treating Abraham and Ishmael. The reports serve singly or are strung together into longer narratives to provide information not found in qur'ānic references to these characters. Whether found in formal qur'ānic exegesis *(tafsīr)* or in other types of Islamic literature, they function as narrative exegesis to the Qur'ān by interpretation through the medium of the story or legend.

The *ḥadīth* reports are recorded in the sources as small units of information that could be remembered and passed on orally. Their records of authentication tend also to link together the names of their transmitters with the terminology of orality, using such connectors as "So-and-so reported to me" *(ḥaddathanī)* or "So-and-so related to us" *(akhbaranā)*.[13] Yet we shall see that in their written form among the sources, reports occasionally betray the influence of a redactor or editor. Since Islamic traditions exhibit characteristics of both "oral" and "written" literature, it will be helpful to preface our examination of the sources with a discussion of the study of orality and literacy.

## ORAL CULTURE AND ORAL LITERATURE

Despite the substantial evidence of writing in northern and southern Arabia prior to Islam, literacy was uncommon in the central western region known as the Ḥijāz.[14] The pre-Islamic culture of this area was almost exclusively oral, with the most famous literature it produced being its poetry. That this pre-Islamic poetry shows all the earmarks of oral literature has been amply demonstrated and need not be repeated here.[15] The Ḥijāz was undoubtedly home to some individuals who could read and presumably even a few who could write, but these individuals were few and had virtually no effect upon the overwhelmingly oral culture.

When Jews, Christians, Zoroastrians, and members of other religious and ethnic groups entered pre-Islamic Arabia to live or trade, they naturally brought their religious traditions and legends with them. If the entering communities or trading groups were large or wealthy enough, they might have had copies of their religious literature with them as well, but they certainly carried along their oral lore in their memories as part of their cultural heritage.[16] I have noted in the previous chapter that legends and lore of biblical origin were indeed known in pre-Islamic Arabia along with the traditions that the native Arab inhabitants considered their own. They entered into the region long before Jewish converts to Islam such as Ka'b al-Aḥbār and Wahb b. Munabbih reported the versions that are attributed to them in Islamic literature. The Qur'ān is the most credible witness to this material when it refers to known stories and motifs with biblical settings that could not have originated from indigenous Arabian religion and tradition.[17]

Because of the oral nature of pre-Islamic Arabia, neither the indigenous nor foreign derivative oral traditions were reduced to writing. One might wonder why biblical motifs are rarely found in the collections of pre-Islamic Arabic poetry if Biblicist legends had penetrated Arabia long before Muḥammad. The answer is simply that pre-Islamic poets had little interest in Biblicist cultural themes; they were concerned with other issues.[18]

As in writing cultures, oral cultures have their own, though oral, literature. The most renowned genre of oral literature is the epic poem, which research in the past half century has characterized as extremely rich in formulae and formulaic expressions.[19] Proper rendition of oral epic poetry is possible only when the bard or rhapsodist has mastered the various formulae of which it is comprised. He does not memorize and recite an oral poem verbatim, but rather relates its matter through the infinitely creative combination and adjustment of oral literary formulae and formulaic expressions. Each rendition of the "same" epic poem is different; the nature of oral literature therefore remains fluid.[20] While most of the classic research on oral literature is devoted to the epic poem, types of oral folk literature have a similar structure of formulaic components.[21]

It is the nature of oral literature, whether poetic song or prose legends, to change and evolve in the course of repeated tellings. Each individual rendition is unique because it consists of interactive communication between the performer (the storyteller or singer of epic poetry) and the audience. The performer reacts to visual and auditory cues that are received from the audience, and will knowingly or unconsciously vary the rendition accordingly.[22] The fluid nature of oral literature therefore lends itself to adaptation to its naturally changing cultural environment. In the case of our study, one could predict that Biblicist legends transplanted into an Arabian clime would naturally bend and evolve into new forms as they were told and retold under the influence of new geographic and cultural surroundings. A common example of this phenomenon is the habit of assigning a new locus to an old tale.[23] Among our sources, we find a classic illustration of this in the sacred pre-Islamic Arabian desert spring associated with an old Biblicist legend of a sacred spring appearing supernaturally in the desert.[24]

Biblicist legends encroaching upon indigenous Arabian culture would not necessarily have found immediate appeal among the native peoples who did not share their religio-cultural world views. But Arabs certainly heard Biblicist legends and were at least vaguely familiar with their heroes. The annual fairs in pre-Islamic Arabia clearly served as occasions for exchanging information as well as merchandise, and we know that Biblicists visited them in the Ḥijāz to proselytize to the indigenous inhabitants.[25] The itinerant preachers undoubtedly found a more receptive response to their stories and legends than to issues of theology or dogma, and Arabs of the Ḥijāz would have heard about biblical characters and tales even if they did not relate them themselves. Furthermore, Arabs who converted to Christianity or Judaism brought their own native traditions with them, which resulted in a mix of indigenous Arab and Biblicist ideas.[26]

The oral process shaped the legends of pre-Islamic Arabia. Particularly with the influx of Biblicist immigrants and their successful integration into Arabian society, hybrid traditions evolved containing characteristics of both Biblicist and native Arabian religio-cultural world views. When early Muslims began collecting some of these traditions soon after the death of the Prophet Muḥammad, they would not have knowingly made significant changes in them, and certainly would not have attempted to make them up. The evidence suggests that early Muslims collected the traditions as they found them and tried to make sense of them as they were. The most convincing testimony for this is the vast number of variant renditions of all kinds of stories and comments in the Islamic collections. A certain range of disagreement *(ikhtilāf)* has always been accepted in Islam. But if the early collectors were not true to their sources, troublesome or conflicting renditions would simply be discarded or made to conform to a single standard. Instead, we note how often variant renditions of the same legend or tale are faithfully collected by the traditionists and cited side by side.

Variations among renditions of a story tend to be accepted more freely in oral cultures than in literate cultures, where written discourse can be closely analyzed and compared to what is assumed to be the "correct" or "accurate" text.[27] During the first Islamic century, the culture of the Muslim Arab leadership was transformed from an oral to a largely literate one.[28] During this period (and during the next century as well), piously motivated Muslims collected hundreds of thousands of oral traditions of all kinds and committed them to writing. This resulted in halting the oral evolution of the traditions within literate religious and political circles—the very leadership that would set the tone for the developing religious civilization of Islam. Among the common folk, however, stories and legends continued to evolve in oral form.

When the Muslims recorded the great mass of oral traditions, they found numerous variations of the same material. Because the various recensions of traditions pertaining to legal issues served to reflect and occasionally promote conflicting interpretations of the law, Muslim authorities were forced to devise a method for establishing which traditions were the most authoritative. The problems they encountered and the solutions they devised during the period of Islamic consolidation and standardization have been the topic of a number of scholarly studies.[29] It is sufficient to point out here that because legends and stories tended not to hold the same immediate primacy in affairs of state and religion as did the legal reports attributed to the Prophet, the sifting process was practiced with less severity on narrative traditions than on legalistic ones. Variations and even competing versions were not regularly omitted nor reconciled through textual emendation.[30] In comprehensive collections of narrative tradition such as al-Ṭabarī's *Commentary*[31] and his *History*[32] one can find numerous renditions of the same story side by side.

To summarize, I suggest that many of the legends in the Medieval Islamic exegetical literature that treat qur'ānic material parallel to the Bible derive from Jewish and Christian, orthodox or heterodox religious traditions. Originating in an oral milieu, the legends continually changed as they incorporated motifs and ideas reflecting the changes taking place in the cultures in and for which the legends themselves evolved. Those legends which were brought into the Arabian Peninsula by Biblicists gradually acculturated to pre-Islamic Arabia as they were repeatedly told and retold in that environment. They became partially "Arabized" as they took on some of the motifs and structures of indigenous Arabian legend, but also retained features of their Biblicist past as well.

## INTERTEXTUALITY IN TRADITION LITERATURE

Any study of literary evolution assumes a movement from one state to another, an approach which is always in danger of begging the question of originality. The classic Orientalist philological-historical studies of Islamic texts tended to do exactly that in assuming *a priori* that Islam "borrowed" its ideas from the "original" (meaning correct) ideas or beliefs of "Judeo-Christianity." They then set out to trace that history through textual analysis. It is true that parallels may often be found between Islamic and Biblicist ideas and texts. But the existence of parallels does not prove direct borrowing. In fact, the question is to a certain extent beside the point. Modern approaches to creativity recognize that no creative act is possible without outside influence. Anyone engaged in literary criticism today acknowledges that no composition is absolutely original and without precedent. There exists no vacuum in which pure creativity is possible without influence from prior or contemporary creations.

In the study of text, whether oral or written, influence must be assumed.[33] At the same time, however, inspiration may also be assumed when examining any creation, whether or not in the form of a written text. No textual approach to Islamic narratives about biblical characters can avoid the problem of dependence and originality, for the parallels with Biblicist material are striking and the historical reality sobering. Recent advances in the study of text have taught, however, that one can and in fact must acknowledge influence and inspiration at one and the same time.[34]

The method of study employed here assumes the basic approach of intertextual studies, acknowledging influence from other sources but transcending the positivist approach that limits the inherent value of the text in question.[35] The narratives examined in this study are analyzed in relation to a whole series of other texts which are not treated as sources, but rather as constituents of a genre whose conventions it is the goal of this study to infer. These conventions include the development and interpretation of character, plot structure and sequence, symbols, and so forth. Although similarities between particular texts will be duly noted, the approach here is to note patterns and conventions providing information about the literary genre in question.

The Islamic legends about Abraham are indeed influenced by the Biblicist legends extant in pre-Islamic Arabia and early Islamic society, but they also exhibit influences from indigenous Arabian culture as well as styles, structures, and motifs that are unique to Islam. The legends in Islamic sources are not "borrowed," but are rather unique creations fully intelligible only when a prior body of discourse—stories, ideas, legends, religious doctrine, and so forth—is taken into consideration along with contemporary Islamic worldviews.

## THE COMPOSITE NATURE OF NARRATIVE TRADITIONS

We have thus far assumed a relationship between Islamic legends on biblical themes and Biblicist legends brought into pre-Islamic Arabia or extant in areas of early Islamicate society. But even a cursory reading of the Islamic legends demonstrates simply from their content that they are not Jewish or Christian, and only rarely may nearly identical legends be found in Biblicist sources. Despite the evidence suggesting that they are influenced by Biblicist world views, the Islamic legends provide information and conclusions that fit far better into any of a number of Islamic contexts than those of either Judaism or Christianity. A close reading of the traditions reveals that many appear to be composite stories with remnants of pre-Islamic Arab elements as well as Islamic and biblical allusions. By subjecting the Islamic narrative traditions on the Abraham-Ishmael story to a form-critical method of textual analysis, it was found that they could be divided into component parts that suggested a consistent and limited choice of origins and evolutionary paths.

The analytic process consisted of collecting recurring traditions from a broad but limited (i.e., consistent and controllable) sample of medieval sources and dividing them into component parts based on the use of literary motifs, language, plot, and style. The various renditions were then compared. By working with a large sample of traditions, patterns could be identified which might otherwise have been missed.

The results of the analysis suggest that the various parts making up the Abraham-Ishmael story can be identified as deriving largely from three sources: communities organized around biblical scripture, pre-Islamic Arabian lore, or Islam.[36] Once the trend was ascertained, a theoretical model was established to represent the ideal-typical traits of traditions having originated in each of these contexts. The various motifs and parts of the legends were compared with the ideal-typical models, and a determination was made as to whether they fit into the model, and if so, where.

The first category of ideal types is Biblicist—that is, those traditions that had evolved out of a biblically based religious milieu. The second category we call Arab. This refers to traditions that had evolved out of a pre-Islamic Arabian environment independent of Biblicist influence. The third ideal-typical category is Islamic, referring to material reflecting Islamic world views that would appear independent of the first two categories.

The ideal-typical Biblicist material would not deviate from the basic chronology of the Bible. Originating in a Bible-centered context, it would not obviously contradict the biblical text. It might parallel a specific narrative found in Jewish or Christian sources extant prior to Islam, and would contain religious motifs found generally in Judaism or Christianity, although perhaps also found in Islam. Biblicist material would include known biblical characters, and might comment upon some aspect of a biblical text or an issue raised by the text. If a geographical locus was provided, it would not be alien to biblical geography. Finally, it would contain motifs that are not inconsistent with available Jewish or Christian legends.

The ideal-typical Arab tradition might parallel an acknowledged pre-Islamic legend[37] and would contain pre-Islamic Arabian religious motifs. It would include well-attested Arab characters and might comment upon an Arabian custom or practice. If a geographical locus was provided, it would be associated with a pre-Islamic Arabian site. Its various motifs would not be inconsistent with Arab lore and legend.

An Islamic component might explain a contemporary Islamic practice or demonstrate how an action or motif in the narrative conforms with the customs and rituals of Islam. It could bind an action in the legend directly to a verse from the Qur'ān or serve to bring two or more qur'ānic references into direct relation with one another within the medium of the narrative legend. The Islamic components of the narratives often appear as comments or brief explanations added to the legends by Muslim storytellers or preachers. They are sometimes short independent reports lacking narrative dialogue or simple editorial remarks inserted into the narrative text. The Islamic components tend to be more formulaic in structure than the more literary Biblicist or Arabian materials because of their technical function, which in all cases is to provide a clear Islamic connection to the story or issue being discussed. These Islamic connectors actually serve as the mortar to bind components of the more ancient legends to the Qur'ān and to Islamic practice. Their role ensured that Biblicist and Arab legends, both of which had become increasingly foreign to the sensibilities of a maturing Islam during the second Islamic century, became islamized and therefore acceptable to the tradition. As a result, the narrative traditions found in Islamic literature assume an authentically Islamic form which is as "original" as Jewish or Christian narrative traditions.

The Muslim exegetical works examined in this study represent a small sample of the hundreds if not thousands of medieval works of this type available in printed editions and manuscripts. Restricting the number of sources for analytically quantifiable analysis is a formidable but obviously necessary task. The investigation is therefore limited to a sample of twenty medieval works which represent some of the major genres of medieval Arabic literature and major approaches to medieval qur'ānic exegesis.[38] The sources examined are still widely read today and are easily accessible in printed editions in most of the Muslim world. They represent Sunnī, Shi'ite, mystical, and Mu'tazilite exegesis as well as major legal schools of Islam, thus typifying the most common and influential medieval Islamic worldviews. They are fairly representative of medieval Islamic exegesis in all its variety and permutations.[39] The methodology employed forces us to relate to all sources equally, despite the greater influence that certain works have had upon Islamic thinking or custom. Those traditions that are repeated most often among the sources are considered to be the most popular approaches to the topic at hand. The assembled sources represent their own historical periods and not necessarily the Islamic views current today. In fact, some opinions found in the works are clearly at variance with what might be considered "normative" modern Islamic views. As a whole, the sample of Arabic sources represents a broad spectrum of Islamic opinion on the Abraham-Ishmael story.

By way of concluding the introductory chapters on the nature of the subject examined by this work and the particular approach to the problem employed here, it will be instructive to note that when pointing our parallels in Biblicist narrative exegesis, this study provides more samples from Jewish than Christian literature. A greater number of Christian parallels are available and would be noted by a scholar specializing in early Christian narratives, and particularly by a specialist in Syriac texts.

PART TWO

# The Syrian Prologue

## INTRODUCTION

The Islamic legends of Abraham begin with his extraordinary birth and childhood in Mesopotamia.[1] Our study takes up the story at the time of Abraham's emigration[2] westward toward Syria[3] and his subsequent journey to Egypt and eventually, Mecca. This is also the point at which the characters of Hagar and Ishmael enter the story.

The sources are not all in accord about the chronology of events following Abraham's emigration. Most agree, however, that Abraham marries Sarah either in the land of his birth or in Haran, where he resides briefly on his way westward. When they continue their journeys, Abraham and Sarah are confronted by a tyrant or king who would possess Sarah sexually because of her stunning beauty. The tyrant is foiled with the help of God, and gives Hagar to Sarah as a maidservant in compensation for his misdeed. Sarah, it turns out, is barren and cannot provide an heir for Abraham. She allows Abraham to have sexual relations with Hagar, who consequently gives birth to Ishmael. By this time, Abraham and his family are living in Syria at the well of Beersheba, where a conflict ensues between him and the native inhabitants. As a result, Abraham moves his family away from Beersheba. In their new abode, Abraham and Sarah are visited by angels on their way to destroy the people of Lot.[4] At about this time, Abraham brings Hagar and Ishmael to Mecca.

# Chapter 3

## ABRAHAM'S EMIGRATION

The legends treating Abraham's emigration mark the transition from his earlier religious development to his maturity as leader and prophet. The culmination of his spiritual journey is reflected in his physical journey from the land of his birth to the land of Syria.[1] According to the legends, Abraham discovers the religious truth of monotheism through a series of personal experiences and trials in the land of the East, culminating in his opposition to the spurious religion of the tyrant Nimrod. Nimrod counters by having him thrown into a fiery furnace, which is miraculously cooled by a miracle of God. Abraham finally leaves his own land and people in order to worship the one God and practice his religion as he knows he must. His emigration is mentioned or assumed in the Qur'ān in Sūras 19:48-9, 21:71, 29:26, and 37:99, but a full picture can be found only in the exegetical literature.

Contrary to many of the later segments of the Abraham-Ishmael story, the traditions treating Abraham's emigration are striking for their variety. They agree neither about where he went nor what he did when he left his native land. Some 32 of these reports have been collected from our sources. Most consist of brief non-narrative comments concerning the path of his journey or the genealogy of Abraham and his family, although they raise a smattering of other issues as well. Some treat Abraham's circumcision or various attributes applied to him, such as his wealth and hospitality or even the kind of food he served his guests. These miscellaneous reports are rarely repeated among the sources, though some thematic repetition can be found.

Of the seventeen descriptions of the route of Abraham's journey, for example, most agree that he emigrated from some land in the Tigris-Euphrates river valley, yet three specify his origins as being in Kūthā,[2] three name the place as *Bābil* or Babylon, two call it the land of Nimrod, and nine fail to provide any name at all. Six mention that he stopped in Haran.[3] Seven include a stop in Egypt to account for the Tyrant episode,[4] and one gives Jordan as the locus for the Tyrant legend. Schematically, then, the emigration stories are distributed as follows:

ABRAHAM'S EMIGRATION

| *Route/Source* | *Authority for Opinion Cited in Sources*[5] |
|---|---|
| *Kūthā* > Ḥarrān<br>Ibn Sa'd 46 | Ibn 'Abbās |
| Babylon > Syria > Jordan > Egypt > Syria<br>Ibn Sa'd 46-7 | Father of<br>Hishām b. Muḥammad |
| Kūthā in Babylon > Holy Land<br>(Ḥarrān > Jordan > Canaan)<br>Ibn Qutayba 30-3 | Wahb |
| Land of Nimrod > Syria[6]<br>al-Ya'qūbī 22-3 | (al-Ya'qūbī) |
| > Egypt > Syria (Beersheba)<br>al-Ṭabarī *History* 270-4 | anonymous |
| Land of Nimrod > desert on way from Yemen to Syria<br>al-Qummī 1:332-5 | (al-Qummī) |
| Kūthā in Iraq > Ḥarān[7] > Egypt > Syria[8]<br>al-Tha'labī 79 | Ibn Isḥāq |
| > Ḥarrān > Jordan > Syria[9]<br>al-Kisā'ī 141 | Ka'b |
| > Egypt > Syria<br>Ibn al-Athīr 102 | (Ibn al-Athīr) |
| > Syria > Egypt > Holy Land<br>Ibn Kathīr *History* 212 | (Ibn Kathīr) |
| > Syria<br>Ibn Kathīr *History* 213<br>(Based on Q.21:71)[10] | Ubayy b. Ka'b, Abū al-'Āliya, Qatāda etc. |
| Babylon ><br>Ibn Kathīr *History* 214 | (Ibn Kathīr) |
| > Mecca<br>Ibn Kathīr *History* 213<br>(Based on Q.21:71 & 3:96) | Ibn 'Abbās |
| Babylon > Ḥarān<br>Ibn Kathīr *History* 213 | People of the Book |
| > Ḥarān > Syria<br>Ibn Kathīr *History* 213 | Ka'b al-Aḥbār |
| > Syria (E. of Jerusalem)<br>> Tayman[11] > Egypt<br>Ibn Kathīr *History* 214 | People of the Book |
| > al-Rahā > Egypt[12] > Syria<br>Mujīr al-Dīn 34-35 | (Mujīr al-Dīn) |

Most of the reports are given on the authority of early Muslim scholars versed in the literature of tradition, though not all include a proper record of authentication.[13] None of the authoritative traditions are repeated in this series, though many are traced to such important authorities as Ibn 'Abbās, Qatāda, al-Suddī, and Ibn Isḥāq. Of the seventeen traditions, ten are authoritative, including two on the authority of "the People of the Book," referring to acknowledged Biblicist lore. Six are the opinions of the exegetes, and one is anonymous.

All but one report marking the route of Abraham's emigration follow the thrust of the biblical rendition that ultimately brings Abraham to the Land of Canaan.[14] The single exception is given on the authority of Ibn 'Abbās in which Abraham's emigration culminates in Mecca.[15] This view is based on Qur'ān 21:71: "WE DELIVERED HIM AND LOT TO THE LAND WHICH WE HAVE BLESSED FOR ALL," and 3:96: "THE FIRST HOUSE APPOINTED FOR MANKIND WAS THAT IN *BAKKA*, FULL OF BLESSING AND GUIDANCE FOR ALL MANKIND." According to the interpretation, the Q.3:96 verse specifically explains that the blessed land, mentioned in both Q.21:71 and 3:96, is the land of Bakka, another name for Mecca. Most exegetes, however, consider Q.21:71 to refer to Syria, particularly in light of Lot's inclusion in the statement. In contrast, the Ibn 'Abbās tradition assumes that Abraham had not finished his emigration until he completed the building of the Ka'ba, the final outcome and ultimate goal of his lifetime of trials and tribulations.[16]

Thirteen traditions provide an identity for Sarah. None follow the biblical genealogy, although one specifically states that it is given according to the Torah.[17] Islamic concern with Sarah's identity suggests an attempt to eliminate the legal problem of incest resulting from marrying one's sibling, despite the fact that the issue is not mentioned in the Qur'ān, although it is raised in the exegetical literature. The problem reflects Abraham's statement in Genesis 20:12 where he claims that Sarah is his sister through a common father though not a common mother.

Only Ibn Kathīr[18] discusses the problem openly by noting that it may have been legal in Abraham's day for a man to marry his sister, although all the exegetes are concerned with the problem of an Islamic prophet committing sin. Despite the biblical claim that Abraham married his own half-sister, they posit that he must have actually married his first cousin, a preferred marriage partner.[19] Only two early opinions suggest that her relationship to Abraham was closer than that. Concern for the infallibility of the prophets *('iṣma)* is the most likely explanation for the variance here from the biblical rendition, a doctrine which was current among some Shi'ites as early as the beginning of the eighth century.[20] This is supported by the "Tyrant" traditions in the following chapter, where Abraham himself explains in a gloss that he and Sarah are "brothers in Islam."

The identity reports appear schematically as follows:

SARAH'S IDENTITY

| *Identity/Source* | *Authority* |
|---|---|
| A* married S in Syria<br>Ibn Sa'd 46 | Father of Hishām b. Muḥammad |
| S = daughter of Hārān, who is brother of A & Nahor[21]<br>Ibn Qutayba 31 | Wahb from the Torah |
| S = daughter of Khārān,[22] A's paternal uncle.<br>al-Ya'qūbī 22 | (al-Ya'qūbī) |
| S = daughter of Haran, A's paternal uncle.[23]<br>al-Tabarī *History* 266 | Ibn Isḥāq |
| S = daughter of King of Ḥarrān.<br>al-Tabarī *History* 266 | (no authority cited) |
| S = daughter of A's maternal uncle<br>al-Qummī 1:332 | (al-Qummī) |
| S = daughter of Bethuel b. Nahor and was A's first cousin.<br>al-Mas'ūdī 1:57 | (al-Mas'ūdī) |
| S = daughter Hārān, A's paternal uncle.<br>al-Tha'labī 79 | Ibn Isḥāq |
| S = daughter of the king of Ḥarān<br>al-Tha'labī 79 | al-Suddī |
| S = daughter of the king of Ḥarrān, named Hārān<br>al-Kisā'ī 141 | Ka'b al-Aḥbār |
| S = daughter of the king of Ḥarān<br>Ibn Kathīr *History* 213 | al-Suddī |
| S = daughter of A's paternal uncle Hārān for whom Harran is named.<br>Ibn Kathīr *History* 213 | (Ibn Kathīr) |
| S = daughter of A's brother Hārān & the sister of Lot<br>Ibn Kathīr *History* 214 | Qutayba & Naqāsh |

*A = Abraham, S = Sarah

Three definitions of kinship between Abraham and Sarah are offered by these sources. According to al-Ya'qūbī, Ibn Isḥāq, and Ibn Kathīr, Sarah is the daughter of Haran, who is Abraham's paternal uncle (i.e., the brother of Teraḥ). Al-Qummī maintains that she is the daughter of Abraham's maternal uncle, although he does not provide his name. According to this genealogy, Sarah would be Abraham's first cousin and a perfectly acceptable marriage partner.

According to the interpretation of al-Suddī, Ka'b al-Aḥbār, and one anonymous comment given by al-Ṭabarī, Sarah is the daughter of the king of Harān and therefore unrelated to Abraham. As in the biblical genealogy (Gen. 11:27-31), the Muslim exegetes noted the similarity between the name for Abraham's brother and the geographical entity Haran. According to their understanding, Sarah was still the "daughter of Haran," although the individual of that name became transposed to the king of a land by that name, thus avoiding the problem of kinship.

According to the rendition attributed to Wahb and repeated by Ibn Kathīr on the authority of Qutayba and Naqāsh, however, Haran is Abraham's brother (as in Gen. 11:26) and Sarah is his daughter. This suggestion is closer but nevertheless still disagrees with the biblical text. It is exactly the same approach, however, of the Jewish rabbinic understanding that Haran's daughter Yiska is none other than Sarah.[24] The rabbinic interpretation explains Wahb's puzzling comment that he found his information in the Torah. Wahb was referring to the rabbinic concept of "Torah," meaning the entirety of Jewish learning and lore,[25] as opposed to "The Torah" or Torah scroll *(sefer torah)*, which refers only to the Pentateuch. Wahb's "Torah" source was, then, extra-biblical rabbinic lore.

The word Torah came into Arabic and is found repeatedly in the Qur'ān, but it is generally understood there to refer to Hebrew Scripture, excluding post-biblical rabbinic writings.[26] Wahb's explanation of Sarah's identity is closest to the biblical genealogy and follows rabbinic lore exactly. It is likely that his comment represents the link between Jewish tradition and the Islamic claims that Sarah was the daughter of Abraham's uncle Haran or the daughter of the King (of) Haran. Muslim religious scholars could not countenance the possibility that Abraham would have married his own sister (according to Abraham's words to Abimelekh in Genesis 20:12). The rabbinic understanding, repeated by Wahb, is that Abraham married his brother's daughter, an acceptable solution according to the Jewish laws of marriageable consanguinity but explicitly forbidden in the Qur'ān (Sūra 4:23). The Muslim scholars were able to solve the problem only be considering Haran Abraham's uncle rather than his brother.[27]

The reports treating Abraham's emigration consist mostly of short and unrelated statements.[28] These help establish a context for more literary narrative reports to be found further along in the Abraham cycle which will fill out the terse qur'ānic references. In the process, the reports provided here serve to collect widely separated qur'ānic verses alluding to Abraham's emigration and bring them into relationship with qur'ānic accounts of Abraham's later adventures.

Qur'ān verses 19:48, 21:71, 29:26, and 37:99 all refer to Abraham or Abraham and Lot leaving their native land for a place in which they can freely worship God. Many of the traditions and comments treating the emigration tie these qur'ānic allusions to the continuing Abraham cycle. As we have noted above, the narrative content of the different statements is inconsistent, but at least with regard to Abraham and Sarah, a good number of them exhibit the common concern of solving the problem of their consanguinity. The various statements in the sources do not represent ancient narrative traditions that have been retained or reinterpreted as they fit into a new Islamic context. Rather, they exhibit all the traits of Islamic editorial comments that bind the ensuing Abraham-Ishmael story to the Qur'ān and place various qur'ānic and traditional sections of the story in coherent relation to one another.

The reports and exegetes' comments pertaining to the route of Abraham's emigration tend to follow the thrust of the biblical rendition, although they exhibit significant variety regarding detail. The lack of consistency demonstrates that no single interpretation achieved dominance and became the accepted view. This fact implies that the traditionists were somewhat familiar with the biblical account, but not well enough acquainted or not interested enough to work through its somewhat confusing and ambiguous details. Wahb's view regarding Sarah's identity originated from Biblicist traditions, as he himself faithfully pointed out. No traces of pre-Islamic Arab traditions on this theme can be found.

Most of the reports treating Abraham's emigration attempt to provide a more thorough accounting of his route than could be gleaned from the qur'ānic references. Many are undoubtedly based on information derived from sources familiar with the biblical story. Their major role, aside from providing detail, is to tie together the Qur'ān references to Abraham as a young man learning about God's truth[29] to his subsequent experiences in Syria,[30] leading eventually to the culmination of his life in building the Ka'ba and establishing the major ritual requirement of Pilgrimage, the famous Ḥajj.[31]

# Chapter 4

# THE TYRANT

The Islamic legend about Abraham, Sarah, and the tyrant is dominated by sixteen reports attributed to Abū Hurayra.[1] Of the total of twenty-eight traditions, sixteen are full narratives, while the remainder consist of narrative fragments or comments referring to some aspect of the story. Half of the narrative traditions are given on the authority of Abū Hurayra,[2] and the other half are given on the authority of a variety of sources which will be detailed below.

A paradigmatic rendition of the legend based on all the narrative traditions attributed to Abū Hurayra follows.

1. Abraham told only three lies: one which can be found in Q.37:89,[3] one in Q.21:63,[4] and his statement to the tyrant when he told him that Sarah was his sister (7/8).[5]
2. ______________________________.[6]
3. The tyrant *(jabbār)* or king of a town through which Abraham passes is told that Abraham is with a beautiful woman (7/8). The tyrant/king sends a message to Abraham asking who she is. Abraham tells him that she is his sister (7/8).
4. ______________________________.
5. Abraham then speaks with Sarah and tells her not to contradict him (8/8), for she is indeed his sister "to God" (1/8) or they are the only believers or Muslims on earth (6/8) or both (1/8).
6. Sarah is brought to the tyrant and begins to pray (4/8), affirming to God that she is a true believer and that she has remained chaste to everyone aside from her husband. She requests that God prevent the infidel from touching her (3/8).
7. The tyrant/king reaches out to her and is stricken (8/8) with a seizure (4/8), or his hand is stricken (1/8).
8. Sarah prays to God to release him (1/8), or the tyrant/king tells her to pray to God to release him, for he says that he will not do it again (3/8).

9. A gloss is inserted here on the authority of Abū Hurayra that Sarah said: "O God, if he dies, they will say that I killed him!" (3/8).
10. When the tyrant is released from his seizure, he reaches for her a second time (2/8), or a total of three or more times (6/8).
11. Foiled, he calls for his chamberlains (3/8) and says that he was not sent a human but rather a devil (8/8).
12. He gives Hagar to Sarah (8/8).
13. Sarah returns to Abraham (6/8), who has been praying all this time (5/8). When he senses her presence, he asks her what happened by using the enigmatic word, *mahyam* (4/8).[7]
14. She tells him that God foiled the plot of the infidel and gave her Hagar (or, a maidservant) (8/8).
15. A final comment is interjected here, stating that Abū Hurayra used to say: "This is your mother, O People of the Water of Heaven (4/8).[8]

The Islamic Tyrant legend parallels a recurring thematic narrative found three times in the book of Genesis.[9] Jewish narrative tradition provides a substantial amount of commentary on the legend, where motifs numbered 5, 6, 7, 11, 12, 13, and 14 from the paradigmatic Abū Hurayra version can be found.[10] Some Jewish versions of the legend can be found in such early sources as the pre-Islamic *Bereshit Rabbah* and Palestinian Targum, as well as compilations of legends contemporary with Islam such as *Pirke de'Rabbi Eliezer* and *Sefer HaYashar.*[11]

The Abū Hurayra version fulfills most of the criteria established for Biblicist material. It remains faithful to the biblical chronology and closely parallels known pre-Islamic Biblicist legends. Referring exclusively to biblical characters, it expands on the biblical narrative in the same way as its Jewish narrative exegetical counterparts by providing a context for the appearance of Hagar as Sarah's handmaiden (motifs 12 and 14).

Two motifs, however, are inconsistent with Biblicist legends. Motif 5 mentions that no Muslims could be found on earth aside from Abraham and Sarah, and motif 15 affirms the matriarchal status of Hagar for the Arabs in a purely Arabian context. The former explains how Sarah is Abraham's "sister" without being his biological sister, thereby eliminating the two problems inherent in the legend for Islam: that of Abraham's apparent incestual relationship with Sarah (discussed in the previous chapter) and Abraham's apparent lie.[12] This motif, which is unnecessary for the smooth narration of the legend and indeed, does not occur in classic Jewish renditions, is a later addition inserted into the legend by a storyteller or redactor and renders it more acceptable to an Islamic world view. The structure of motif 15, given independently on the authority of Abū Hurayra (like the tradition as a whole), points to the motif's independence form an earlier stage of the legend. It is actually a metanarrative sign commenting on the significance of Hagar in terms of Arab genealogy, thereby functioning as a gloss. Although it parallels the biblical world view concerning Hagar as the mother of Ishmael and therefore a progenitor of Arab peoples, it specifically assigns her matriarchal status as the "mother of the Arabs," a specifically Islamic Arab genealogical view.[13]

Only the prologue of the Abū Hurayra version (motif 1) remains to be discussed. This introductory statement represents later Islamic material prefaced in order to connect Qur'ān verse 37:89 with 21:63 and attach both to the legend of Abraham and Sarah with the Tyrant. The comment can actually be found without the subsequent narrative in eight renditions in al-Ṭabarī[14] and in Ibn al-Athīr.[15] In view of the foregoing, it would be difficult to assign the origin of the Abū Hurayra version of the Tyrant tradition to anything but a Biblicist milieu. The three non-Biblicist motifs (1, 5, and 15) represent Islamic material that was added to an earlier version of the legend in order to place the context and characters firmly into an acceptable Islamic framework.

The eight narrative traditions of the Tyrant story not given on Abū Hurayra's authority comprise a second version of the legend. Referred to as "Version 2," two of these traditions are found on the authority of "some scholars,"[16] one each on the authority of al-Suddī[17], Ka'b al-Aḥbār[18] and Abū Sa'īd,[19] and three are given without any record of authentication *(isnād)*.[20] Ibn Qutayba provides a report given on the authority of Wahb b. Munabbih,[21] although this rendition is a brief editorial narration and not a true narrative. It is not factored in the paradigmatic rendition provided here.

The paradigmatic Version 2 (based on eight narrative traditions):

1. Abraham only told three lies: one in Q.37:89, one in Q.21:63, and his statement to the tyrant when he told him that Sarah was his sister (1/8).
2. Sarah is an exceptional woman and would never disobey her husband (3/8).
3. Pharaoh of Egypt (6/8), King Nimrod (1/8), or King Zadok *(Ṣādūq)* in Jordan (1/8) is the person who takes Sarah from Abraham after he is told of her beauty (3/8). Pharaoh sends a message to Abraham asking who Sarah is. Abraham tells him that she is his sister (4/8), fearing that the ruler would take her and kill him if he said she was his wife (4/8).
4. Pharaoh tells Abraham to adorn her and send her to him, which he does (3/8).
5. Abraham then speaks with Sarah and tells her not to contradict him (2/8), for she is indeed his sister in religion (5/8), or they are the only believers or Muslims on earth (2/8).
6. ______________________________.
7. When Pharaoh reaches out to touch her, his hand or arm is stricken (6/8).

8. Pharaoh asks her to pray to God to release him (6/8). She asks God to release Pharaoh only if his claim that he will not do it again is honest (4/8), or God says that he will release him only if King Zadok gives his entire kingdom in Jordan to Abraham, which he does (1/8).
9. ______________________________.
10. Pharaoh reaches for her three times (2/8).
11. Foiled, he calls for his chamberlains (1/8) and says that he was not sent a human but rather a devil (1/8).
12. He gives Hagar to Sarah (7/8).
13. Sarah returns to Abraham, who has been praying all this time (1/8). When he senses her presence, he asks her what happened by using the enigmatic word, *mahyam* (1/8).[22]
14. She tells him that God foiled the plot of the infidel and gave her Hagar (1/8).
15. ______________________________.
16. God raised up the veil that was between Abraham and Sarah so that Abraham would be assured of Sarah's chastity even in the face of such a trial (2/8).

Version 2 appears to be quite similar to the Abū Hurayra version. In addition to fulfilling the same Biblicist criteria, however, most renditions of Version 2 provide the same Egyptian setting as the biblical account in Genesis 12:10-20, and Pharaoh's withered hand parallels BR 41:2. As in the earlier verison, Version 2 satisfies no criteria of Arabian legends aside from the fact that its motifs are not inconsistent with Arab folklore. This story appears to hold no importance for establishing a basis for Arab customs or practice.

When the two versions are lined up in parallel columns, they appear as follows:

| *Abū Hurayra (8 Renditions)* | *Motif No.* | *Version 2 (8 Renditions)* |
|---|---|---|
| Abraham told only three lies (7) | 1 | Abraham told only three lies (1) |
| ______________ | 2 | Sarah exceptional and never disobeys (3) |
| Tyrant or king (8) | 3 | Pharaoh (6/8) Nimrod (1/8) Zadok (1) |
| Ruler is told of S's beauty (7) | 3 | Ruler is told of S's beauty (3) |
| A asked and says S is his sister (7) | 3 | A asked and says S is his sister (4) |
| ______________ | 3 | Ruler would kill A if he told truth (4) |
| ______________ | 4 | A told to adorn S and send her (3) |
| A tells S not to contradict (8) | 5 | A tells S not to contradict (2) |
| Sarah is his sister "to God" (2) | 5 | ______________ |

| *Abū Hurayra (8 Renditions)* | *Motif No.* | *Version 2 (8 Renditions)* |
|---|---|---|
| ______ | 5 | Sarah is his sister in religion (5) |
| They are the only believers (7) | 5 | They are the only believers (2) |
| Sarah prays for God's help (4) | 6 | ______ |
| Ruler's hand is stricken (1) | 7 | Ruler's hand is stricken (6) |
| Ruler stricken with seizure (4) | 7 | ______ |
| S prays to God to release him (1) | 8 | ______ |
| He asks her prayer for release (3) | 8 | He asks her prayer for release (6) |
| ______ | 8 | She does on condition he is honest (4) |
| ______ | 8 | God releases only if A given kingdom (1) |
| If he dies S will be blamed (3) | 9 | ______ |
| Ruler accosts her repeatedly (8) | 10 | Ruler accosts her repeatedly (2) |
| Foiled, ruler calls attendant (3) | 11 | Foiled, ruler calls attendant (1) |
| Ruler not sent human but devil (8) | 11 | Ruler not sent human but devil (1) |
| Ruler gives Sarah Hagar (8) | 12 | Ruler gives Sarah Hagar (7) |
| S returns to A, who is praying (5) | 13 | S returns to A, who is praying (1) |
| A asks what happened *(mahyam)* (4) | 13 | A asks what happened *(mahyam)* (1) |
| God foiled infidel and gave Hagar (8) | 14 | God foiled infidel and gave Hagar (1) |
| "This is your mother . . ." (4) | 15 | ______ |
| ______ | 16 | God raised veil so A assured (2) |

When all motifs occurring two or fewer times are eliminated, two distinct versions emerge:

| *Abū Hurayra* | *Motif No.* | *Version 2* |
|---|---|---|
| Abraham told only three lies (7) | 1 | ______ |
| ______ | 2 | Sarah exceptional and never disobeys (3) |
| Tyrant or king (8) | 3 | Pharaoh (6) |
| Ruler is told of S's beauty (7) | 3 | Ruler is told of S's beauty (3) |
| A asked and says S is his sister (7) | 3 | A asked and says S is his sister (4) |
| ______ | 3 | Ruler would kill A if he told truth (4) |
| ______ | 4 | A told to adorn S and send her (3) |
| A tells S not to contradict (8) | 5 | ______ |

| *Abū Hurayra* | *Motif No.* | *Version 2* |
|---|---|---|
| ______________ | 5 | Sarah is his sister in religion (5) |
| They are the only believers (7) | 5 | ______________ |
| Sarah prays for God's help (4) | 6 | ______________ |
| Ruler reaches to touch her | 7 | Ruler reaches to touch her |
| ______________ | 7 | Ruler's hand is stricken (6) |
| Ruler stricken with seizure (4) | 7 | ______________ |
| He asks her prayer for release (3) | 8 | He asks her prayer for release (6) |
| ______________ | 8 | She does on condition he is honest (4) |
| If he dies S will be blamed (3) | 9 | ______________ |
| Ruler accosts her repeatedly (8) | 10 | ______________ |
| Foiled, ruler calls attendant (3) | 11 | ______________ |
| Ruler not sent human but devil (8) | 11 | ______________ |
| Ruler gives Sarah Hagar (8) | 12 | Ruler gives Sarah Hagar (7) |
| S returns to A, who is praying (5) | 13 | ______________ |
| A asks what happened *(mahyam)* (4) | 13 | ______________ |
| God foiled infidel and gave Hagar (8) | 14 | ______________ |
| "This is your mother . . ." (4) | 15 | ______________ |

As may be observed by noting the number of times each motif is found in the sources (given in parentheses), those of the Abū Hurayra version tend to be repeated more consistently than those of Version 2. In fact, we have found quite consistently throughout this study that groups of traditions attributed to a single authority are more regular than those attributed to a variety of sources or given anonymously. The Abū Hurayra version is also more substantial and includes more details than Version 2.

Version 2 tends to be slightly closer to the biblical text. The episode takes place in Egypt, as in Genesis 12:10, while no Abū Hurayra rendition mentions any geographical locus. Secondly, Abraham explains his strange request to Sarah that she pose as his sister in Version 2, just as in Genesis 12:12. The Abū Hurayra version provides no explanation. As intriguing as their literary proximity to the biblical text, however, is the fact that neither of our two versions draws a *close* parallel to any of the post-biblical Jewish versions of the legend, although Version 2 is somewhat closer than Abū Hurayra (perhaps because of its closer parallels with the biblical text).

Certain motifs found in the few renditions not corresponding to either of the two versions given above will occasionally parallel some aspect of a

Jewish version. Thus, for example, in a rendition given by al-Qummī,[23] Abraham carries Sarah concealed in a chest, which parallels *Bereshit Rabbah* 40:5.[24]

It is likely that Version 2 originated as a narrative legend based on the wife/sister story of Genesis 12:10-20, while the Abū Hurayra version developed originally in relation to the theme found in Genesis 20:1-28. In the latter rendition of the legend, King Abimelekh of Gerar[25] is the antagonist and has no connection with Egypt. An interesting parallel can be found in al-Kisā'ī's rendition given on the authority of Ka'b al-Aḥbār, where the episode takes place in Jordan and a king named Zadok[26] takes Sarah to be his wife. Similar data are also given by Ibn Qutayba on the authority of Wahb b. Munabbih, where a Coptic tyrant named Ṣādūf[27] tries to take Sarah from Abraham. Neither Ka'b nor Wahb are considered reliable transmitters of tradition,[28] but Abū Hurayra is.[29] If the Abū Hurayra version did indeed enter into Islam through Abū Hurayra,[30] he must have received the material from Biblicist sources,[31] which may have omitted the setting of the story and the identity of the antagonist in order to eliminate the conflict between the biblical renditions of Genesis 12:10-20 and 20:1-28.

It appears clear that the Tyrant legend evolved out of a Biblicist milieu, since it satisfies most of the criteria for Biblicist material but exhibits almost no influence of pre-Islamic Arab traditions. Only Abū Hurayra's insert that the Arab people are "the People of the Water of Heaven" suggests an Arab component. Neither version of the legend provides a sacred historical justification for any Arab custom or practice. On the other hand, the Abū Hurayra version includes comments that were undoubtedly added after the tradition had entered the Islamic world. The introductory motif (1) of the "three lies" binds the legend to two vaguely related Qur'ān verses. Furthermore, Abū Hurayra's attribution of "People of the Water of Heaven" to Hagar dates that motif as Islamic. The evidence for this can be found in Arabic genealogies, which appear to connect the Northern Arabs and the tribe of Muḥammad to Hagar and Ishmael only in late—that is, Islamic—texts.[32] Pre-Islamic pagan Arab genealogies appear to have no awareness or concern for the connection, which probably evolved only after the Qur'ān made such a strong case for Abraham being the first Muslim.[33] Version 2, meanwhile, has remained intact even to the extent that it does not contain Islamic additions.

Both versions were most likely learned from Biblicist sources after the beginning of Islam, without their having absorbed significant pre-Islamic Arab motifs. In fact, there appears to be no reason why pre-Islamic Arabs would be interested in a legend in which foreign characters acted out a strange story that took place in a distant land. Aside from the genealogical connection (which we have noted is probably an Islamic development), the Tyrant legend would hold little interest to Arabs until the Qur'ān and Islam opened up the world of biblical legends and traditions for the Arab people. As Glick has pointed out, ideas do not cross cultural boundaries unless they are congruent with the dominant modes of thought of the recipient culture.[34] For Biblicist legends to have been absorbed into non-Biblicist pre-Islamic Arabian culture, they must either have exhibited enough inherent congruence or must have evolved sufficiently so that they eventually did. We shall attempt to demonstrate below that some legends did indeed go through enough of a transformation to do just that, while others remained effectively incongruent until the beginning of Islam. The revelation of the Qur'ān with its many allusions and references to biblical stories and themes quickly placed many of these previously incongruent legends within a recognized framework which made them intelligible, rendering their acceptance reasonable.

It is not within the scope of this study and, indeed, virtually impossible to detail the process of transition the legend underwent upon leaving its Biblicist sources.[35] It is sufficient to demonstrate that it originates from a biblically oriented tradition and is derivative neither of the culture or religions of pre-Islamic Arabia nor of the religious civilization of Islam.

The logical question that must be raised at this juncture is, why is this clearly foreign legend found in important religious and historical works of Islam, particularly in light of the fact that its story is not specifically mentioned or even directly alluded to in the Qur'ān? We posit two reasons why the legend was brought into the Islamic corpus, both of which satisfy Islamic interests. To begin with, once the genealogical connection with Hagar was established in the Islamic period, the Abū Hurayra version became an authoritative vehicle for establishing the origin of the matriarch of the northern Arabs. The second reason is that the story was simply a good source for much-needed information about Abraham, the first Muslim.[36] It became a natural exegetical narrative *(midrash)*, filling the gaps within qur'ānic references to Abraham's emigration *(hijra)* and subsequent adventures. Its association with the Qur'ān was natural because of the qur'ānic references to Abraham and Ishmael, although the connection was reinforced in the Abū Hurayra version with the motif of the three lies. The legend supplied genealogical information even without the Islamic additions,[37] although the Abū Hurayra version again provided a stronger context with its gloss regarding the "People of the Water of Heaven." It is most likely because of its success in placing a Biblicist legend into a recognizable framework for Islam that the rendition attributed to Abū Hurayra became the dominant tradition among the sources.

# Chapter 5

## THE BIRTH OF ISHMAEL

The Bible assigns special significance to the birth of Ishmael. Although Ishmael and his progeny will not remain within the covenant-bound inheritance of Abraham through Isaac, he nevertheless receives God's blessing:

> And the angel of the Lord said to her, 'I will greatly increase your offspring, and they shall be too many to count.' And the angel of the Lord said to her further, 'Behold, you are with child and shall bear a son; you shall call him Ishmael (i.e. 'God heeds'), for the Lord has paid heed to your suffering. He shall be a wild ass of a man; his hand against everyone, and everyone's hand against him. He shall dwell alongside of all his kinsmen.' (Genesis 16:10-12).

> As for Ishmael, I have heeded you. I hereby bless him. I will make him fertile and exceedingly numerous. He shall be the father of twelve chieftains, and I will make of him a great nation. (Genesis 17:20)

Later Jewish tradition follows the biblical lead in assigning significance to his birth, but by the time the earliest extant anthologies of this material were committed to writing, the rabbis had associated Ishmael with enemies of the Jews. It is apparent from the general cosmological thrust of Genesis that Ishmael, like Esau in the following generation, represented neighboring peoples having occasional but ongoing relationships with the Israelites. The biblical prophecy is less a statement of reproach (as it is understood by the rabbis) than it is a description of a particular people's way of life understood by the biblical world view to have derived from Ishmael. Nevertheless, even early rabbinic legendary texts such as BR 45:9 understand Genesis 16:10f to be words of rebuke.[1]

In contrast to the Bible and the collections of Jewish narrative exegesis, the Islamic sources rarely assign special significance to the birth of Ishmael.[2]

References to his birth tend to be made in passing and are often connected to the story of the Tyrant,[3] a chronology which is basically in keeping with that of the Bible.[4] The most common Islamic version of the Tyrant story, however, the Abū Hurayra version, does not even mention the birth of Ishmael. The appended statement of Abū Hurayra about Hagar being the mother of the "people of the water of heaven" is clearly a reference to her status as matriarch of the Arabs, but it does not refer specifically to Ishmael in any sense. Most references to Ishmael's birth are given at the end of the Tyrant narratives which are *not* attributed to Abū Hurayra. Others are connected to Abraham's emigration.[5] We find only one repeated tradition[6] and none that exhibit the specific qualities of earlier Jewish, Christian, or pre-Islamic Arab traditions. Most references consist of a simple comment by the exegete providing a chronology for Ishmael's birth within the sequence of the full Abraham story.

Ibn Sa'd[7] mentions Ishmael's birth after his brief rendition of the Tyrant tradition given "on the authority of more than one scholar":[8] ". . . [The Tyrant] called for Hagar, who was his most trusted servant. He gave her to Sarah and gave her clothing. Then Sarah gave her to Abraham, who had sexual intercourse with her. She gave birth to Ishmael, who was the eldest of his children. His name was *Ashmūwīl*, but it was changed in Arabic [to *Ismā'īl*]."

This rendition calls no special attention to Ishmael's birth. The fact of Ishmael being the oldest son follows the biblical account, and *Ashmūwīl* may have been understood (incorrectly)[9] to be the Hebrew name corresponding with the Arabic *Ismā'īl*. In Ibn Sa'd's rendition, Sarah offers Hagar to Abraham immediately after receiving her as a handmaid. According to the biblical story, Sarah did not offer Hagar to Abraham until long after their return from Egypt.[10]

Ibn Qutayba attaches a brief comment of Abū Muḥammad to Wahb's rendition of the Tyrant story:[11] "in the Torah, Sarah paired up Abraham with Hagar saying: 'God has prevented me from having children. Go in unto my handmaid. Perhaps we will be consoled with a child through her." As Abū Muḥammad said, this rendition does indeed parallel the biblical account by providing a similar logic to that in Genesis 16:2: "And Sarah said to Abraham, 'Look, the Lord has kept me from bearing. Consort with my maid; perhaps I shall be built up with a child through her.' "[12]

Al-Ya'qūbī includes no Tyrant story in his history but refers to the battle of the kings of Genesis 14 in its place.[13] We then read:

> God greatly increased Abraham's wealth. Abraham said: 'Lord, what will I do with my wealth without a son?'[14] So God provided him with a revelation [saying]: 'I will increase your progeny such that they will equal the number of the stars.'[15] Sarah had a maidservant named Hagar. She gave her to Abraham and he had intercourse with her. She became pregnant and gave birth to Ishmael. Abraham was 86 years old at that time.

God said: 'I will increase your progeny and will give them such dominion throughout time that no one will know their number.'[16] When Hagar gave birth, Sarah became jealous and said: 'Send her and her child away from me!' He sent her and Ishmael away and brought them to Mecca. . . ."

AL-Ya'qūbī attaches the prophecy of Genesis 15:5 and 16:10 directly to Ishmael. The latter verse is clearly applied to Ishmael in the biblical text, but 15:5 is understood in Jewish tradition to apply to Isaac.[17] Despite the fact that al-Ya'qūbī's narrative is unique within our pool of sources, it is clearly informed by the biblical version of the story.

Al-Ṭabarī relates a tradition on the authority of Ibn Isḥāq:[18] "Hagar was a female slave of special mien. Sarah gave her to Abraham saying: 'I view her as a pure woman, so take her. Perhaps God will bestow a son upon you from her,' for Sarah had grown old without bearing children. Abraham had invoked God to give him a pious son, but his prayer was delayed until Abraham had grown old and Sarah had become barren. Thereupon, Abraham had relations with Hagar, and she bore him Ishmael."

Al-Mas'ūdī simply writes: "Ishmael was born to Abraham when he was 86 or 87 years old; and some say, 90 years old. He was born of Hagar, Sarah's slave girl."[19]

Al-Tha'labī appends the same tradition found in al-Ṭabarī to the Tyrant story: "They say: Hagar was a female slave of special mien. Sarah gave her to Abraham saying: 'I view her as a pure woman, so take her. Perhaps God will bestow a son upon you from her,' for Sarah had grown old without bearing children. So Abraham had intercourse with Hagar and she gave birth to Ishmael."[20]

Al-Ṭabarsī's brief reference to Ishmael's birth is given on the authority of al-Ṣādiq:[21] "Abraham settled in the Syrian Desert, and when Ishmael was born to him from hagar, Sarah became worried and grieved because she could not have a child. . . ."[22]

Al-Kisā'ī's account[23] occurs after a rendition of the Tyrant legend attributed to Ka'b: "It was said: The king had a daughter of extreme goodness and beauty named Hagar. He gave her to Sarah. Then Gabriel came to Abraham and gave him the good news that God would provide him with a child through Sarah, from whom would be born many prophets; and through Hagar a son through whom would appear a prophet by the name of Muḥammad, the seal of the prophets. So when Sarah had grown old and had not provided a son, she gave her maidservant Hagar to Abraham. Perhaps God would bestow a son upon him from her. So Abraham had intercourse with her and she became pregnant. When she gave birth to Ishmael, his face shone like the moon with the light of our prophet Muḥammad."[24]

This rendition provides a "double prophecy" regarding Ishmael and Isaac that parallels that of Genesis 17:19-21 (also referring to both sons). In al-Kisā'ī's account, however, the meaning of the prophecies are essentially the opposite of the biblical rendition, with Ishmael rather than Isaac receiving the dominant blessing.[25]

Ibn al-Athīr's reference follows a chapter heading entitled: "The Story of the Birth of Ishmael and His Transfer to Mecca":[26] "It is said: Hagar was a female slave of special mien. Sarah gave her to Abraham saying: 'Take her. Perhaps God will bestow a son upon you from her', for Sarah had grown old without bearing children. So Abraham had intercourse with Hagar and she gave birth to Ishmael. For this reason, the Prophet said: 'When you conquer Egypt, make its people your concern, for they have protection *(dhimma)*[27] and relationship—that is, the offspring of Hagar.' "

The most interesting rendition of the birth of Ishmael is found in Ibn Kathīr[28] under the heading, "The Birth of Ishmael from Hagar":[29]

> The People of the Book say:
>
> Abraham requested a sound progeny from God, and God gave him good news about having descendents. After Abraham had been in the Holy Land[30] for twenty years,[31] Sarah said to Abraham, "God has forbidden me from having a child. Go in unto my maidservant;[32] perhaps God will provide you with a son through her."
>
> When she gave her to him, he had sexual relations with her and she became pregnant. When she became pregnant her soul was exalted and she became proud and arrogant to her mistress,[33] so Sarah became jealous of her. Sarah complained to Abraham, who said to her, "Do with her as you desire."[34] Hagar was frightened and fled. She stopped at a spring.
>
> An angel said to her, "Do not fear, for God will do good for this boy that you are carrying." He commanded her to return and announced to her that she would give birth to a boy whom she would name Ishmael. He would be a wild man. His hand would be over everyone, and the hand of everyone would be against him.[35] His brethren would rule over all the lands.[36] Then she thanked God.
>
> [This prophecy is appropriate for his offspring, Muḥammad, for he was the one through whom the Arabs ruled. They ruled all of the lands throughout the east and west. God bestowed upon them useful knowledge and virtuous acts which were not given to any of the peoples before them. This is because of the honor of their messenger above all of the other messengers, the blessing of his mission, the good fortune of his revelation, the perfection of that which he brought, and the universality of his mission to the people of the earth.]

When Hagar returned, she gave birth to Ishmael when Abraham was 86 years old, thirteen years before the birth of Isaac.[37] When Ishmael was born, God gave a revelation to Abraham informing him of the impending birth of Isaac from Sarah. He fell to his knees in prayer and [God] said to him, "I responded to you[38] with Ishmael[39] and blessed him and made him extremely great and very lucky; twelve[40] great sons will be born to him and I will make him the head of a great people."

[This is also the prophecy regarding this great [Islamic] nation,[41] and these twelve great sons are the twelve great rightly guided caliphs, about whom the prophecy is given in the report of ʿAbd al-Malik b. ʿUmayr on the authority of Jābir b. Samra from the Prophet, who said: "There will be twelve commanders." Then he [ʿAbd al-Malik] said, "I did not understand one word, so I asked my father, who said, "All of them are from among the Quraysh."[42]

Al-Bukhārī and Muslim included in their standard collections of Prophetic Tradition:[43] 'According to one account, "That decree is still in force", and according to a variant, "That decree is still notable until twelve caliphs will all be from among the Quraysh".' These include the four Masters *(al-a'imma al-arbaʿa)*: Abū Bakr, ʿUmar, ʿUthmān, and ʿAlī,[44] and they also include ʿUmar b. ʿAbd al-ʿAzīz,[45] and some of the ʿAbbāsids.[46] The intent of the account is not that the twelve caliphs be in chronological order, but simply that they will exist.

Neither is the intent that the twelve *Imāms* are those in whom the *Rāfiḍa*[47] believe, the first of them being ʿAlī b. Abī Ṭālib and the last of them being the awaited one in the cistern of Sāmarrā—he being Muḥammad b. al-Ḥasan al-ʿAskarī according to their claims. Of those, there were none more beneficial than ʿAlī and his son Ḥasan b. ʿAlī when they left the fighting and surrendered the rule to Muʿāwiya,[48] extinguished the fire of revolt *(fitna)*, and calmed the fighting between the Muslims. Those remaining[49] from the group of supporters had no authority over the [Islamic] nation concerning any matter.

As for believing in the one who is in the cave of Sāmarrā, that is foolishness in their heads and madness in their souls. There is no truth to it, and no substance or evidence.]

This tradition of Ibn Kathīr's given on the authority of the People of the Book parallels the biblical story more closely than any of the other traditions and is the only instance where Hagar is given some responsibility for Sarah's jealously, as in Genesis 16:4. It faithfully follows the biblical chronology where Hagar flees from Sarah in Genesis 16:6 and comes to a well, only to return after receiving the blessing and instructions of an angel; she gives birth to

Ishmael upon her return. Abraham then receives the "double prophecy" regarding Isaac and Ishmael, just as in Genesis 17:1ff.[50]

It appears as if the editorial remark, "His brethren will rule over all the land," has been inserted into this tradition immediately after the prophecy regarding Ishmael's birth in order to explain its meaning in Islamic terms. The preceding sentences are parallel with the biblical prophecy of Genesis 16:12 nearly word for word, but the biblical meaning is clearly inappropriate for Islam. The difficulty is solved by the slight change of "his hand above" *(yaduhu 'ala . . .)* from the Hebrew "his hand against" *(yado ba . . .)*. Even so, an additional line is inserted into the prophecy to leave no doubt as to its proper meaning. The insert occurred before Ibn Kathīr, who is careful to separate his comments from the traditions he cites,[51] explains the meaning of the prophecy with his comments in the following paragraph.

Ibn Kathīr cites authoritative traditions within his commentary in support of his mainstream Sunnī political and religious views. He feels the need to take issue with the powerful Twelver Shi'ite claim of the twelve Imāms deriving from the blessing of Ishmael, a far more symmetric answer than his own to the question of who are the twelve "sons" referred to in the blessing.[52]

Among ten traditions treating Ishmael's birth, only three attach a prophecy to the event. At first sight it appears odd that so little is made of the biblical prophecy regarding the birth of the Arab patriarch. The Bible itself provides an invaluable source for the enhancement of Ishmael's personality within Islam. Why then did so few commentators use such a valuable tool? The most likely answer is that few or no Biblicist traditions were available that took up the issue of prophecy connected with Ishmael's birth in a positive light. As we have seen above, the large compendium of Jewish tradition had little positive to say about the character of Ishmael, and Christianity agrees with the biblical view the Ishmael was rejected for the covenant in favor of his younger brother Isaac.

Although less likely, the lack of qur'ānic reference to prophecy connected with Ishmael may have also influenced the use of traditions.[53] Muslim exegetes hesitated to relate reports that might be perceived as contradicting the plain meaning of the Qur'ān, and its lack of reference to Ishmaelite prophecies may have prevented their inclusion. The exegetes who did relate such traditions are al-Ya'qūbī, al-Kisā'ī, and Ibn Kathīr. The first did not adopt the practice of careful analysis of records of authentication found in al-Ṭabarī and many other historians[54] and includes material considered suspect by others. Al-Kisā'ī's and Ibn Kathīr's traditions were attributed to non-authoritative transmitters who tended to follow the biblical renditions closely.[55] None of the prophecy traditions are found in Qur'ān commentaries, but rather appear in the histories or collections of popular hagiographic literature, which tend to be more lenient about including possibly suspect traditions and their sources.[56]

A careful examination of the qur'ānic references to Ishmael reveals that very little is actually said about him. Of the twelve times Ishmael's name is given in the Qur'ān, only Q.19:54-5 provides specific information about his character. In Q.2:125, God commands Ishmael along with Abraham to purify *(ṭahhara)* the Ka'ba for those who would use it as a place of prayer.[57] In Q.2:127, Ishmael assists Abraham in raising the foundations of the Ka'ba. The peculiar syntax of the latter reference alludes to Ishmael's inclusion only as an afterthought. As we shall see in Chapter 11 below, some exegetes assumed, despite Ishmael's explicit presence in the qur'ānic text, that Abraham raised the foundations even without his son's assistance. Both these verses and their contexts center on the character of Abraham. Ishmael is most definitely a secondary character.

In the nine verses enumerated below, Ishmael is mentioned along with a list of other prophets. His name appears to be included only because he too was considered a prophet. No specific information is offered that might lend insight into the qur'ānic conception of his character. In Q.2:133, Ishmael is included along with Abraham and Isaac as a pure monotheist. In Q.2:136, Ishmael is said to have received revelation along with Abraham, Isaac, Jacob, the tribes [of Israel], Moses and Jesus. In Q.2:140, Ishmael, along with Abraham, Isaac, and Jacob, is considered a pure Muslim or indigenous pre-Islamic monotheist *(ḥanīf)* rather than a Jew or a Christian. According to Q.4:163, Ishmael is to have received revelation along with Noah, Abraham, Isaac, Jacob, the tribes, Jesus, Job, Jonah, Aaron, Solomon, and David. Ishmael is included with Elisha, Jonah, and Lot in Q.6:87 as being preferred by God above His other creatures. In Q.14:39, Abraham gives a prayer of thanksgiving saying: PRAISE BE TO GOD WHO HAS GIVEN ME, IN MY OLD AGE, ISHMAEL AND ISAAC! In Q.21:85, Ishmael, Idrīs[58] and Dhū al-Kifl[59] are singled out as being steadfast. And in Q.38:48, Ishmael, Elisha *(Al-yasā')* and Dhū al-Kifl are described as being "chosen."

The only place in the Qur'ān where Ishmael is mentioned alone is in Sūra 19 *(Maryam)*, verses 54-5: MAKE MENTION IN THE SCRIPTURE OF ISHMAEL. HE WAS TRUE TO HIS PROMISE. AND HE WAS A MESSENGER, A PROPHET. HE ENJOINED WORSHIP AND ALMSGIVING UPON HIS PEOPLE AND WAS ACCEPTABLE IN THE SIGHT OF HIS LORD. Surprisingly, there is extremely little exegesis on these verses. One might assume that this Qur'ān locus would serve as an ideal place to bring many diverse reports to bear on the character and the history of the first Arab prophet and the progenitor of the northern Arabs.[60] But here we find an extreme scarcity of traditional material. Most likely, this is due to the simple lack of reports available that would paint Ishmael in a favorable light. By the sixth century C.E., Jewish exegesis had already long considered Ishmael an enemy of the Jews and contained few traditions that would supply positive information.[61] Pre-Islamic Arabian traditions had virtually nothing to say about Ishmael, since we see no Arabian material about him among the exegetes.[61]

Nevertheless, one narrative tradition responding to Sūra 19:54 . . . FOR HE WAS TRUE TO HIS PROMISE . . . repeats itself in a number of different forms among our sources. Al-Ṭabarī[63] explains that Ishmael would never lie or substitute concerning a promise he made because he was a man of his word. He cites a tradition ". . . on the authority of Sahl b. 'Uqayl that Ishmael promised a man to meet him at a [certain] place. He came, but the man forgot. Ishmael remained there and stayed all night until the man came the next day. He said: 'You did not leave?' Ishmael said: 'No.' He said: 'But I forgot!' He replied: 'I would not leave until you came.' Thus, he was true and sincere *(ṣādiq)*."

Al-Qummī[64] picks up the same tradition in shortened form but identifies his Ishmael as different from Abraham's son: "He made a promise, and he waited for his friend for a year. That was Ishmael b. Ezekiel."[65] Al-Qummī points out that this legend specifically does *not* refer to the Ishmael of the Qur'ān verse (therefore, not the prophet) but to another extraordinary person of the same name, Ishmael.

Al-Zamakhsharī gives the tradition on the authority of Ibn 'Abbās: "He promised a friend that he would wait for him in a [certain] place, and he waited for him for one year." Al-Zamakhsharī understands this to refer to Ishmael, son of Abraham, and connects Ishmael's trait of being true to his promise to his comment in 37:102: IF GOD WILLS, YOU WILL FIND ME MOST PATIENT AND ENDURING. Ishmael here is "promising" to be patient and enduring, even in the face of his own sacrifice at the hands of his father.[66]

The Shi'ite al-Ṭabarsī,[67] like a number of other exegetes, considers Ishmael to have been the prophet to the Jurhum tribe which had adopted him:

> Ibn 'Abbās said that he made an appointment *(wa'ada)* with a man. He waited for him in a [certain] place. The man forgot, but he waited for him for a year until the man came. That was transmitted from Abū 'Abdallāh. But Muqātil said that he waited for him for three days. It is said that Ishmael son of Abraham died before his father Abraham, and that that [person] is Ishmael son of Ezekiel, whom God sent to his people. They tore off the skin of his face and scalp. But God preferred him because of his desire for their torment.[68] He asked for pardon and God was pleased with his merit. He entrusted the matter of his people to God for His forgiveness or punishment. In the end, an angel of his Lord came to him and gave him greetings, saying: "I have seen what was done to you. God commanded me to obey you, so tell me what you desire." Ishmael said, "Let me be an example like Ḥusayn." Our companions transmitted this on the authority of Abū 'Abdallāh.

Al-Ṭabarsī points out the conflict of opinion over which Ishmael is the subject of this tradition. The Shi'ite coloring is obvious from Ishmael b. Ezekiel's desire to die as a martyr like Ḥusayn.[69]

Ibn Kathīr quotes al-Ṭabarī:[70] "... Sahl b. 'Uqayl related that the prophet Ishmael promised a man that he would meet him at a certain place. He came, but the man forgot. Ishmael remained there and slept there that night until the man came the next day. He said: 'You did not leave from here?' Ishmael replied: 'No.' The man said: 'But I forgot.' Ishmael replied: 'I would not leave until you came.' For that reason, HE WAS TRUE TO HIS PROMISE (Q.19:54). Sufyān al-Thawrī said: 'I heard that he stayed in that place and looked around for him until he came.' Ibn Shawdhab said: 'I heard that he decided to make that place his home.' "

Ibn Kathīr continues with an interesting tradition told on the authority of 'Abdallāh b. Abī al-Ḥamsā' that equates the behavior of Muḥammad with the legendary patience of Ishmael: "I had something of the Prophet's and I promised that I would bring it to a certain place. I forgot for two days, but I brought it to him on the third day. He was still in that place and said to me: 'O lad, you made it hard for me here. For three days I waited for you!' "

There is clearly some confusion regarding this tradition and the character of Ishmael, son of Abraham, in general. It is probable that the legend referring to his patience did not originally refer to our Ishmael, son of Abraham, but was assigned to him because of the lack of traditional information painting him in a positive light available to the early Muslims, the original Ishmael b. Ezekiel having been largely forgotten.

In conclusion, we note that the qur'ānic Ishmael is a vague and cloudy figure.[71] All we know about him is that he is an apostle and a prophet, and that he is connected with both biblical and non-biblical prophets, but especially with Abraham. He keeps his promise. He is a religious man who received divine revelation and urged his people to do pious deeds. We know nothing more from the Qur'ān and little more from the traditions attached to Q.19:54f. In fact, we shall observe below that the traditions that do provide information about the Islamic Ishmael tend to derive from legends and stories concerning Abraham. Had Ishmael not been associated with Abraham in the Qur'ān and therefore in Islamic narrative exegesis, his character would have developed even less.

# Chapter 6

# BEERSHEBA

The Beersheba story is a minor tale that parallels the story of Genesis 21:25-31 and occurs only five times in our sources. Because it has no direct connection to any qur'ānic reference, it is not played out in the Qur'ān commentaries and occurs in only half of the histories or story collections that cover Abraham's adventures in Syria.[1] Four renditions consist of full narratives. Ibn Sa'd gives another in the form of a simple reference:[2] "Abraham returned to Syria and stayed at Saba', a land in the vicinity of Jerusalem[3] and Palestine. There he dug a well and built a place of prayer *(masjid)*. But some of the inhabitants wronged him so he withdrew from them and settled in a place between Ramle and Jerusalem."

The narrative renditions of al-Ṭabarī, al-Tha'labī, and Ibn al-Athīr are identical in all essentials. That of Mujīr al-Dīn follows the same plot but adds more detail. None of the renditions are attributed to any traditionist or carry a chain of authorities *(isnād)*.

According to the legend, Abraham settles in al-Saba', which is in the land of Palestine. He digs a well there, builds a place of prayer, and finds the water of the well is good and pure. But the people of al-Saba' wrong him in some unspecified manner, so he leaves them and moves to *Qit* or *Qat*, also in Palestine.

As soon as Abraham departs, the water of the well dries up. The residents of al-Saba' pursue him and repent of their wrong, asking him to return and live with them again, but Abraham refuses and notes that he will not return to a place from which he was expelled. The people then complain that the well has gone dry. Abraham thereupon takes seven goats and gives them to the people, explaining that when the seven goats are brought to the well, plenty of fresh water will appear for them and everyone will be able to use it. But they must not allow any menstruating woman to draw near or ladle water from the well.

The people do as Abraham instructs them, and abundant water appears when the goats are brough near. The system works well until a menstruating woman ladles from it or drinks from it. As a result, the water recedes or becomes still, as it remains to this day.

The Mujīr al-Dīn version supplies additional information: Abraham comes to the Saba' valley *(wādī saba')* when he is still a young man with no property. As he grows older, his property and livestock increase until the people of the area complain that his large flocks and possessions are causing harm to them. Finally, they ask him to move away.[4] After Abraham leaves, some of the younger men of the town urge the others to take half of his wealth from him by force since he grew wealthy at the townspeople's expense. When they overtake Abraham and make this claim he replies: "O people, you are correct. I came to you when I was but a youth, and today I have become an old man. Return to me my youth and take whatever you desire from my wealth." With that, he defeated them in argument and they let him go.[5]

All the full renditions provide an etymology for the name al-Saba', where Abraham resided, although this is never explicitly spelled out. Saba' is the Arabic word for the numeral seven, which is the special number of goats that Abraham gave to the people of that place.[6] The Arabic name of that place is therefore *bi'r saba'* (Beersheba), the "Well of Seven". No editorial comment explicitly points out the connection, although the etymology is clear from the specific number of animals given to the people of al-Saba'.[7] The story depicts Abraham as a deeply religious man who, like the character depicted in Genesis, establishes places of worship wherever he settles and is fair and generous to his neighbors. It also warns of the consequences of women in an "impure" state (at the time of menses) drawing water from a well.

The Beersheba legend satisfies many criteria of Biblicist legends. It remains within the basic biblical chronology and has a geographical locus that is connected to a biblical site. All the named characters are biblical. The entire story is entirely consistent with Jewish legend, but appears to satisfy few criteria of Arab legends and has no connection to Arabian religious practice nor to any Arabian site.[8] Only the expulsion of the Abraham tribe from the oasis may reflect a nomadic Bedouin practice,[9] although the issues of menses and pure/impure states can be found both within Arab-Muslim and Israelite-Jewish tradition as well as others. No Islamic editorial comments can be found in our five renditions. For all intents and purposes, it appears that the Beersheba legend originated in a Biblicist milieu and was taken into Islam with only minor variations to reflect an Arab environment.

Despite its affinity with the form and content of Biblicist legends, however, the Islamic legend does not follow any known pre-Islamic Jewish or Christian legend that is available to us, although its motifs are not foreign to Biblicist material.[10] It strays far enough from the Genesis versions to suggest a relationship that is removed from our recension of the Bible.

The Islamic legend does in fact provide an alternative to the official etymology for Beersheba given in the biblical text of Genesis 21:22-34. The official biblical etymology bases the second component of the Hebrew name *be'er sheva'* (Beersheba) on the root meaning to make an oath or swear *(sh-b-')*.[11] The meaning of the name would therefore be "the well of oath," the oath referred to being the covenant sworn between Abraham and Abimelekh in Genesis 21:31. A similar story providing the same etymology for Beersheba is told further on in Genesis 26:26-33, where an oath is sworn between Isaac and Abimelekh.[12]

A second etymology for Beersheba's name is provided though not officially recognized in the biblical Abraham story of Genesis 21 (it does not occur in the Isaac version of the tale in Genesis 26). According to this explanation, the word *sheva'* in Genesis 21:32f (*shava'* in its pausal form) is derived from the number of animals Abraham gives Abimelekh as a legal signature to the pact they made. The root for the word seven in Hebrew is identical to the root for making an oath *(sh-b-')*, and some Semitic philologists have derived the latter meaning from the number seven.[13] Without the editorial gloss of Genesis 21:31, the name *be'er sheva'* would be easily understood from the context of the biblical passage to mean "the well of the seven," referring to the symbolic number of sheep Abraham gave Abimelekh as witness to their agreement. This, in fact, may have been the original significance of the name, which was superseded by a later "official" etymology in order to distance the holy site of Abraham's sojourns from any connection with magic or perhaps polytheist meaning. The last bit of evidence in favor of this interpretation is the word *sheva'* in Hebrew, which is attested in the Hebrew Bible only in the meaning of "seven"—never as "oath", which is found only in the form *shvu'ah*.[14]

In contrast to most Islamic legends that appear to have evolved from Biblicist exegetical narratives, the Islamic Beersheba story may have evolved directly out of a telling of the Genesis 21 version. As the biblical story was taken in oral form farther and farther away from its original locus in the minds of generations of emigrants or traveling traders, it would have passed through a series of transformations that could result in the hybrid version we find in our sources. It has no connection, for example, with the biblical Abimelekh, Philistines, or any petty ruler or king for that matter. It portrays only anonymous local inhabitants as Abraham's antagonists. There is presumably no reason for the biblical names to completely fall out unless they were forgotten.[15]

Of greater significance, the Islamic legend knows nothing of the official biblical etymology for Beersheba. We have noted that it does, however, provide the alternative etymology based on the seven goats Abraham gives to the people to restore the water of their well. The reason for its variant etymology on Beersheba is that the "official" biblical explanation made no sense for an

Arabic-speaking people. The Hebrew meaning of the root *sh-b-‘* for making an oath does not occur in Arabic.[16] The basic meaning of the Hebrew *sh-b-‘*, however, is a common Semitic word for seven found in both languages. When the legend came into an Arabic-speaking environment without a close connection with the Hebrew Bible, the official biblical etymology would make no sense. In an Arabic-speaking world, the root *sh-b-‘* (or in Arabic, *s-b-‘*) would have no connection to swearing an oath, but only to the number seven. The official biblical etymology therefore dropped out, and the alternative etymology became the only explanation for the name Beersheba.[17]

The Beersheba story adds no essential data to Islam, although it does provide information supporting the honesty and righteousness of Abraham (equally of interest to Judaism and Christianity). By virtue of Abraham's righteousness, the legend supports the justice of his being the patriarch for the monotheistic religions. It also establishes his perfected sense of fairness and duty, which will become important in the face of the subsequent conflict between Sarah and Hagar. Yet despite these contributions, it is unnecessary for the remainder of the Abraham-Ishmael story and in fact supplies no critical information regarding the unfolding story of Abraham, Ishmael, and the Meccan sanctuary. This and the fact that it has no relation to any qur'ānic text are the most plausible reasons why it was not utilized by more sources.

## Chapter 7

# THE ANGELS VISIT

The Islamic legend of the angels' visit to Abraham on their way to destroy the people with whom Lot lived is generally found in relation to Qur'ān 11:69-74 and 51:24-30, both of which parallel the biblical text of Genesis 18:1-16.[1] The relevant sections of the two major qur'ānic renditions follow:

> Qur'ān 11:69-74:
>
> OUR MESSENGERS CAME TO ABRAHAM WITH GOOD NEWS. THEY SAID: "PEACE!" HE ANSWERED: "PEACE!" AND DID NOT DELAY IN BRINGING A ROASTED CALF. BUT WHEN HE SAW THAT THEIR HANDS DID NOT GO TOWARD IT [TO EAT] HE BECAME MISTRUSTFUL OF THEM IN FEAR. THEY SAID: "DO NOT FEAR, FOR WE HAVE BEEN SENT TO THE PEOPLE OF LOT." HIS WIFE WAS STANDING [THERE] AND SHE LAUGHED. BUT WE GAVE HER THE ANNOUNCEMENT OF ISAAC, AND AFTER ISAAC, JACOB. SHE SAID: "ALAS FOR ME. SHALL I GIVE BIRTH, BEING AN OLD WOMAN? AND THIS, MY HUSBAND HERE IS AN OLD MAN! THAT IS A STRANGE THING INDEED!" THEY SAID: "DO YOU WONDER AT GOD'S DECREE? GOD'S GRACE AND BLESSINGS ARE UPON YOU, O NOBLE PEOPLE *(AHL AL-BAYT)*. HE IS INDEED THE PRAISEWORTHY AND GLORIFIED."
>
> Qur'ān 51:24-30:
>
> HAVE YOU HEARD THE STORY OF THE HONORED GUESTS OF ABRAHAM? THEY CAME TO HIM AND SAID: "PEACE!" AND HE ANSWERED: "PEACE!" A STRANGE PEOPLE. THEN HE TURNED QUICKLY TO HIS WIFE *(AHLIHI)* AND BROUGHT A FATTED CALF. HE SET IT BEFORE THEM AND SAID: "WILL YOU NOT EAT?" BUT HE WAS APPREHENSIVE OF THEM IN FEAR. THEY SAID: "FEAR NOT." AND THEY ANNOUNCED THE GOOD NEWS OF A KNOWLEDGEABLE SON *(GHULĀM 'ALĪM)*. THEN HIS WIFE CAME FORWARD WITH A CRY. SHE STRUCK HER FOREHEAD AND SAID: "A BARREN OLD WOMAN?!" THEY SAID: "THAT IS WHAT YOUR LORD HAS SAID, AND HE IS MOST-WISE AND KNOWLEDGEABLE." ABRAHAM SAID: "SO WHAT IS YOUR BUSINESS, O MESSENGERS?" THEY SAID: "WE HAVE BEEN SENT TO A SINFUL PEOPLE. . . ."[2]

Both of these widely separated passages of the Qur'ān refer to the same episode: the visit of a group of messengers[3] to Abraham on their way to destroy the cities and people of Lot.[4] Aside from announcing the birth of a son to Abraham and Sarah, the narrative contains no particularly useful information regarding the Abraham-Ishmael story. It is included in our sample because of its location within the Abraham/Ishmael sequence.

Five of the histories and folk literature collections provide a definite chronology for the angels' visit, although all agree that it occurred sometime during Abraham's sojourns in Syria.[5] Al-Ṭabarī, al-Mas'ūdī, and al-Tha'labī place it before the transfer of Ishmael and Hagar to Mecca. Al-Ya'qūbī and al-Kisā'ī place it afterward.[6] In fact, there is no reason for the episode to necessarily occur before or after the move to Mecca since it is essentially unrelated to the Ishmael story. Al-Kisā'ī, for example, never mentions any interaction or even meeting between Ishmael and Isaac. It is therefore completely logical for the visit of the angels to have taken place after Abraham had taken Hagar and their son to Mecca. According to al-Tha'labī, on the other hand, the natural competition between the half-brothers Ishmael and Isaac brought about Sarah's jealousy toward Hagar.[7] This could only have occurred after Isaac's birth, which was announced by the visiting angels. It was therefore necessary for al-Tha'labī to place the angels' visit before the transfer to Mecca.

The episode of the angels' visit to Abraham presents a unique situation within our sequence of stories because it serves to explain a narrative that is firmly and clearly established in both the biblical and qur'anic revelations.[8] In al-Ya'qūbī's rendition, we read:

> When the acts of deviance of the people of Lot increased, God sent angels to destroy them. They descended to Abraham who was very hospitable to guests. When they stayed with him, he served them a roasted calf, but when he saw that they did not eat he disapproved. They disclosed who they were to him and said, "WE ARE MESSENGERS OF YOUR LORD (Q.11:81) for the destruction of the people of this city"—meaning Sodom, the city in which lived the people of Lot.
>
> Abraham said to them, "BUT LOT IS THERE!" THEY ANSWERED, "WE KNOW VERY WELL ABOUT WHO IS THERE. WE WILL MOST CERTAINLY RESCUE HIM AND HIS FAMILY EXCEPT HIS WIFE" (Q.29:32). Abraham's wife, Sarah, had been standing and was surprised at their words.[9] They gave her the good news of [her giving birth to] Isaac, and she said, "SHALL I GIVE BIRTH, BEING AN OLD WOMAN? AND THIS, MY HUSBAND HERE IS AN OLD MAN!" (Q.11:72). Abraham was one hundred years old and she was ninety.

Al-Ya'qūbī generally does not provide a chain of authorities for his reports. His comments above, however, represent neither a tradition in the formal sense of the term nor his own rendition of a narrative tale, but rather a running commentary on two widely separated Qur'ān sections treating the story of the angels' visit to Abraham. He ties Qur'ān 11:69ff with 29:32 simply through his choice of words in explaining the plot of the story. He makes no attempt to identify a Qur'ān verse through formal language,[10] but rather weaves the words of Scripture into his own commentary.[11]

In the first paragraph, al-Ya'qūbī expalins that the messengers were angels *(malā'ika)*, emphasizes Abraham's hospitality, and clarifies that the city referred to in the Qur'ān is Sodom, using a Biblicist term to establish the locus for the qur'ānic "People of Lot."[12] All three of these details are assumed in the Qur'ān verse, but al-Ya'qūbī feels the need to explain. In the second paragraph, the only new information not already supplied by the Qur'ān are the ages of Abraham and Sarah.[13] Al-Ya'qūbī's depiction of the angels' visit, therefore, serves as an Islamic commentary that binds together two sections of the Qur'ān and clarifies data already assumed but not spelled out in the scriptural text.

Al-Ṭabarī's rendition of the angels' visit consists of both a narrative tradition and a running commentary:[14]

> The messengers were commanded to descend to Abraham and to give him the good news of Isaac through Sarah AND AFTER ISAAC, JACOB (11:71). By the time they had come down to Abraham, guests had been withheld from him for 15 nights until it had become unbearable to him. According to what they say, no one visited him or came to him. So when Abraham saw them [the messengers], he was delighted with them, seeing quests whose loveliness and beauty he had not previously beheld.
>
> He said, "I will serve these people with my own hands". So he went out to his wife and brought, as is written:[15] A FATTED CALF (Q.51:26) which he roasted. Roasting is cooking it well (wal-taḥnādh[16] al-inḍāj), as it is written in the Qur'ān: HE BROUGHT A ROASTED CALF (Q.11:69) AND SET IT BEFORE THEM (Q.51:27). But they kept their hands away from it. WHEN HE SAW THAT THEIR HANDS DID NOT GO TOWARD IT, HE BECAME MISTRUSTFUL OF THEM IN FEAR (Q.11:70) when they did not eat from his food. They said, "DO NOT FEAR, FOR WE WERE SENT TO THE PEOPLE OF LOT" (Q.11:70). His wife Sarah got up and laughed about what she knew of God's command and about what she knew of the people of Lot. Then they gave her the prophecy of Isaac AND AFTER ISAAC, JACOB a son and a grandson. And then she said AS SHE STRUCK HER FOREHEAD (Q.51:29)– she struck her brow–"ALAS FOR ME! SHALL I GIVE BIRTH, BEING AN OLD WOMAN? AND THIS, MY HUSBAND HERE IS AN OLD MAN! THAT IS A STRANGE THING INDEED!" THEY SAID: "DO YOU WONDER AT GOD'S DECREE? GOD'S GRACE AND BLESSINGS ARE UPON YOU, O NOBLE PEOPLE. HE IS INDEED THE PRAISEWORTHY AND GLORIFIED." (Q.11:72-3).

> Sarah was at that time, according to what some of the scholars[17] have reported to me, ninety years old, and Abraham was one hundred and twenty years old. WHEN FEAR HAD PASSED FROM ABRAHAM AND THE GOOD TIDINGS HAD REACHED HIM (Q.11:75) of Isaac, and Jacob was born of the loins of Isaac, and he felt safe from that which he was afraid of, he said: "PRAISE BE TO GOD WHO GRANTED ME IN OLD AGE ISHMAEL AND ISAAC. MY LORD IS MOST CERTAINLY THE HEARER OF PRAYER" (Q.14:39).

Al-Ṭabarī begins this section with a tradition about guests being withheld from Abraham for fifteen days. This is repeated by al-Tha'labī[18] and may have been derived from Jewish traditions. In the Jewish renditions, God withheld guests because Abraham had just circumcised himself, and his penchant for hospitality would have made recovery from his circumcision difficult.[19] The Islamic version has no connection with circumision, and the motif of the withheld guests in the Islamic context is puzzling. If God withheld guests from Abraham for a reason other than to allow his recent circumcision to heal, what was it? The tale implies that guests were withheld from him in order to make him a better host. But if that were the case, his excellent hospitality toward the angels would have been precipitated by godly intervention and would therefore be unnatural.

Nevertheless, the Islamic version clearly connects the withholding of guests from Abraham with his special eagerness to be hospitable to the visiting angels. Al-Tha'labī and al-Kisā'ī note that Abraham was so intent upon being hospitable that he would not eat without guests, which would explain his eagerness for guests when the angels finally arrived.[20] Yet Abraham's hunger would still fail to provide a suitable explanation for his exceptional hospitality. The motif of withholding guests simply does not fit naturally into the Islamic version. The confusion suggests that it derived from the Jewish tradition in which Abraham's circumcision was used to stress his hospitality toward the angels even while recuperating from a painful operation at the age of ninety-nine.[21]

The remainder of al-Ṭabarī's exegesis is a running commentary drawing together the Qur'ān renditions of Sūras 11 and 51. By closing with Qur'ān 14:39, al-Ṭabarī not only provides an appropriate response from Abraham to the miraculous tidings brought to him by the angels, he also places the angels' visit into the larger Abraham sequence by connecting it to Abraham's journey with Ishmael and Hagar to Mecca (Q.14:37). As in al-Ya'qūbī's exegesis, al-Ṭabarī's comments here serve to connect separate but related Qur'ān texts with a running commentary. He surpasses al-Ya'qūbī's weaving of qur'ānic quotes, however, by connecting an Abrahamic story in Syria with his experience in Mecca. The full and complete Abraham cycle emerges when the relevant Qur'ān texts are placed together in sequence.

In addition to his own coments, al-Ṭabarī produces a traditional commentary on the authority of al-Suddī:[22]

> Mūsā b. Hārūn reported to me going back to the authority of al-Suddī who said: "God sent a band of angels for the death of the people of Lot. They drew near walking in the form of young men until they came to Abraham and stayed as his guests. When Abraham saw them, he honored them and went to his wife. He brought a fatted calf and slaughtered it. Then he roasted it on a hot stone—this is the meaning of *ḥanīdh*: "when he roasts it"—and he came to them and sat with them, and Sarah got up to serve them. That was when the Qur'ān said, "HIS WIFE WAS STANDING (Q.11:71) and he was sitting," according to the recitation of Ibn Mas'ūd.[23] Then, when HE SET IT BEFORE THEM AND SAID, "WILL YOU NOT EAT?" (Q.51:27) They replied, "O Abraham, we do not eat food except through compensation." He said, "Then there is a price for this." They asked, "What is the price?" He said, "Say the *Basmalla* at the beginning of the meal and *al-ḥamdu lillāhi* at the end of the meal."[24] Then Gabriel looked toward Michael and said, "It is fitting to this one that his Lord take him as his friend.[25] BUT WHEN HE SAW THAT THEIR HANDS DID NOT GOT TOWARD IT (Q.11:70) he said: They are not eating. He was afraid of them—AND HE WAS APPREHENSIVE OF THEM IN FEAR (Q.11:70/51:28). When Sarah looked toward him and noticed that he honored them, she got up to serve them, laughed, and said, "How strange are these guests of ours; we serve them ourselves with great honor to them, but they do not eat our food."

Like al-Ṭabarī, al-Suddī's exegesis is mostly a running commentary. His explanation for the enigmatic word *ḥanīdh*, like al-Ya'qūbī's, is an attempt to explain both the word and the different descriptions of the calf in Q.11:69 *('ajal ḥanīdh)* and Q.51:26 *('ajal samīn)*. Al-Suddī also includes a narrative tradition connected to Q.51:27: WILL YOU NOT EAT?. He explains the hesitation of the angels by citing the story of Abraham's pious example of preaching the ways of Islam at every opportunity.[26] Requiring the blessing before the meal and the giving of thanks afterward parallels the Palestinian Targum(TJ1) on Genesis 18:5: "Refresh yourselves and give thanks for the sake of God's word. Afterwards, you can go on your way" *(Us'idu libkhon v'odu l-shum meimra dadonai uvatar k'dein ta'avirun)*.[27] Like the others, al-Suddī's words represent a running commentary originating after the beginning of Islam but including some earlier Biblicist material. His commentary serves to bind together separate sections of the Qur'ān as well as clarify parts of the text.

In al-Tha'labī's section treating the visit of the angels, we find the following:[28]

When God desired the destruction of the people of Lot, he sent his messengers to him [Lot] telling him to leave them. He ordered [the messengers] to begin [by visiting] Abraham, and they gave Sarah the good news ABOUT ISAAC AND AFTER ISAAC, JACOB (Q.11:71). When they came to Abraham, he had not had any guests for fifteen days. It had become unbearable for him, for as much as possible he would eat only when he had guests. So when he saw [the messengers] in the form of men, he was delighted. He beheld guests whose grace and beauty he had never hosted before. He said: "No one will go out to [welcome] these guests but me!" So he went and brought a fat *"ḥanīdh"* calf, which means that it was roasted on embers, and he brought it near them. But they withheld their hands from it. He said to them: "Will you not eat?" BUT WHEN HE SAW THAT THEIR HANDS DID NOT GO TOWARDS IT, HE DID NOT UNDERSTAND, AND BECAME APPREHENSIVE OF THEM IN FEAR (Q.11:70) when they did not eat of his food. But they said: "O Abraham, we do not eat food without [paying the] price." He said: "Well, then, there is a price for it." They asked: "What is its price?" He said: "You will mention God's name before [you eat], and give praise to God after [you finish].[29] [At that point] Gabriel looked toward Michael and said: "It is certainly fitting for him that his Lord has taken him as His friend." Then they said to him: "Do not fear. We have been sent to the people of Lot." Sarah at this time was standing and serving them while Abraham was sitting with them.[30] When they told him why they had been sent to him and gave him the good news about [the birth of] Isaac and Jacob, Sarah laughed.

The religious scholars differed over the reason for her laughing.[31]

Al-Suddī said: Sarah laughed when they did not eat from their food. She said: "How strange of these guests of ours. We serve them ourselves with great honor, yet they do not eat our food!"

Qatāda said: She laughed at the foolishness of the people of Lot as their punishment drew near.

Muqātil and al-Kalbī said: She laughed on account of the fear of Abraham toward [the] three [of them], for they were situated between his servants and his family dependents.

Ibn 'Abbās said: She laughed in shock that she would have a child in her old age and because of the age of her husband, for she was 90 while Abraham was 120 years old.

Al-Suddī said: When Gabriel gave her the good news about a son in her old age, she said to him: "Give me a sign of that." So he took a dry stick in his hand and twisted it between his fingers until it trembled and sprouted green. Abraham then said: "Verily, he will be a sacrifice to God!"[32]

> Mujāhid and 'Ikrima said: AND SHE LAUGHED (Q.11:71): that is, she menstruated at that moment. The Arabs say that rabbits laugh when they menstruate.[33]

Al-Tha'labī's commentary includes the two brief narrative traditions discussed earlier along with a series of authoritative comments explaining why Sarah laughed in Qur'ān 11:17. Unlike the earlier examples, this is not a running commentary but rather a collection of traditions that were woven together to form a narrative whole. Al-Tha'labī includes only a few Qur'ān verses in his comments and quotes only from the passage in Sūra 11. He makes no attempt to bind qur'ānic sections together.

Some of the explanations for Sarah's laughter are standard comments that are repeated in the Qur'ān commentaries.[34] Al-Suddī's tradition about the dry twig sprouting green as a sign or proof is also known in the Pentateuch.[35]

Al-Tha'labī's exegesis is a weave of traditions with few or no personal comments. The first part is made up of unauthoritative narratives while the series of short comments on Sarah's laughter represent typical authoritative Islamic exegesis.[36]

The qur'ānic story of the angels' visit is closely parallel to the biblical tale. As such, it is not surprising to note similarities in its exegesis. Nothing resembling Arab legends can be found in the exegesis collected here. Most of the commentary about the angels' visit consists rather of running Islamic commentaries, unauthoritative[37] traditions with many of the earmarks of Biblicist legends, and brief authoritative non-narrative exegesis dating from the Islamic period. Since the story of the angels' visit is both part of the sacred history of the Hebrew Bible and the history of prophecy in the Qur'ān, the similarities between Islamic and Jewish exegesis should not be unexpected. When the story was brought to the attention of the Arabs through its appearance in the qur'ānic revelation, the early Muslims naturally turned to Jews and Christians, from whom they knew they would find related information about it. The connection between Sarah's laughter at the angels' visit and the meaning of Isaac's name at his birth fell out in Islam, hastened by the fact that the etymological relation in Arabic between laughing *(ḍ-ḥ-k)* and Isaac *(s-ḥ-q)* did not parallel the exact correlation in the Hebrew cognate *tz-ḥ-q*.[38]

Since the story of the angels' visit originated and evolved largely outside of the pre-Islamic Arabian consciousness, there were no Arab legends available that could serve to shed light on the qur'ānic text.[39]

The five sections of exegetical material reviewed in the Syrian Prologue make up the major occasions of Abraham's experience in Syria among the Islamic sources. Part of their role in the Abraham cycle is to set the stage for bringing

Ishmael and Hagar to Mecca, where Abraham and Ishmael will build the Ka'ba and Abraham will establish the Pilgrimage. In addition to building up to the climax of the Meccan experience, however, the Syrian Prologue also supplies important information that serves to fill out the terse qur'ānic statements about Abraham.

Virtually all the exegetical material on the Syrian Prologue originates from two places. Many narrative traditions find clear parallels among the People of the Book, and can be said to have derived largely from Biblicist sources. The second source is the Muslim exegetes, who sought to establish a coherent Abraham story from the mass of disparate comments spaced throughout the Qur'ān by connecting widely separated texts in their commentaries. They also tried to understand enigmatic qur'ānic words or phrases by supplying their own explanations or quoting earlier Muslim scholars.

We encounter virtually no trace of indigenous Arab legends in the Syrian Prologue, nor would they be expected. By placing the terminus of Abraham's emigration in Syria, most early Muslims naturally sought clarifying traditions from among Biblicist legends. Despite the substantial dependence upon "foreign" traditions, however, the Islamic Abraham cycle remains uniquely Islamic and even Arab in character. The reason for this is that foreign traditions were not accepted into the Islamic corpus of legends in a wholesale manner. Certain motifs or even whole legends were rejected as being irrelevant or contrary to developing Islamic perspectives. Those of biblical roots that were accepted had already passed through a series of adaptations such that they would satisfy the basic religious and ethnic requirements of the new Muslim-Arab world view. In our sample of traditions, the Biblicist parallels may appear striking to one who is familiar with Jewish or Christian legends, but they in no way detract from the style and ultimate design of the Islamic Abraham cycle. No matter their origin, they have evolved into fully Islamic traditions that serve a different purpose from their Biblicist forebears. In the analysis of the Meccan Sequence which follows, we will observe how Biblicist and pre-Islamic Arab material serve together to provide legendary authority for newly Islamized ritual and religious sites.

PART THREE

# The Meccan Sequence

## INTRODUCTION

After Abraham's emigration to Syria and his encounter with the tyrant, the birth of Ishmael, the incident at Beersheba, and the visit of the angels, virtually all action in the Abraham cycle moves to the environs of Mecca. Abraham brings Hagar and Ishmael to Mecca, settles them there, and then returns to Syria. Although his permanent residence remains in Syria, all the narrative action takes place in Mecca, where he periodically visits his son. Sarah drops out of the story after Abraham settles Ishmael and Hagar in Mecca, and Hagar soon drops out as well as Ishmael grows up, marries a local Arab woman, and acculturates to Arabian life. He is later associated with his father building the Ka'ba and making the Ḥajj pilgrimage during one of Abraham's visits. Despite the fact that Abraham does not appear in every narrative of this collection, he remains a pervasive presence throughout.

The Meccan Sequence essentially establishes Mecca and its environs as Holy Land through Abraham's association with its sacred sites. Although it does not negate the holiness of that area of Syria sometimes referred to as the Holy Land in our Arabic sources,[1] it establishes the precedent of an equally holy geography in the Arabian Ḥijāz which will eventually surpass it. Abraham establishes the earliest monotheism in Mecca, even pre-dating the monotheism of the Jews and Christians.[2] The ancient monotheistic origin of the Ka'ba is authenticated through his and Ishmael's actions as its founders. Abraham and Ishmael also establish the foundations of a sacred genealogy that will produce the Northern Arabs and eventually, the important tribe of Quraysh, keepers of the Ka'ba and the tribe of the last and greatest prophet, Muḥammad. And finally, Abraham calls all humanity to take part in the first postdeluvian Ḥajj or Pilgrimage to the sacred sites, thus authenticating their monotheistic roots.

# Chapter 8

# THE TRANSFER TO MECCA

While the Qur'ān refers to Abraham and Ishmael in Mecca,[1] it provides no explanation as to how they arrived there. The traditions found in this chapter fill out the qur'ānic references by establishing a context for the transition of our two main protagonists from Syria to the Ḥijāz. Three versions of the transfer are found repeated often in the sources. Each is told on the authority of a separate early traditionist: Ibn 'Abbās,[2] 'Alī,[3] and Mujāhid.[4]

## THE IBN 'ABBĀS VERSION

The "Ibn 'Abbās" version of the transfer to Mecca is made up of twelve full narratives,[5] an additional two which are incomplete,[6] and five fragments referring to one or two motifs from the full story.[7] Nineteen full and partial renditions make up the paradigmatic Ibn 'Abbās version which follows:

1. The narrative takes place subsequent to Sarah's behavior toward Hagar. Sarah's jealousy of her handmaid after the birth of Ishmael causes conflict and strife between the two women (8/19).
2. Hagar lets down her dress or soaks the bottom of her dress to hide her tracks from Sarah (9/19).
3. Abraham gives Hagar and Ishmael a saddlebag of dates and a water skin (4/19), or a water skin only (8/19).
4. Abraham personally brings Hagar and Ishmael to Mecca (9/19), to the House[8] (6/19), or to the location of Zamzam[9] (6/19), and leaves them under a large tree (9/19)[10] (in all versions Abraham brings them to Mecca without God commanding him to do so and without any supernatural assistance).
5. After depositing them there, Abraham departs on his return to Syria, and arrives at Kadā (7/19).[11]

6. Hagar follows him and asks him to whom he is entrusting them in that desolate place. When he finally answers: "to God", or that God commanded him, Hagar is satisfied (13/19). Abraham then recites Qur'ān 14:37: O LORD! I HAVE MADE SOME OF MY OFFSPRING LIVE IN AN UNCULTIVATED *WĀDĪ* BY YOUR SACRED HOUSE, IN ORDER, O LORD, THAT THEY ESTABLISH REGULAR PRAYER. SO FILL THE HEARTS OF SOME WITH LOVE TOWARD THEM, AND FEED THEM WITH FRUITS SO THAT THEY MAY GIVE THANKS (7/19); or the following verse (14:38): O LORD! YOU KNOW WHAT WE CONCEAL AND WHAT WE REVEAL, FOR NOTHING ON EARTH OR IN HEAVEN IS HIDDEN FROM GOD (2/19).
7. Ishmael was still being suckled at the time (2/19). The water in the water skin runs out (11/19) and Hagar's milk stops flowing for her son (11/19). Ishmael gets thirsty and begins writhing or having a seizure (6/19). Hagar cannot bear to see him die (8/19).
8. She climbs the nearby hills of Ṣafā and then Marwa[12] (15/19) and runs between them seven times (11/19) like someone exerting himself (2/19), or in distress (4/19), or *not* like someone in distress (1/19).
9. A comment is inserted here on the authority of the Prophet or Abū al-Qāsim[13] that this is why people run between Ṣafā and Marwa, or this is the manner in which people run between Ṣafā and Marwa (8/19).
10. Hagar is desperate because of the worsening condition of her son. She thinks she hears a voice (10/19), which turns out to be an angel (8/19) or Gabriel (6/19), who scratches the ground with his heel (14/19) or wing (3/19), bringing forth water. Or, when she returns to Ishmael, she finds him scratching the ground with his heel, which brings forth the water (2/19).[14]
11. Hagar immediately dams up the flow (13/19), or scoops water into her water skin (12/19), or both.
12. A second comment is inserted here on the authority of the Apostle, Abū al-Qāsim or the Prophet (15/19),[15] or Ibn 'Abbās (1/19) to the effect: "May God have mercy on the mother of Ishmael. If she had not done that, then Zamzam would be flowing forever with a great volume of fresh water."
13. The angel tells Hagar not to worry about perishing, for the boy and his father will build the House of God there (7/19).

This Ibn 'Abbās version of the transfer legend exhibits all the earmarks of a Biblicist tradition that has evolved to the point where it has become acceptable to an Arab Islamic milieu. It is, first of all, very closely associated with the biblical rendition in its structure, content and style, and follows the biblical telling of Genesis 21:9-21 in almost perfect order:

Motif 1 parallels Genesis 21:9-10.
Motif 3 parallels verse 14.
The tree of motif 4 parallels the bush of verse 15.
Motif 7 parallels verses 15-16.
Motif 8 parallels verse 16.
Motif 10 parallels verses 17-19.
Motif 11 parallels verse 19.
Motif 13 parallels verse 18.

And as in the biblical rendition, only the miracle of the well points to supernatural intervention. Even the destination of their journey at Mecca is easily equated with the Paran desert of Genesis 21:21, an area in the northeastern Sinai Peninsula[16] inhabited by desert nomads during most of the biblical period and associated with Arab peoples.[17] This Biblicist connection is confirmed by the Muslim geographer Yāqūt, who writes: "*Fārān* . . . an *arabized* Hebrew word. One of the names of Mecca mentioned in the Torah."[18]

The Ibn 'Abbās version also parallels extra-biblical Jewish tradition, such as the parallel of motif 2 (of Hagar hiding her tracks) with PRE 67a-b: "[Abraham] took a water barrel *(dardūr)* and tied it around her waist so that it would drag behind her in order to demonstrate that she was a bondwoman."[19] Hagar's mistake in motif 12 parallels BR 53:14: " 'And she went and filled the bottle with water' (Genesis 21:19). This proves that she was lacking in faith."[20]

Despite the many Biblicist parallels, the Ibn 'Abbās version exhibits traits of Arab lore as well. It explains the old Arab religious practice of running between Ṣafā and Marwa, though it reinterprets the act in monotheistic terms by substituting Hagar's actions for the pre-Islamic practice of running between the idols that graced the peaks of the two hills.[21] It also provides an explanation for the miraculous nature of the Zamzam well in Mecca. And of course, the setting for the narrative takes place in a central Arabian religious site.

Islamic material is clearly evident as well. Motif 6 binds an action in the drama directly to Qur'ān verse 14:37 or 14:38, and the authoritative section making up motif 9 explains the running ritual between Ṣafā and Marwa in clearly acceptable Islamic terms. Finally, motif 12 consists of another authoritative insert that explains why the supposedly miraculous Zamzam well had very little water.[22]

It is not difficult to identify the legend's many parallels with Biblicist material. But the narrative as a complete entity clearly exhibits all the qualities of an Islamic legend. It demonstrates this both in its particular rendering of foreign parallels and with details that are inconsistent or unrelated to other sources. Abraham, for example, personally brings Hagar and Ishmael to Mecca rather than simply sending them away as in the biblical rendition.[23] The spring is identified as the Arabian Zamzam rather than Miriam's well or the well created on the sixth day of creation found in Jewish sources.[24] Moreover, after hearing from Abraham that her new home in inhospitable Mecca is God's decree, she is satisfied with her lot rather than straying after false gods as in Biblicist tellings.[25] And of course, the entire section of Hagar's running between Ṣafā and Marwa is completely foreign to Biblicist accounts; its parallel with pre-Islamic Arabian religious practice is masked by the acceptable reinterpretation of the ritual act through the actions of Hagar and Ishmael.

It is clear from the preceding that the Ibn 'Abbās version originated at least in part as Biblicist tradition based on exegesis of the Bible. As it evolved in oral form, however, it incorporated pre-Islamic Arab elements that anchored it to the sanctuary tradition of Mecca.[26] The Islamic material was added last, reflecting an Islamic outlook and making what originated as irrelevant or inadmissable material perfectly acceptable to Islam.

In addition to the nineteen traditions making up the Ibn 'Abbās version, a number of traditions lacking records of authentication fit the same paradigm with slight variations. These unauthoritative traditions are less regular and tend to mix motifs from the more consistent authoritative traditions, often resulting in composite narratives that appear to have been collected or even created by later redactors. They may also represent traditions whose original sources were dropped because they were not recognized as reliable by later transmitters, and they are sometimes quite unique.

Al-Ya'qūbī's brief unauthoritative rendition incorporates the Ibn 'Abbās version's motif numbers 6, 7, 8, and 11.[27] It begins with a prophecy immediately before the birth of Ishmael: "God said: 'I will increase your progeny and will give them a dominion that will last throughout time such that no one will know their number.' When Hagar gave birth Sarah became jealous . . ." The Ṣafā and Marwa section is largely eliminated, and a bird rather than an angel brings forth the water of Zamzam.

The rendition found in al-Kisā'ī's collection includes motif numbers 7, 8, 10, 11, and 12.[28] Although the story line follows the Ibn 'Abbās version, the wording and details are often quite different. Ishmael, for example, is born with the light of Muhammad shining from his face,[29] and God specifically directs Abraham to bring Ishmael and Hagar to the sacred land of Mecca. After their water runs out, Hagar tries to shade Ishmael from the intense heat of the sun with a piece of cloth that she hangs on the tree. And the narrator himself rebukes Hagar for damming up the well rather than placing the words in the mouth of Muḥammad (motif 12).

Ibn al-Athīr's rendition[30] includes motif numbers 1, 4, 5, 6, 7, 8, 9, 11, and 12. As in al-Kisā'ī's rendition, God tells Abraham to bring them to Mecca. Motif 9 about the running ritual is given by the narrator rather than on the authority of the Prophet. No angel or supernatural intervention appears in this rendition. The spring begins to flow after Ishmael scrapes his heel on the ground.

Mujīr al-Dīn's rendition contains motif numbers 1, 3, 4, 5, 6, 7, 8, 9, 10, 11, 12, and 13.[31] This telling is one of the more complete narratives and follows the Ibn 'Abbās version almost verbatim. The only variant detail is that God authorizes Abraham to take Ishmael and Hagar to Mecca.

A particularly interesting and unique telling of the story is given by al-Ṭabarī on the authority of al-Suddī and includes motif numbers 1, 2, 4, 5, and 6.[32] In a jealous rage, Sarah sends Hagar out, brings her back and then sends her out again.[33] Sarah is beside herself with anger and vows to cut Hagar to pieces, but then decides to circumcise Hagar, who uses the bottom of her skirt to wipe off the blood. This, the narrator notes, is the origin of female circumcision and the practice of using a feminine napkin.[34]

Al-Tha'labī has a related rendition given on the authority of al-Suddī, Ibn Yasār, and other transmitters *(ahl al-akhbār)* containing motif numbers 1, 4, 5, 6, 7, 8, 10, 11, 12, and 13.[35] Isaac and Ishmael are born at the same time and grow up together. The two brothers compete with one another one day in the presence of their father, and Ishmael wins. Abraham rewards him by giving him his own seat and setting Isaac down beside him, an act apparently reflecting the status of primogeniture and inheritance. As a result, Sarah is furious at Abraham for treating Hagar's son as if Hagar were his second legal wife.

> She got angry and said, "You took the son of the slave woman and sat him on your seat, but took my son and sat him next to you. But you swore by God that you would not take a second wife! Do not vex me!" Female jealousy had taken ahold of her. She swore to cut off a piece of [Hagar's] flesh in order to change her physical state. When she came back to her senses, she became confused about what happened. Abraham then suggested: "Reduce her status by boring a hole in her ear."[36] She did that, and it became a custom among women. Then Ishmael and Isaac fought with one another as young boys tend to do. But Sarah got angry with Hagar and said, "You will not live with me in the same place!" She commanded Abraham to dismiss Hagar. God then gave Abraham a revelation that he bring Hagar and her son to Mecca.

At this point, the rendition follows an authoritative version attributed to Mujāhid.[37] This telling of the legend provides an Arabic etymology for Ishmael when Hagar hears the angel who saves them from thirst,[38] and also gives a folk-etymology for an alternative name for the Zamzam well: *rakdat jibrīl*, meaning "the impulse of Gabriel."[39]

One motif common to most of these last renditions but absent from the Ibn ʿAbbās version is that God personally directs Abraham to bring Hagar and Ishmael to Mecca. This aspect is prominent in all the other authoritative versions of the legend listed below.

## THE ʿALĪ VERSION

A different tale is told on the authority of ʿAlī b. Abī Ṭālib.[40] According to the "ʿAlī" version, Abraham proceeds to Mecca because God commanded him to establish the site of the Kaʿba. He brings Hagar and Ishmael along, but no mention is made of any conflict with Sarah. The ʿAlī version is found in two forms. The first, cited in two sources,[41] reports that after God commanded Abraham to build the Sacred House or Kaʿba, a supernatural being called the *sakīna*[42] guided him to Mecca and showed him its proper location. In al-Ṭabarī's *History*, Ishmael and Hagar accompany Abraham on his journey as the *sakīna* guides them on their way. When they arrive in Mecca, it circles around the site of the House and says "Build upon me! Build upon me!" In al-Ṭabarī's *Commentary*, the *sakīna* guides Abraham alone from Armenia to the House, and Ishmael and Hagar are not mentioned. The *sakīna* shows him the location "as a spider ascends to its house, and it is raised up from stones that 30 men could not lift."[43]

The second form of the ʿAlī version is made up of three somewhat more consistent renditions.[44] When Abraham is commanded to build the House, Ishmael and Hagar go out with him. They arrive in Mecca and see something like a white cloud with a head in it floating over the site of the Kaʿba.[45] This cloud tells Abraham to build exactly on its shadow or measurement, but not to exceed or fall short of the specified dimensions. After Abraham builds the House, he leaves, and Hagar and Ishmael follow him. When Hagar asks to whom he is entrusting them, Abraham replies: "To God." Hagar is satisfied, but Ishmael soon becomes thristy so she runs from Ṣafā to Marwa seven times looking for help. She cannot bear to see the death of her child, but she nonetheless returns to Ishmael, who is scratching up the ground with his heel. She finds the angel Gabriel there, who asks her who she is. She replies that she is the mother of Abraham's son. He asks: "To whom did he entrust you?" She answers: "To God." Gabriel is satisfied, the boy scratches the ground with his finger, and the water of Zamzam flows out. Hagar begins to hold back the water and is chastised by Gabriel, who says: "Stop that, for the water is fresh!", or in another rendition, "for it quenches thirst!"

The first form of the ʿAlī version entirely omits the long section about Ishmael's thirst and the well of Zamzam. Aside from the names of the characters and the term, *sakīna*, it has no parallels in Biblicist legends. The second form includes the thirst and the Zamzam sequence and therefore finds more natural parallels with the biblical legend.[46] Both variants contain motifs that contradict or are unrelated to the biblical text: Abraham personally brings Hagar and Ishmael to Mecca and is guided by a supernatural being. Hagar asks Abraham to whom he is entrusting them, and runs between Ṣafā and Marwa in search for help (as in the Ibn ʿAbbās version).

We note hints of pre-Islamic Arab influence in the ʿAlī version. The description and function of the *sakīna* and the speaking cloud are not inconsistent with Arab folklore.[47] The geographical locus is obviously connected with the ancient pre-Islamic religious site, and Hagar's running between Ṣafā and Marwa reflects a known pre-Islamic Arab rite. Neither variant contains any new Islamic material.

The ʿAlī version does not relate to the biblical story as does the Ibn ʿAbbās version. It is only vaguely related to the biblical text and appears to be largely unconscious of the Bible account. Although affected indirectly by Biblicist material (minimally by the names of the characters), it does not derive from a Biblicist environment. It most likely originated as an Arab or otherwise non-biblically oriented legend that evolved into a hybrid containing some components of Biblicist as well as pre-Islamic Arabic material.

## THE MUJĀHID VERSION

According to the "Mujāhid" version, Abraham brings Ishmael and Hagar with him to Mecca, where God shows him the site of the Kaʿba. This version is made up of six renditions, four on the authority of Mujāhid[48] and one each on the authority of Ibn Isḥāq[49] and al-Ṣādiq.[50] Five are complete narratives while one is a fragment on the authority of Mujāhid. The paradigmatic Mujāhid version follows:

1. God shows Abraham the site of the House (4/6),[51] or Gabriel shows him (1/6), and Ishmael and Hagar come along (5/6). God (3/6) or Gabriel (1/6) also show Abraham the sites of the Sacred Precinct *(ḥarām)* of Mecca.
2. They come from Syria (3/6) when Ishmael is still suckling (3/6).
3. Gabriel guides them (5/6) and they ride on the legendary supernatural steed, Buraq (4/6).[52]
4. On their way, they never pass a town (4/5) or a pleasant location (1/5) without Abraham asking Gabriel if that is where he should build the Kaʿba. Gabriel answers: "No, keep going!" When they come to Mecca (5/5), it is full of rocks and three varieties of thorn trees (4/5).[53] the Amalekites live in the area (3/5), and the site of the House is a reddish clay hill (4/5).[54] Abraham asks again if this is the place and Gabriel answers: "yes" (4/5).[55]

5. Abraham leaves Hagar and Ishmael at al-Ḥijr and tells Hagar to build a shelter there (4/5).
6. Abraham then recites Q.14:37 (5/5) and departs (3/5), returning to Syria (2/5).

Only two of the six renditions include the Ṣafā and Marwa sequence. In al-Ṭabarī's *History*, Hagar hears a voice on Ṣafā and climbs the hill looking for help. She prays to God for rain and then hears the voice again, this time near Marwa. She runs there, climbs that hill, and prays again. When she hears the sounds of wild animals in the wadi, she rushes to Ishmael and finds him drinking water from a spring gushing forth under his hand. She drinks and begins to draw water into her water skin. If she had not done that, then Zamzam would be a spring of pure water forever. A comment on Mujāhid's authority is appended to the story, stating that some say it was Gabriel who dug out Zamzam with his heel.

Al-Ṣādiq's rendition has Hagar calling out for help and climbing Ṣafā. She sees a mirage in the wadi so runs toward it. Then she climbs Marwa and sees another mirage, so runs to it as well, repeating the maneuver seven times. On her seventh circuit at Marwa, she sees water underneath Ishmael's legs so she races to him and dams it up with sand. The narrator remarks that the well is called Zamzam because she collected *(zammat)* the water.

All renditions of motif numbers 1 through 6 are virtually identical with the exception of that of al-Ṣādiq, who mixes in some aspects of the Ibn 'Abbās version. According to al-Ṣādiq, the story takes place after the conflict with Hagar, and God tells Abraham to bring Hagar and Ishmael to the safety of Mecca. Before leaving, Abraham promises Sarah that he will not descend from his mount until he returns to Syria.[56] Hagar ties a garment on a tree for shade when they arrive, and tells Abraham that it is not like him to leave them in such a desolate place. Abraham replies that God commanded him to bring them there and then departs to Kadā where he recites Qur'ān 14:37.

The Mujāhid version has little in common with Biblicist legends aside from the names of the characters. Abraham's supernatural guide and steed in the form of Gabriel and Buraq are nowhere found in the entire series of Genesis legends. The motif of the magic steed, Buraq, may have originated in Arabia.[57] And Gabriel, though officially an angel, seems to take on the traits of a jinni *(jinn)* who takes Abraham on a magic horse and speaks in riddles until arriving at their destination in Mecca. Even the two renditions of the Zamzam motif omit any mention of an angel or divine intervention with the sudden flow of the spring as may be found in the Genesis rendition. The one Islamic editorial insertion found in every rendition of this version is where Abraham recites Qur'ān 14:37, thus binding the legend to Islamic Scripture.

Like the 'Alī version, the Mujāhid version appears to be a hybrid that contains both Biblicist and Arab elements. The two versions display enough similarities to suggest the possibility of their having been derived from the same ancient *milieu*.[58]

To summarize our findings, the Ibn 'Abbās version of the transfer legend appears to be quite conscious of the Bible and careful not to contradict it, connecting Abraham and his Ishmaelite descendants to Mecca and its environs in a manner that is consistent with the biblical narratives. There are no major contradictions and no one could claim fairly that it distorts the biblical meaning. It is, rather, an *extension* of the biblical story, lengthening a tale that comes to an abrupt halt in the Bible. As will become evident in the following chapters, the Ibn 'Abbās version of the Transfer tradition is part of a longer Ibn 'Abbās narrative that follows the story of Abraham and Ishmael to its logical conclusion with the construction of the Ka'ba and Abraham's famous call to the Pilgrimage.

The Mujāhid version also brings Abraham with Hagar and Ishmael to Mecca, but is not concerned about being consistent with the biblical narrative. The major goal of Abraham's Meccan journey in this version was for God to show him where to build the Ka'ba. Like the Ibn 'Abbās version, it also establishes Abraham's Ishmaelite line in Mecca, although is not nearly as detailed (two thirds of the traditions know nothing of the Ṣafā-Marwa or Zamzam sections).

The 'Alī traditions connect Abraham directly to the site of the Ka'ba and also have no direct consciousness of the biblical story. Their portrayal of Ishmael and Hagar is inconsistent and even omitted entirely in one rendition, suggesting that their involvement in the story may have been an addition to an earlier legend depicting only Abraham journeying alone to Mecca.

Both the 'Alī and Mujāhid versions appear to have the goal of connecting Abraham directly to the Ka'ba, whereas the Ibn 'Abbās version connects Abraham, Ishmael and Hagar with the larger area of Mecca.[59] The 'Alī and Mujāhid versions are highly dependent on the supernatural with the *sakīna*, the magic cloud, angelic guide and supernatural steed, while the Ibn 'Abbās version is not.

The Ibn 'Abbās version evolved out of a Biblicist tradition that underwent a series of changes in pre-Islamic Arabian and Islamic settings until it came into the form we observe in our sources. The 'Alī and Mujāhid versions, on the other hand, appear to have originated as Arab traditions, explaining the sanctity of the Ka'ba. These versions also evolved until they too would satisfy the needs of Islam with its incorporation of biblical themes. both represent hybrid versions that include aspects from various sources. Despite their varied origin, all three now function effectively as Islamic traditions with their particular religious and cultural agenda.

# Chapter 9

# THE JURHUM

The Jurhum legend serves the role of assimilating Ishmael into Arab culture from that of the Biblicist world, and at the same time establishes his prominent role in traditional Arab genealogy. Consequently, its significance cannot be fully understood without understanding the basic thrust of the classic Arab genealogical world view. The genealogists agree that all Arab tribes are derived from one of two great ancestors, Qaḥṭān or 'Adnān. The former is generally associated with the True or Original Arabs *(al-'arab al-'āriba)*, ancient tribes such as 'Ād, Thamūd, Ṭasm, and Iram, most of which had disappeared long before the beginning of Islam and are therefore designated also as the Lost Arabs *(al-'arab al-bā'ida)*. The descendants of Qaḥṭān are the southern Arabs *(qabā'il al-yaman)* and include such famous groupings as the Ḥimyar, Kahlān, Ṭayyi', and the famous Aws and Khazraj of Medina, who figured so prominently in Muḥammad's emigration there from Mecca.

'Adnān is associated with the Arabised Arabs (*al-'arab al-muta'arriba* or *al-'arab al-musta'riba*), those non-indigenous tribes who became Arabized when they migrated into the Arabian Peninsula. The descendants of 'Adnān are the northern Arabs, including such well known groupings as the Thaqīf, Tamīm, Kināna, and most important, the Quraysh, from which Muḥammad, the Umayyad and 'Abbasid imperial dynasties, and the Imāms of the Shi'ites all derive. Ishmael is considered an ancestor of the tribal descendents of 'Adnān. He is the progenitor of the northern Arabs, those who re-established the new-old religion of Islam and who led the faithful in its great conquests.[1]

Arab genealogical tradition considers the Jurhum one of the ancient True Arab tribes derived from Qaḥṭān. The Jurhum migrated from Yemen to Mecca, where they are assumed to have controlled the religious rites of the Ka'ba or even to have built it, but were eventually forced to concede control of the holy city and then died out long before the beginning of Islam.[2]

Ibn 'Abbās is the only consistent authority for the Jurhum legend, with eleven narratives attributed directly to him.[3] Three additional renditions of the legend but without records of authentication are also found among our sample.[4] We have found, in addition, two narrative fragments of the legend, one without a chain of authorities[5] and one attributed to Saʿīd b. Jubayr,[6] and two unique narratives that are clearly informed by the Ibn ʿAbbās version: one is told on the authority of Wahb,[7] and one on the authority of al-Ṣādiq.[8]

The following plot sequence of the Jurhum legend is based on the fourteen complete narratives.

1. The Jurham live in a wadi near Mecca (3/14), or a caravan or group of Jurhum pass Mecca (10/14) on their return from Syria (2/14) or on their way to Syria (4/14) from Yemen (1/14). They pass through Kadā (3/14) or the lower part of Mecca (7/14).
2. The Jurham notice a bird circling over the Meccan wadi (14/14). Birds only circle[9] over water, but the Jurhum know that no water can be found in the Mecca valley. Curious, they send one or two scouts who report back that there is indeed water there (7/14).
3. The Jurhum enter, find Hagar, and request of her to allow them to live there. She agrees (14/14), but the water will remain in the possession of Hagar and Ishmael (9/14).
4. A statement is interjected on the authority of the Prophet (or Abū al-Qāsim): Hagar was happy to allow the Jurhum there because she loved humanity (5/14).
5. Ishmael grows up with the Jurhum (12/14),
6. learns Arabic from them (5/14),
7. impresses them with his abilities (4/14),
8. and marries a Jurhumite woman (11/14).
9. Hagar dies before (6/14) or after (3/14) Ishmael's marriage.
10. Ishmael also learns to hunt from the Jurhum (2/14).

The narrative ends rather abruptly here in most renditions and immediately picks up with Abraham's visits to Ishmael to inspect his legacy.[10] Only a few renditions, none of which are attributed to Ibn ʿAbbās, specifically take up the genealogy of Ishmael's descendents.[11] The only direct parallel with the biblical narrative is Ishmael learning to hunt, which occurs only twice.[12] Aside from this and the fact that the main characters are also biblical, the narrative appears to have no connection with Biblicist literature. Despite the lack of parallels, however, the legend perfectly fits the paradigm of narrative exegesis on Genesis 21:20f, "And God was with the boy and he grew up; he dwelt in the wilderness and became an archer. He lived in the wilderness of Paran. . . ."[13]

Of the two renditions attributed to sources other than Ibn ʿAbbās, the earliest is given by Ibn Qutayba[14] on the authority of Wahb and includes motif numbers 5, 6, 8, and 11. It adds that the Jurhum give Ishmael seven goats, which become the basis of his possessions.[15]

The second is given by al-Ṭabarsī[16] on the authority of al-Ṣādiq and includes motif numbers 2, 3, and 5. The Jurhum tribe is living in the Ḥijāz and at ʿArafāt[17] when Abraham settles Hagar and Ishmael in Mecca. Animals as well as birds draw near to the water of Zamzam. When the Jurhum request permission of Hagar to live with her and her son, she cannot respond until she asks Abraham, who visits them on the third day. Abraham agrees, so the Jurhum pitch their tents there. When Abraham visits a second time, he is exceptionally pleased with the large number of people who have settled there. Each one of the Jurhum give Ishmael one or two sheep.

Other reports provide more information about the Jurhum, although they do not always connect the tribe with Ishmael. Al-Thaʿlabī[18] includes a poem that was part of a pre-Islamic ritual litany uttered during parts of the Pilgrimage ritual and known as *talbiya*:[19] "For this reason, the Arabs used to recite in their *talbiya*:

> Nay. The Jurhum are Your servants
> All people are your acquisition, but they are Your original possession.
> In ancient times, they built Your cities.

Two reports declare that because of their sins, the Jurhum are no longer blessed with the glories and miracles of the Kaʿba and Zamzam.[20] Al-Ṭabarī's mentions that the second Caliph ʿUmar b. al-Khaṭṭāb preached a sermon noting that God destroyed the Jurhum because of their desecration of the Kaʿba.

Both al-Thaʿlabī and Ibn al-Athīr note that Ishmael is the father of the Arabized Arabs but provide no traditions in support of their claims. In fact, no authoritative tradition specifically supporting the claim that Ishmael is the father of the northern Arabs could be located in any of the traditions from our sample. His lofty position within Arab genealogy is assumed, but aside from the Jurhum legend, has little authoritative support in the tradition. Recent research in the sources of Arab genealogy supports the view that Ishmael's status is a late idea among the Arabs, having developed only after the beginning of Islam.[21]

Although lacking a parallel among Biblicist legends, the Jurhum legend actually serves to inform the biblical Ishmael story in a style similar to Jewish midrashic exegesis by extending it and depicting what happened after Ishmael and his mother left Abraham and Sarah. At the same time, it also features the well-attested pre-Islamic Arab tribe of Jurhum and centers on an ancient Arab religious site. The circling bird auguring good tidings (motif 2) also represents a pre-Islamic Arab motif.[22] The metanarrative sign of motif 4 represents an Islamic gloss affirming that Hagar, the matriarch of the line resulting in the tribe of Quraysh and the Prophet Muḥammad, was a pious and praiseworthy woman, an addition which may have been a polemical response to the Biblicist view that she lacked true faith in God.[23]

Like the previous legends in the Meccan Sequence, the story of the Jurhum is a hybrid tradition. It serves in typical style as exegesis on Genesis 21:20 ("And God was with the lad") and is carefully constructed in such a way that it remains entirely consistent with the biblical text. Yet despite its role as a logical extension of Genesis 21:10-21, its content is made up primarily of pre-Islamic Arab material and provides for the arabization of Ishmael through his upbringing among the Original Arab tribe of Jurhum. In its final and Islamic form, the legend serves to establish the transition from the biblical Ishmael to the Arab Ishmael, progenitor of the Northern Arabs and of course, Muḥammad. It functions effectively both in preparing Ishmael for his role of patriarch of the northern Arabs and in assisting his father to build the holiest shrine of Islam (Qur'ān 2:127: AND REMEMBER, ABRAHAM RAISED THE FOUNDATIONS OF THE HOUSE, AND ISHMAEL ...). In its final form, therefore, this Ibn 'Abbās legend assumes the role of exegesis on the Qur'ān, but in a manner that never contradicts or deviates from the biblical story of Abraham and Ishmael.

But Ishmael's preparation is not yet complete. His father Abraham has yet to ensure that Ishmael's wife, a matriarch of the northern Arabs and founders of Islam, is of the proper calibre and refinement to fit her task.

# Chapter 10

## ABRAHAM'S VISITS

Of all the various components of the Islamic Abraham-Ishmael cycle, the story of Abraham's visits to Ishmael in Mecca draws the closest parallel to Biblicist sources.[1] Ibn 'Abbās is the only consistent authority for these traditions, with eleven narratives attributed to him.[2] Six anonymous narratives[3] bring the total to seventeen. As one would already begin to expect from previous sections of the Abraham-Ishmael cycle, the anonymous tellings tend to be less consistent than those attributed to an early authority. The following plot sequence of Abraham's visits is based on the seventeen narratives.

1. Abraham comes to Mecca to visit Ishmael or inspect his legacy (10/17), or he asks Sarah's permission to visit (7/17) Ishmael. She agrees on the condition that Abraham will not dismount from his steed or remain away (5/17).
2. When Abraham arrives in Mecca, Ishmael is not at home (17/17) because he is out seeking food (5/17), or hunting (10/17). He would always leave the Sacred Precinct whenever he went out to hunt (4/17).
3. Abraham meets Ishmael's wife, who is rude and inhospitable to him (8/17), shrewish and complaining (4/17), or lacking intelligence (1/17). She never asks who he is and he does not volunteer his name.
4. Abraham tells her to give greetings from him to her husband, and asks her to convey to her husband the message to "change the threshold of your door" (11/17) or "house" (5/17).
5. Ishmael returns and smells the scent of his father (5/17), or senses that someone came by (3/17). He asks his wife or she volunteers to tell him the story of the visit. When he hears his father's message, he divorces her and marries another woman (7/17) or specifically another Jurhumite (9/17).[4]
6. After a period of time, Abraham visits again. Ishmael's second wife is friendly and hospitable (16/17). She never asks who he is and he does not volunteer his name.

7. She offers him food (8/17) or a feast of bread, meat, water, and grilled poultry (1/17).
8. Abraham asks what food they eat. The wife answers "meat and water" (9/17) or "milk and meat" (5/17). Abraham calls for God's blessing on whatever she answers (12/17) three times (2/17).
9. An anonymous comment is added here stating that no one could survive on eating only milk and meat except in Mecca (3/17). The Prophet, Apostle, Abū al-Qāsim[5] (4/17) or the narrator (5/17) explains that that is why there is no agriculture in Mecca, or it is stated that Abraham's prayer is like a blessing (2/17).
10. In seven renditions, Ishmael's wife then washes his head while he remains on his mount (6/7, see motif 1), or anoints his hair with oil (1/7). In order to remain on his mount, he stands on a stone called the Maqām Ibrāhīm and his footprint remains upon it (4/7), or he stands on a water jug (2/7).[6]
11. Abraham tells Ishmael's wife to give greetings from him to her husband, and asks her to convey the message that "the threshold of your house (or door) is sound".
12. Ishmael returns and smells the scent of his father or senses that someone came by. He asks his wife or she tells him the story of the visitor. Ishmael tells her that the visitor was Abraham (10/17) and that she is the threshold.

The image of Ishmael portrayed in this story is the dutiful husband and son. He is the breadwinner who is busy providing food for his family, and he demonstrates his devotion to his father by immediately obeying whatever his father wishes. The legend also assures its audience that Abraham cared so much for his son that he would visit him repeatedly even long after the move to faraway Mecca.

The story likewise establishes a proper wife for the dutiful son and ensures that the second generation matriarch of the leadership of Islam is fitting for her role.[7] Abraham calls God's blessings upon the forebears of the Muslims, and the ancient Arab custom of showing hospitality is confirmed as a religious as well as cultural value. The metanarrative gloss in motif 9 explains the barrenness and lack of agriculture in and around the holy city of Mecca, a characteristic that might appear incongruous to someone first visiting the city known as the blessed Mother of Cities.

A few renditions provide names for one or the other of Ishmael's wives, but none are authoritative. Ibn Sa'd[8] provides two variants on the name of Ishmael's second wife: Ri'la bt. Muḍāḍ b. 'Amr al-Jurhumī and Ri'la bt. Yashjub b. Ya'rub.[9] Al-Ya'qūbī[10] gives al-Ḥayfā' bt. Muḍāḍ al-Jurhumiyya. Al-Mas'ūdī names her as Sāma bt. Mahlahl b. Sa'd b. 'Awf b. Hayni b. Nabat.[11] Al-Kisā'ī has Hāla bt. 'Umrān b. al-Hārith.[12] Ibn Sa'd[13] and al-Mas'ūdī[14] provide names also for Ishmael's first wife, where she is an Amalekite in both renditions, possibly reflecting the Jewish view that she was a Moabite.[15] Al-Mas'ūdī gives the name al-Jadā' bt. Sa'd al-'Imlāqī,[16] and al-Kisā'ī calls her the daughter of Sabda.[17]

The unauthoritative traditions contain more embellishments.[18] Both al-Tha'labī and al-Kisā'ī claim that Abraham travelled to Mecca to visit Ishmael on Buraq or a horse that Gabriel brought to him from Paradise.[19] The hagiographic folk literature collections all carry the motif of washing Abraham's head and the miraculous mark of his footprint, while only five of the other fifteen sources include any aspect of this motif.

The Biblicist versions of the legend most likely evolved to explain Genesis 21:21: "[Ishmael] lived in the wilderness of Paran; and his mother got a wife for him from the land of Egypt." The Islamic legend, however, set in an Arabian context, evolved to find Ishmael a wife of good Arab (not Egyptian) character. The names associated with Ishmael's wives in the unauthoritative renditions reflect pre-Islamic Arab roots, as do the renditions containing the motif of the Maqām Ibrāhīm (#10). Only a few renditions carry these Arab motifs, however, and they cannot be said to typify the legend as a whole.

Editorial glosses are interspersed throughout the narrative. Four renditions of motif 2, for example, take pains to point out that Ishmael would leave the sacred precinct of Mecca before hunting, thus acknowledging the religious sanctity of the Sacred Precinct of Mecca *(ḥarām)* where the taking of life is strictly forbidden. The prohibition of hunting reflects a pre-Islamic as well as Islamic religious rule, of course, and may have entered the legend before it became canonized under Islam (though it appears in four of seventeen renditions).[20]

Motif 9 consists of editorial glosses explaining either the special sanctity or the odd barrenness of the holy city of Mecca. Three explain how people who could not normally survive on the diet Ishmael and his family ate in Mecca could nevertheless thrive because of the sanctified nature of the place.[21] A second and more popular version explains that the lack of agriculture in Mecca resulted from the specific food brought by Ishmael's second wife to Abraham for his blessing. "If she had brought wheat or barley or dates, then that land would be full of agriculture."[22] Both of these additions explain various aspects of Islamic or current Arab realia that were inserted into an older legend.[23]

The legend of Abraham's visits to Ishmael draws the closest parallel with available Biblicist material while also exhibiting Arab and Islamic material. It probably evolved originally as biblical exegesis, although it naturally satisfied important Islamic considerations as well, such as the fact that Abraham did not reject his oldest son. The fact is that both the Biblicist *and* the Islamic versions serve to explain the biblical story by extending the narrative beyond the abrupt end given in Genesis 21:21. The Islamic version affirms that Ishmael was never rejected in favor of his younger half brother Isaac. The forebear of the northern Arabs and the Quraysh continued to receive his father's blessing; his second wife, befitting the status of the Arab matriarch and the progenitor of Muḥammad, received explicit approval from father Abraham.[24] Ishmael remains closely connected with his father and in doing so, remains firmly within the Abrahamic monotheistic tradition. The legend also confirms the special awareness and sensitivity of Ishmael. He feels his father's presence as soon as he returns from hunting. He has no difficulty understanding his father's coded message and demonstrates his unquestionable filial piety and obedience. He also portrays the image of the responsible provider, all highly respected Arab cultural traits.

In neither the Biblicist nor the Islamic tellings of the legend did Abraham expel Hagar and Ishmael from the sphere of his love and concern. But in the Jewish renditions, Abraham returns home without giving his eldest son a blessing, while the Islamic renditions overwhelmingly note God's blessing invoked by Abraham upon Ishmael's family, thus proving Abraham's love for his Arab progeny and for Arabian monotheism (motifs 8 and 9). Abraham approves of Ishmael living in Mecca and marrying a proper Arab woman. He gives his blessing to their way of life.

The only disonance between the Islamic legend and the biblical text is in the identity of Ishmael's wife, who is Egyptian in Genesis 21:21. The Jewish narrative midrash follows up on the verse through the story of Abraham's visits.[25] Abraham disapproves of Ishmael's first Moabite wife whom Ishmael had himself chosen, so Hagar sends for a more appropriate wife from Egypt. Abraham approves of Hagar's choice on his second visit, thus explaining Genesis 21:21.[26] The Jewish renditions, therefore, appear to have evolved as exegesis on Genesis 21:21.[27]

The Islamic renditions, however, have no direct association with the Genesis verse. On the contrary, their purpose appears to be the establishment of Ishmael and his progeny among the Arab people—a very different goal. If Ishmael had taken a wife from Egypt in the Islamic version of the legend as in the biblical story and its Biblicist exegesis, Ishmael's *arabization* would not have been accomplished. Moreover, the story would hardly have held any relevance in an Arabian context. This particular aspect is noteworthy because it is the only segment of the Ibn 'Abbās Abraham-Ishmael cycle that obviously contradicts the biblical text. It appears that there was little alternative to establishing Ishmael's Arab identity.[28] Its importance was greatly enhanced by the fact that he married into one of the legendary pre-Islamic Arab tribes associated with the holy city of Mecca.

# Chapter 11

# BUILDING THE KA'BA

Building the Ka'ba in Mecca, the spiritual and ritual center of the Islamic world, marks a climax in the Abraham-Ishmael cycle and signals the culmination of Abraham's religious career according to at least one school of early Islamic tradition. This observation may not be immediately clear from a casual reading of the sources, for most append traditions to Abraham's building of the Ka'ba which tell of his centrality in the Pilgrimage ritual, an act which might be seen as the true acme of his life since it establishes a sacred precedent for the Islamic requirement of Pilgrimage. But the Pilgrimage traditions are inconsistent in structure, content, and attribution, suggesting a later association.[1] They represent more recent developments that did not form part of a coherent early group of traditions making up the epic Abraham story.

The reports about building the Ka'ba are divided into three major types distinguished by the ultimate authorities of their records of authentication: Ibn 'Abbās, 'Alī, and al-Suddī.[2] Abraham is always depicted as the primary builder, with Ishmael sometimes assisting him, but it is not always clear whether the entire Ka'ba is built or whether only the foundations are raised. The most consistent and often recurring version is that attributed to Ibn 'Abbās.

## THE IBN 'ABBĀS VERSION

This version is dominated by fourteen traditions attributed directly to Ibn 'Abbās. Twelve are complete narratives[3] and two are fragments.[4] One additional narrative, identical to the Ibn 'Abbās version, is given without a chain of authorities,[5] and one fragment is attributed to Sa'īd.[6] Thirteen of the sixteen traditions, therefore, are complete narratives.

The paradigmatic Ibn 'Abbās version:

1. Abraham comes to Ishmael a third time (10/16) and finds him trimming arrows (15/16) under a tree (*dawha* 9/16) next to the well of Zamzam (12/16).
2. He informs his son that God has given him a command. Ishmael replies that if God gave Abraham a command, he must carry it out. In response, Abraham either asks Ishmael for help or tells him that he was commanded as well, and explains that the command was to build God's House (13/16).
3. Abraham points to a small hill raised up above the surrounding area or above the winter flash-floods and tells Ishmael that that is to be the site of the House (7/16).
4. Abraham thereupon begins building while Ishmael hands him the stones.
5. When Abraham tires or the building gets too high for him to reach, Ishmael brings him a large rock upon which he stands (13/16). That is the Maqām Ibrāhīm (5/16).
6. As they continue, they recite Qur'ān 2:127: OUR LORD, ACCEPT [THIS] FROM US, FOR YOU ARE THE ALL-HEARING, THE ALL-KNOWING (13/16).

The Ibn 'Abbās version is consistent, displaying little variation among its sixteen renditions. The *dawha* tree and Zamzam well motifs seen also in previous Ibn 'Abbās narratives demonstrate the literary consistency of the Ibn 'Abbās cycle in its identification of the site of the Ka'ba.[7] Here as well as in the other sections of the Ibn 'Abbās cycle, we find no supernatural intervention as Abraham and Ishmael carry out their work. Ishmael is characterized as a pious man who fully supports his father in carrying out the command of God. He continues to demonstrate filial piety first made obvious in the previous chapter by assisting his father, even bringing the large stone for him to stand upon and moving it along the side of the Ka'ba as they work their way around its walls.

The Ibn 'Abbās version explains the ancient sanctity of the Ka'ba as well as the pre-Islamic structure now called the Maqām Ibrāhīm,[8] but it does so in monotheistic, even Biblicist terms by virtue of the names of the characters in the story. No supernatural or magic traits are associated here with the holy places, despite supernatural traits found in other sources.[9] And aside from God's House being built in Mecca rather than Jerusalem, none of the motifs are inconsistent with Biblicist material. They do appear to be incongruous, however, with what one would expect from pre-Islamic Arab lore because they have been purged of pre-Islamic religious content. The old religious sites were explained simply through an overlay of Biblicist material that was entirely consistent with the thrust of the book of Genesis.[10] And closure for the episode is provided by motif 6, an Islamic insertion that binds the entire narrative to the Qur'ān.[11]

A legend establishing the sanctity of the Ka'ba as God's House would not have developed in Biblicist communities as we know from today. Nevertheless, its content, style, and literary motifs fit perfectly with the previous narratives attributed to Ibn ʿAbbās, some of which we have suggested earlier derive from Jewish narrative exegesis. This version of building the Kaʿba is neither predominantly Biblicist nor pre-Islamic Arab in nature, and it needed little modification through Islamic insertions to place it fully within the rubric of classic Islamic text (only motif 6). The legend functions to cap Abraham's life with his establishing the Kaʿba, thereby extending the Abraham cycle to its appropriate conclusion in the Meccan setting. Since the core of the legend revolves around establishing Abraham as the founder of the Kaʿba even without the help of Islamic editorial additions, it suggests the possibility of this episode and the full Abraham cycle attributed to Ibn ʿAbbās having evolved in a pre-Islamic Arab environment in which Biblicist influence was already strong—in a world in which Abraham's association with the Kaʿba was established even before Muḥammad's extensive contact with the Jews of Medina.[12] Abraham is frequently associated with establishing sacred sites in the Hebrew Bible (Genesis 12:7; 13:4, 13:18; 21:33), and this association was probably the source for his pre-Islamic connection with the founding of the Kaʿba.

In the earlier episodes of the Ibn ʿAbbās Abraham cycle, the plot appears to follow the biblical story of Abraham and Ishmael quite closely. Once Ishmael is established in Mecca and remains outside the framework and purpose of the biblical story, however, the traditions take on more typically Arabian concerns that relate more directly to ancient Meccan associations. We note fewer biblical parallels and greater freedom in the use of Arab and Islamic components as the legend unfolds further away from the setting and chronology of the biblical story. The Ibn ʿAbbās cycle extends the biblical story of Abraham and Ishmael to its logical conclusion in an Arabian setting, suggesting the possibility of the use of this (or similar) legend, among pre-Islamic heterodox Biblicists (or Arabian *ḥanīf* monotheists) who worshiped at the holy sites in Mecca.

## THE ʿALĪ VERSION

This version is dominated by sixteen traditions traced back to ʿAli b. Abī Ṭālib. Five located in the sources under the rubric of Abraham's transfer of Ishmael and Hagar to Mecca have already been discussed above in Chapter 8. Of those five, four refer to Hagar and Ishmael accompanying Abraham to Mecca when he is commanded to build God's House. The remaining eleven renditions are found among discussions on the actual building of the Kaʿba and exclude any reference to Hagar and Ishmael accompanying Abraham to Mecca. Because the two groups represent tellings of the same tradition, we have presented the entire sample of "ʿAlī" traditions here, including those already examined in Chapter 8.

The 'Alī version actually comprises three covariant traditions. All portray Abraham's journey to Mecca as an immediate response to God's command to build the Ka'ba.[13] They all depict Abraham receiving supernatural assistance in locating the site upon which to build the Ka'ba, and all but one portray the *sakina* as providing him with that assistance. Apart from these commonalities, a degree of variation may be observed between the covariants, delineated below as 1) Maqām, 2) Cloud, and 3) Spider. We also note a certain amount of confusion among the traditions, a phenomenon not surprising since the three related accounts of Abraham building the Ka'ba are attributed to the same authority.

### *The Maqām Tradition*

The "Maqām Tradition" consists of seven nearly identical renditions (7/16).[14]

1. One or two men approach 'Alī and ask him if the House[15] is the first dwelling place on earth (6/7).[16] 'Alī answers them (6/7) or begins the narrative (1/7) by saying that it was not the first house *(bayt)*, but was the first with the blessing of the Maqām Ibrāhīm. Whoever enters it is safe.[17] 'Alī then asks permission of his questioner to complete his explanation, and continues.
2. God commanded Abraham to build Him a House, but Abraham was very uneasy because he did not know where to build it (7/7).
3. To remedy this, God sent him the *sakīna*, a gale wind with two heads (6/7) or one head (1/7), which leads him to Mecca (6/7) or to the correct location (1/7).
4. The *sakīna* coiled itself up on the site of the Ka'ba like the round Arab shield of overlapping leather skins sewn one over the other (6/7), or like a snake (1/7).
5. Abraham is told by God to build where the *sakīna* came to rest (6/7) or to actually build upon it (1/7).[18]
6. He builds, but one stone remains to be put in place (5/6), or Abraham reaches the location of the stone *(al-ḥajr)* (1/6). Ishmael is playing nearby, and Abraham tells him to find a stone (6/6). When Ishmael returns,[19] he finds Abraham mounting the Black Stone.[20] He asks his father who gave it to him (6/6). Abraham answers that it was someone who did not trust in Ishmael's (5/6) or Ishmael's and Abraham's (1/6) building. It was Gabriel (6/6) who brought it from heaven (5/6).

An eighth rendition of this tradition contains a slight variant, though also given on 'Alī's authority.[21] It excludes 'Alī's remarks regarding the first house and commences with God commanding Abraham to build the House and call the people to the Pilgrimage:

> Ibn Humayd reported to us on the authority going back to ʿAlī b. Abī Ṭalib that he used to say: "When God commanded Abraham to build the House and call for the pilgrimage among humanity, Abraham went out from Syria with his son Ishmael and Ishmael's mother, Hagar. God sent the *sakīna* with them, a wind that has a tongue for speaking. Abraham followed it wherever it went until it arrived in Mecca. When it came to the site of the House, it circled around it and said to Abraham, 'Build upon me! Build upon me!' Abraham thereupon laid the foundations and raised up the House along with Ishmael until they arrived at the location of the corner support *(al-rukn)*. Abraham said to Ishmael: 'O my son, find me a stone that I may establish as a sign for humanity!' He brought him a stone, but Abraham was not satisfied with it so he said: 'Find me a different one!' So Ishmael went to search for a [different] stone. But when he came back, it had already been brought and Abraham had placed it in its proper location. He said: 'O father, who brought you this stone?' Abraham answered: 'Someone who did not let me depend on you, my son.' "

These renditions of the Maqām Tradition contain three instances of supernatural intervention: the *sakīna* leading Abraham to Mecca, the *sakīna* showing him the exact location of the Kaʿba, and Gabriel bringing the Black Stone to Abraham from Heaven. They have nothing in common with Biblicist legends aside from the biblical names of the characters, but they contain the motifs of the Jinni-like *sakīna* and the Black Stone, which are not found in Jewish folklore.[22] The site is the ancient Arab religious shrine, and the coiling up of the *sakīna* is described in terms of a traditional Arab battle shield. With the combination of biblical characters and Arab lore, the Maqām Tradition explains the sanctity of the Kaʿba and the Black Stone in terms recognizable in both Biblicist and ancient Arab environments. The introduction, on the other hand, locates it in relation to the Qur'ān, thereby placing it in an Islamic context. The Maqām Tradition associates the Maqām Ibrāhīm with the entire Sacred Precinct of Mecca (the *Ḥarām*)—not from the contents of the narrative itself but rather by the introductory comment of ʿAlī (motif 1), which sets up the tradition as exegesis on the term Maqām Ibrāhīm found in Qur'ān 3:97.[23]

Only one of eight tellings mentions that Abraham brought Hagar and Ishmael to Mecca, yet six depict Abraham telling Ishmael to seek out a stone for the corner support. Ishmael's unsuccessful search and lack of assistance to his father point to the assumption that he is too young to assist in building the Kaʿba. This episode would therefore seem to have taken place when

Abraham first brought his family to Mecca, although only one rendition affirms this explicitly.

The Maqām Tradition exhibits a concern for the sanctity of the Ka'ba and the Black Stone, with only the introduction referring to the Maqām Ibrāhīm and no significant concern for a history of Hagar and Ishmael. It strongly reflects pre-Islamic Arab legends surrounding the supernatural sanctity of the Ka'ba and the Black Stone, although it too is influenced by Biblicism through the names of its characters.

*The Cloud Tradition*

The "Cloud Tradition"[24] features a supernatural cloud that floats over the site of the Ka'ba in order to mark its exact measurements for Abraham. Only three complete narratives were located in the sources, although it is referred to on other occasions.[25]

1. Abraham is commanded to build the House.
2. He comes to Mecca bringing Hagar and Ishmael.
3. When they reach Mecca, Abraham sees a cloud floating over the site of the Ka'ba. It speaks to Abraham saying: "Build on my shadow (or measurements), but do not exceed or diminish [them]".
4. When Abraham finishes and leaves to return to Syria, Hagar asks him to whom he is entrusting her and Ishmael. He answers, "To God," which Hagar accepts by saying, "He will not allow us to perish".
5. A shortened Ṣafā-Marwa and Zamzam story then follows.[26]

The Cloud Tradition contains one motif probably deriving from Biblicist material in addition to its use of biblical names. The cloud resting over the site of the Ka'ba is reminiscent of the biblical cloud resting over the Tabernacle in the desert; but as in the case of the *sakīna*, this portrayal is substantially removed from the biblical view.[27] By explaining the sanctity of the Ka'ba through the supernatural cloud, the legend confirms the holiness of the site in terms that might be recognized by both Biblicists and pre-Islamic Arabs.

Though incorporating Biblicist motifs, the Cloud Tradition also has the feel of an Arab legend accounting for the sanctity of the Ka'ba. It provides less information about the holy site than the Ibn 'Abbās version or the Maqām tradition by its omission of references to the Black Stone or the Maqām Ibrāhīm, and it is not particularly popular, although it clearly had enough merit to allow for al-Ṭabarī and then Ibn Kathīr to include it in their works.

*The Spider Tradition*

The "Spider Tradition" is also repeated less often than the others, and centers on a comparison of the way the *sakīna* showed Abraham the location of the Ka'ba with the way in which a spider marks out its home. The *sakīna* marked the perimeter of the Ka'ba as a spider would first thread a single strand around the perimeter of its web before filling it in.[28]

1. Abraham came from Armenia (3/4) with the *sakīna* guiding him. Joining them were Gabriel and the Surad bird[29] (1/4).
2. The *sakīna* guided him in marking off the site like a spider marks off the site of its home (4/4).
3. Abraham or the *sakīna*[30] lifted stones that only thirty men could lift (4/4) in building the House (1/4), exposing the foundation of the earlier House (2/4), or bringing the stones of the semi-circular enclosure to the side of the Ka'ba (*al-Ḥijr*, 1/4).[31]
4. One rendition continues with a sequence of the Cloud Tradition: after the foundations are exposed, a cloud floats over the site and gives Abraham instructions about building the House.[32]

Two variant Spider renditions are given on the authority of Mujāhid[33] and on the joint authority of Ibn Jurayj and Bishr b. 'Āṣim.[34] The Mujāhid rendition reads: "Abraham drew near from Syria with the *sakīna*, a Surad bird, and an angel. The *sakīna* said: 'O Abraham, establish the House upon me!' For that reason, no king or desert Arab pilgrim will circumambulate the House unless he is in a state of [religious] tranquility."[35]

The other rendition has: "Abraham came from Armenia with the *sakīna*, the angel, and the Surad bird guiding him, marking the location of the House like the spider marks the location of its home. He/it lifted a rock that thirty men could not lift. The *sakīna* said: 'Build upon me!' For that reason, the desert Arab pilgrim and the tyrant will not enter it unless he is in a state of [religious] tranquility."

The Spider Tradition presents some intriguing difficulties for analysis. The story has no connection to Biblicist content aside from Abraham's name. His origin in Armenia nevertheless raises the possibility of an earlier legend in Christian narrative exegesis. The Spider motif (2) may be a simple comparison of the actions of the *sakīna* to the natural habits of a spider, or it may represent a deeper but obscure level of association.[36]

The Spider Tradition explains the sanctity of a pre-Islamic Arab religious shrine through the supernatural *sakīna*. The Surad Bird is a local creature found in the Arabian Peninsula, but its significance, as well as that of the spider and Armenia, still remains unclear. No clearly Islamic material may be found in this story.

As in the case of the two previous covariants on the authority of 'Alī, this is a fantastic tale that accounts for the sacred nature of the Ka'ba in Mecca. Like the others, it brings Abraham to Mecca, although in this tradition he comes from Armenia rather than Syria. Abraham is the only human character in the tradition. The Spider Tradition lacks any component treating the Black Stone or the Maqām Ibrāhīm and appears to be a minor tradition that was probably retained because of its authoritative source, 'Alī. Like the Cloud Tradition, it remains incomplete and somewhat obscure in that it does not include Ishmael or provide an explanation for the Black Stone or the Maqām Ibrāhīm.

It is notable that the more fantastic traditions in this series, and particularly the *sakīna* traditions, are associated with 'Alī b. Abī Ṭālib. In every rendition of the three 'Alī versions, Abraham is credited with building the House without any help from Ishmael, a notion that appears to contradict Q.2:127. Even when Ishmael is asked to help (as in the Maqām Tradition), he fails in what he was asked to do.

*The Suddī Version*

An outline of the "Suddī" version, represented by three complete renditions,[37] two incomplete renditions,[38] and one brief synopsis,[39] follows:

1. God entrusts Abraham and Ishmael with the purification of the House[40] (3/5) or commands them to build the House (2/5).
2. Abraham goes to Mecca (4/5).
3. Abraham and Ishmael take pick axes (4/5) but do not know where to dig the foundations (5/5).
4. God sends a wind called the Gale Wind (*Rīḥ khajūj*, 5/5) which has two wings and a head in the shape of a snake (5/5). It sweeps around the Ka'ba for Abraham and Ishmael and lays bare the foundations of the first House[41] (5/5).
5. Abraham and Ishmael follow with their tools until they establish the foundations, to which the Qur'ān refers in 22:26: BEHOLD! WE GAVE THE SITE OF THE HOUSE TO ABRAHAM (5/5).[42]
6. When they reach the corner in which the Black Stone is to be set, Abraham sends Ishmael to find a good stone to put there. Ishmael complains that he is "lazy from exhaustion," but goes anyway (3/3). When he returns with a stone, Abraham is not satisfied and sends him back to find a better one (1/3).
7. While he is gone, Gabriel brings the Black Stone from India (3/3). It was originally a pure white sapphire, white as the *thighāma* plant,[43] which Adam brought down from Heaven (3/3). But it became black from menstruating women (1/3) or the sins of humanity (2/3).
8. Ishmael brings a stone and finds Abraham next to the corner *(rukn)*. Ishmael asks who brought the Black Stone, and Abraham answers: "Someone livelier than you!" (3/3).

9. Then they both build it together (3/3) reciting Qur'ān 2:127: O LORD, ACCEPT [THIS] FROM US, FOR YOU ARE THE ALL-HEARING, THE ALL-KNOWING (2/3).

Aside from the biblical characters again and Abraham's association with founding religious sites, this version has no connection with Biblicist material and probably evolved around the pre-Islamic shrines at Mecca. The act of purifying the Ka'ba in motif 1 and motifs 5 and 9 connect it to the Qur'ān, thereby bringing it into the realm of acceptable Islamic tradition.

The image of al-Suddī's "Gale Wind" is quite similar to 'Alī's *sakīna*, and the definition *(rīḥ khajūj)* is identical.[44] It is more closely connected to the Qur'ān than any traditions of the 'Alī version, however, and provides a narration that is more consistent with Qur'ān 2:127 because Abraham and Ishmael are credited with building the House together, despite the fact that Ishmael's stone is not acceptable. The Suddi version also makes it clear that they establish the foundations upon those of the original Ka'ba and build the structure in one act.[45] In both the Ibn 'Abbās and the 'Alī versions, it is unclear whether Abraham (and Ishmael) merely lay the foundations or raise the building.[46]

The Black Stone segment of the Suddī version provides the fullest legendary explanation for that sacred relic of the Ka'ba. And by referring to the establishment of the original Ka'ba prior to Abraham, it provides a full and satisfying historical perspective.[47] The lack of a Maqām Ibrāhīm component is surprising, since in all other ways, this version appears to rank with the most complete. Al-Suddī's version is unique with its inclusion of Q.22:26 (BEHOLD! WE GAVE THE SITE OF THE HOUSE TO ABRAHAM) as a focal point for the narrative tradition.

The traditions about Abraham building the Ka'ba make up the largest number and exhibit the widest variety of reports on any topic of the Abraham-Ishmael cycle outside of the story of the Sacrifice.[48] The many hybrid renditions drawing from parts of the three major versions, as well as the number of unique renditions point to the importance attached to the Ka'ba's origins.

The hybrid traditions include a mix of the Ibn 'Abbās and 'Alī-Cloud tradition,[49] the Ibn 'Abbās and 'Alī versions,[50] and others. Al-Ya'qūbī's rendition gives only a brief explanation of the building of the Ka'ba and uses it as a vehicle to arrive at the Pilgrimage ritual, which he deems most important.[51] The most complete rendition of all is given by al-Azraqī on the authority of Muḥammad Ibn Isḥāq.[52] It incorporates the Ibn 'Abbās version, 'Alī-Maqām, Cloud, and Spider traditions, the Suddī version, and a number of unique components that appear in no other renditions. This telling was clearly an attempt to weave together a comprehensive history of the Ka'ba and its major features:

> When Abraham the Friend of God *(khalīl Allāh)* was commanded to build the Sacred House, he drew near from Armenia on Buraq. With him was the *sakīna* which had a face that spoke. It is a blowing wind.

He also had an angel that showed him the location of the House when he arrived in Mecca. Ishmael, who was 20 years old at the time, was also with him. His mother had died before that and was buried at the site of al-Ḥijr.[53] He said: "O Ishmael, God has commanded me to build Him a house." Ishmael said to him: "Where is its site?"

An angel showed him the site of the House. They both got up and began digging at the foundations. They were alone. Abraham arrived at the foundations of the primordial Adam.[54] He dug to the very foundation of the House and found great stones that 30 men could not [lift]. Then they both built on the foundations of the primordial Adam and the *sakīna* curled up like a snake on the original foundations saying: "O Abraham, build upon me!" So they built. That is why desert Arab pilgrims or tyrants do not circumambulate the House unless they are in a state of [religious] calm.

So they built the House. Its height was 9 cubits. Its measurement from the corner of the Black Stone *(al-rukn al-aswad)* to the north corner toward the area called al-Hijr was 32 cubits. Its measurement from the north corner to the west corner at which is the Ḥijr wall *(al-ḥijr)* was 22 cubits. The length of its back side from the west corner to the south corner was 31 cubits. The measurement of its southern side from the corner of the Black Stone to the south corner was 20 cubits. The reason it is called the Ka'ba is because it was created as a cube.

The foundation of Adam was like that building [in terms of its dimensions]. Its door was in an unspecified location until [the time of] As'ad al-Ḥamīrī. He is the one who made a door and Persian lock for it, covered it with a complete embroidered cloth covering *(kiswa)* and sacrificed there.

Abraham built an arbor of *arāk* trees from the *ḥijr* to the side of the House for the protection of his she-goats. It became a corral for the goats of Ishmael.[55]

Abraham dug a pit in the middle of the House to the right of its entrance as a treasury for the House, in which objects brought to it were placed. This is the pit upon which 'Amrū b. Nuḥayy raised up the idol Hubal that the Quraysh used to worship. Divination was practiced with arrows by the idol after he brought it from Hīt in the land of the Jazīra.

Abraham would build while Ishmael would pass the stones to him on his shoulder. When the building was raised up, Ishmael brought the *Maqām* near to him. He would stand upon it and build as Ishmael would move it around the sides of the House until he came to the site of the corner of the Black Stone. Abraham said to Ishmael: "O Ishmael, look for a stone for me to put here so that it will be a sign for the people.

They will begin their circumambulations from it[s location]." So Ishmael went to look for a stone for him. He returned, but Gabriel had already come and brought the Black Stone. God had deposited the corner *(al-rukn)* with the Black Stone at Abū Qubays when he submerged the earth at the time of Noah.[56] He said: "When you see My Friend *(Khalīlī)* building My House, bring it out to him.

When Ishmael came to him and said: "O Father, where did you get that?", he replied: "Someone brought it who did not entrust me with your stone. Gabriel brought it." When Gabriel put the stone in its place and Abraham built above it, it sparkled and glistened with a powerful whiteness and radiated its light to the east, west, south and north.

Its light shone in all directions of the Sacred Precinct until there were no idols there. Its deep blackness was a result of the fires that burned it time after time during the pre-Islamic period and during Islam. In the pre-Islamic period, a woman came during the time of the Quraysh and prepared a fire at the Ka'ba. A spark flew off onto the curtains covering the Ka'ba and burned it. The corner containing the Black Stone was burned, it became blackened, and the Ka'ba was weakened. That is the reason that the Quraysh were all stirred up about demolishing and [re]building it. In the Islamic period, during the period of Ibn al-Zubayr, al-Ḥuṣayn b. Numayr al-Kindī surrounded it and burned the Ka'ba. The corner [containing the Black Stone] was burned and [the Black Stone] split into three pieces until Ibn al-Zubayr put them back together with a silver [setting]. Its blackness is because of that. If only the impure during the shameful pre-Islamic period had not touched the corner, but only the pure!

Al-Qummī[57] and al-Ṭabarsī[58] provide a unique rendition in which Ishmael carries the Black Stone from *Dhū Tuwwin*, a location near Mecca.[59] Al-Azraqī, who provides more traditions on this subject than any of the other exegetes, also gives a tradition on the authority of Wahb b. Munabbih that ties Abraham's building of the House very closely with Adam's original structure and includes the 'Alī-Cloud tradition within it.[60]

Finally, Ibn Kathīr twice mentions a tradition that he found in al-Azraqī, in which Dhū al-Qarnayn happens upon Abraham and Ishmael building the Ka'ba: "Ibn Abī Hātim said . . . on the authority of 'Aliyā b. Aḥmar that Dhū al-Qarnayn came to Mecca and found Abraham and Ishmael building the foundations of the House from five mountains.[61] He said: 'What are you doing?' Abraham replied: 'We have been commanded to build this Ka'ba.' He said: 'Then prove what you claim!' So five wild sheep got up and said: 'We bear witness that Abraham and Ishmael are the two who have been commanded to build this Ka'ba.' He then said: 'I am satisfied [with this proof]'."[62] With that, Dhū al-Qarnayn joins Abraham in circumambulating the Ka'ba.

The remainder of the exegetical material consists of attempts to clarify a variety of issues raised by the Qur'ān or the legends, and a number of miscellaneous comments center on descriptions of the *sakīna.* Some explain that it had a head that looked like a cat, that it came down like a fog or a cloud, that it had a human head, or that it was a kind of white vulture.[63] Others record the tradition that the Ka'ba was built from the stones of five mountains: from Mt. Sinai, the Mount of Olives, Lebanon, Jūdī, and Ḥirā'; or from Ḥirā', Thabīr, Lebanon, al-Ṭur (sometimes referred to as Ṭūr Sīnā'-Mt. Sinai), and al-Jabal al-Aḥmar.[64] A popular issue for discussion was whether Abraham raised up the foundations of the House by himself or whether he was assisted by Ishmael.[65]

Certain issues were regarded as problematic by the exegetes, such as whether God actually commanded Abraham to build the Ka'ba since the Qur'ān implies but does not explicitly say as much.[66] Another problem, as we have seen, is whether Abraham actually built the original Ka'ba or whether an earlier structure associated with Adam was already in existence. The tradition literature tends to support the latter claim, which may be the message of the Qur'ān as well.[67] Ibn Kathīr presents all of the relevant qur'ānic verses for the reader to examine.[68]

Ibn Kathīr does not hesitate to offer his own comments regarding the soundness of certain traditions and their chains of authorities. He presents a number of different traditions regarding the origins of the Ka'ba and then writes: "All of these traditions are from the Israelites *(banū isrā'īl).* We have determined that they are not truth nor lies, for there is no support for either. Generally, they are rejected as not being the truth."[69]

Both al-Ṭabarī and Ibn Kathīr tended to follow the Ibn 'Abbās version of the building of the Ka'ba. Al-Ṭabarsī, as would be expected from his Shi'ite background, follows the 'Alī version, stipulating that Abraham built it alone when Ishmael was too young to help. The mystic Ibn 'Arabī draws from both the 'Ibn Abbās and 'Alī versions in order to draw attention to his esoteric views. The other exegetes tend to withhold their own personal views regarding the building of the Ka'ba but express themselves through their citation of traditions.

The building of the Ka'ba attracted the attention of most of our exegetes and many of the early traditionists. It was natural for the early Muslims to establish a plausible sacred history for the founding of their holiest religious shrine. Two basic approaches evolved for providing such a sacred Islamic history, and both followed the Qur'ān (as well as the Bible) by including Abraham and Ishmael in the founding process. The approach represented by the 'Alī and Suddī versions, which includes the motif of the Black Stone, minimizes Ishmael's role, while the other approach, represented by the Ibn 'Abbās version and excluding any mention of the Black Stone, maximizes it.

Each approach draws from a different tradition literature for the bulk of its material.

The Ibn 'Abbās version represents a unique and consistent approach to the tradition literature which may be found throughout its account of the Abraham-Ishmael cycle. It draws heavily from Biblicist traditions and is typically concerned about following a historical outline that does not contradict the biblical version of the story. The Ibn 'Abbās style can be found throughout its coherent account of Abrahamic history, beginning with the Patriarch's emigration from the land of Nimrod. It ends with the final authentication of the major Islamic religious site by anchoring it in the person and history of the first monotheist, Abraham. The 'Alī traditions and the Suddī and Mujāhid versions represent an approach that draws more of its material from pre-Islamic Arab traditions. They appear to be either unaware of or unconcerned about the coherence or relevance of biblical history and stories.[70]

The total omission of the Black Stone in the Ibn 'Abbās renditions beckons our attention. This version probably ignored the Black Stone purposefully in consonance with the view of some Companions such as 'Umar b. al-Khaṭṭāb, who is credited with being uncomfortable with the pagan-like veneration of such an object. According to al-Bukhārī's report on the authority of 'Ābis b. Rabī'a:[71] "'Umar came near the Black Stone and kissed it and said, 'I know that you are a stone and can neither benefit nor harm anyone. Had I not seen the Apostle of God kissing you I would not have kissed you.' " Al-Bukhārī cites a second report on the authority of the father of Zayd b. Aslam:[72] "'Umar b. al-Khaṭṭāb addressed the corner [of the Ka'ba in which was situated the Black Stone] *(rukn)* saying, 'By God, I know that you are a stone and can neither benefit nor harm. Had I not seen the Prophet touching you, I would never have touched you.' "

The Ibn 'Abbās version is a complex literary work that was woven together with special concern for consistency of plot and the use of various literary motifs. It takes the listener or reader on a long journey with Abraham, who successfully passes a series of difficult trials culminating in the establishment of God's holy House in Mecca and the ritual Pilgrimage. These trials include his realization of monotheism during his youth in the land of Nimrod,[73] the threats and attempts of his own people to kill him there because of his belief,[74] the long journey from his native land and people to God,[75] the trial of the tyrant who would steal his wife Sarah,[76] the family conflict resulting from Sarah's jealousy of Hagar, his having to leave his son Ishmael with Hagar in an inhospitable desert, the challenge to care properly for his entire family and particularly his son in Mecca, the trial of the Sacrifice,[77] and finally, the command to build God's House.

All of these nine trials, with the exception of the tyrant legend, are found in renditions attributed to Ibn 'Abbās.[78] These trials are similar to those enumerated in PRE chapters 16-31.[79] A tenth and final trial in the Islamic context might be God's command to Abraham to call all humanity to perform the Pilgrimage,[80] although it is not referred to as such in the sources. The Islamic sources do not specifically consider Abraham's adventures trials nor do they enumerate ten trials as do some Jewish sources, but Qur'ān 2:124 reads: REMEMBER! ABRAHAM WAS TRIED BY HIS LORD WITH *KALIMĀT*, a term meaning "word" but quite enigmatic in this context and provoking a good deal of exegetical comments. Some exegesis views the *kalimāt* as being a series of ten trials, but they are generally different from our narratives and from PRE.[81] Only one view, which is not widespread in the sources, suggests a sequence somewhat similar to the Ibn 'Abbās cycle: the trials are the star, the moon, and the sun when Abraham was tempted to believe that they were gods, the fire of Nimrod, his emigration, his circumcision, and the Sacrifice.[82]

Despite the fact that the Abraham-Ishmael cycle attributed to Ibn 'Abbās ends with the building of the Ka'ba, a large number of traditions evolved describing the next logical step: sacred Pilgrimage to the holy sites as prescribed by the Qur'ān. This will be the topic of the last chapter in the Meccan Sequence.

# Chapter 12

# THE PILGRIMAGE

One of the Five Pillars of Islam *(al-arkān al-khamsa)*, the annual pilgrimage to Mecca and its environs during the month of *dhū al-ḥijja*, is known as the Ḥajj and is a requirement for all Muslims who are able (Q.3:97).[1] Traditions referring to Abraham's Pilgrimage are organized around either of two narrative foci: one is Abraham's response to the divine command in Qur'ān 22:27[2] to summon all humanity to perform the Ḥajj; the other is Abraham's own actions during his first and divinely guided Pilgrimage. Some traditions include both these events. The Pilgrimage traditions do not display the same kind of consistency noted in many of the earlier sections, nor do they exhibit the kind of literary consistency among traditions grouped according to the names of the ultimate authorities of their records of authentication. Only a few are descriptive narratives, while most are simple non-narrative comments.

Of thirty-six traditions treating the topic, eleven are attributed to Ibn 'Abbās[3] and six are attributed to Mujāhid.[4] Both groups of authoritative traditions consist mostly of brief statements, and only one rendition in each could be considered a narrative.[5] These as well as other narratives examined in this chapter are actually descriptive accounts of Abraham's act of calling humanity to take part in the Pilgrimage or his ritual activities on his own Pilgrimage. Of the nineteen traditions not attributed to Ibn 'Abbās or Mujāhid, twelve are narratives[6] and seven are brief comments.[7]

## THE SETTING FOR THE PILGRIMAGE

The chronological setting for the Pilgrimage traditions in the histories and story collections is immediately after Abraham's construction of the Ka'ba. In the Qur'ān commentaries the traditions center on two Qur'ān verses. One series focuses on the meaning of *manāsik* or "ritual stations"[8] in Qur'ān 2:128: OUR LORD, MAKE US MUSLIMS TO YOU AND A MUSLIM PEOPLE OF OUR PROGENY.

SHOW US OUR *MANĀSIK* AND TURN TO US [IN FORGIVENESS] FOR YOU ARE THE ALL-FORGIVING AND ALL-MERCIFUL. The second focus is a verse understood by most exegetes to be a command directed by God to Abraham:[9] CALL THE PEOPLE FOR THE PILGRIMAGE. THEY WILL COME TO YOU ON FOOT AND ON EVERY KIND OF CAMEL, LEAN FROM THE JOURNEYS THROUGH DEEP AND DISTANT MOUNTAIN HIGHWAYS (22:27).[10]

Half of the thirty-six traditions specify that they occurred immediately after Abraham built the Ka'ba, and the remaining eighteen do not mention when they took place. There is some confusion among the sources as to whether Abraham only called upon humanity to make the Pilgrimage, made the Pilgrimage himself, or both.

In seven of the eighteen traditions providing a chronology, Abraham calls for the Pilgrimage immediately after building the House.[11] In four he makes the Pilgrimage himself after building the House.[12] Three renditions have Abraham build the House, make the Pilgrimage and then call the people to make the Pilgrimage as well.[13] Two renditions have Abraham build the House, call the people for the Pilgrimage, and then make the Pilgrimage himself.[14] In one he builds the House, makes the Pilgrimage, calls the people for the Pilgrimage, and then shows them how to do it.[15] Finally, al-Ya'qūbī provides an anonymous narrative rendition in which Abraham builds the House and then makes the Pilgrimage, although an editorial remark contradicts the narrative by explaining that Abraham built the House, called for the Pilgrimage, and then made the Pilgrimage himself.

The following chart diagrams this data with the exception of al-Ya'qūbī's rendition:

| | | |
|---|---|---|
| | *BUILD-CALL* | |
| al-Ṭabarī | *Commentary* 17:144 | Ibn Jubayr |
| al-Ṭabarī | *Commentary* 17:145 | 'Ikrima[16] |
| al-Ṭabarī | *History* 286 | Ibn 'Abbās |
| al-Ṭabarī | *History* 286-7 | Ibn 'Abbās |
| al-Ṭabarī | *Commentary* 17:144 | Ibn 'Abbās |
| al-Ṭabarī | *Commentary* 17:144 | Ibn 'Abbās |
| al-Qummī | 2:83 | anonymous |
| | *BUILD-HAJJ* | |
| al-Ṭabarī | *Commentary* 1:555 | 'Alī |
| al-Qummī | 1:62 | anonymous |
| al-Ṭabarsī | 1:471-2 | al-Ṣādiq |
| Ibn Kathīr | *Commentary* 1:183 | Mujāhid |
| | *BUILD-HAJJ-CALL* | |
| al-Azraqī | 33-4 | Ibn Isḥāq |
| al-Tha'labī | 88 | anonymous |
| al-Kisā'ī | 145 | anonymous |

| | *BUILD-CALL-HAJJ* | |
|---|---|---|
| al-Ṭabarī | *Commentary* 1:554 | al-Suddī |
| Ibn al-Athīr | 107 | anonymous |
| | *BUILD-HAJJ-CALL-SHOWS HAJJ* | |
| al-Ṭabarī | *History* 287-8 | 'Ubayd b. 'Umayr[17] |

The lack of consistency regarding the order of events is clear from the chart,[18] and the confusion points to the likelihood that the early traditionists had no traditions that could provide a consistent account of the tale. The ambiguous nature of the traditions suggests that the early Muslims could find few if any legends treating the Abrahamic pilgrimage, a situation quite different from Abraham establishing the Ka'ba, an act which appears to derive from pre-Islamic tradition.

The connection between the Pilgrimage (with its major act in the plain of 'Arafāt some thirteen miles east of Mecca) and the Meccan Ka'ba was important to Islam, despite the fact that the pre-Islamic Ḥajj ritual was probably independent of the religious shrines in Mecca itself.[19] Among Muslims who naturally associated Abraham with both the pre-Islamic shrines in Mecca and the pristine monotheism of ancient Islam, the newly interpreted *Islamic* Hajj may have seemed impossible without a standing Ka'ba. This logic would have required all the reports touching on the Pilgrimage to be placed after Abraham had completed enough of the structure of the Ka'ba for it to be circumambulated.[20]

The connection between Abraham building the Ka'ba and his own Pilgrimage now becomes clearer. Yet the versions of the story we find in the tradition literature are contradictory and confused. No single version can be followed through the sources as was the case in our earlier sections, and no meaningful patterns can be ascertained. It is likely, therefore, that the Pilgrimage traditions originated as Islamic material providing a link between God's command to Abraham that he call humanity to make the Pilgrimage (Q.22:27) and the qur'ānic references (and pre-Islamic associations) of Abraham in Mecca. Their origin being neither among Biblicist nor pre-Islamic Arab traditions, the Pilgrimage stories evolved as Muslim interpretations that served to complete the Abraham cycle and connect the Ka'ba to the Islamic Hajj.

## ABRAHAM CALLS FOR THE PILGRIMAGE

Twenty-eight of the thirty-six reports treat Abraham's call for the Pilgrimage, and six of these also include a segment about his own first Pilgrimage. Most are brief and consist of two or three short sentences; only four or five include any narrative detail. Ten of the eleven Ibn 'Abbās renditions[21] and five of the six Mujāhid renditions[22] treat only Abraham's call for the Pilgrimage. Despite the consistency in theme between the two groups, however, there is no consistency in the style and content of the individual renditions. Each report attributed to Ibn ʿAbbās or Mujāhid describes Abraham's act of calling for the Pilgrimage differently; each emphasizes different aspects of his actions. Some concentrate on Abraham's fear that his voice will not reach all the people on earth. Others emphasize that everything on earth heard him, specify where he stood to make the call, or mention that the response to his call was the liturgical refrain known as the *talbiya*.[23] Nearly every telling offers a different version of what Abraham said. The following paradigmatic sequence for Abraham's call for the Pilgrimage is based on these twenty-eight renditions:

1. Abraham is commanded to call humanity for the Pilgrimage (Q.22:27).
2. He responds by saying that he does not understand how his voice will reach. God tells him to call anyway and that it will be up to God to make Abraham's call reach the people (7/28).
3. Abraham climbs onto the *Maqām* (7/28), on al-Ḥijr[24] (2/28), Mt. Abū Qubays (2/28), al-Ṣafā (1/28), or Mt. Thabīr (1/28), or stands at the corner *(al-rukn)* (1/28), or between the two great mountains of Mecca (1/28).
4. The mountains lower themselves or he is raised up above the mountains to allow his voice to reach all humanity (4/28).
5. Abraham puts his fingers in his ears (3/28) and calls in all directions (4/28), summoning humanity to the Pilgrimage.[25]
6. Everyone or everything on earth, including the Jinnis and those not yet born hear his call (10/28).
7. Everything or everybody responds (6/28), or every believer responds (5/28) by reciting the liturgical *talbiya* (15/28).
8. Everyone who makes the Pilgrimage today actually heard Abraham's original call (3/28).

Motif 3 features a variety of choices for where Abraham stood when he enjoined humanity to make the Pilgrimage, the most popular of which provides yet another explanation for the Maqām Ibrāhīm.[26] Yet despite the fact that this association is repeated more often than most, it is rendered by only one third of the tellings of Abraham's call to humanity. In fact, the very few times that each motif of this story is rendered demonstrates the brief and inconsistent nature of most of the renditions.[27] Only motifs 6 and 7 occur consistently, with the former establishing the ancient sanctity of the Pilgrimage and the universal responsibility to take part as pious Muslims. The latter provides a sacred monotheistic justification for the pagan practice of uttering the *talbiya* refrain during the Pilgrimage ritual.[28] Both might be expected in a sacred historical tale about Abraham's call for the Pilgrimage. The lack of consistency among the renditions suggests that they do not rely on any single pre-Islamic tradition, although various motifs may reflect pre-Islamic customs or mental associations.

## ABRAHAM MAKES THE PILGRIMAGE[29]

Fourteen traditions treat Abraham's first Pilgrimage.[30] Only two are attributed to the same authority (Qatāda), and six overlap with the traditions about Abraham calling humanity to the Pilgrimage. The renditions range from a one-sentence list of Abraham's actions during his first Pilgrimage to a narrative consisting of three paragraphs. Only three renditions refer to the component of the Pilgrimage known independently as the Minor Pilgrimage *('umra)*, although two others refer to a ritual part of the Minor Pilgrimage known as the *sa'ī*.[31] Most renditons begin the Ḥajj Pilgrimage with the journey from Mecca to Minā, an aspect of the Islamic Pilgrimage that disagrees with pre-Islamic accounts.[32]

The paradigmatic Abrahamic Pilgrimage:

1. Abraham finishes building the House (9/14).
2. Abraham calls for the Pilgrimage (4/14).
3. Gabriel (8/14) or God (3/14) shows Abraham the Pilgrimage ritual.
4. Abraham circumambulates the House (3/14) seven times (1/14).
5. He then makes two prostrations behind the Maqām Ibrāhīm (1/14).
6. He goes to Ṣafā and Marwa or is referred to Ṣafā and Marwa by his guide (4/14).
7. He begins the Ḥajj ritual proper on the Day of Watering *(Yawm al-Tarwiya)* (7/14), and a folk-etymology for the name of the day is given based on quenching thirst *(rawiya)* (3/14).
8. He goes on to Minā[33] (11/14) where he stays overnight (9/14) and prays the noon, afternoon, evening, night, and dawn prayers (5/14).[34]

He goes to 'Arafa/'Arafāt[35] (8/14), builds a mosque (1/14), prays the morning and noon prayer (1/14) or combines the noon and afternoon prayers (4/14), and does the Waiting Ritual *(waqafa)* until sunset (6/14). A folk-etymology for 'Arafāt is given based on the root "to know" *('arifa)* (4/14).

On his way from Minā to 'Arafa, Abraham encounters the Devil *(iblīs)* at 'Aqaba, throws stones at him three times,[36] and then completes the ritual stations (1/14).

Or, at a tree at 'Aqaba, Abraham meets the Devil and throws stones at him while saying "God is most great!" *(Allāhu akbar)*.[37] He does the same at al-Jamra al-Thāniya and at al-Jamra al-Thālitha (1/14).

Or, on the way to Minā,[38] Abraham meets the Devil twice. Gabriel tells him to throw stones and recite "God is most great!", which he does (1/14).

Or, after Minā, at Jamrat al-'Aqaba, Satan opposes Abraham. He throws seven stones and then meets him at al-Jamra al-Wusṭā and again at al-Jamra al-Qiswā. Gabriel takes him to Jam', which he tells Abraham is al-Mash'ar. They then proceed to 'Arafāt (1/14).

After the 'Arafāt station, Abraham does the *ifāḍa*[39] (3/14) to al-Ma'zamayn (1/14), or to Jam' (1/14) with a folk-etymology given for Jam' based on "gathering together" *(jam')*, or to al-Muzdalifa (6/14) with a folk-etymology for Muzdalifa given based on "drawing near" *(izdalafa)*. At al-Muzdalifa, he combines the evening and the night prayers (3/14), remains the night (4/14), or stays *(waqafa)* (4/14) at Quzāha (3/14).

In other renditions, he does the *ifāḍa* to Jam' (2/14), which is the same as al-Mash'ar (1/14), and combines the evening and the night prayers (1/14), which supplies another folk-etymology for Jam' based on the root *j-m-'*,[40] and stays there *(waqafa)*, where he does another lapidation.

It is also said that he goes to al-Mash'ar (2/14) and sleeps there (1/14).

After spending the evening and night at al-Muzdalifa/Jam'/al-Mash'ar,[41] he returns to Minā (4/14), where he goes through the process of sacrificing his son Ishmael (1/14),[42] makes a sacrifice of an animal (4/14), shaves[43] (4/14), and does another lapidation (2/14).[44] Or, he does an *ifāḍa* to Minā (2/14), where he does another lapidation (2/14), or he does the *ifāḍa* from Jam', where he does another lapidation (2/14).

He does the *ifāḍa* from Minā back to the Ka'ba (3/14) and does another series of circumambulations (1/14).

He returns to Minā for another lapidation (4/14).[45]

At this point or at any point in the account after going to the plain of 'Arafāt, renditions may end with the note that Abraham continues and finishes the Ḥajj (9/14). When he is finished, he recites Qur'ān 2:126: MY LORD, MAKE THIS A CITY OF PEACE AND FEED ITS PEOPLE WHO BELIEVE IN GOD AND THE LAST DAY WITH FRUITS (2/14). He calls the people for the Pilgrimage (1/14), or charges Ishmael to live at the Ka'ba and teach the people the Pilgrimage sequence (1/14).

There is general agreement among the traditions on the following aspects of the Ḥajj:

1. It takes place after Abraham finished building the House (9/14).
2. Gabriel shows Abraham the ritual (8/14).
3. The Ḥajj ritual begins on the Day of Watering (7/14).
4. On that day, Abraham goes to Minā (11/14), where he spends the night (9/14).
5. The next day he goes to 'Arafāt (8/14) and does the Waiting Ritual (6/14).

6. After leaving ʿArafāt, he goes to al-Muzdalifa, al-Mashʿar, or Jamʿ (10/14).[46]
7. After spending the night at al-Muzdalifa/al-Mashʿar/Jamʿ, he returns to Minā (8/14).

Because this series of ritual activities corresponds with and at times explains the general progression of the Pilgrimage ritual practiced by contemporary Islam, Abraham's acts represent the first occasion of the rituals that are carried out even by pious Muslims today. His throwing stones at the devil corresponds with the ritual of lapidation, and indeed, explains the reason for the stoning custom. His sacrifice corresponds with the *naḥr* or ritual sacrifice of the Ḥajj, and the act of shaving his head explains the current custom of shaving the head or cutting off a lock of hair.

Abraham's Pilgrimage, then, represents the quintessential Ḥajj, and his very actions provide the reason and inform the meaning of the various rituals of the Islamic Pilgrimage. It was Abraham, the first true monotheist, who performed the same acts that pious Muslims carry out today. The association of the Ḥajj with pre-Islamic paganism would be understood, therefore, as only a temporary aberration from the original monotheistic act represented by Abraham and restored by Muḥammad. The true Pilgrimage rite, these traditions teach, was not instituted on the basis of pagan beliefs, but was rather an act of monotheistic obeisance decreed by God through the angel Gabriel.[47]

Despite the clear intent of associating Abraham with the original Pilgrimage, the sources display a good deal of confusion about the order and specifics of many of the ritual acts. The confusion may be partially due to certain features of the Pilgrimage ritual itself. Different names are associated with the three stone pillars at Minā where the stoning takes place, for example.[48] The lapidation also occurs at two different points in the ritual process, and the pilgrims remain at Minā or pass through it at least twice during the ritual sequence. These factors may account for part of the confusion, but not all. Some accounts such as that of al-Yaʿqūbī, al-Ṭabarī, al-Qummī and al-Thaʿlabī make no mention of Abraham's lapidation at all, and no more than two sources ever agree about when and where he did it. The greatest variation among the sources occurs with the activities at al-Muzdalifa after the station at ʿArafāt and at the return to Minā after al-Muzdalifa.

Because some of the sources are quite terse in their list of ritual stations and activities, one must be circumspect about drawing conclusions from their variety or omissions. Some reports such as the brief list supplied by Qatāda consist of a single sentence.[49] Others provide a brief exposition that ends abruptly with Gabriel teaching Abraham the Ḥajj ritual "just as he taught Adam."[50] Many of these sources, therefore, had no intention of describing the entire Pilgrimage sequence in detail. In order to draw significant conclusions about possible chronological or juristic variations between schools of law or religious movements, one must collect and analyze a very large pool of Pilgrimage traditions, a worthwhile endeavor but beyond the scope of this study.[51]

It is instructive to note here that according to all the traditions, Abraham's directions for the Pilgrimage were given by Gabriel or God. This detail sets up the Pilgrimage traditions as prototypes for the proper Pilgrimage ritual. It is all the more puzzling that there should be so much confusion and disagreement among the sources. The confusion suggests that the Islamic Pilgrimage was not yet standardized among the early Muslims, despite Muḥammad's precedent of his Farewell Pilgrimage during the year of his death.

If any significant legend connecting Abraham to a Pilgrimage rite were in existence at the beginning of Islam, we would expect more consistency among the traditions. The broad range of specifics regarding the Abrahamic Ḥajj sequence suggests that no such legend was in existence. In fact, the pre-Islamic Pilgrimage rite itself had never been standardized. Because it consisted of paying homage to several deities in various locations outside of Mecca, whoever wished to emphasize obeisance to specific deities would naturally alter their worship accordingly.[52]

The evidence suggests, therefore, that the early Muslims simply had no Abrahamic traditions connected to the Ḥajj that they could incorporate into the interpretive literature of Islam.[53] The early Islamic view of the Pilgrimage was undoubtedly colored by the new Muslims' immediate knowledge of the pre-Islamic pagan pilgrimage and its associations. Muḥammad worked toward eliminating the pagan associations with the Pilgrimage.[54] Yet perhaps because of the great changes taking place during the last year of Muḥammad's life and the fact that he made the *Islamic* Pilgrimage only once, the rite simply did not have enough time to become established before his death.[55]

It may appear less surprising, then, that we are confronted with a variety of routes and orders of activity for Abraham's first Pilgrimage. Abraham's pre-Islamic association as founder of the Ka'ba suggested a natural link between him and the Pilgrimage as the latter became more closely associated with the Ka'ba under Islam. And the early Muslims learned more about Abraham and the various episodes of his life as they acquired more Abraham legends during their contacts with Biblicists during the first few generations of Islam. It would therefore be natural to connect him more closely with the activities of the Pilgrimage, which had already been largely Islamized and connected to Mecca by Muḥammad. As the specific episodes of Abraham's life were assimilated into Islam, some centered on the Pilgrimage ritual itself.

Before the Great Pilgrimage became as standardized as it would become among the various acceptable interpretations of Islam, Muslim scholars laid out the order and significance of Abraham's actions differently, corresponding, presumably, to their own views of the proper ritual sequence. As their views were written down they became fixed; it became somewhat problematic to correct or smooth over contrary explanations in written texts. The Pilgrimage reports, then, represent an Islamic development that evolved in response to the pre-Islamic association of Abraham with Mecca, the growing knowledge among the Muslims of the character and activities of Abraham, and the specifics of the ritual acts that made up the Ḥajj itself.

## THE IBN ʻABBĀS TRADITIONS

Unlike the series of traditions attributed to Ibn ʻAbbās found earlier, the eleven traditions found here do not represent renditions of a single Ibn ʻAbbās legend. They represent, rather, a series of largely unrelated reports attributed to the same source. All but one are brief tellings of Abraham calling humanity to perform the Pilgrimage. Of these ten, eight are found in al-Ṭabarī's two works.[56] They average three or four lines in length and treat Abraham's call in a variety of ways. The only true narrative describes Abraham's first Ḥajj pilgrimage and is eight lines in length.

It is unclear why such a variety of traditions are all attributed to Ibn ʻAbbās. They may have been assigned to him after they were inserted into renditions of the Abraham cycle attributed to Ibn ʻAbbās. Or they may have originated as unconnected traditions that were attached to Ibn ʻAbbās simply because of his fame for being such a prolific early traditionist.[57] Less likely, they may have originated with Ibn ʻAbbās but then evolved slightly before being written down and "frozen" in the written works.[58] Whatever the case, there is no evidence to suggest that the ten Ibn ʻAbbās "Call" traditions originate among either Biblicist or pre-Islamic Arab traditions. They function rather as editorial comments that bring the Abraham cycle to a *finale*. All are connected to Abraham's call for the Pilgrimage in Qur'ān 22:27, but they hardly agree about any particulars regarding the substance and location of his call.

## THE MUJĀHID TRADITIONS

Similar to the Ibn ʻAbbās series, five of the six Mujāhid traditions depict Abraham calling the people to the Pilgrimage. These reports consist of only two or three lines and tend to be even briefer than those attributed to Ibn ʻAbbās. All are found in al-Ṭabarī, connected with Qur'ān 22:27, and like the Ibn ʻAbbās traditions, display a marked lack of consistency. The only narration of Abraham's Pilgrimage is about 12 lines in length.[59] There is no reason to assume that the Mujāhid traditions served a different function from the Ibn ʻAbbās traditions. They appear as reports that evolved during the early Islamic period to tie together the various sections of the Qur'ān treating Abraham's experiences in Mecca.

In summary, the traditions treating Abraham's call for the Pilgrimage represent Islamic material that binds together Qur'ānic verses treating Abraham's association with Mecca and provides closure to the legend. Most are brief and provide little consistent information regarding Meccan sites or ritual activities apart from the single motif of the liturgical pilgrim recitation known as the *talbiya*.

The reports treating the Pilgrimage are generally fuller than those treating Abraham's call to humanity. Most eliminate the 'umra section of the Great Pilgrimage and concentrate on the ritual proper, beginning in Mecca because of Abraham's association with building the Ka'ba. This fact indicates an Islamic innovation, since evidence suggests that the pre-Islamic Pilgrimage began with the journey to 'Arafāt from 'Ukāẓ and Majanna.[60] The great variety among the traditions reflects both the lack of a standardized pre-Islamic Pilgrimage ritual and the absence of pre-Islamic traditions connecting Abraham to the Ḥajj. The many variations in detail among our traditions correspond with the flexible approach regarding the rites of the Pilgrimage attributed to Muḥammad in the Prophetic Tradition:

> Ibn 'Abbās: A man said to the Prophet, "I did the visitation ritual before the lapidation." The Prophet replied, "There is no harm." He said, "I shaved [my head] before the ritual sacrifice." The Prophet replied, "There is no harm." He said, "I have slaughtered the ritual sacrifice before the lapidation." The Prophet replied: "There is no harm."[61]

> 'Abdallāh b. 'Amr b. al-'Āṣ: I witnessed the Prophet when he was delivering the sermon on the Day of the Sacrifice *(yawm al-naḥr)*. A man stood up and said: "I thought that such and such was to be done before such and such." Then another stood up and said, "I thought that such and such was to be done before such and such. I shaved [my head] before slaughtering." [Another said]: "I slaughtered the ritual sacrifice before doing the lapidation." And similar things [were said to him]. The Prophet said, "Do it [now] and there is no harm in all these cases." Whenever the Prophet was asked about anything on that day, he replied, "Do it [now], and there is no harm.[62]

PART FOUR

# The Sacrifice

## INTRODUCTION

The "Sacrifice," or more accurately, near-sacrifice of Abraham's son, is known in Arabic as the *dhabīḥ*. The root meaning of the word is to tear, cut, rend, or slit, and has the technical meaning of slaughtering or sacrificing in the manner prescribed by law. The word *dhabīḥ* can be synonymous with *madhbūḥ*, signifying the thing that is cut or rent, or a sacrificial animal slaughtered in accordance with religious practice. It also has the meaning of an animal that is ritually fit and *intended* for sacrifice—the intended victim.

The word has therefore come to be used as an honorific epithet *(laqab)* for Ishmael, since Islam has come to view him as the intended victim of Abraham's sacrifice. It is not at all clear from the story of the Sacrifice found in the Qur'ān, however, that Ishmael was the intended victim.[1] In fact, neither he nor Isaac is named, and early Muslim exegetes were divided over which one they believed was intended to be the sacrifice.[2] The exegetes were concerned with other issues raised by the legend as well, but the issue of which son was the intended victim was by far the most pressing. They often gave their own opinion about who it was and cited early scholars and collectors of traditions in support of their views. Yet they also included reports and opinions supporting the contrary point of view. A significant amount of material is therefore available which relates to the issue of who was the intended sacrifice. Not only do we find a variety of tellings of the sacrificial act itself, but we also find recurring reports supporting one or the other of the sons as being the intended victim. While the purpose of this study is not to determine who the intended victim actually was or which son was intended in the Qur'ān, we will examine the various traditions and opinions in the exegetical literature in order to understand the way in which they fit and function within the cycle of Abraham legends.

# Chapter 13

# PRELUDE TO SACRIFICE

Qur'ān 37:99-113 reads:

> 37:99. [ABRAHAM] SAID: "I WILL GO TO MY LORD HE WILL SURELY GUIDE ME. 100. O MY LORD; GRANT ME A PIOUS SON!" 101. SO WE GAVE HIM THE GOOD NEWS OF A PATIENT AND FORBEARING SON. 102. WHEN HE REACHED THE AGE OF RUNNING WITH HIM, HE SAID: "O MY SON. I SEE IN A VISION THAT I WILL SACRIFICE YOU. SO LOOK, WHAT IS YOUR VIEW?" THE SON SAID: "O MY FATHER! DO AS YOU ARE COMMANDED. IF GOD WILLS, YOU WILL FIND ME PATIENT AND ENDURING!"[1] 103. SO WHEN THEY HAD BOTH SUBMITTED, HE LAY HIM ONTO HIS FOREHEAD. 104. AND WE CALLED OUT TO HIM, "O ABRAHAM! 105. YOU HAVE ALREADY FULFILLED THE VISION!" THUS DO WE REWARD THOSE WHO DO RIGHT. 106. FOR THIS WAS A CLEAR TRIAL. 107. WE REDEEMED HIM WITH A MAGNIFICENT SACRIFICE. 108. AND WE LEFT FOR HIM [THIS BLESSING] AMONG OTHERS: 109. "PEACE UPON ABRAHAM." 110. THUS DO WE REWARD THOSE WHO DO RIGHT. 111. FOR HE WAS ONE OF OUR BELIEVING SERVANTS. 112. AND WE GAVE HIM THE GOOD NEWS OF ISAAC—A PIOUS PROPHET. 113. WE BLESSED HIM AND ISAAC. BUT OF THEIR PROGENY ARE THOSE THAT DO RIGHT AND THOSE THAT CLEARLY DO WRONG. THEY REAP THEIR OWN REWARDS.[2]

The brief qur'ānic telling of the Sacrifice occurs within a homily exhorting cynics and mockers to believe in God and the way of righteousness. After comparing the inevitable hellish fate of unbelievers with the paradise for those who accept God, it launches into a historical synopsis of the fate of ancient peoples: MOST OF THE ANCIENTS HAD EARLIER GONE ASTRAY, THOUGH WE SENT [MESSENGERS] TO WARN THEM. CONSIDER THE FATE OF THOSE WHOM WE WARNED! [ALL PERISHED] EXCEPT GOD'S TRUE SERVANTS (Qur'ān 37:71-74). The homily continues with a brief summary of the prophetic acts of Noah, Abraham, Moses and Aaron, Elijah *(Ilyās)*, Lot, and Jonah, repeating the recurring qur'ānic warning that the great prophets and their followers were rewarded while those who did not heed their call were doomed to utter destruction. Abraham's is the longest narration in the series and includes the extra-biblical story of his destruction of the idols and being cast into the fiery furnace as well as the Sacrifice.[3]

The exegetes placed the brief Sacrifice story into the larger context of the Abraham cycle in various ways. One response was to connect Q.37:106 (FOR THIS WAS A CLEAR TRIAL) to Q.2:124: REMEMBER THAT ABRAHAM WAS TRIED BY HIS LORD WITH *KALIMĀT* WHICH HE FULFILLED.[4] Al-Ṭabarī understood this verse to refer to the religious requirements of Islam with which Abraham was tested after he had demonstrated a steadfast belief in one God: "[God] tested him with them [the *kalimāt*] after testing him with the affair of Nimrod b. Kuth, who attempted to burn him with fire.[5] It was also after his test through the command to sacrifice his son AFTER HE REACHED THE AGE OF RUNNING WITH HIM (37:102), hoping for his welfare and succor by bringing him close to his Lord; and after his raising up the foundations of the House and establishing the stations of the pilgrimage."[6] According to al-Ṭabarī, then, the attempted sacrifice was one of a series of tests that Abraham had to pass in order to merit being the patriarch of Islam, an approach that parallels that of Jewish legend.[7]

A slightly different opinion is attributed to al-Ḥasan:[8] "Abraham was tested with the stars, the moon, the sun, circumcision, the sacrifice of his son, with the fire, and with the emigration, and he passed all of them.[9] Despite the existence of this tradition and al-Ṭabarī's personal view, the association of the Sacrifice with the trials of Qur'ān 2:124 is not well attested, occurring only a few times among the sources.

Others understood the meaning of *dhabīḥ* to be a sacrifice that fulfilled a personal vow.[10] Abraham's vision in Q.37:102 was interpreted to be the divine call to fulfill a vow he had made previously regarding his son. The trial *(balā')* referred to in Q.37:106 was to determine whether Abraham would be willing to carry out his word, even if it meant that he must slaughter his own son. When had Abraham made this vow? According to the exegetes, it was in response to the divine message of his son's impending birth given by the angels during their visit on the way to destroy the people of Lot.[11] This interpretation held that the son intended was Isaac because it was his birth that was announced by the angels in Q.11:71 (... AND WE GAVE HER THE GOOD NEWS ABOUT ISAAC, AND AFTER ISAAC, JACOB).

The tradition is first reported in our sample by al-Ṭabarī on the authority of al-Suddī:[12]

> Gabriel said to Sarah, "I am giving you the good news of a son named Isaac, and after Isaac, Jacob." She slapped her forehead in surprise. Thus the verse, SHE STRUCK HER FOREHEAD AND SAID: "A BARREN OLD WOMAN?

> (51:29) AND THIS, MY HUSBAND HERE IS AN OLD MAN! THAT IS A STRANGE THING INDEED"! ... (11:72). Sarah said to Gabriel: "What is a sign of this?" He took a dry twig in his hand and bent it between his fingers. It quivered and turned green. Then Abraham said, "He will therefore be a sacrifice to God!" When Isaac grew up, Abraham was visited in his sleep and was told, "Fulfill your vow that if God bestowed upon you a boy from Sarah, you would offer him as a sacrifice!" He said to Isaac, "Let's go and offer a sacrifice *(qurbān)* to God." He took a knife and rope and set out with him until they came between some mountains. The boy said to him, "O Father, where is your offering?" He answered, "O MY SON. I SEE IN A VISION THAT I WILL SACRIFICE YOU. SO LOOK, WHAT IS YOUR VIEW?" THE SON SAID: "O MY FATHER! DO AS YOU ARE COMMANDED. IF GOD WILLS, YOU WILL FIND ME PATIENT AND ENDURING!" (37:103).

The tradition occurs three more times in the sources, although it is attributed to al-Suddī only twice in all.[13] The second "Suddī" rendition is shorter than that found in al-Ṭabarī:

> Abraham separated from his people and emigrated to Syria in flight for his religion, as the Qur'ān says: I WILL GO TO MY LORD. HE WILL SURELY GUIDE ME! (37:99). He prayed to God that he be given a pious son from Sarah, saying: LORD, GIVE ME A PIOUS SON! (37:100). When the guests, who were angels sent to the cities of Lot *(al-mu'tafika)* came to him, they gave him the good news of a pious son. When Abraham was given the news, he said: "He will therefore be a sacrifice to God!" So when the boy was born and REACHED THE AGE OF RUNNING WITH HIM (37:102), it was said to him: "Fulfill your vow that he would be an offering to God!" That is the reason for the command of God to Abraham to sacrifice his son.

Al-Ṭabarī provides another rendition with a different record of authentication culminating in "... some of the Companions of the Prophet." This rendition is virtually identical with his telling attributed to al-Suddī.[14] Our fourth and last rendition is also found in al-Ṭabarī's *History*, but again with a different record of authentication: "Abraham was shown in a dream and instructed to 'carry out the oath you made that if God granted you a son through Sarah, you would sacrifice him.' "[15] The same tradition is referred to twice more but not provided by al-Ṭabarī,[16] al-Ṭabarsī[17] and Ibn al-Athīr[18] in support of the view that the intended sacrifice was Isaac, and by al-Zamakhsharī.[19]

Abraham's vow to sacrifice his son does not appear to parallel known Biblicist legends, although certain of its motifs have biblical parallels. Note, for example, the story of Jephthah in Judges 11:30-40, where he must slay his daughter as the result of a vow to God.[20] The motif of the sprouting twig also has a parallel in Aaron's staff in Numbers 17:16-26, which sprouts leaves and blossoms as a supernatural sign.[21] Neither does our tradition find a clear parallel in pre-Islamic Arab legends, although a similar child-sacrifice story is found in Ibn Isḥāq's biography of Muḥammad, where the Prophet's grandfather 'Abd al-Muṭṭalib vows to sacrifice a son.[22] Moreover, pre-Islamic Arabia knows of a vow to have the son of a previously barren mother serve the cult at Mecca.[23]

The major significance of this tradition lies in the fact that it provides a context for the attempted sacrifice. The qur'ānic rendition implies that it took place soon after Abraham's emigration from the land of his birth in the east.[24] He asks God for a son (Qur'ān 37:100) and is told that his request will be granted (37:101). But as soon as the son is old enough, Abraham has a vision in which he learns he must offer that son in sacrifice (37:102). The obvious lacuna in the qur'ānic text is the period between the granting of Abraham's request and his vision. Yet other Qur'ān sections provide narrative material to fill that gap, namely, the visit of the angels on their way to destroy the people of Lot. This would suggest to most exegetes that the Sacrifice took place in Syria before the transfer to Mecca, and therefore that Isaac was the intended victim.[25]

This reconstruction is quite possible from the standpoint of the Qur'ān text itself. The missing item is the connection between the announcement of Isaac's birth and the vision to offer him in sacrifice. That connection is supplied in some sources with the mention of Abraham's vow, a very simple sentence inserted into the telling of the angel's announcement of Isaac's birth in classic exegetical manner. In other words, the tradition of Abraham's vow represents an Islamic addition that serves to bind together two disparate Qur'ān sections. Because the precedence of a vow to sacrifice a child can be found in both Biblicist and pre-Islamic pagan Arab milieus,[26] the Islamic addition could have been influenced by either environment or may have developed within nascent Islam.

It must be noted, however, that the legend does not appear to be particularly popular among the sources. It occurs only four times on the authority of at least two early figures, and is referred to but not quoted another five times by other sources, providing one of several explanations for the setting of the sacrifice.[27]

## SATAN ATTEMPTS TO INTERFERE

After Abraham receives his vision in which he learns he must sacrifice his son (Q.37:102), he immediately sets out, determined to accomplish his task. On his way he is confronted by Satan *(al-Shayṭān)*, who tries to divert him from his mission. This sequence is found in three different versions distinguished in two cases by the ultimate authorities of their records of authentication, Ka'b al-Aḥbār and Ibn Isḥāq. The third version is anonymous.[28] The Ka'b version is the most complete and occurs five times among the sources.[29] A composit telling follows:

> Ka'b asks Abū Hurayra if he would like to hear the story of Isaac, son of Abraham. Abū Hurayra responds in the affirmative, so Ka'b narrates:
>
> After Abraham is shown his vision about the sacrifice, Satan says: ". . . if I do not beguile the family of Abraham [now] I will never beguile them!" Satan appears as a man known to Abraham and Sarah and goes to Sarah after Abraham and Isaac had already left home for the place of sacrifice. Satan asks Sarah where they went and she replies: "To do an errand" or "to gather firewood". Satan says it is not so, and tells her that Abraham actually took Isaac out to sacrifice him. Sarah responds that Abraham would never do that, or that he is more compassionate toward the boy than even she but asks why he would ever wish to sacrifice him. Satan answers that Abraham claimed that God commanded him. Sarah replies: "If God commanded that of him, then he should do it!"
>
> Foiled, Satan leaves and finds Isaac walking next to his father. He tells Isaac that his father is going to sacrifice him or asks Isaac where Abraham is taking him, to which the son answers: "To do an errand" or "to gather firewood". Satan counters: "No by God . . . he is going to sacrifice you!" Isaac does not believe him and asks why he would do that. Satan replies that Abraham claimed that God commanded him, to which Isaac answers: "If God commanded that, then he should obey Him!"
>
> Foiled again, Satan hastens to Abraham and asks him where he is going. He replies that he must do some errands with Isaac. Satan says: "Well, by God, you took him to sacrifice him!" Abraham says: "Why would I sacrifice him?" Satan answers: "You claimed that your Lord commanded you." Abraham replies: "By God, if my Lord commanded that of me, I would do it!"[30]

The "Ibn Ishaq" version is represented by two traditions given on his authroity, the second essentially a duplicate of the first but omitting some of the detail and dialogue.[31] The full account is as follows:

> After Abraham is commanded to sacrifice his son but before his son knows about the command, Abraham says to him: "O my son, take the rope and the knife, and let's go gather firewood." When Abraham turns onto the path, the devil *(iblīs)* appears in the form of a man who

tries to deter him, asking "Where are you going old man?" He replies that he is going to do an errand. The devil says: "I see that Satan has come to you in your sleep and has commanded you to sacrifice this little boy of yours!" But Abraham recognizes him and says: "Away, you enemy of God!"

Foiled, the devil comes to Ishmael, who is carrying the rope and knife behind his father. He asks him where his father is taking him and Ishmael replies: "To gather firewood." The devil tells him that his father plans to sacrifice him, but Ishmael does not believe him. When asked why, the devil says: "He claims that his Lord commanded that of him." So Ishmael replies: "Then let him do what his Lord commands in perfect obedience!"[32]

Foiled again, the devil goes to their home where he asks Hagar the same question. She tells him that Abraham and Ishmael went to gather firewood. When he tells her that Abraham went to sacrifice her son, she says: "Certainly not! He is even more compassionate toward him than I! But if his Lord would command that of him, then he would submit to the command of God!"

So the "enemy of God" failed in his desire because of God and because Abraham's entire family submitted to God's will.

Our third version of this legend is found in two Shi'ite sources: al-Qummī and al-Ṭabarsī.[33]

An old man approaches Abraham and asks him what he plans to do with the boy. Abraham replies that he will sacrifice him. The man responds: "Heaven forbid! You will sacrifice an innocent boy?" Abraham answers that God commanded him. The man counters by saying that it must have been Satan who commanded that. Abraham replies: "Woe to you! I know that I received a truly Godly revelation." The man repeats that it must have been Satan, but Abraham refuses to speak with him further. He is resolved to obey his Lord, but the old man says: "O Abraham, you are a leader whom people follow. If you sacrifice him, then [all the] people will sacrifice their children!" But Abraham spoke with him no longer.

The devil[34] then goes to the boy's mother when she is engaged in what appears to be the 'umra pilgrimage to the Ka'ba. He tells her that he just saw an old man, and she tells him that that is her husband. He says that he saw a boy with him, and she tells him that that is her son. He continues: "Then I saw him laying him down and taking up the knife to sacrifice him!" She says: "You lie! Abraham is the gentlest of men. Why would he sacrifice his own son?" The devil insists that he

> saw it and she asks why. He replies: "He claimed that his Lord commanded him." She concurs: "It is true that he would obey his Lord." She becomes agitated but finishes her ritual responsibilities, and then runs toward Minā with her hand on her head saying: "O Lord! Do not punish me for what I did to the mother of Ishmael!"

The second rendition adds: "When Sarah came and was told the story, she went to her son and saw the sign of the knife scratched into his throat.[35] She was terrified and was stricken with a paroxysm of sickness that killed her.

Finally, one miscellaneous rendition is given by al-Kisā'ī without record of authentication.[36]

> When the two of them left, the Devil approached Sarah and said to her: "Abraham has resolved to sacrifice your son, Isaac! Catch up with him and stop him!" But she recognized him and said: "Away, God's cursed one! He has set out with him to please God!" So he left her and caught up with Isaac. He said to him: "Your father wants to sacrifice you!" But Abraham said to him: "O my son, come along. Do not pay attention to him, for he is the Devil."

The three versions represent covariants of the same basic theme: the devil or an old man approaches each of the three characters in the story and tempts them to disobey the command of God. In every case, the tempter brings forth compelling and logical arguments that should convince the protagonists to desist from carrying out the awful act of child sacrifice. Yet in every case absolute obedience to God prevails, the tempting arguments are ignored, and the drama of the sacrifice continues.

The most prevalent of the three versions is the Ka'b version, attributed to the well-known early Jewish convert to Islam who is credited with bringing many Jewish traditions into the corpus of Islamic religious literature. The Ibn Isḥāq version is probably a later rendition of the Satan story.[37] Version 3 is given anonymously, but both renditions are located in Shi'ite sources and may represent a Shi'ite version of the tradition.

The Ka'b version and Version 3 understand the intended sacrifice to be Isaac, and it is indeed consistent for Ka'b to have transmitted coherent legends from Jewish tradition assuming Isaac to be the victim. Shi'ites have been associated with borrowing more freely from Jewish legends than Sunnis, which may explain the view of Version 3 that the intended sacrifice was Isaac.[38] Only the Ibn Isḥāq version places Ishmael in the role of the intended sacrifice.[39] This may have been a later view[40] or may simply reflect a different opinion as it was passed down in the tradition literature.

The story of Satan trying to prevent Abraham and his family from carrying out the sacrifice is a well-known theme in Jewish legendary literature. Post-Muḥammad Jewish sources such as *Tanhuma*, *Sefer HaYashar*, and *Midrash VaYosha'* closely parallel the Islamic legends.[41] Pre-Islamic Jewish sources also contain the story of Satan's enticing, with the closest parallel found in *Bereshit Rabbah*.[42] Another pre-Islamic legend connecting Satan with the attempted sacrifice and taken up repeatedly in later midrashic literature can be found in the Babylonian Talmud.[43]

The few available pre-Islamic Arab parallels to the sacrifice theme include no mention of Satan or any wicked power challenging the authority or morality of the decision to sacrifice a child, although they are not completely silent on the issue. The most famous Arab child-sacrifice story is that of 'Abd al-Muṭṭalib vowing to sacrifice the son who was destined to become the father of the Prophet Muḥammad.[44] A parallel to the Shi'ite version can be found in the argument of the Quraysh against 'Abd al-Muṭṭalib's decision to carry out his vow when they say: "If you do a thing like this, there will be no stopping men from coming to sacrifice their sons, and what will become of the people then?"[45] This compares with the claim of the old man in Version 3: "O Abraham! you are a leader that people follow. If you sacrifice him, then [all the] people will sacrifice their children!"

While the prevalence of this theme in early Jewish legendary literature does not preclude the possibility of its independent existence in pre-Islamic Arabia, it appears more than likely that the legendary Satan story evolved out of a Biblicist milieu.[46] The Islamic renderings of Satan's temptation closely parallel early Jewish exegesis of the biblical text. In most of the Jewish versions (except those originating from the text of BT *Sanhedrin* 89b) Satan challenges Abraham during the three days mentioned but not accounted for in Genesis 22:4: "On the third day Abraham looked up and saw the place from afar." The Jewish narrative exegesis points out that the lag between God's command and the actual occasion of the ordeal teaches that with three days to come to terms with the true meaning of the command, Abraham did not attempt to carry out the Sacrifice in a state of shock.[47] Despite Satan's temptation at that time, Abraham, Isaac, and Sarah all overcome their own personal wishes and needs in order to fulfil the ultimate wish of God.

The Islamic sources have no need to explain the three days, since Qur'ān 37:102 mentions Abraham's vision and his words to his son that he must sacrifice him in the same breath. They nevertheless match the biblical sequence despite the fact that the Qur'ān text presents no similar problem, therefore suggesting a development from Jewish literary forebears. Moreover, the geographical locus of many of the legends is in Syria, a biblical site,[48] while no motifs are found to be inconsistent with Jewish legends.

We have noted that Version 3, however, finds a parallel in an Arab legend[49] which may have explained away a pre-Islamic practice of vowing a human sacrifice,[50] and the traditions considering Ishmael to have been the intended victim place the story in pre-Islamic Arabia. None of the three versions appears to contain any Islamic editorial material.[51]

To summarize, the "Satan" legend derived originally from Biblicist sources, but naturally served to provide information about the qur'ānic rendition of the sacrifice as well. It taught a similar lesson in both religious traditions: that Abraham and his family overcame their own personal obstacles in order to fulfill the ultimate command of their Lord.

## SATAN AND THE LAPIDATION

A very different tradition about Satan occurs five times among the sources and is given on the authority of Ibn 'Abbās.[52]

The setting is Abraham's first Pilgrimage, where Abraham is shown the stations of the pilgrimage or is commanded with the sacrifice. Satan appears to him at the place of the Running Ritual, or at al-Mash'ar al-Ḥarām and tries to get the better of him, but Abraham surpasses him.

Then Gabriel takes him to al-Jamra al-'Aqaba,[53] or Abraham goes there himself where Satan again appears to him. Satan departs or sinks into the ground when Abraham throws seven stones at him. Satan appears again at al-Jamra al-Wusṭā, Abraham throws the stones, and the scene repeats itself. He then appears again at al-Jamra al-Quṣwā (1/5) or al-Jamra al-Kubrā (1/5), where the scene is repeated (2/5).

Abraham then flings Ishmael, who is wearing a white shirt, onto his forehead, or begins to go through with the sacrifice of Isaac.[54] Ishmael says: "O father, I have no other garment for a shroud, so please take off my shirt and use it for that," or Isaac says: "O father, tie me up so I will not shake and my blood splash you when you sacrifice me". Abraham turns around for a moment and sees a horned ram with dark eyes and white wool or is called from behind: O ABRAHAM, YOU HAVE ALREADY FULFILLED THE VISION! (Q.37:105).

Ibn Kathīr refers to a sixth rendition without citing it, saying that it is the same as the Ishmael tradition given here except that the intended sacrifice was Isaac.

These tellings are independent of the previous Satan tradition and center on the native pre-Islamic custom of stoning the three pillars in Minā. Substituting Satan for the pre-Islamic association of the lapidation purged the act of its pagan meaning and set it into an acceptable Islamic framework.[55]

# Chapter 14

# THE SACRIFICIAL ACT

The story of the sacrificial act occurs in three coherent versions, one each attributed to al-Suddī or Ibn Isḥāq, and a third found only in Shi'ite sources. The first two are quite similar, and actually represent covariants of the same tradition. The Shi'ite version differs substantially, although it also appears to derive ultimately from the same environment.

The paradigmatic "Suddī" version is represented by five renditions:[1]

1. When Abraham is given the good news of a son, he vows to offer him as a sacrifice to God. After the son grows up, Abraham is shown a vision in his sleep telling him that he must fulfill his vow (5/5) and sacrifice Isaac (4/5).
2. Abraham tells Isaac to come and make a sacrifice[2] to God. He takes along a knife and a rope (5/5).
3. When they come between some mountains, the boy asks where the offering is (5/5).
4. Abraham answers with Q.37:102: ... O MY SON, I SEE IN A VISION THAT I WILL SACRIFICE YOU. SO LOOK, WHAT IS YOUR VIEW?" THE SON SAID: "O MY FATHER! DO AS YOU ARE COMMANDED. IF GOD WILLS, YOU WILL FIND ME PATIENT AND ENDURING!" (5/5).[3]
5. Isaac continues by telling his father to:
   a. tighten his bonds so he will not squirm (3/3),
   b. keep back his clothes from him so that no blood will soil them and cause Sarah grief (3/3),
   c. move the knife quickly to his throat so that death will be easiest (3/3),
   d. ____________________________________________,[4]
   e. give greetings *(salām)* to his mother when he returns (3/3),
   f. ____________________________________________
6. ____________________________________________

7. Abraham draws near, kisses Isaac, and binds him (3/3). They both cry so much that the ground is soaked underneath Isaac's cheek where he is lying (2/3).
8. ______________________________
9. Abraham draws the knife onto Isaac's throat but it does not cut (3/3) because God had pounded a sheet of copper over his throat (2/3).
10. So Abraham throws Isaac onto his forehead and [tries to] make a gash on the back of his neck.[5] Thus Q.37:103: SO WHEN THEY HAD BOTH SUBMITTED, HE LAY HIM [THREW HIM] ONTO HIS FOREHEAD (2/3).[6]
11. AND WE CALLED OUT TO HIM, "O ABRAHAM! YOU HAVE ALREADY FULFILLED THE VISION!" (Q.37:104-5) (3/3).
12. Abraham turns and sees a ram. He takes it, unties his son, and kisses him (3/3).
13. Abraham says: "O son, you have been given to me!" Therefore verse Q.27:107: WE REDEEMED HIM WITH A MAGNIFICENT SACRIFICE (2/3).
14. When Abraham returns to Sarah and tells her what happened, she is unhappy and says: "You would sacrifice my son and not inform me?" (2/3).

The rendition of Mujīr al-Dīn never mentions the name of the son, which could be either Isaac or Ishmael. Despite the fact that the Mujīr al-Dīn rendition is attributed to al-Suddī, it is actually a hybrid tradition incorporating the following numbered motifs from the Ibn Isḥāq version below:

5d. The son asks his father to lay him on his forehead for he is afraid that compassion will overcome his father and prevent him from carrying out God's command.[7]
5e. He also asks him to return his shirt to his mother, for it may give her some comfort.
6. Abraham tells his son that he is truly a wonderful help in carrying out God's command.
9. Abraham puts the knife to his son's throat but God turns it over to its blunt side in Abraham's hand.
13. Gabriel, Abraham, his son, and the ram all say "God is most great!"[8] and Abraham sacrifices the ram at al-Manḥar in Minā.

The paradigmatic "Ibn Isḥāq" version is represented by four traditions.[9]

1. Abraham would visit Hagar and Ishmael by riding to Mecca on Buraq. He would leave Syria in the morning and would return home before nightfall so that he could spend the night with his wife in Syria. This continued until Ishmael ... REACHED THE AGE OF RUNNING WITH HIM. (Q.37:102) (2/4).

2. Abraham tells his son to take some rope and a knife and to come onto a trail to gather firewood.
3. ______________________________
4. When they are alone on the Thabīr[10] trail, Abraham says (Q.37:102): "O MY SON, I SEE IN A VISION THAT I WILL SACRIFICE YOU (3/4). He continues: SO LOOK, WHAT IS YOUR VIEW?" THE SON SAID: "O MY FATHER! DO AS YOU ARE COMMANDED. IF GOD WILLS, YOU WILL FIND ME PATIENT AND ENDURING!" (2/4).
5. Ishmael continues by telling his father to:
   a. tighten his bonds (4/4),
   b. keep back his clothes from him so that no blood will soil them (3/4), cause Hagar grief (2/4), and diminish his reward (2/4); or be careful not to allow anything to prevent him from his task so that Ishmael's recompense will not be diminished, for death is severe and he may waver (1/4),
   c. Sharpen his knife to finish him off quickly (4/4) to give him rest (1/4) or so death will be easier, for death is severe (2/4),
   d. Throw him onto his forehead and not on his side,[11] for Ishmael is afraid that compassion will overcome his father and prevent him from carrying out God's command (3/4),[12]
   e. Please return his shirt to his mother, for it may give her some comfort (3/4),
   f. "Now proceed!" (3/4).
6. Abraham tells his son that he is truly a wonderful help in carrying out God's command (4/4).[13]
7. Abraham binds his son just as Ishmael had directed him (3/3).
8. Abraham sharpens his knife (2/3) and then, HE LAY HIM ONTO HIS FOREHEAD (Q.37:103) (3/3) and Abraham is careful to avoid looking at him (1/3).
9. He puts the knife to his son's throat but God turns it over to its blunt side in Abraham's hand (3/3).
10. ______________________________
11. When Abraham is about to draw the knife across his son's throat to end his life, he is called: "O ABRAHAM! YOU HAVE ALREADY FULFILLED THE VISION!" (Q.37:104-5) (3/3).
12. He is told that a different sacrifice will be the redemption for his son, so he should slaughter it in Ishmael's place (2/3).

Al-Tha'labī's version attributed to Ibn Isḥāq and included in the paradigmatic version above is actually a hybrid that includes the following motifs from the Suddī version:

5e. He asks his father to give greetings *(salām)* to his mother when he returns.

7. Abraham draws near, kisses Isaac, and binds him. They both cry so much that the ground is soaked underneath Isaac's cheek where he is lying.
9. God had pounded a sheet of copper onto Isaac's throat. So Abraham throws him onto his forehead and tries again, but this time God turns the knife over in his hand (as in the Ibn Isḥāq version).

In fact, the Thaʿlabī and Mujīr al-Dīn renditions are virtually identical in their renditions of motifs 5 through 12. Although each is attributed to a different source, they demonstrate the close affinity between the Suddī and Ibn Isḥāq versions.[14]

The two versions display important differences as well. The Suddī version understands the intended sacrifice to be Isaac, who must be sacrificed as a result of Abraham's vow.[15] Although the sacrifice takes place in a non-specific location, the narrative assumes that Abraham had not moved since receiving his revelation about Isaac in Syria, therefore placing the action in accordance with Biblicist tradition. But according to the Ibn Isḥāq version, Ishmael is the victim of the attempted Sacrifice in Mecca. Abraham spans the distance between his home in Syria and Ishmael in Mecca by riding on the supernatural creature al-Burāq.

Both the Suddī and Ibn Isḥāq version have close parallels in later (post Muḥammad) Biblicist sources, where motif numbers 3, 4, 5a, 5b, 5c, 5e, 7,[16] 11, and 12 are found repeatedly in Jewish Midrash.[17] Some of the motifs would be expected in any narrative exegesis of the biblical or qur'ānic story of the sacrifice, since both include mention of divine intervention (motif 11), the substitution of a sacrificial animal for the human victim (motif 12), and so forth. Yet other motifs such as 5a, 5b, 5c, 5e, and 7 are unlikely to have evolved independently. Their commonality points either to borrowing or the use of common traditional lore. Of major importance in this regard is the fact that motifs 5a and 7 occur in the pre-Islamic *Bereshit Rabbah*, and 5a also occurs in the Palestinian Targum.[18]

Although they both parallel pre-Islamic Jewish legends and feature biblical (as well as qur'ānic) characters, only the Suddī version remains totally within the biblical chronology and setting. But even the Ibn Isḥāq version refrains from straying too far outside of the biblical parameters by providing for Abraham's transportation to Mecca, thus preserving the biblical view of his home in Syria. Since Ishmael is assumed by the Bible to live in an Arab land, the Ibn Isḥāq version remains roughly within the Biblicist worldview. The supernatural Buraq, of course, points to greater native Arab influence in the Ibn Isḥāq version.[19]

Motif 5d represents an Islamic addition in both versions explaining the problematic Qur'ān verse 37:103, which appears to contradict normal Islamic slaughtering practice.[20] And in both, the tale is structured to fit between Qur'ān verses 37:102-107, thereby providing a fuller account of the legend than can be found in Islamic scripture.

To conclude our discussion of the Suddī and Ibn Isḥāq versions, we note that although many motifs find parallels in Biblicist sources, neither version derived wholly from Biblicist legends. They represent rather two depictions of an authentic Islamic tradition incorporating Biblicist, Islamic, and in the case of the Ibn Isḥāq version, old Arab motifs.

Motif 5a represents a good example of how a motif with a specific purpose in one environment is retained in a new environment despite the fact that its original *raison d'etre* no longer applies. In the Jewish renditions, Isaac tells his father to tighten his bonds so that he will not strain in fear of the knife and damage himself, thereby rendering himself ritually unfit as an offering according to Jewish law. The significance of Isaac's request was lost as the motif came into the Arabian or Islamic milieu because the guidelines for determining a proper sacrifice are different in Islam.[21] Nevertheless, the request to tighten the bonds was retained without explanation in the Islamic legend because it served in a powerful manner to demonstrate the son's perfect willingness to serve as the sacrificial victim.[22]

The "Shi'ite" version is represented by four traditions found only in Shi'ite sources and without consistent records of authentication.[23] The motif sequence for each separate rendition is provided below.

Al-Ya'qūbī:

1. After building the Ka'ba and calling the people to the Pilgrimage, Abraham begins his own Pilgrimage under Gabriel's guidance on the "Day of Watering" *(yawm al-tarwiya)*[24]
2. As part of the Pilgrimage, Abraham sleeps at al-Mash'ar, and during the night God commands him to sacrifice his son.
3. When Abraham arrives at Minā, he tells his son that God commanded him to sacrifice him. Ishmael replies: "O MY FATHER, DO AS YOU ARE COMMANDED. (37:102).
4. ______________________________
5. ______________________________
6. Abraham takes the knife and lays his son down on top of a donkey saddle at Jamrat al-'Aqaba.
7. Abraham places the blade on his son's throat. When he turns his face away so that he will not look at his son, Gabriel turns the blade over onto its dull side. Abraham notices that it is inverted and turns it over again. He does that three times.
8. Then Abraham is called: O ABRAHAM! YOU HAVE ALREADY FULFILLED THE VISION! (Q.37:104-5).
9. Gabriel takes the boy and Abraham puts the sheep that was brought from the summit of Mt. Thabīr in his place. He sacrifices the sheep.

10. When Abraham is finished with the pilgrimage and intends to leave [Mecca], he charges Ishmael to dwell in the Sacred Precinct and instruct the people in the Pilgrimage.

Al-Qummī:

1. Gabriel comes to Abraham on the "Day of Watering" and takes him on his first pilgrimage.
2. Abraham stays overnight at al-Mash'ar al-Ḥarām and receives a vision in his sleep. He must sacrifice his son Isaac, who came along with his mother Sarah to make the Pilgrimage. When they get to Minā, Abraham and Sarah do the lapidation, and then Abraham tells her to return to the Ka'ba. He keeps the boy with him.
3. Abraham takes Isaac to al-Jamra al-Wusṭā [in Minā] and says: "O MY SON, I SEE IN A VISION THAT I WILL SACRIFICE YOU. SO LOOK, WHAT IS YOUR VIEW?" The boy tells him to carry out God's command, as in the verse: O MY FATHER! DO AS YOU ARE COMMANDED. IF GOD WILLS, YOU WILL FIND ME PATIENT AND ENDURING. (Q.37:102). They both submit *(aslamā)* to God's command.
4. The motif of the old man arguing with Abraham about God's command occurs at this point.[25]
5. Then the boy tells Abraham: "Hide my face and tighten my bonds!"
6. Abraham responds that he will not add to God's command, but will only do the sacrifice. He takes the donkey saddle, lays his son upon it, and takes the knife.
7. He places it upon his son's throat, looks toward heaven, and leans to pull the knife, but Gabriel turns it over to its back side.
8. ______________________________
9. A ram is brought from Thabīr. Abraham puts the ram in place of the boy and is called from a distance: "O ABRAHAM, YOU HAVE ALREADY FULFILLED THE VISION! (37:04-5).

Al-Ṭabarsī 1 (nearly identical with al-Qummī):

(2.) It is said that Abraham saw in a vision that he would sacrifice his son Isaac.

1. When Abraham and Sarah make the Pilgrimage and come to Minā, they do the lapidation. Abraham tells Sarah to go visit the Ka'ba, but the boy stays with him.
3. He takes Isaac to al-Jamra al-Wusṭā (in Minā) and tells him what he must do. The boy answers that he must carry out God's command. So they both submit to God's command.

4. The motif of the old man arguing with Abraham about God's command is inserted at this point.[26]
5. Then the boy tells Abraham: "Hide my face and tighten my bonds!"
6. Abraham responds that he will not add to God's command, but will only do the sacrifice. He takes the donkey saddle, lays his son upon it, and takes the knife.
7. Abraham places it upon his son's throat, looks toward heaven, and leans to pull the knife, but Gabriel turns it over to its back side.
8. ________________________________________
9. A ram is brought from Thabīr. Abraham puts the ram in place of the boy and is called from a distance: "O ABRAHAM, YOU HAVE ALREADY FULFILLED THE VISION! (Q. 37:104-5).

Al-Ṭabarsī 2:

1 and 2. After the conflict with Sarah in Syria, Abraham has a vision in his sleep. He must sacrifice his son, Ishmael, during the festival period in Mecca.[27] When the proper month for making the Pilgrimage *(dhū al-ḥijja)* arrives, he takes Hagar and Ishmael to Mecca. He raises up the foundations of the Kaʿba, goes to Minā in pilgrimage, returns to Mecca for one week to perform the circumambulations, and then does the running ritual *(al-saʿi)*.

3. As Abraham and Ishmael are doing the running ritual, Abraham says: "O MY SON, I SEE IN A VISION THAT I WILL SACRIFICE YOU during this yearly festival. SO WHAT IS YOUR VIEW? He answers, ... DO AS YOU WERE COMMANDED. (Q.37:102).
4. ________________________________________
5. ________________________________________

3 and 6. When they complete the Running ritual, Abraham takes him to Minā on the Day of the Sacrifice *(yawm al-naḥr)*.[28] He takes him to al-Jamra al-Wusṭā, lays him onto his left side, and takes the blade to slaughter him.

7. ________________________________________
8. He is called: O ABRAHAM, YOU HAVE ALREADY FULFILLED THE VISION ... (Q.37:104-5).
9. Ishmael is redeemed with a magnificent ram.
10. Abraham slaughters it and gives its meat as charity to the unfortunate.[29]

Even a cursory reading of the three versions suggests that the Shiʿite legend differs substantially from the other two. The most striking difference is that the Shiʿite version carefully weaves the sacrificial act into Abraham's precedental Ḥajj Pilgrimage, placing the Sacrifice in the setting of the pre-Islamic pilgrimage slaughtering ritual which was retained in the Islamic Pilgrimage. Abraham's vision occurs at al-Mash'ar (3/4), where pilgrims customarily remain overnight before coming to Minā for the sacrifice. Abraham's sacrifice also takes place in Minā (4/4), where the Pilgrimage sacrifice is enacted. Neither the Suddī nor Ibn Isḥāq versions connect Abraham's Sacrifice with the Pilgrimage in any way.

The various renditions of the Shi'ite version name both Isaac and Ishmael as the intended sacrifice. Only one rendition is repeated, and it is quite striking because it considers Isaac to be the intended sacrifice at the same time that it places the act within the context of the Meccan Ḥajj.[30] Both renditions connect Isaac to Mecca by having him make the Pilgrimage along with his mother Sarah. Al-Ya'qūbī appears almost ambivalent about who the intended sacrifice was, but eventually names him as Ishmael. Only the Ṭabarsī #2 rendition provides a context for Ishmael representing the Sacrifice, and does so effectively by transferring Ishmael and Hagar from Syria to Mecca in response to God's command to Abraham to sacrifice Ishmael during the Pilgrimage. This reasoning is unique among all the traditions.

Despite the marked differences between the Shi'ite and other versions, they share a number of similarities. The motifs 3, 5, 7, and 9 of the Shi'ite renditions reflect motifs 4, 5a, 9, 11 and 12 of the other two versions. Some parallels, such as motifs 3 and 9 corresponding to motifs 4, 11, 12, represent natural commonalities because they respond to the same Qur'ān verses. But motifs 5 and 7 of the versions in Shi'ite sources corresponding to motifs 5a and 9 must assume borrowing or the use of a common source.

All the Shi'ite renditions explain the pre-Islamic practice of making a sacrifice during the Islamic Pilgrimage. As such, the Shi'ite version in its entirety serves as a kind of Islamic commentary, although it offers less commentary than the Suddī and Ibn Isḥāq versions on specific Qur'ān verses. The core of the Shi'ite version may have originated from the same sources as the Suddī and Ibn Isḥāq versions but evolved into a legend more closely tied into the Islamic ritual concerns of the Pilgrimage and retaining fewer motifs with direct Biblicist parallels.

Few comments or fragments other than the three versions related above treat the sacrificial act. One brief rendition found in Ibn Ḥanbal's *Musnad* connects the sacrifice to the Ḥajj Pilgrimage by placing it immediately after the lapidation ritual:[31] "Gabriel brought Abraham to Jamrat al-'Aqaba. Satan appeared to him, so he threw seven stones at him and he sank into the ground. . . . When Abraham desired to sacrifice his son Isaac, he said: 'O my father, tie me up so that I will not shake and my blood splash onto you when you sacrifice me.' So he tied him up. When he took the butcher knife to sacrifice him, he was called from behind: O ABRAHAM, YOU HAVE ALREADY FULFILLED THE VISION! (Q.37:105).

Another rendition given twice by al-Ṭabarī[32] has: ... WHEN THEY HAD BOTH SUBMITTED THEIR WILLS AND HE HAD FLUNG HIM DOWN ON HIS FOREHEAD (Q.37:103). They both submitted their wills together to the command of God. The boy was resigned to the sacrifice and the father was resigned to sacrificing him.[33] He said, 'O father, throw me unto my face so that you will not look upon me and have mercy for me, and I would look at the knife and be anxious. Rather, insert the knife from underneath me and carry out the command of God.' Thus the verse, WHEN THEY HAD BOTH SUBMITTED THEIR WILLS AND HE HAD FLUNG HIM DOWN ON HIS FOREHEAD. WHEN HE DID THAT, WE CALLED UNTO HIM, O ABRAHAM! YOU HAVE ALREADY FULFILLED THE VISION. THUS DO WE REWARD THE GOOD!" (Q.37:104-5).

Al-Ṭabarī also provides a fragment attributed to Mujāhid:[34] "... AND HE HAD FLUNG HIM DOWN ON HIS FOREHEAD (Q.37:103): He put his face to the ground. He said, 'Do not sacrifice me while you look into my face lest you have mercy upon me and do not complete the sacrifice. Tie my hand to my neck. Then put my face to the ground.' "

Al-Tha'labī offers a brief comment on the authority of al-Sha'bī:[35] "Abraham was thrown into the fire when he was 16 years old, Isaac was sacrificed when he was 7 years old, and Sarah gave birth to him when she was 90 years old. The location of the sacrifice was 2 miles from Jerusalem,[36] and when Sarah found out what Abraham intended with Isaac, she remained [alive] for two days, and died on the third."[37]

Finally, the fullest rendition of the sacrificial act is found in al-Kisā'ī[38] under the title: "The Story of Isaac":

> Ka'b al-Aḥbār said: Sarah conceived Isaac on the night that God destroyed the people of Lot. After a full term of pregnancy, she gave birth to him on the Friday evening of the tenth day of the month of Muḥarram.[39] A light shone from his face that illuminated what was around him. [The moment] he touched the ground, he fell prostrate in prayer to God. He then raised up his hands to heaven in a motion [signifying] the Unity of God.[40] Abraham praised his Lord and called the poor and unfortunate. He fed them and gave them drink in thanks to God.[41]
>
> When Isaac reached the age of seven years, he went out with his father to Jerusalem.[42] Abraham slept for an hour [there], and a visitor came [in a dream] and said: "O Abraham, God commands you to make an offering to Him." When he awoke, he took a fat bull, slaughtered it, and divided it among the unfortunate. On the second night, the voice came to him and said: "O Abraham, God commands you to make a greater offering than that bull." When he awoke, he slaughtered a camel and divided it among the poor. On the third night, the voice came to

him and said: "God commands you to make a greater offering to Him than that camel." He said: "What is greater than that?" It pointed to Isaac, and he woke up in fright.

He said to Isaac, "O my son, are you not obedient to me?" He answered: "Certainly, O father. If you desired to sacrifice me, I would not [try to] prevent you from it." So Abraham went to his home and took a knife and rope. He said to Isaac: "O my son, come with me to the mountains!"

When the two of them left, the Devil[43] approached Sarah and said to her: "Abraham has resolved to sacrifice your son, Isaac! Catch up with him and stop him!" But she recognized him and said: "Away, O cursed of God! They have set out to please God!" So he left her and caught up with Isaac. He said to him: "Your father wants to sacrifice you!" But Abraham said to him: "O my son, come on. Do not pay attention to him, for he is the devil."

When they arrived at the mountain,[44] Abraham said: "O MY SON, I SEE IN A VISION THAT I WILL SACRIFICE YOU." HE SAID: "O MY FATHER, DO AS YOU ARE COMMANDED. IF GOD WILLS, YOU WILL FIND ME MOST STEADFAST!" (Q.37:102).[45] He said: "O father, if you want to sacrifice me, take my shirt off my back so that my mother will not see it [bloodied] and cry a long time over me. Tie up my shoulders lest I squirm between your hands and it cause you pain. When you place the knife on my throat, turn your face from me lest compassion for me overcome you and you fail [to carry out your task]. Seek help in God for your bereavement over me. And when you return [home], bring my shirt to my mother so that she may find some comfort in it over me. Give her greetings from me, but do not tell her how you slaughtered me, nor how you took off my shirt, nor how you bound me up with rope so that she will not be sorrowful over me. And when you see a young boy like me, do not look at him, so that your heart will not grieve on my account."

The voice from heaven called him: "O Friend of God, how can you not be compassionate for this small child who speaks to you with such words?" Abraham thought that it was the mountain who spoke to him, so he said: "O Mountain, God has commanded this of me! Do not distract me with your words!"[46] Abraham then took off Isaac's shirt, bound him with the rope, and said: "In the name of God the Powerful and the Excellent!" He put the knife on his throat. He raised up his hand [with the knife] and brought it down again. But the knife turned over and said: "There is no might nor power save with God the Most High and Magnificent!" He sharpened the knife on a stone until he made it as hot as fire. Then, he returned to Isaac with it. But it turned over [again] and spoke with God's permission, saying: "Do not blame me, O prophet of God, for I have been commanded to do this!" At that, Abraham heard a voice calling: "O ABRAHAM, YOU HAVE [ALREADY] FULFILLED THE VISION! (Q.37:105). And God said: AND WE REDEEMED HIM WITH A MAGNIFICENT SACRIFICE (Q.37:107). That is, with a magnificent ram.

He was called: "O Abraham, take this ram and redeem your son with it. Sacrifice it as an offering. God has made this day a [holy] festival for you and your children.[47] The ram said: "O Friend of God, sacrifice me instead of your son, for I am more appropriate for sacrifice than he. I am the ram of Abel, son of Adam, who gave me as an offering to his Lord and whose offering was accepted. I have grazed in the meadows of the Garden for forty autumns!"[48]

Abraham praised his Lord for delivering Isaac. He went to untie him from [his] bonds, but he was already free. He said: "O my son, who untied you?" He answered him: "The one who brought the sacrificial ram." Then Abraham went to the ram and sacrificed it. A white smokeless fire[49] from heaven came, burned up the ram and consumed it so that the only thing that remained was its head.

Abraham and Isaac departed with the ram's head and told Sarah about [all that happened]. She fell down prostrate in thanks to God.

The legend of the Sacrifice is also rendered in two slightly different covariants of a poem attributed to 'Umayya b. Abī al-Ṣalt, a poet living at the time of the Prophet, Muḥammad.[50] Al-Ṭabarī's version[51] has:

To Abraham, the Fulfiller of the vow
with consideration, and bearing generosity.

His first born would not resist him
when he saw him among a troop of enemies.

"O my lad, I have pledged you a sacrifice to God,
so be patient, for I will be your redemption."[52]

"Tighten the bond so I will not resist the knife,
like the manacled captive turning away."

Its blade reflected the flesh [of the]
slave boy curved over like a crescent.

While doffing his dress
His Lord released him with a splendid ram.

"Take it, and release your son, for by Me,
what you have done is no simple thing."

A God-fearing father, and another—his son,
created from him in obedience.

Perhaps the souls severed from the act
he has relief after suffering, like release from bondage.

Al-Tha'labī's rendition[53] has:

Abraham, who fulfills [his] vow
with consideration, and bearing generosity.

His first born would not resist him
even if he saw him in a troop of enemies.

"O my lad, I have pledged you a sacrifice to God,
be patient for that is my lot.

Be steadfast as I draw the knife
the way a captive pulls at his shackles."

Its blade reflects the flesh,
the boy's forehead [reflected] in the crescent [of the knife].

While doffing his clothes
His Lord released him with a splendid ram.

"Take this redemption for your son, for by Me,
what you have done is no simple thing.

Perhaps the souls severed from the act
he has relief after suffering, like release from bondage.

As in the case of the other miscellaneous traditions, the two renditions of the poem include a number of motifs found in the Suddī and Ibn Isḥāq versions. The redemption of Ishmael is assumed early on in al-Ṭabarī's rendition of the poem. This represents a significant change from the prose accountings, which offer no hint that the Sacrifice would be halted before Abraham actually started to slaughter his son.

Because the poem can be traced back only as far as a poet of Muḥammad's generation, it offers no firm evidence in support of the view that the story of the sacrifice was known among pre-Islamic Arabs. 'Umayya was in all likelihood an Arab monotheist and is said to have been familiar with Biblicist tradition.[54]

Some exegetes such as al-Ṭabarī, al-Ṭabarsī, and Ibn Kathīr include their own comments and explanations as well as traditional reports on the story of the Sacrifice, many of them explaining problematic words or difficult syntax in the Qur'ān text.[55] The mystic Ibn 'Arabī, however, only mentions the bare outline of the traditional narrative so that he can expand on the esoteric meaning of the act. According to his understanding, both the father and the son achieved a kind of perfect annihilation of the self[56] by carrying out the ultimate command of God.[57]

In conclusion, we note that the three major versions of the Islamic sacrifice legend contain a significant number of motifs that closely parallel Biblicist sources, some of which are clearly pre-Islamic. Despite the existence in pre-Islamic Arabia of infanticide and perhaps even occasional child-sacrifice, the legend of the Sacrifice in the Qur'ān and the tradition literature appears to have evolved out of a Biblicist setting. As suggested earlier, however, this does not prove that the Islamic traditions are simply copies of "original" Biblicist traditions. On the contrary, the various renditions found in the sources have evolved into unique Islamic traditions that serve to explain a difficult and obscure qur'ānic text. As in previous segments of the Abraham-Ishmael cycle, the most fanciful and unique rendition of the Sacrifice story is found in a collection of popular literature (al-Kisā'ī). Of the nineteen narrative renditions and fragments (including the two poetic renditions), ten assume the intended victim to have been Isaac while nine assume it to have been Ishmael. The significance of the identity of the intended victim will be discussed below in Chapter 16.

# Chapter 15

# THE REDEMPTION

According to the qur'ānic narrative, God redeemed Abraham's son with a "MAGNIFICENT SACRIFICE."[1] The traditionists were not all in agreement regarding the exact nature of this sacrifice, although most considered it to have been a ram as in the biblical story.[2] Few narrative traditions were available to support this view, and most exegetes simply relied on the opinions and statements of early traditionists.

The opinion of Ibn 'Abbās is cited thirty-three times by the exegetes, and he is generally credited with the view that the redemption was a ram (fourteen renditions) or a sheep (one rendition),[3] although he is also cited five times as saying that it was a mountain goat.[4] Ibn 'Abbās is credited five times with a tradition that the ram sacrificed in place of Abraham's son was the identical animal that was sacrificed by Adam's son Abel: "The ram that Abraham slaughtered was the ram that the son of Adam offered up *(qarrabahu)* and was accepted."[5] ". . . the ram that redeemed him was the ram that Abel son of Adam offered and was accepted."[6] The only detailed rendition is given by Ibn Sa'd, who recounts an unusual version of the story of Cain and Abel:

> Adam had four children from two sets of twins, each set consisting of one male and one female. The sister of the farmer was pretty while the sister of the herdsman was ugly. The farmer said that he had more of a right to the pretty one, while the herdsman said that he had a greater claim on her. The herdsman said: "Fie on you! You desire to have preference over me because of her beauty? Let us each make an offering. If your offering is accepted, you have the right to her, but if mine is accepted, I have the right to her." They each made an offering. The herdsman offered a white dark-eyed horned ram while the farmer offered a pile of food. The ram was accepted and God kept it in the Garden for forty autumns. That is the ram that Abraham sacrificed. The farmer then said: "I AM GOING TO KILL YOU!" (Q.5:29). The herdsman replied:

"EVEN IF YOU STRETCH OUT YOUR HAND TO SLAY ME, I WILL NOT STRETCH OUT MY HAND AGAINST YOU TO KILL YOU, FOR I FEAR GOD, THE LORD OF THE WORLDS. I PREFER THAT YOU TAKE ON MY SIN AS WELL AS YOUR OWN, FOR YOU WILL BE ONE OF THOSE CONSIGNED TO THE FIRE. THAT IS THE REWARD OF EVILDOERS" (Q.5:31-2).[7]

The motif of the identical ram is referred to frequently in the Islamic sources. In addition to the reports mentioned above, Ibn 'Abbās is credited five times with saying that the ram that redeemed Abraham's son grazed in Heaven[8] for forty autumns. Although this motif has no exact parallel in Biblicist tradition,[9] it reflects a similar interest in recurring religious symbolism, and Jewish tradition assigns the redemptive ram's origin to the first days of Creation when God brought it into existence for the specific purpose of redeeming Isaac.[10]

Both al-Ṭabarī and Ibn Kathīr[11] credit Ibn 'Abbās with a legal decision regarding a man who vowed to slaughter himself.[12] In order for the man to redeem himself from his vow, Ibn 'Abbās ". . . ordered him [to redeem himself] with 100 camels. After that, he said: 'If I had made the legal opinion [concerning the redemption] with a ram, I would have been content that he [only] sacrifice a ram." Ibn 'Abbās considered either solution sufficient to redeem a vow to sacrifice a human life. The 100 camels, which may have derived from 'Abd al-Muṭṭalib's vow to sacrifice his son or from other pre-Islamic Arab sources,[13] was remembered immediately by Ibn 'Abbās. Only as an afterthought did he cite the sacrifice of the ram. If this story is accurate, then the satisfactory bloodwit of 100 camels was well-imbedded in the minds of the traditionists of Ibn 'Abbās' day, while the legend of the Sacrifice was less easily called to mind. Perhaps the attempted sacrifice still retained a foreign tinge and had not yet become fully integrated into the Islamic corpus of tradition.

Sa'īd b. Jubayr is also credited with saying that the redemptive ram grazed in Heaven for forty autumns. Al-Ṭabarī, al-Ṭabarsī and Ibn Kathīr cite him a total of six times and mention that this ram had speckled reddish wool. Ibn Kathīr mentions that the ram grazed in Heaven until Mt. Thabīr was split open for it to appear to Abraham,[14] a theme reminiscent of the story of Mt. Abū Qubays splitting open to bring forth the Black Stone to Abraham.[15] It also parallels the story of the Arab prophet Ṣāliḥ, who brought forth a camel from a rock.[16] This motif represents pre-Islamic Arab legendary material that became integrated into one particular rendition of the sacrifice story.

Al-Ṭabarī and al-Ṭabarsī together credit Mujāhid and al-Ḍaḥḥāk with the opinion that the redemption was a ram. Al-Ṭabarī also cites al-Suddī and Ibn Zayd with that opinion and credits the People of the Book as the original source for the description of the ram being horned, salt-and-pepper colored, and with dark eyes.[17]

The minority view regarding the nature of the son's redemption is held by al-Ḥasan, who is quoted seven times by al-Ṭabarī, al-Tha'labī, al-Zamakhsharī, al-Ṭabarsī, Ibn al-Athīr, and Ibn Kathīr as saying that it was a goat which came from Thabīr.[18] Ibn Kathīr, however, mentions a tradition on al-Ḥassan's authority that the redemption was a ram by the name of Jarīr, but proceeds to explain how that tradition cannot be sound. Of interest for our study is the surprising fact that Ibn Kathīr cites the absence of this tradition among Israelite Tales as an argument *against* its soundness.[19]

It is clear from the foregoing that most of the early exegetes considered the redemption of Abraham's son to be a ram, though a minority supported the view that it was a goat. Either view would seem to be at variance with the meaning of "magnificent sacrifice" *(dhibḥ 'aẓīm)* within the pre-Islamic Arab context. But what may we surmise is a magnificent sacrifice for pre-Islamic Arabs? We know that 'Abd al-Muṭṭalib could not redeem his son with less than 100 camels, which must have been a magnificent sacrifice indeed.[20] According to al-Kisā'ī's distinctive rendition of the sacrifice legend,[21] Abraham considers a camel to be a much greater sacrifice than a fat bull, and then asks in wonder what could possibly be greater than a camel. Only human sacrifice could be more dear, yet the redemptive sacrifice for Abraham's son is nothing more than a ram or a goat. Since this notion simply would not fit into the pre-Islamic Arab context of a magnificent sacrifice, the ram as sacrifice could not have evolved out of native Arabia.[22] It came naturally from a Biblicist environment where Genesis 22:13 had clearly spelled out the nature of the redemption. The connection with Abel's sacrifice must have come from the same Biblicist milieu. Arab folklore simply offers no precedent for that theme, despite the fact that Ibn Sa'd's rendition of the Cain and Abel story surely incorporates aspects of Arab legend in its rendering of the Cain and Abel legend.[23] The only motif representing a pre-Islamic pagan Arab milieu is that of the mountain splitting open to produce the animal, a theme that occurs only one time among our exegetical sources.

Ibn 'Abbās is credited four times with a narrative tradition associating the ram with the lapidation ritual of the Ḥajj. Al-Ṭabarī and al-Ṭabarsī provide the tradition in full, while al-Zamakhsharī merely makes reference to it.[24] According to the tradition, the redemptive ram comes from the Garden after grazing there for forty years. Abraham sends his son to watch over it, but after he throws seven stones at it at al-Jamra al-'Ūlā, it escapes from him. He overtakes it at al-Jamra al-Wusṭā and throws another seven stones, but it flees again. He catches up with it once more at al-Jamra al-Kubrā and throws another seven stones. Abraham then takes it and brings it to al-Manḥar in Minā and sacrifices it there. As al-Zamakhsharī points out, ". . . it has remained the custom *(sunna)* to throw stones."[25]

One cannot but associate this legend with the tradition about Abraham throwing stones at the devil who is attempting to prevent him from carrying out the sacrifice of his son in Mecca,[26] or the story of Satan appearing to Abraham and Gabriel during the first Abrahamic Ḥajj.[27] Both versions associated with the Sacrifice are attributed to Ibn ʿAbbās, while the legend connecting the devil to Abraham's first Pilgrimage is attributed to a number of different traditionists. As in the other lapidation stories, Abraham's son herding the redemptive ram by throwing stones at the location of the three pillars in Minā served to substitute a monotheistic origin for the original pagan association of the lapidation ritual. It represents an Islamic development that expanded on a qur'anic/biblical theme in order to provide a monotheistic basis for a pagan practice.

## ISAAC'S WISH

A recurring legend describes a scene in which God offers to grant Isaac a wish after the ordeal of the Sacrifice. This tradition occurs six times among the sources and most likely originates with Kaʿb al-Aḥbār. Two versions have come down in the sources, with the earliest consisting of four renditions and attributed directly to Kaʿb.[28] The wording varies considerably among the renditions, but the message remains constant. Immediately after Isaac's redemption, God tells him personally that He will answer any prayer that Isaac wishes. Isaac replies: "O God, I pray to you that you grant me [this]: When any person in any era who does not attribute any partner to You meets You [at the gates of Heaven], allow him to enter Paradise." (3/4); or "Lord, I ask that you do not punish anyone who believes in You" (1/4).

The second version is attributed to Abū Hurayra, who reports that the Prophet said:

> God allowed me to choose between having Him forgive half of the Muslim people, or having Him respond to my intercession on their behalf. I chose my own intercession, for I hoped [that would bring God's] forgiveness for most of the Muslim people. If a pious Muslim dies after me, then let my prayer hurry [on his behalf]. When God comforted Isaac from the terror of the Sacrifice, it was said to him: "O Isaac, ask and you will be granted!" So he said: "O He who has my soul in His hand, will You hasten it [into Paradise] before Satan incites it to evil? O God, whoever dies and does not associate any partner with You, forgive him and bring him into Paradise!"[29]

Ibn Kathīr criticizes this tradition for coming from only a single source and for being inferior and objectionable.[30] He is particularly concerned with the fact that Isaac is listed as the intended sacrifice since Ibn Kathīr believed it to have been Ishmael.[31]

This tradition developed out of the feeling that either the Sacrifice ordeal was unfair to its intended victim and that he was therefore deserving of recompense, or that Isaac's merit was so great for having agreed wholeheartedly to the act that he was deserving of reward. In response to the extraordinary divine gift, Isaac demonstrates his exceptional piety by asking God to keep him from sinning (the second version) and to forgive the sins of others (both versions).

This tradition is reminiscent of a story in the Jewish *Tanhuma*.[32] After God tells Abraham to cease and desist from the sacrifice, Abraham remains at the altar with knife in hand allowing the emotion of the ordeal to pour forth. He tells God that because of the awful command to sacrifice Abraham's son after all of God's promises for progeny through Isaac, and because Abraham was willing to do God's will without a word of regret, so should God remember the merit of the sacrifice when Isaac's descendants sin or find themselves in difficult straits. God should attribute merit to them as if Isaac had actually been slaughtered and burned on the altar. God should forgive them and redeem them from their troubles when they arise. This legend attributes to Isaac's near-sacrifice the power of atonement for the entire Jewish people.[33]

A second parallel can be found in the Babylonian Talmud[34] where Rabbi Shmuel b. Naḥmani asks in the name of Rabbi Yonatan what is the meaning of Isaiah 63:16:

> Surely You are our Father:
> Though Abraham regard us not,
> And Israel recognize us not,
> You, O Lord, are our Father;
> From of old, Your name is "Our Redeemer."

He posits an answer in a fashion typical of Jewish narrative exegesis: God asks Abraham if he would forgive his future progeny who will sin against God. Abraham is of the opinion that the sinners should be destroyed. God then asks Jacob (Israel), who is the father of many children and might have greater compassion. But Jacob gives the same answer. Finally, when God asks Isaac what he would do, Isaac gives a long and moving defense of man's proclivity to sin. He then asks God to forgive them. If that is not possible, he willingly takes responsibility for half their sins. But even if Isaac took over all the sins of the Jewish people, he has already offered himself up as a sacrifice to God, so it is only fitting that God forgive them on his merit. Isaac calls upon the Jewish people to praise and see God with their own eyes. When they do, they exclaim: "You, O Lord, are our Father; From of old, Your name is "Our Redeemer" (Isaiah 63:16b).

That Isaac is the protagonist in every rendition of this Islamic tradition of God granting the intended sacrifice one wish, and that he rather than his father is credited for the merit of the sacrifice suggests that Christianity was the vehicle that brought the legend into the Islamic world. Isaac was credited with volunteering for the sacrifice in Christian tradition, and his near-sacrifice even became a paradigm for the crucifixion of Jesus.[35] Israel Levi and Geza Vermes have demonstrated, however, that the motif of atonement through voluntary sacrifice of the righteous existed in pre-Christian Judaism as well.[36] Particularly in the earliest Jewish versions of the Palestinian Targum and in *Bereshit Rabba,* Isaac is credited with volunteering quite eagerly for the Sacrifice.[32] It is therefore just as possible that Ka'b al-Aḥbār derived this tradition from his own Jewish religious training as well as from other Biblicist lore.[38] Whatever the specific origin of this motif, the concept derives from a Biblicist world view.[39]

# Chapter 16

# ISAAC OR ISHMAEL?

Most reports treating the Sacrifice directly or indirectly relate to the issue of who was the intended victim, and the intensity of interest in this matter is reflected in the great amount of space devoted to it. Exegetes cite traditions supporting both Isaac and Ishmael, and many even cite full lists of the early traditionists who took one position or the other.[1] Some of the most well-respected traditionists, such as Ibn ʿAbbās, Saʿīd b. Jubayr, al-Suddī, Mujāhid, al-Ḥasan al-Baṣrī, and ʿAlī, are cited in support of both, with some reports giving their opinion that it was Isaac and others claiming that it was Ishmael. When all the traditions are collated we find a surprisingly close count. One hundred thirty authoritative statements consider Isaac to be the intended victim; one hundred thirty three consider it to have been Ishmael.[2]

## THE ARGUMENTS

Aside from citing evidence in favor of one or the other son on the basis of authoritative opinions, the exegetes did not hesitate to propose arguments in support of their views. Al-Yaʿqūbī[3] is the first to do this in our sample and cites the most basic and recurring opinion: "Some people say that it was Ishmael because he was the one who settled [in Mecca], while Isaac remained in Syria. Other people say that it was Isaac because [Abraham] sent him [Ishmael] and his mother out when [Isaac] was a young boy, and Ishmael was a grown man with children. There are many traditions about each view and people disagree about them."

Al-Ṭabarī proffered detailed arguments in favor of Isaac.[4] He says that because every announcement of a child in the Qur'ān refers to Isaac, Abraham's prayer for a child at the beginning of the Sacrifice story in Qur'ān 37:100 must also refer to Isaac. He derives support for his view from Qur'ān 11:71: AND WE GAVE HIM GLAD TIDINGS OF ISAAC, AND AFTER ISAAC, JACOB; and indeed,

Isaac is referred to in Qur'ān 51:28 without mention of his name. Al-Ṭabarī adds that Abraham would not have asked God to grant him a son in Qur'ān 37:100 if he already had a pious son. In fact, he did not have such a son until his prayer for Isaac was answered.[5]

Despite al-Ṭabarī's opinion that it was Isaac, he dutifully cites the arguments of the supporters of Ishmael. How could God have commanded the sacrifice of Isaac if God had already promised Abraham in Qur'ān 11:71 that Isaac would have a son? If God had commanded Isaac's sacrifice then the divine promise to Abraham would have been broken. This would be a theological impossibility, since God, by definition, does not break promises. The intended sacrifice must therefore be Ishmael. Al-Ṭabarī cites a second argument in favor of Ishmael which refers to Q.37:112 occurring immediately after the narrative of the Sacrifice: AND WE GAVE HIM GLAD TIDINGS OF ISAAC, A PIOUS PROPHET. According to some, this proved that Isaac was born only *after* the Sacrifice. The intended victim, therefore, must have been his older brother, Ishmael. Al-Ṭabarī responds by pointing out how the purpose of the verse is to emphasize the reward for Isaac's and Abraham's steadfast obedience to God. The Sacrifice proves that Isaac is no ordinary man, and the Qur'ān verse is not an announcement of his birth. It is, rather, the announcement that Isaac will be counted among the prophets as a reward for his pious obedience.[6]

Al-Ṭabarī encounters a third argument based on the recurring tradition that the horns of the redemptive ram were seen hanging inside the Ka'ba. What better proof that the Sacrifice took place in the Ḥijāz where Ishmael lived? But there is no reason, says al-Ṭabarī, to exclude the possibility that the horns were carried from Syria to Mecca, and wistfully concludes: If only the Qur'ān were explicit in naming the son who was intended! He sums up the gist of the problem in his *History*:[7]

> The early sages and religious scholars of the nation of our Prophet differed about which one of Abraham's sons he was commanded to sacrifice. Some said it was Isaac and others said it was Ishmael. Both statements are given on the authority of the Apostle of God. If either was completely sound, we would not bother with any other, unless proof from the Qur'ān made the view that it was Isaac the clearest and most evident.

Ten pages later he asserts that the qur'ānic evidence is indeed available:[8]

> "As for the evidence in the Qur'ān that we have quoted, [the view that it was] Isaac is more reliable. God's word [in the Qur'ān] is related about Abraham's prayer when he parted from his people to emigrate to his Lord in Syria with his wife Sarah: HE SAID: "I WILL GO TO MY LORD.

> HE WILL SURELY GUIDE ME. O MY LORD, GRANT ME A RIGHTEOUS SON!" (Q.37:99-100). That was before he knew Hagar and before she became the mother of Ishmael. Then our Lord answered his prayer with the announcement of a gentle son and the narrative about the vision of Abraham. He would sacrifice that boy WHEN HE REACHED THE AGE OF RUNNING WITH HIM (Q.37:102).

Al-Mas'ūdī notes the disagreement regarding the identity of the intended sacrifice and repeats the logic expressed by al-Ya'qūbī in slightly stronger terms: "If the Sacrifice occurred in the Ḥijāz, it was Ishmael, because Isaac never entered the Ḥijāz. If the Sacrifice took place in Syria, then it was Isaac because Ishmael did not enter Syria after he was taken from there."[9] Al-Asadābādī considers the intended victim to be Ishmael and cites the Prophetic tradition of Muḥammad being the son of two intended sacrifices in support of his view.[10]

Al-Tha'labī believes the intended sacrifice was Ishmael but also provides arguments supporting both points of view. He adds: "The Jews claim that it was Isaac, but the Jews lie,"[11] an obvious reference to the suspicion cast upon Biblicist traditions after the first few Islamic generations. His main arguments in support of Ishmael rest on reasoning already provided by al-Ṭabarī: Qur'ān 37:112 is essentially a birth announcement that occurs after the Sacrifice, and since God had already promised progeny for Isaac he could not have been the intended victim.[12]

Al-Zamakhsharī claims that if Abraham had known from Isaac's birth that his son would become a prophet, he could not have been truly tested with his sacrifice and the trial would be a sham. This is the reasoning behind verse 37:112: AND WE GAVE HIM THE GOOD NEWS OF ISAAC, A RIGHTEOUS PROPHET. The verse occurs only after the Sacrifice in order to allow for a fair test; Abraham learns only afterward that the son he intended to sacrifice would indeed be a prophet.[13] Al-Zamakhsharī is nevertheless an adherent of the Ishmael school and writes in his commentary,[14] ". . . the announcement [to Abraham that he would have a son] included three things: that the child would be a boy, that he would reach sexual maturity, and that he would be gentle and patient *(ḥalīm)*.[15] What patience could be greater than his when his father proposed the Sacrifice to him, and he replied: YOU WILL FIND ME, IF GOD WILLS, PATIENT AND ENDURING"?[16] The term *ḥalīm* could refer to either son, but further along in his commentary[17] al-Zamakhsharī ties the meaning of *ḥalīm* (patience) to its synonym *ṣabr* and restricts it to Ishmael: "Another indication that it is him is that God describes him as patiently enduring,[18] but not his brother Isaac, in the verse: ISHMAEL, ELISHA AND DHŪ AL-KIFL, ALL OF THEM PATIENTLY ENDURING.[19]

Al-Ṭabarsī also considers Ishmael to have been the intended victim despite his citing of the "Shi'ite" version of the Sacrifice in which Isaac was laid on the altar near Mecca: "Both opinions are given by our companions from our religious masters *(a'immatinā)*. Nevertheless, the clearer of the traditions is that it was Ishmael."[20] He cites reasoning already given but adds: "The proof for those who say that it was Isaac is that the Christians and Jews[21] agree about it. The answer to that is that their agreement is no proof and their view is not acceptable."[22]

Ibn al-Athīr only quotes one tradition on the issue, and that tradition supports Ishmael.[23] Ibn Kathīr also believes the intended sacrifice to be Ishmael, but gives al-Suhaylī's unique argument in support of Isaac just the same.[24] Al-Suhaylī is arguing against the pro-Ishmael view that because God had already promised Isaac his son Jacob and would not contradict His own revelation, Isaac could not have been intended. His argument is based on grammatical analysis. Says al-Suhaylī:

> AND WE GAVE HER THE GOOD NEWS OF ISAAC (Q.11:71) is a complete sentence. The words: AND AFTER ISAAC, JACOB is a different sentence which is not part of the first. It is impossible in Arabic to make a single sentence [out of these two] without a preposition. It is not possible, for example, to say "I passed by Zayd, and after him, 'Amr" without [using the preposition "by" a second time in the second phrase] "and after him *by* 'Amr". The words AND AFTER ISAAC, JACOB is in the accusative case with the unstressed meaning [that it is the complete sentence] "We gave to Isaac Jacob."[25]

According to the argument, the revelation could have occurred at two different times if it were made up of two separate sentences. The first revelation would have occurred before the command to sacrifice Isaac; the second afterwards, therefore solving the problem of contradictory revelations. He adds to the argument with evidence from Q.37:102: WHEN HE REACHED THE AGE OF RUNNING WITH HIM. "Ishmael could not have been with him, for he was very little when he was with his mother in the Meccan mountains. How could he have reached the age of running with him?" According to this view, Abraham brought Hagar and Ishmael to Mecca and left them there, never to return. Their only experience together was therefore when Ishmael was too young to be at "the age of running with him." Ibn Kathīr counters al-Suhaylī's argument with the tradition about Buraq: "Abraham often rode upon Buraq to Mecca, coming suddenly to his son and then returning. God knows best!"[26]

Ibn Kathīr's negative argument in support of Ishmael is particularly interesting.[27]

> AND WE GAVE HIM THE NEWS OF A PATIENT AND FORBEARING *(ḤALĪM)* SON (Q.37:101). That boy is Ishmael. He is the first son announced to

Abraham in revelation.[28] The Muslims and the People of the Book agree that he was older than Isaac. However, in their book, Ishmael was born when Abraham was 86 years old, while Isaac was born when Abraham's age was 99 years. According to them, God commanded Abraham to sacrifice his only son, but according to another version, [he commanded him to sacrifice] his oldest son. They dishonestly and slanderously introduced Isaac here by forcing him in. But this is impossible because it contradicts their own book. They forced this understanding because Isaac is their father while Ishmael is the father of the Arabs. They envy them, so they added it and distorted "your only son" in the sense that "you have no other than he." But [Abraham] took Ishmael and his mother to Mecca[29] so theirs is subjective exegesis and distortion.[30] That is because "your only son" can refer only to one for whom there is no other. . . . A group of scholars are of the opinion that the intended sacrifice was Isaac. They relate this on the authority of the sages *(al-salaf)* that quote the authority of some of the Companions of the Prophet, though it is only an oral tradition and not an accepted practice.[31] I am of the opinion that this comes from none other than the sages *(aḥbār)* of the People of the Book.[32] It was taken [into Islam] uncontested and without proof. But this Book of God is a witness and a guide to the right path that it was Ishmael, for it mentioned the announcement of a pious boy [Q.37:100] and stated that he was the intended sacrifice. Only after that does it say: AND WE GAVE HIM THE GOOD NEWS OF ISAAC, A PROPHET . . . (37:112). . . .

Ibn Kathir continues further along in his Commentary:[33]

The account that it was Isaac came from Ka'b al-Aḥbār. . . . All of these statements, and God knows best, are taken from Ka'b al-Aḥbār. Now when he converted to Islam during the caliphate of 'Umar, he began to report traditions to 'Umar on the authority of his ancient books. Perhaps 'Umar listened to him and permitted the people to listen to his sources and to transmit what he had on his [Ka'b's] authority, [both] the corrupt ones and the good ones. Now this Islamic nation *(umma)* has no need for one word of [those traditions] he possessed. . . . Those who follow Ka'b al-Aḥbār's traditions include Sa'īd b. Jubayr, Qatāda, Masrūq, 'Ikrima, 'Atā', Muqātil, al-Zuhrī, and al-Suddī. Even Ibn 'Abbās uses him in one of his two chains of authorities, and one report is given with it. If it were reliable, I would gladly give it [myself], but its chain of authorities is not sound.

In his *History*[34] he writes:

> The basis of the claim that it was Isaac is from the Israelite Tales *(isrā'īliyyāt)*. But their book is full of distortions *(wakitābuhum fīhi taḥrīf)*. It is especially true in this case. According to them, God commanded Abraham to sacrifice his only son, but in the Arabic copy[35] his first-born was Isaac. Putting Isaac here is an insertion without reason, a lie, and a falsehood, for he is neither the only son nor the first-born. Rather, it is Ishmael.

Mujīr al-Dīn does not overtly provide his opinion about who was the intended victim, but cites one or two well-known arguments in support of each candidate. If the Sacrifice took place in Mecca, it was Ishmael, but those who support Isaac ". . . say that the place of sacrifice was in Syria about two miles from Jerusalem *(īlyā)*—that is, *bayt al-maqdis*. The Jews claim that it was on the rock of *bayt al-maqdis*."[36]

## THE TRADITIONS

The preoccupation with determining the identity of Abraham's intended victim is expressed in the use of narrative traditions within the sources. Certain legends innocently identify the intended sacrifice in the course of detailing a related story. Others refer to either Isaac or Ishmael with the honorific title *(laqab)* "Sacrifice of God" attached to the name. In one case, a legend is told about an "expert witness," who in the court of an Umayyad Caliph, identifies the true victim. Five recurring traditions and one citation of evidence are found in the sources. Three are cited in support of each candidate.

All three narrative traditions supporting the candidacy of Isaac occur in similar form. Their testimony lies in the formulaic citation of Abraham Isaac and Jacob, where Isaac's connection with the Sacrifice is explicitly pointed out. One tradition found six times among the sources portrays Joseph giving his genealogy to a king identified in one rendition as Egyptian. He uses the honorific title, *dhabīḥ Allāh* ("the Intended Sacrifice of God") when referring to his grandfather Isaac. The story is brief and consistent, with four renditions given on the authority of Abū Maysara[37] and two on the authority of Ibn Abī Hudhayl:[38] "Joseph told the king to his face: 'Do you wish to eat with me, for by God, I am Joseph, son of Jacob the Prophet of God, son of Isaac the Intended Sacrifice of God, son of Abraham the Friend of God.' "[39]

A second narrative has God telling Moses that Isaac was given exceptional merit for submitting fully to the Sacrifice. This tradition occurs seven times with great consistency and is attributed to a family chain of authorities connected to 'Ubayd b. 'Umayr:[40]

> Moses said: "O Lord, why will you be called, 'O God of Abraham, Isaac and Jacob?" God replied: "Abraham never considered anything equal to me but always chose Me above all things. Isaac was generous to Me in the Sacrifice and was most generous in other things. As for Jacob, the more I put him through trials, the better he thought of Me."[41]

A variation is found in al-Zamakhsharī on the authority of Muḥammad b. Ka'b al-Quraẓī in which the intended victim is Ishmael.[42]

> A pious Israelite[43] used to say when praying, "O God, God of Abraham, Ishmael and Israel." And Moses said: "O Lord what should the pious children of Israel say when praying? O God of Abraham, Ishmael and Israel, I should be included among them. You let me hear Your words. You have chosen me as Your messenger!" God replied: "O Moses, no one ever loved me with Abraham's love and nothing ever tempted him away from Me. Ishmael was most generous with his own blood. And as for Israel, he never despaired of My spirit despite the hardships that befell him."

The third narrative tradition is found four times among the sources and is attributed to Abū al-Aḥwaṣ:[44] "A certain man boasted before Ibn Mas'ūd saying: 'I am so-and-so son of so-and-so son of noble shaykhs.' 'Abdallāh [Ibn Mas'ūd] said: 'That is Joseph son of Jacob, son of Isaac the Intended Sacrifice of God, son of Abraham the Friend of God.' "

All three of these narrative reports are quite similar in their formulaic style of listing the biblical patriarchs. Their style and content is reminiscent of the Jewish recitation of the central daily prayer known as the *avot* (patriarchs) in which the litany "God of Abraham, God of Isaac, and God of Jacob" is recited.[45] Our Islamic traditions cite the patriarchs in reverse order because they provide a sacred genealogy moving from most recent to most ancient member, and include a formulaic use of the Arabic *laqab* or honorific title. These three legends reflect normative pre-Islamic Jewish tradition and probably developed among the pre-Islamic Arabic-speaking Jewish communities of Arabia.[46]

Two narrative traditions and a series of authoritative citations are found in support of Ishmael being the intended sacrifice. The most often repeated are the citations which occur fourteen times according to six different authorities.[47] Twelve consist of simple statements confirming the fact that the horns of the ram which redeemed Ishmael once hung in the Ka'ba, thereby suggesting that the Sacrifice took place in the vicinity. Al-Sha'bī even claimed to have seen them there himself. According to the Ibn 'Abbās renditions, the entire head of the ram was hanging by its horns on the drain spout[48] of the

Ka'ba. The head had become *wakhusha*, a problematic term defined within the tradition as meaning "dried out."

The reports concerning the horns serve as evidence that the intended victim was Ishmael because they imply that the Sacrifice took place in Arabia where Ishmael would have been the intended victim. Had it taken place in Syria, the intended victim would have been Isaac. The horns are no longer hanging in the Ka'ba, however, because they were burnt along with the Ka'ba in the days of Ibn al-Zubayr and al-Ḥajjāj.[49]

Ṣafya bt. Shayba's rendition offers the most substantial report about the horns: "A woman of the Banū Salīm . . . said to 'Uthmān b. Ṭalḥa: 'Didn't the Apostle of God call you?' He said: 'The Apostle of God said to me: I used to see the two horns of the ram when I entered the House, and I forgot to tell you to cover them up.' So he covered them because it is not fitting to have anything in the House that would distract those who pray."[50]

A narrative tradition supporting Ishmael's candidacy as the sacrificial victim occurs seven times on the authority of al-Ṣunābiḥī and is referred to another four times among the sources.[51] Its full rendition is quite consistent among all the renditions. Al-Ṣunābiḥī says:

> We were with Mu'āwiya b. Abī Sufyān[52] when they said: "Was the intended sacrificial victim Ishmael or Isaac?" He answered: "You have come to someone well-informed about the matter! We were with the Apostle of God when a man came up and said: 'O Apostle of God, repeat to me [the knowledge] that God has bestowed upon you, O son of two intended sacrifices!' " So he laughed. Then I said to him, "O Commander of the faithful, who are the two intended sacrifices?" He answered: "When 'Abd al-Muṭṭalib was commanded to dig Zamzam, he vowed to God that if it were made easy for him, he would sacrifice one of his sons. The lot [arrow] fell on 'Abdallāh. But his maternal uncles prevented him, saying, 'Redeem your son with one hundred camels!' So he redeemed him with camels. Ishmael was the second."

The four brief references to this narrative simply mention that the Prophet said: "I am the son of two intended sacrifices,[53] and al-Ṭabarsī considers the Prophet's comment to be sound. 'Abd al-Muṭṭalib's vow to sacrifice his son refers to the famous story in Ibn Isḥāq's biography of the Prophet,[54] where 'Abd al-Muṭṭalib began to re-dig the well of Zamzam despite Qurayshite opposition. He vowed that if he would have ten sons to grow up and protect him, he would sacrifice one of them at the Ka'ba. The story reflects the actual history of pre-Islamic Mecca whether or not the incident occurred as found in Ibn Isḥāq's biography, since it treats the problematic issue of who owned the rights to the waters of Zamzam and therefore the coveted office of distributing the water to pilgrims.

After making his vow, 'Abd al-Muṭṭalib succeeds in prevailing over the opposition and intrigue of the Quraysh and attains control over the water of Zamzam. Since he is required to fulfill the vow he made, he casts lots to determine which son must be sacrificed. The lot falls upon 'Abdallāh, his youngest and favorite son and the future father of the Prophet Muḥammad. Immediately, . . . "His father led him by the hand and took a large knife; then he brought him up to Isāf and Nā'ila[55] to sacrifice him; but the Quraysh came out of their assemblies and asked what he was intending to do. When he said that he was going to sacrifice him, they and his sons joined together saying, 'By God! you shall not sacrifice him until you [first] offer the greatest [possible] expiatory sacrifice for him.[56] If you do a thing like this there will be no stopping men from coming to sacrifice their sons, and what will become of the people then?' "[57] A sorceress eventually determines through the casting of lots that 'Abdallāh could be safely redeemed with one hundred camels, so 'Abd al-Muṭṭalib redeems him.

The final tradition is a story that takes place in the court of the Umayyad Caliph 'Umar b. 'Abd al-'Azīz.[58] Found eight times and with virtually no variation in the sources (though three are incomplete),[59] Muḥammad b. Ka'b al-Quraẓī reports that he asked 'Umar b. 'Abd al-'Azīz in Damascus about who he believed was the true intended victim of the sacrifice.

> 'Umar said to him: "I would never have considered that issue before, but I think it is as you say." Then he sent for a man who was with him in Syria. He was a Jew who had converted to Islam and became a good Muslim. It became apparent that he was one of the religious scholars[60] of the Jews, so 'Umar b. 'Abd al-'Azīz decided to ask him about it. Muḥammad b. Ka'b al-Quraẓī said: "I was with 'Umar b. 'Abd al-'Azīz when he said: 'Which of Abraham's two sons was he commanded to sacrifice?' He answered: 'Ishmael. And by God, O Caliph, the Jews know that. However, they envy the Arab community because their father was the one commanded [to be sacrificed] and he is the one who is ascribed for merit for his steadfastness. But they deny that and claim that it was Isaac because Isaac was their father.' "[61]

Unlike the Isaac traditions, the two traditions and series of citations supporting Ishmael are quite different from one other in form and style, although they all have the appearance of Islamic (as opposed to pre-Islamic) legends. The popular comment about the horns of the ram hanging inside the Ka'ba tends not to be credited only to early traditionists,[62] and there appears to be no reference to horns hanging in the Ka'ba in pre-Islamic accounts. Al-Ṣunābiḥī's tradition about Muḥammad being the son of two intended sacrifices stresses the story of 'Abd al-Muṭṭalib and only mentions the reference to Ishmael in the last sentence as a kind of afterthought. Finally, the story of ‘Umar II and the Jew is obviously a late tradition. The Ishmael traditions therefore represent Islamic material that evolved in an effort to affirm the view that Ishmael was the intended sacrificial victim.

## THE CHRONOLOGY AND SETTING FOR THE SACRIFICE

The many arguments presented in favor of one or the other of Abraham's sons being the intended victim of the Sacrifice point to the significance of establishing the context of the act. Abraham's adventures and journeys in the land of the east, in Syria, and in Mecca unfold with considerable detail within the Islamic tradition literature, and most accounts end with Abraham establishing the foundations of the Ka‘ba and calling the people to the Pilgrimage, although some even include a narrative tradition describing the occasion of his death.[63] Despite the extensive information, however, there is little agreement as to how the episode of the Sacrifice fits into the full Abraham story. Some sources even omit the story of the Sacrifice from the Abraham cycle altogether and place it in a separate section. Even among those sources that set the Sacrifice into the Abraham story one finds a good deal of variation as to when and where it takes place, not to mention who was the intended victim.

Ibn Sa‘d does not consider the Sacrifice in his work, and though Ibn Ḥanbal alludes to it in some of his traditions, he is not concerned with its chronology or setting. Neither does al-Azraqī consider these issues, nor does al-Bukhārī mention the Sacrifice. Ibn Qutayba is the first in our sample of sources to publish a roster of the supporters of Isaac or Ishmael as the intended victim, but he does not take up the issue of the legend's spatial or chronological setting.

The first exegete among our sources to posit a chronology and location is al-Ya‘qūbī, who sets the action in Mecca after Ishmael helps Abraham build the Ka‘ba. Al-Ya‘qūbī is careful to provide the alternate view that it may have been Isaac, and if so, it would have taken place in the Amorite desert in Syria.[64]

In typical fashion, al-Ṭabarī lays out the largest number and greatest variety of opinions among the many traditions he cites in his comprehensive works. His own view is that the Sacrifice took place in Syria as a result of Abraham's vow upon receiving the angels' announcement of Isaac's impending birth. According to al-Ṭabarī, this is the view of al-Suddī[65] and of ‘Abdallāh and Companions of the Apostle of God.[66] The Sacrifice occurs before Abraham raised up the foundations of the Ka‘ba and before he established the stations of the Pilgrimage.[67] Al-Ṭabarī also quotes Shu‘ayb al-Jabā'ī as saying that "Isaac was sacrificed when he was seven . . . The location of the Sacrifice was about two miles from Jerusalem."[68]

Most of al-Ṭabarī's traditions, however, place the location of the Sacrifice in the area of Mecca. Ibn 'Abbās places it at Minā during Abraham's first Pilgrimage.[69] Other brief authoritative reports confirm its location in Minā but do not specifically connect it with Abraham's Pilgrimage. This is the view of many of al-Ṭabarī's sources which describe the ram or goat that redeemed Isaac. 'Alī is credited with saying that the ram was found bound to a tree in Thabīr.[70] Others say that it was sacrificed at the Place of Sacrifice[71] in Minā[72] or at a variety of other places in that vicinity. According to Ibn Isḥāq's tradition, Abraham commenced with the sacrifice of Ishmael on one of his day-long journeys from Syria to Mecca on the supernatural steed, Buraq. The exact location was on a trail at Mt. Thabīr just outside of Mecca.[73] 'Ubayd b. 'Umayr al-Laythī is credited with a full narrative tradition detailing Abraham's first Pilgrimage, during which Abraham takes Ishmael and the people he called to the Pilgrimage and shows them its entire ritual sequence.[74] Although the ritual sacrifice of the Pilgrimage is counted among the many stations they complete, no reference is made to this sacrifice being equated with the attempted sacrifice of Abraham's son.[75]

Al-Qummī cites a tradition attributed to Abū 'Abdallāh in which the Sacrifice takes place in Minā within the context of Abraham's first Pilgrimage.[76] The sacrificial victim, however, is to be Isaac, who had made the Pilgrimage with his mother, Sarah.[77]

Al-Mas'ūdī's sequence of the Abraham-Ishmael story begins with Ishmael's birth, soon after which he is brought to Mecca, where the Jurhumites and Amalekites befriend him and his mother Hagar. God destroys Sodom and Gomorrah[78] and then commands Abraham to sacrifice his son. After the attempted sacrifice, Abraham and Ishmael raise up the foundations of the Ka'ba. Only after all this has transpired is Isaac born.[79] According to al-Mas'ūdī's chronology, the only possible candidate for the sacrifice is Ishmael, although he provides the standard explanation that if the Sacrifice took place in Syria, it was Isaac.[80]

Al-Asadābādī does not consider the chronology nor the location of the Sacrifice. His view that the intended victim was Ishmael draws on the pro-Ishmael argument based on Qur'ān 37:112: AND WE GAVE HIM THE GOOD NEWS OF ISAAC, A PIOUS PROPHET.[81]

Al-Tha'labī follows al-Ṭabarī closely and gives nearly the same traditions. These include a report of al-Sha'bī that is nearly identical to that of al-Jabā'ī quoted by al-Ṭabarī, in which Isaac "was sacrificed" about two miles from Jerusalem at the age of seven years.[82] Al-Tha'labī also provides the al-Suddī tradition found in al-Ṭabarī[83] that has Abraham attempting to sacrifice Isaac in Syria in compliance with his vow. Like al-Ṭabarī, al-Tha'labī cites the Ibn Isḥāq tradition in which Abraham visits Ishmael on Buraq and attempts his sacrifice near Mecca.[84] He also cites the Ibn 'Abbās traditions that place the location of the Sacrifice in Minā,[85] some clearly within the context of Abraham's first Pilgrimage, while others are more vague.

Al-Zamakhsharī establishes the context of the Sacrifice within Abraham's first Pilgrimage and bases it on unnamed traditions.[86] The entire episode is a result of Abraham's vow to sacrifice his son after being given the divine announcement of his birth. Al-Zamakhsharī quotes a number of traditions specifying the exact location of the redemptive sacrifice as at al-Ḥijr, at the rock *(al-ḥajr)* near the Minā mosque, or at the Place of Sacrifice *(al-manḥar)* in Minā. He cites al-Ḥasan's tradition that the mountain goat that was used in place of Abraham's son came from Thabīr[87] and provides some traditions found in earlier sources.

Al-Ṭabarsī considers the age of Abraham's son to be thirteen years when the Sacrifice took place, although he does not provide a setting.[88] Later, he cites al-Aṣma'ī, who is told that the Sacrifice had to have taken place in Mecca where Ishmael lived and where the place of sacrifice is located.[89] Al-Ṭabarsī repeats al-Suddī's tradition in support of the Sacrifice taking place in Syria[90] but also provides a tradition in which Isaac is the intended victim of the Sacrifice that takes place in Mecca during the Ḥajj.[91] He repeats Ibn Isḥāq's tradition of Abraham attempting to sacrifice Ishmael during one of his visits on Buraq[92] and gives a tradition on the authority of Barīd b. Mu'āwiya al-'Ajalī in which Ishmael is the intended victim of the Sacrifice that takes place during the festival period in Mecca.[92]

Al-Kisā'ī's setting is a mountain in Syria and Ka'b al-Aḥbār his authority.[94] After receiving his vision in a dream at Jerusalem, Abraham sets out to sacrifice Isaac, who is seven years old.

Ibn al-Athīr also understands the location to be about two miles from Jerusalem and the intended victim to be Isaac.[95] The act was a result of Abraham's vow when he prayed to God to grant him a pious son (Q.37:100). But he also gives the opposing view that Ishmael was the intended victim at Mecca and cites a few traditions specifying the location in that area.[96] Ibn Arabi does not express any interest in the location or chronology of the Sacrifice.

Ibn Kathīr cites the Ibn 'Abbās tradition connecting the intended Sacrifice of Ishmael to the Pilgrimage, but also mentions a virtually identical tradition except that the intended victim is Isaac.[97] He also cites a large number of traditions discussed above which specify a particular location of the redemptive sacrifice.[98]

Mujīr al-Dīn cites al-Suddī's tradition but leaves the location of the Sacrifice vague until the last sentence, when Abraham brings the redemptive offering to al-Manḥar in Minā in order to slaughter it.[99] This last line is clearly a change from the other al-Suddī renditions that consistently locate the Sacrifice in Syria. According to Mujīr al-Dīn, those who say it was Isaac believe that it took place two miles from Jerusalem *(īlyā)*. The Jews say that it took place on the rock of Jerusalem *(bayt al-maqdis)*. Whoever says it was Ishmael believes that it took place in Mecca.[100]

Our pool of sources provides a great variety of suppositions regarding the chronology and location of the Sacrifice. The most often repeated and presumably earliest coherent account assumes the Sacrifice to have taken place in Syria and Isaac to have been the victim. According to this report, Abraham asks God for a pious son[101] and is given the divine announcement of Isaac's birth when the angels visit on their way to destroy the people of Lot.[102] Upon hearing the miraculous news he vows to offer his son as a sacrifice in thanks to God. Some unspecified time later, Abraham receives a vision stating that he must fulfill his vow.[103] He takes his son Isaac and proceeds to carry out the Sacrifice while they are both in Syria.

This account is found repeatedly and its rendition on the authority of al-Suddī is repeated more often than any other among the sources. Al-Ṭabarī mentions that this must have taken place before Abraham and Ishmael laid the foundations of the Ka'ba.[104] Although it is not stated specifically, we assume that the Sacrifice was to have taken place before Abraham settled Ishmael and Hagar in Mecca.[105]

Aside from the issue of Abraham's vow, the chronology given in these traditions provides a near-perfect parallel with that of the biblical rendition.[106] It is popular with al-Ṭabarī and turns up in five other exegetical sources. The strength of this account may have rested originally in its close proximity to the biblical story, although that very fact is seen by later Islam as a source of weakness. Its greatest weakness from the perspective of the religious institution of Islam lies in the fact that it in no way connects the Sacrifice to Mecca, the Ka'ba, or the Ḥajj. It therefore serves no Islamic purpose beyond its exegesis of the Qur'ān, which, it is true, is no inconsiderable achievement in itself. But as we shall suggest, other scenarios managed to establish the chronology and location of the Sacrifice in such a way that they could tie it into Mecca and the Islamic Pilgrimage, a role that required a different exegesis.

The second most popular narrative account is associated with Ibn 'Abbās. According to this scenario, the Sacrifice occurs in Mecca and is viewed within the context of Abraham's first and precedential Pilgrimage. When Abraham is taught the Meccan Ḥajj, Satan appears, but Abraham throws stones at him and he departs. Abraham then begins to carry out the sacrifice on Ishmael, although Isaac is considered the intended victim in two renditions.[107] This scenario ties the action into the Mecca Pilgrimage, although it does not relate to Abraham's association with the Ka'ba.

A closely related fragmentary tradition connects the Sacrifice to the throwing of stones at the redemptive ram near Mecca. This is also given on the authority of Ibn 'Abbās, whom we have noted is associated with all the Abrahamic lapidation traditions.[108] The incomplete narrative begins only after

Ishmael has been released and will be redeemed with a ram, but when the redemptive ram is brought down from Paradise it escapes. Ishmael or Abraham runs after it, throwing seven stones at it at each of the stations of the lapidation.[109] When it is finally captured, it is brought to al-Manḥar in Minā, where it is sacrificed.

Ibn Isḥāq's tradition about Abraham riding on Buraq to Mecca where he visits Ishmael is found three times among the sources.[110] Abraham was accustomed to taking day-trips to Mecca in order to check up on his son, and on one of these visits he takes Ishmael to the Sacrifice. This tradition provides no connection with the Pilgrimage or building the Ka'ba, although it does connect the Sacrifice firmly to Mecca.

The other depictions of the chronology and location of the Sacrifice each occur only once among the sources. Al-Zamakhsharī gives a unique anonymous tradition in which the Sacrifice is connected to the Pilgrimage through a series of etymological explanations for the popular names of the days of the Pilgrimage ritual.

> It is said that on the Day of Tarwiya *(yawm al-tarwiya)*, it seemed as if someone said [to Abraham]: "God commands you to sacrifice this son of yours!" When he awoke, he considered that *(rawwaya fi dhālika)* from the morning until late whether that dream came from God or from Satan. From that time [onward], it was called the Day of Consideration *(yawm al-tarwiya)*. In the evening he saw something similar and knew *('arifa)* that it was from God. From then on, [that day] was called the Day of 'Arafa.[111] He saw something similar on the third night and was very distressed with [the thought of] slaughtering him, so it was named the Day of Slaughtering *(yawm al-naḥr)*.[112]

Al-Ṭabarsī[113] provides a chronology that is fully in keeping with the religious sensibilities of Islam. According to this understanding, Abraham received his vision about the sacrifice of Ishmael immediately after Sarah had demanded the expulsion of Hagar and her son from their family. The vision informed Abraham that he would sacrifice Ishmael during the festival period of Mecca, so when the Pilgrimage month approached, Abraham brought Ishmael to Mecca. After laying the foundations of the House, Abraham brought Ishmael with him to perform the Ḥajj. During the running ritual, he informed his son of his task. (Q.37:102), and lay him down for the Sacrifice at al-Jamra al-Wusṭā.[114]

Perhaps the most appropriate chronology according to what became standard Islamic views would be al-Ya'qūbī's, which weaves the Sacrifice into the most complete version of the Abraham-Ishmael story.[115] After Sarah expresses her jealousy of Hagar, Abraham takes her and Ishmael to Mecca and settles them near the Kaʿba. The episode of Hagar searching for water and the miracle of Zamzam ensues, followed by the story of the destruction of the people of Lot. Ishmael has meanwhile attained manhood and has married a Jurhumite woman. Abraham visits Mecca twice in order to ensure that his son marries a proper wife. God then commands Abraham to build the Kaʿba, call the people to the Pilgrimage, and show them the proper [Pilgrimage] rituals. Abraham and Ishmael build the Kaʿba and Abraham calls the people to the Pilgrimage. Gabriel leads Abraham through the Pilgrimage on the "Day of Watering." While at al-Mashʿar, Abraham receives his vision that he must sacrifice his son, which he proceeds to do at Minā. Gabriel ultimately prevents him from carrying out the act and provides him with a sheep from Thabīr. Abraham charges Ishmael to dwell at the Sacred House after the ordeal is over in order to teach the people the proper Pilgrimage and ritual stations. Abraham then returns to Syria after telling his son that God will increase his family and progeny and will give his children much blessing and goodness.

This scenario connects the Sacrifice to the full story of Ishmael, patriarch of the northern Arabs and the progenitor of the Quraysh. Ishmael is old enough to help build the Kaʿba with his father as in Qur'ān 2:127, and significantly, is also old enough to resist his father's attempt to sacrifice him had he desired to do so, thus demonstrating his perfect willingness to submit to God's command. The Sacrifice is intimately associated with the Kaʿba and the Pilgrimage, thereby establishing their ancient monotheistic origins. It is a perfect chronology from the Islamic perspective. Yet it occurs only once and is never picked up completely by any later exegetes. The reason for this may lie in the fact that al-Yaʿqūbī did not include records of authentication in his history, thus rendering his data suspect. He is also accused of Shiʿite partiality in his History, which affected general regard for his work.[116]

The nature of the Islamic traditions regarding the Sacrifice suggests that those locating the act in Syria and assuming Isaac to have been the intended victim were earliest. Early Muslims naturally turned to Biblicists for information regarding legends found both in the Qur'ān and the Bible,[117] and the traditions they learned that followed the biblical orientation of the Sacrifice in Syria clearly derived from a Biblicist milieu. The pre-Islamic association of Abraham with Mecca, however, naturally encouraged the growth of counter traditions positing the location of the Sacrifice in the sacred Islamic center. The fact that many traditions treating the first Abrahamic Pilgrimage exclude any mention of the Sacrifice lends credence to the view that the connection between the Abrahamic Sacrifice and the pre-Islamic pilgrimage sacrifice was a late (Islamic) development. Once Abraham's association with Mecca was affirmed by the authority of the Qur'ān, the growth and development of legends about his adventures in Mecca were accelerated. It is only to be expected that all possible sources of tradition were consulted during the early

Islamic period: those deriving from Biblicist, pre-Islamic native Arabian, and other backgrounds.[118]

It is not clear whether traditions placing the Sacrifice in Mecca existed side by side with traditions locating the Sacrifice in Syria in the earliest Islamic period. None of the sources we consulted that are dated before the very end of the ninth century cite traditions that posit any kind of chronology for the Sacrifice.[119] Whether or not this was the result of a unanimity of opinion is impossible to answer based on the data from this study. On the other hand, it has long been established that even the most reliable records of authentication should not be relied upon without additional evidence. Yet one notes a consistency among traditions attributed to certain early transmitters that strongly supports the view that the traditions represent coherent legends that were transmitted intact for a long period of time.

The series of traditions attributed to Ibn ʻAbbās is a case in point. These form a single coherent "Ibn ʻAbbās" Abraham-Ishmael cycle that takes Abraham on his journey from the east to Syria and eventually to Mecca. They are the most consistent series of traditions, are found in sources of all the periods we treated, and contain almost no contradictions. Even the Sacrifice is placed into an Ibn ʻAbbās context by being the last act in the Abraham story, occurring only after Abraham builds the Kaʻba and calls the people to the Pilgrimage.[120] With the completion of that episode, the Abraham story is complete. According to Ibn ʻAbbās, there is nothing more to tell.

It is extremely unlikely that anyone was able to collect the hundreds of traditions attributed to Ibn ʻAbbās among our twenty sources and edit them in such a way as to eliminate contradictions. The only way to account for their consistency is to assume that they derive from a coherent account of the Abraham story that was reported by Ibn ʻAbbās or by an early source that could successfully attribute the work to him. In either case, if the less consistent traditions attributed to Ibn ʻAbbās about the Sacrifice were a part of this full account, then both the Syria-Isaac and Mecca-Ishmael Sacrifice scenarios would have been extant during the early Islamic generations.[121]

We know that the Syria-Isaac exegesis would have been available, at least among Arabian Biblicists, during the sixth and seventh centuries. The Mecca-Ishmael exegesis was probably a later development, when the figure of Ishmael was more firmly established as the progenitor of the northern Arabs.[122] The question that must now be raised is why the older Syria-Isaac exegesis came to be essentially replaced by the Mecca-Ishmael view. The most likely answer is that according to an Islamic world view by the ninth or tenth century, C.E., the Syria-Isaac exegesis had two major weaknesses. First, it was a nearly perfect parallel to the biblical version. This trait would have provided it with great authority in the first century of Islam when the new Arab Muslims were searching for information that would shed light on the difficult passages of the Qur'ān. But as Islam preferred to rely only on its own authoritative sources at the intellectual height of the Abbasid Caliphate, and as the genealogical connection with Abraham, Ishmael, and the northern Arabs became more firmly established, the Isaac legend was deemed increasingly suspect until it was eventually rejected.

The second weakness of the Syria-Isaac exegesis lies in the fact that it has absolutely no relation to the holy city of Mecca nor to the Pilgrimage. The opposing exegesis of the Ishmael-Mecca school served not only to explain difficult passages of the Qur'ān, but also to provide an acceptable origin for some of the important ritual acts of the Islamic Pilgrimage. The lapidation and the sacrifice of the Pilgrimage, both holdovers from a pagan pre-Islamic past, were re-interpreted through the narrative exegesis of the Sacrifice legend to derive from the pure and pristine monotheism of Abraham. What could be more authentically monotheistic than the classic test of God's servant Abraham through his willingness to sacrifice his son? Both father and son proved themselves worthy of being the progenitors of the greatest and most powerful religious civilization of its age. The story of the Sacrifice could provide the unifying and politically powerful act of Pilgrimage with a strong and effective monotheistic religious base that would forever shape its concept in the eyes of Islam.

The battle between the two kinds of exegesis was probably won by the Mecca-Ishmael school even before the time of al-Ṭabarī, but the psychological power of an earlier revelation (the Torah and the Gospel) and the bits of doubt that it could induce among Muslims managed to keep the Syria-Isaac exegesis alive and healthy among some exegetes. By taking into account the fact that this exegesis had been written down and disseminated within the first two centuries of Islam, we can understand how it survived so well. Yet if one asks a Muslim on the street today which son of Abraham was offered by his father in sacrifice, the answer would undoubtedly be that Ishmael was the intended victim of the Sacrifice in Minā.[123]

# Conclusion

This study has engaged in a process of analysis that involved not only the contextualization but also the decontextualization and recontextualization of selections representing a genre of literature. Hundreds of narrative traditions were examined both within and outside of their contexts in the sources. The advantage of this double method is that it included but then went beyond the analysis of a narrative's contextualized meaning; examining a narrative out of its immediate context eliminated a certain portion of meaning that was imposed by the authors or redactors who placed it in a purposeful order within the sources. It should not be forgotten that as traditions were passed orally between people over generations, their contextualization within the sources already represented a synthesis undertaken by the exegetes and not necessarily reflective of earlier stages in their meaning. Removing a large number of tellings of legends out of context and comparing them with one another as well as with related lore shed new light onto patterns of content and structure which, in turn, suggested a logic to their intertextuality.

We can rest the case of authorship or origin for the material in the foggy history of oral literature. There was no single author nor "source," but rather, as we learn from studies in oral literature, a long process of creation and influence. The teller of an oral tradition, and even the redactor of one who provided a context for it in a written source, is a living part of the creative process resulting in its current meaning. If there is a last stage in the process it can only be temporarily last, for it is represented by the occasion of the most recent discourse—that is to say, the circumstances of the most recent reading (or hearing) of the text, which must take into consideration the makeup of the reader (mental associations, cultural "baggage," etc.) and the context of the communicative act.

The written form of the traditions in our sources is a conservative medium which discourages the kind of fluidity that allowed oral traditions to change and bend to the needs and interests of a changing environment. This is the reason, for example, that modern Muslim scholars have occasionally been embarrassed or apologetic when confronted with the problem of making sense out of medieval narrative exegesis.[1] One cannot say, however, that as soon as an oral telling of a tradition was transcribed during the first few generations of Islam it became frozen in its written form, never to change or evolve further. The Muslims transcribing traditions lived in a stratum of culture for which writing was a reality, but for which oral literature was also of extreme importance. If a collector of tradition acquired a written telling of a legend that was contrary to the popular oral version with which he was already familiar, to which version would he remain faithful? This is a question we cannot answer, but we allow for the probability of further evolution of traditions even in their written form through scribal errors, glosses, or outright alterations. This thesis is fully supported by this study's identification of the Islamic components of the legends. Some were undoubtedly added during a late oral stage of evolution, but others were clearly added by transcribers or redactors as well.

Despite the possibility of continued evolution in written form, it must be acknowledged from the continuity between renditions and sources in our sample that the written medium is far more conservative than the oral medium.[2] This observation is further supported by the fact that in all but one instance,[3] only individual motifs but not coherent narratives could find close parallels in Biblicist sources. The traditions evolved actively during their oral stage. Many moved from Biblicist to pre-Islamic Arabian and then Islamic environments, but once they were transcribed in the sources they remained relatively stable, with little variation among renditions of specific versions among our sources spanning the ninth to the sixteenth centuries.

It should be noted here also that reducing oral traditions to writing at different periods or at different locations could be reflected in differences between the written renditions. Let us assume theoretically that a tradition is carried in a linear fashion from the Galilee to the Ḥijāz and is transcribed twice, once in Taymā in the northern district and a year later in al-Ṭā'if in the south. The two transcripts would differ to the extent that the oral tradition had undergone changes based on changes in the environment in which it was remembered and retold. This undoubtedly resulted in some of the variation among the renditions and probably influenced the creation of the hybrid traditions we observed as well.

Our discussion inevitably leads back to the question of origins. Is there somewhere an "original" version of a legend? From the perspective of personal experience, what is considered the original is of course the specific version that any particular audience (whether hearer or reader) came to know first. The audience becomes familiar with a particular telling and relates all other subsequent discourse to the so-called "original," meaning the one known first and regarded as the quintessence of the paradigm. Subsequent renderings are considered variants carrying the stigma of secondary importance or even mistakes, a phenomenon encountered often among children who, having learned a specific rendition of a fairy-tale from a written source will inevitably "correct" any other versions encountered.

From the religious perspective as well there is an "original": the specific rendering of legend or sacred myth derived from Scripture. But the religious orientation, like the personal orientation, is governed by the culture from which the world view evolved. For a Jew who learns the biblical Abraham legends through the culture of Jewish tradition and learning, a Christian understanding of even the identical biblical text, based as it is on the culture of Christian exegesis, will appear foreign, "incorrect." Abraham's character and role and the meaning invested in his activities are understood differently by Jews and Christians, even when reading the same text. How much the more so when comparing a religious reading of the biblical rendition with a religious reading of the qur'ānic. Each understands an "original," meaning "True" telling, against which all others are judged.

From the literary perspective, however, there really can be no original. The famous Cinderella story cited so effectively by Barbara Herrnstein Smith is a case in point.[4] Over one thousand renditions of the tale have been collected and analysed from Europe, Africa, the Middle East, and the Far East. The variations between tellings and cultures have multiplied so often that many renditions of the story would hardly be recognized by any of us as the story we know. Origins for the tale have been proposed as being in such far away places as North Vietnam.[5]

Like language itself, renditions of narratives can be understood to vary through dialects and even particular "accents" among specific cultures of discourse, subcultures, and even individuals. One cannot speak of an original legend any more than one can speak of an original language. But just as a certain dialect of London English became accepted as the proper or authentic English speech, so certain renditions of narratives, largely frozen in their written form and enjoying a wide distribution through published works such as those of the Brothers Grimm, may be mistakenly regarded as the authentic or original telling.

When treating legends found in the Bible, it is sometimes difficult to dispel the personal and religious connections that predispose one to assume their originality, despite the massive number of parallels in ancient Near Eastern texts uncovered during the past century.[6] Unlike Cinderella stories and other fairy tales, the stories about Abraham and other characters known from the Bible tend to evoke a deeper emotional response among audiences that have grown up in a Biblicist environment such as that of the West. The discussion in Chapter One outlined some of the historical responses to the problem of biblical/qur'ānic legends occurring in both scriptures, and the bulk of this study took up the very issue of intertextuality in the legends about Abraham and Ishmael found in Islamic and Biblicist tradition. Having traced influence upon the Abraham-Ishmael narratives to the three primary sources of Biblicism, pre-Islamic indigenous Arab culture, and Islam, we concluded that the traditions as found in the Islamic sources nevertheless represent uniquely Islamic creations. They cannot be reduced simply to inaccurate reproductions of biblical legends. Like all human creations, they are indebted to an infinite series of associations with earlier and contemporaneous creations. Now having summarized our methodology and findings, it is possible to reexamine some of the themes discussed earlier in light of the results of the study.

The historical and literary evidence is consistent in supporting the existence of Biblicist legends in the Arabian Peninsula before the birth of Muḥammad. Various Biblicist groups had entered and lived in the Peninsula, brought their lore with them, and in the course of daily life shared it with their non-Biblicist neighbors. While Biblicist lore clearly existed, Arabs who did not share the same religio-cultural environment would not necessarily have found it particularly meaningful. Legends were heard but largely forgotten, and names such as Abraham or Moses or Jesus were recognized but the characters not necessarily known.

Cross-cultural diffusion does not occur unless there is enough congruence between cultures to allow new information to fit into a recognized framework, making it intelligible to the host culture. Part of the sublimity of the Qur'ān was its success in rendering Biblicist traditions that had found their way into Arabia meaningful to the indigenous non-Biblicist Arab population—to provide the framework for successful diffusion. Its audience certainly knew many of the Bible-oriented stories and may have enjoyed hearing them told by their Biblicist neighbors, but had not previously considered them relevant to their own history and welfare. Through his recitation of the qur'ānic revelation, Muḥammad taught that the legends were a part of universal history and that they related directly to every individual's personal salvation. This, in turn, effected a synthesis between an interpretation of biblical history and the history of the Arab peoples, resulting somewhat later in the classic Arab genealogical anthropology. Convincing the Arabs of the profound meaning and relevance of this new Islamic world view was a difficult endeavor, as we know from the qur'ānic portrayals of Muḥammad's Arabian opposition.

The qur'ānic stories, references, and allusions to characters found in the Bible were not made up or adapted from biblical texts.[7] The revelation rather drew heavily upon the corpus of monotheistic oral traditions extant in the Arabian Ḥijāz of the late sixth century, which was at least recognized if not well-known by most of its inhabitants. Much of it derived from a Biblicist milieu,[8] although some was derivative of other sources as well[9] and had evolved during the course of time to continue reflecting local issues and concerns. The mass of extant Biblicist and hybrid Biblicist-Arabian material represented a pool of monotheistic lore that was recognizable and available as a basis for the sacred history of a newly evolving monotheism, Islam. It was a natural source of monotheistic wisdom in relation to which the revelations of the Qur'ān would be meaningful.

When the Jews of Medina criticize Muḥammad for reciting legends which they considered inaccurate,[10] they call our attention to the probability that by virtue of their oral nature, the legends Muḥammad faithfully retold had evolved to the point that they no longer corresponded well to the written versions known to educated Rabbinite Jews in the Bible and the Midrash. For his part, Muḥammad sincerely believed that he knew the legends correctly. He, in turn, accused the Jews of distortion when he recited Qur'ān 2:78-79: "And there are illiterates *(ummiyyūn)* among them who do not know the Book, but only fancies, and they do nothing but conjecture. Woe to those who write the Book with their own hands and then say: 'This is from God.' " In the context of his relations with the Jews of Medina, Muḥammad's attitude can hardly be construed as anything but genuine anger and even shock at what he considered the complete Jewish disregard for the true story. The Qur'ān portrays the tension resulting from two different versions of parallel scriptural tales. Each version is claimed by separate parties as being the unchangeable word of God. The standard against which the Medinan Jews judged the legends and sermons recited by Muḥammad would have been their Hebrew Bible and Midrash, although they were undoubtedly familiar with the versions to which Muḥammad referred as well. Muḥammad's was a version known in oral form in Mecca and Medina and common to Jews and Christians as well as his followers and Arab pagans. Muḥammad's anger at their rejection was not merely a reaction to personal insult, but rather a natural response to the rejection of what he believed was authentic scripture, which indeed it was, although not identical to the scripture that the Jews considered authentic.[11]

Before Muḥammad, the conflict between the oral and written versions of biblically based legends was irrelevant. They existed side by side with little conflict because no one claimed the oral lore to be exclusively authoritative. But when the oral versions were made pertinent to the Arabs through the medium of the Qur'ān, they became invested with divine authority. As they achieved canonical status in qur'ānic revelation, they attained supreme importance as God-given lore that would become forever relevant to adherents of the new/old religion of Islam.

This theoretical reconstruction of the history of early Islamic narrative implies that the material found in qur'ānic narratives on biblical themes and the traditions collected during the first two centuries of Islam represent essentially the same *genre* of literature. Any comparison of the two, however, would reveal that there are distinct differences between the Qur'ān and the legends found in later exegetical literature. First, the literary style of the qur'ānic legends is shaped by the fact that many are given in the form of a revelation to Muḥammad. Its literary form is known as *saj'* in Arabic, a kind of rhymed Arabic prose which is substantially different from the language in which the exegetical stories are typically told.[12] Second, much of the Qur'ān is rendered in a homiletical fashion which is different from the style of the traditions as we know them in the exegetical sources. The Qur'ān is not merely a collection of simple tales and legends, but an instrument of inspiration and education. Legends found in the Bible tend to be alluded to in sermonic utterances in order to promote a feeling or an idea, but they are rarely provided in full. Even in the longest and most complete legends such as the story of Joseph in the twelfth chapter of the Qur'ān *(Sūrat Yūsuf)*, many anticipated details are omitted and are assumed already to be known. Finally, because the qur'ānic legends are part of the Sacred Book of Islam, they have attained a sanctified status that is not open to comparison. They can have no competing versions because they are considered God's word and are therefore beyond criticism or relative meaning.

The revelation of the Qur'ān set the parameters for traditions that would be acceptable to early Islam. Because, as has been mentioned, the indigenous Arabs prior to Islam were not particularly interested in knowing the details of Biblicist lore, the first Muslims naturally searched among Jews and Christians for information that would shed light on the brief qur'ānic narratives and allusions to biblical tales. Legends from other foreign environments such as Persia and India no doubt had also penetrated the Arabian Peninsula, but because they did not obtain the same kind of relevance through the text of the Qur'ān, they tended more to fall out of existence. Both native and foreign traditions circulating in pre-Islamic Arabia that did not relate to the new Islamic Scripture or practice went the way of unrepeated oral lore: they were forgotten and disappeared.

This process was hastened by the conscious Islamic practice of eradicating all that belonged to what was to be henceforth referred to as the ignorant pagan period of Arabia *(al-jāhiliyya)*.[13] The fact, however, that Jewish and Christian (orthodox and heterodox) as well as indigenous *(ḥanīf)* expressions of monotheism were clearly extant and apparantly well-organized in pre-Islamic Arabia suggests that the coming of Islam to Arabia may not have represented as radical a departure from pre-Islamic times as generally assumed.

Muslim historiographers have regularly claimed that Islam represented an absolute religious break from pre-Islamic times, an assumption that may now be questioned. Modern scholarship still tends to take for granted the classic Islamic view of a revolutionary separation in thinking and institutions between pre-Islamic and Islamic times, based on the radical changes brought about by the new Islamic power and its conquest of so much of the world. This habit, however, tends to deny or ignore the overwhelming logical and natural continuity in thinking as well as in the structure of social, economic, and political institutions between these two periods, despite the acknowledged changes caused by Islam. By assuming a new genesis in the first quarter of the seventh century, this approach tends to ignore the important and lasting influence of pre-Islamic Arabian religious thought (monotheistic as well as pagan) and institutions on nascent and early Islamic civilization. This pre-Islamic influence existed linearly in the continued existence of pre-Islamic lore and legal, social, and religious practices, and less directly as pre-Islamic institutions and thinking evolved into more recognizably Islamic forms.[14]

The legends of Abraham and Ishmael represent one small example of the continuity from pre-Islamic to Islamic times and are particularly intriguing because they depict important figures that are viewed quite differently by Judaism, Christianity, and Islam. They of course represent only a small part of the large mass of Islamic legends on themes found both in the Qur'ān and the Bible. The clear continuity between Islam and pre-Islamic religious ideas and institutions represented by these legends is tempered, however, by the unique content and form that they exhibit in the Islamic sources. Just as they display continuity from earlier and contemporaneous literature, they also exhibit originality as new literary works. They represent the synthesis of new ideas based upon both influence and inspiration, forming part of the religious and sacred historical foundations upon which the religious civilization of Islam rests.

PART FIVE

# Appendices

# Appendix 1

## THE EXEGETES AND THEIR SOURCES

### IBN SA'D, *KITĀB AL-TABAQĀT AL-KABĪR*[1]

Abū Abdallāh Muḥammad b. Sa'd b. Manī' al-Baṣrī al-Hāshimī (d. 230/845) was born in Basra around 168/784 and died in Baghdad. He was an orthodox traditionist who traveled in search of traditions and studied under many scholars, but eventually settled in Baghdad, where he attached himself to the famous scholar and historian of the Islamic conquests, al-Wāqidī (d. 207/822). He became his secretary and transmitted his works. Ibn Sa'd studied genealogy under Hishām b. al-Kalbī. His famous work of early history is organized around biographies of individuals in each age, and was probably intended as an aid to the study of *Ḥadīth*, giving information about some 4,250 individuals.[2] He generally includes records of authentication and collected a significant amount of legendary material about the pre-Islamic period.

### IBN ḤANBAL, *AL-MUSNAD*[3]

Aḥmad b. Muḥammad b. Ḥanbal (d. 241/855-6), was known simply as "the Imām" of Baghdad. Born in Baghdad, he spent time in Basra, Kufa, and Mecca, and travelled widely in pursuit of traditions. Like Ibn Sa'd, Ibn Ḥanbal was persecuted by the Mu'tazilite-led inquisition, the *mihna*, but refused to accept Mu'tazilite dogma required by the Abbasid authorities at the time. He studied law and *Ḥadīth* under a great many teachers and was immensely popular and extremely well respected as a traditionist.[4] Strongly orthodox or traditional in outlook, he is the founder of the Ḥanbalite school of religious law, known as the most rigid approach to the use of tradition. His *Musnad* is a collection of about 30,000 *ḥadīths*, organized according to the Companions of the Prophet, who are the last link in the chains of tradition he cites.[5] Most traditions he cites are brief.

## AL-AZRAQĪ, *AKHBĀR MAKKA*[6]

Abū al-Walīd Muḥammad b. Abdallāh b. Aḥmad al-Azraqī (d. 244/858). His grandfather, Aḥmad b. Muḥammad b. al-Walīd b. 'Uqba (d. 222/837) was interested in the history of Mecca and its sanctuary and gathered a huge mass of materials from Sufyān b. 'Uyayna, Sa'īd b. Sālim, al-Zanjī, Dāwūd b. 'Abd al-Raḥmān al-'Aṭṭār, and other inhabitants of Mecca. His grandson (Abū al-Walīd) considerably expanded upon his efforts in *Akhbār makka*, which has become the standard work on the history of the holy city. The traditions are often traced back to Ibn 'Abbās and his "school," and tend to represent its approach to qur'ānic exegesis. He also quotes Ibn Isḥāq, al-Kalbī, and Wahb b. Munabbih in his work on pre-Islamic history.[7] *Akhbār makka* is organized both historically and topically.

## AL-BUKHĀRĪ, *AL-ṢAḤĪḤ*[8]

Abū 'Abdallāh Muḥammad b. Ismā'īl b. Ibrāhīm b. al-Mughīra b. Bardizbah Abū 'Abdallāh al-Ju'fī al-Bukhārī (d. 256/869) was given the *nisba* al-Ju'fī because his great grandfather al-Mughīra was a client *(mawla)* of Yaman al-Ju'fī, the governor of Bukhara, from whom he accepted Islam. Known and respected in his lifetime as an excellent traditionist, he travelled widely in search of *ḥadīth* reports. He was expelled from Nishapur and went to Bukhara because of his alleged heterodox views regarding the status of the Qur'ān. According to his view, the Qur'ān was indeed uncreated, although that status did not apply to its recitation (this is the 'Asharite view). He was eventually expelled also from Bukhara and died in the village of Khartank, near Samarkand. Al-Bukhārī did not hold consistently to the doctrines of any particular school of law, although al-Subkhī included him among the Shafi'ite legalists.[9] His *Ṣaḥīḥ* is considered the most highly respected collection of *Ḥadīth* in Sunni Islam.

## IBN QUTAYBA, *KITĀB AL-MA'ĀRIF*[10]

Abū Muḥammad 'Abdallāh b. Muslim b. Qutayba al-Dīnawarī (d. 276/889-90). Some biographers add "al-Kūfī," referring to his place of birth. He is of Persian origin and was a theologian and writer of *Adab* as well as a philologist. He was influenced by the Ḥanbalite Sunni theologian al-Ḥanẓalī (d. 851), became the religious judge *(qāḍī)* of Dīnawar and probably spent time in Basra as well. He spent the last seven or eight years of his life in a district of Baghdad. Ibn Qutayba wrote on philology and practical astronomy, and gave religious decisions on drinking alchohol and gambling. He was also a prolific writer on poetry and *Ḥadīth*, and participated in the polemics against the *Shu'ūbiyya* movement, the Mushabbihas, and the Mu'tazilites.[11]

## AL-YA'QŪBĪ, *TA'RĪKH*[12]

Aḥmad b. Abī Ya'qūb b. Wāḍiḥ al-Ya'qūbī (d. 277/891-2) was an Imāmī Shi'ite historian and geographer, who spent his youth in Armenia and served the Ṭāhirids in Khurasan. He traveled widely and wrote an important geographical work, *Kitāb al-buldān* while in Egypt. His *History (Ta'rīkh)* is typical of the early Shi'ite interest in the history of ancient religions and includes that of the patriarchs of Israel, Jesus and the Apostles, rulers of Syria, Assyria, Babylon, Indians, Greeks, Romans, Persians, Turks, Chinese, etc. He includes in his work the bequest or willed essence *(waṣīya)* of each prophetic figure. Because his work is earlier than al-Ṭabarī, who influenced most later works, al-Ya'qūbī is of particular interest.[13]

## AL-ṬABARĪ, *JĀMI' AL-BAYĀN 'AN TA'WĪL ĀY AL-QUR'ĀN*[14] AND *TA'RĪKH AL-RUSUL WAL-MULŪK*[15]

Muḥammad b. Jarīr al-Ṭabarī (d. 310/923) was of Persian extraction. He traveled widely in Syria, Iraq, and Egypt to seek out well-known teachers, and settled in Baghdad. Accused of Mu'tazilite tendencies for his stand on free will, he was also accused of being a Shi'ite, although he was clearly a traditionalist who leaned toward Ash'arism. He was a part of the Shāfi'ite school, but later formed his own independent school of law, the "Jarīrite" school, which was similar to the Shāfi'ite school. His school has not survived. In his Qur'ān commentary, al-Ṭabarī is said to have collected all of the extant traditions available to him and assembled the various interpretations through verse-by-verse comments. He included full records of authentication in his work and added his own philological comments as well as his own views, comments, criticisms, and evaluations of various traditions. His collection of traditions contained historical and dogmatic information, "occasions of revelation" *(asbāb al-nuzūl)*, and apparently, nearly everything available. In his introduction he himself mentions that his work ". . . is so comprehensive that with it there is no need to have recourse to other books . . . We shall present the reasons for every school of thought or opinion and elucidate what we consider to be the right view with utmost brevity."

Similar in philosophical approach to his *Commentary*, Tabari's *History* is relatively impartial and includes various versions and aspects of historical events. He includes records of authentication in this as well as his Qur'ān commentary. Like most medieval histories, al-Ṭabarī begins his work with Creation and includes the stories of biblical and extrabiblical figures known to him through the Tradition. He is said to have taken much material for his *History* from oral as well as literary sources.[16]

## AL-QUMMĪ, *TAFSĪR AL-QUMMĪ*[17]

Abū al-Ḥasan ʻAlī b. Ibrāhīm b. Hāshim b. Mūsā b. Bābawayhī (d. 328/939) was born in Khurasan, but moved to Baghdad. He was an Imāmī Shiʻite commentator, jurist, and historian, who studied under al-Kūlinī (d. 939). He is also known as a compiler of *Ḥadīth*, and is not unanimously well-thought of in this regard, although Shiʻite sources generally view him more favorably than Sunnī. Al-Qummī represents what has been called the formative and somewhat extremist stage of Imāmī Shiʻite *Ḥadīth* development. His *Commentary* is clearly weighted heavily in favor of Shiʻite interpretation. Unlike al-Ṭabarī, Ibn Kathīr, and others, al-Qummī neither analyzes nor evaluates his *ḥadīth* reports.[18]

## AL-MASʻŪDĪ, *MURŪJ AL-DHAHAB WA-MAʻĀDIN AL-JAWĀHIR*[19]

Abū al-Ḥasan ʻAlī b. al-Ḥusayn (d. 345/956-7) was a Muʻtazilite historian and geographer. He traveled widely through Persia, India, Ceylon, Zanzibar, the area of the Caspian Sea, and Palestine, and lived both in Syria and Egypt, where he died in Fostat. He was knowledgable in geography, ethnography, and history. His *Murūj al-dhahab* is a briefer form of his long history entitled *Kitāb akhbār al-zamān waman abādahu ʼlḥidthān min al-umam al-māḍiya waʼl-ājyāl al-khāliya waʼl-mamālik al-dāthira*, which is said to have been thirty volumes in length but has been lost. His *Murūj al-dhahab* is broader than a regular historical work and includes interesting items treating the history of ancient peoples and Islam until the year 336/947-8. The title: "Golden Meadows and Mines of Precious Stones" appears appropriate to this collection of history and legend.[20]

## AL-ASADĀBĀDĪ, *TANZĪH AL-QURʼĀN*[21]

Abū al-Ḥasan al-Qādī ʻAbd al-Jabbār b. Aḥmad b. ʻAbd al-Jabbār al-Hamadhānī al-Asadābādī (d. 415/1025) is considered the last great Muʻtazilite. He lived in Baghdad and was appointed the Qadi of Rayy. With regard to legal issues, he followed the Shāfiʻite school. His work treats linguistic questions concerning the language of the Qurʼān but does not treat verses about ritual and social or moral questions. His is a basically dialectical approach to interpretation.[22]

## AL-THAʻLABĪ, *ʻARĀʼIS AL-MAJĀLIS*[23]

Abū Isḥāq Aḥmad b. Muḥammad b. Ibrāhīm al-Thaʻlabī al-Nīsābūrī (d. 427/1036) was part of a mystically oriented circle acknowledging al-Junayd

(d. 910) as its founder. His hagiography, *'Arā'is al-majālis*, grew out of his own commentary: *al-Kashf wa'l-bayān 'an tafsīr al-Qur'ān*, and employs a great deal of tradition taken from formal exegetical literature in general. He used al-Ṭabarī, among other works, and his traditions often parallel those of al-Ṭabarī. His collection is considered to be more sober, less fantastic than al-Kisā'ī's hagiography, also entitled *Qiṣaṣ al-anbiyā'*.[24]

## AL-ZAMAKHSHARĪ, *AL-KASHSHĀF 'AN ḤAQĀ'IQ AL-TANZĪL WA'UYŪN AL-AQĀWĪL FĪ WUJŪH AL-TA'WĪL*[25]

Abū al-Qāsim Maḥmūd b. 'Umar b. Aḥmad al-Zamakhsharī (d. 538/1143-4), born in Persian Khwarizm, was a great philologist, scholar, and Mu'tazilite theologian. His long stay in Mecca earned him the honorific title *(laqab) Jār Allāh* ("neighbor of God"). Al-Zamakhsharī is best known for his grammatical works and his philologically oriented commentary to the Qur'ān, *al-Kashshāf*, although he wrote works in other fields as well. His *Commentary* is considered a rationalist work including philosophical as well as philological interpretation of Scripture. He deals with grammar and lexicography and brings proofs from old Arabic poetry. Because his Mu'tazilite affiliation tended to affect his interpretation of the Qur'ān in only a few points, his *Commentary* has been regarded by the Sunni religious scholars as one of the most important works. He pays little regard to records of authentication which he generally omits, and tends to include little tradition.[26]

## AL-ṬABARSĪ, *MAJMA' AL-BAYĀN FĪ 'ULŪM AL-QUR'ĀN*[27]

Radī al-Dīn Abū 'Alī al-Fadl b. al-Ḥasan Amīn al-Dīn al-Ṭabarsī (d. 518/1153) was an Imāmī Shi'ite theologian and traditionist. His place of birth is obscure, but it is known that he taught in Mashhad and composed his commentary in Khurasan, where he died. In addition to his commentary, he composed a number of particularistic Shi'ite tracts. His *Majma' al-bayān* is considered a classical Qur'ān *Commentary* because it presents the views of other major commentators. Nevertheless, it gives prominence to Shi'ite exegesis. Because it includes material including even Mu'tazilite and Sunni traditionalist theological comments, it is not generally considered a strictly "Shi'ite" work, as is that of al-Qummī. Nevertheless, al-Ṭabarsī tends to transmit traditions on our subject from very few sources, most of them going back to Ja'far. His work is carefully organized, and every section of commentary includes introductory comments, variant readings of the qur'ānic verses, philological, lexical and syntactic analysis, traditions, and often his own opinion, including esoteric interpretations.[28]

## AL-KISĀ'Ī, *QIṢAṢ AL-ANBIYĀ'*[29]

Muḥammad b. 'Abdallāh (twelfth century) is the name given to the unknown compiler of this work. Eisenberg believed him to be Abū al-Ḥasan 'Ali b. Hamza b. 'Abdallāh, the famous philologist under Harūn al-Rashīd, but this is contested by Nagel and others. Schussman considers the work to be earlier than the twelfth century.[30]

## IBN AL-ATHĪR, *AL-KĀMIL FĪ AL-TA'RĪKH*[31]

'Izz al-Dīn Abū al-Ḥasan 'Alī (d. 630/1232) spent most of his adult life in Mosul as a private scholar, but studied in Baghdad, Jerusalem, and Syria as well. His two brothers, Majd al-Dīn and Diyā' al-Dīn also achieved literary fame in their respective fields of philology and religious studies (Majd al-Dīn) and literary criticism (Diyā' al-Dīn). 'Izz al-Dīn spent some time in Aleppo and Damascus, and probably fought with Salaḥ al-Dīn ("Saladin") against the Crusaders. His *Kāmil* is an annalistic history from Creation to 628 A.H., and as such, includes legendary material about the pre-Islamic period.[32]

## IBN AL-'ARABĪ, *TAFSĪR AL-QUR'ĀN AL-KARĪM*[33]

Muḥyi al-Dīn Abū 'Abdallāh Muḥammad b. 'Alī b. Muḥammad b. al-'Arabī al-Ḥātimī al-Ṭā'ī (d. 638/1240) was born in Murcia, Spain, and studied in Seville. He was one of the greatest Sufi mystics and undoubtedly the most prolific writer. He travelled a great deal and lived last in Damascus, where he died. He is purported to have written a mystical commentary that has not come down to us. It is not clear, therefore, whether the work attributed to him was indeed written by him or by one of his disciples, al-Razzāq al-Qashānī (d. 1329). Whether it was written by Ibn 'Arabī or not, it is understood to represent his school of thought and exegesis. *Tafsīr al-Qur'ān al-karīm* is an esoteric commentary that would be classified in the category of esoteric exegesis *(ta'wīl)*. The author sees hidden allegorical meaning throughout the qur'ānic utterances and has very little interest in legendary material. As such, this commentary contains the least amount of material for this study.[34]

## IBN KATHĪR, *TAFSĪR AL-QUR'ĀN AL-'AẒĪM*[35] AND *QIṢAṢ AL-ANBIYĀ'*[36]

'Imād al-Dīn Ismā'īl b. 'Umar b. Kathīr (d. 774/1373) was born in Basra and died in Damascus. He was a Syrian traditionist and one of the best-known historians under the Baḥrī Mamluks. Ibn Kathīr was trained by the Shāfi'ite Burhān al-Dīn al-Fazārī, but was strongly influenced by Ibn Taymiyya (d. 1328) and the Ḥanbalī school. In his *Tafsīr*, which is considered traditional and "conservative," he includes full records of authentication and liberally gives his own comments regarding the veracity of traditions. Ibn Kathīr collects a large number of traditions in both his *Commentary* and *History* and does not hesitate to include variant reports. Both Ibn Kathir and al-Ṭabarī clearly provide the largest number of traditions for this study.[37]

## MUJĪR AL-DĪN, *AL-UNS AL-JALĪL BITA'RĪKH AL-QUDS WAL-KHALĪL*[38]

'Abd al-Raḥmān b. Muḥammad Abū al-Yaman Mujīr al-Dīn al-Ḥanbalī (d. 927/1520-1) was born in Jerusalem and studied with a number of local scholars. He is the least known exegete of our pool of sources. *Al-Uns al-jalīl* is a local history of the cities of Jerusalem and Hebron, the former receiving far greater attention than the latter. Like other historians, Mujīr al-Dīn begins his study with an account of Creation and continues with legendary history up until his own generation. He includes traditions but generally omits their records of authentication.[39]

# Appendix 2

# TRADITIONISTS NAMING ISAAC OR ISHMAEL AS THE INTENDED SACRIFICIAL VICTIM

## OPINIONS OF THE TRADITIONISTS REGARDING WHO WAS THE INTENDED SACRIFICE (LISTED BY EXEGETE)

*Supporters of Isaac:*

*Ibn Qutayba:*
Most of *ahlu al-'ilm* & the Torah
al-'Abbās b. 'Abd al-Muṭṭalib
'Abdallāh
Masrūq
al-Suddī + Abū Mālik
Ibn 'Abbās
Ibn Mas'ūd
Ka'b, who told Abū Hurayra

*al-Ṭabarī (Commentary):*
'Ikrima
Qatāda
al-'Abbās b. 'Abd al-Muṭṭalib
al-'Abbas b. 'Abd al-Muṭṭalib + Prophet
Ibn 'Abbas (3x)
Abū Hurayra + Ka'b
Ibn Isḥāq + Masrūq
'Ubayd b. 'Umayr
Ibn Abī al-Hudhayl
Ibn Sābiṭ

*al-Ṭabarī (History):*
al-'Abbās b. 'Abd al-Muṭṭalib
Ibn 'Abbās (3x)
Ka'b al-Aḥbār
Ibn Sābiṭ
Masrūq

*al-Tha'labī:*
People of the Book are unanimous that it was Isaac
'Umar b. al-Khaṭṭāb
'Alī b. Abī Ṭālib
Ka'b al-Aḥbār
Sa'īd b. Jubayr
al-Qāsim b. Abī Barra
Masrūq b. al-Ajdā'
'Abd al-Raḥmān b. Abī Sābiṭ
Abū Hudhayl
al-Zuhrī
al-Suddī
al-'Abbās b. 'Abd al-Muṭṭalib + Apostle

*al-Zamakhsharī:*
'Alī b. Abī Ṭalib
Ibn Mas'ūd
al-'Abbās
'Atā'
'Ikrima

*al-Ṭabarsī:*
'Alī
Ibn Mas'ūd
Qatāda
Sa'īd b. Jubayr
Masrūq
'Ikrima
'Atā'
al-Zuhrī
al-Suddī
al-Jabā'ī

*al-Kisā'ī:*
Ibn 'Umar

Ḥasan
Ḥusayn
Qatāda

*Ibn al-Athīr:*
al-'Abbās b. 'Abd al-Muṭṭalib + Apostle
Ibn 'Abbās
'Umar b. al-Khaṭṭāb
'Alī
al-'Abbās b. 'Abd al-Muṭṭalib
his son 'Abdallāh
'Ikrima
'Abdallāh b. Mas'ūd
Ka'b
Ibn Sābiṭ
Ibn Abī al-Hudhayl
Masrūq

*Ibn Kathīr (Commentary):*
Abū Maysara
Ibn Abī al-Hudhayl
The father of 'Abdallāh b. 'Ubayd b. 'Umayr
'Abdallāh b. Mas'ūd
Ibn 'Abbās
al-'Abbās
'Alī b. Abī Ṭālib.
'Ikrima
Sa'īd b. Jubayr
Mujāhid
al-Sha'bī
'Ubayd b. 'Umayr
Zayd b. Aslam
'Abdallāh b. Shaqīq
al-Zuhrī
al-Qāsim b. Abī Yarza
Makḥūl
'Uthmān b. Abī Ḥāḍir
al-Suddī
al-Ḥasan
Qatāda
Abū Hudhayl
Ibn Sābiṭ

Ibn Jarīr
The tradition that it was Isaac came from Ka'b
Abū Hurayra + Ka'b al-Aḥbār.
al-Baghawī said so on the authority of 'Umar
'Alī Ibn Mas'ūd
al-'Abbās.
Those who follow Ka'b al-Aḥbār are Sa'īd b. Jubayr, Qatāda, Masrūq, 'Ikrima, 'Atā', Muqātil, al-Zuhrī, and al-Suddī.
Ibn 'Abbās is also the ultimate authority for this tradition but the *isnād* is not reliable.
Ibn Kathīr criticizes al-Ṭabarī's *isnād* on the authority of al-'Abbās b. 'Abd al-Muṭṭalib + Prophet that it was Isaac. (The weaknesses are al-Ḥasan b. Dinār al-Baṣrī [*matrūk*] and 'Alī b. Zayd b. Jid'an [*marfū'*]).
al-Ṭabarī's *isnād* on the authority of Ibn 'Abbās is more sound.

*Ibn Kathīr (History):*
Ka'b al-Aḥbār
'Umar
al-'Abbās
'Alī
Ibn Mas'ūd
Masrūq
'Ikrima
Sa'īd b. Jubayr
Mujāhid
'Atā'
al-Sha'bī
Muqātil
'Ubayd b. 'Umayr
Abū Maysara
Zayd b. Aslam
'Abdallāh b. Shaqīq
al-Zuhrī
al-Qāsim
Ibn Abī Burka
Makḥūl
'Uthmān b. Ḥāḍir
al-Suddī
al-Ḥasan
Qatāda
Abū Hudhayl
Ibn Sābiṭ, who is Ikhtiyār b. Jarīr

*Mujīr al-Dīn:*
The People of the Book
'Alī
Ibn Mas'ūd
Ka'b
Muqātil
Qatāda
'Ikrima
al-Suddī

*Supporters of Ishmael*

*Ibn Qutayba:*
Mujāhid + Ibn 'Umar
Abū Hurayra

*al-Tabari (Commentary):*
Mujāhid + Ibn 'Umar
Ibn 'Abbās (6x)
al-Sha'bī + Ibn 'Abbās (3x)
Mujāhid + Ibn 'Abbās
Mujāhid
'Āmir
al-Sha'bī
Yūsuf b. Mihrān
al-Ḥasan (2x)
Ibn Isḥāq said he heard Muḥammad b. Ka'b al-Quraẓī say it often.

*al-Ṭabarī (History):*
Ibn 'Umar
Ibn 'Abbās (9x)
al-Sha'bī + Ibn 'Abbās
'Āmir
al-Sha'bī
Yūsuf b. Mihrān
Mujāhid
al-Ḥasan (2x)
Ibn Isḥāq said he heard Muḥammad b. Ka'b al-Quraẓī say it often.

*al-Qummī:*
Abū 'Abdallāh

*al-Tha'labī:*
'Abdallāh b. 'Umar
Abū al-Ṭufayl
'Āmir b. Wā'ila
Sa'īd b. al-Musayyib
al-Sha'bī
Yūsuf b. Mihrān
Mujāhid
al-Ḥasan al-Baṣrī
'Abdallāh b. 'Abbās
Ibn Isḥāq + Muḥammad b. Ka'b al-Quraẓī

*al-Zamzkhsharī:*
Ibn 'Abbās
Ibn 'Umar
Muḥammad b. Ka'b al-Quraẓī,
Other Followers

*al-Ṭabarsī:*
Ibn 'Abbās
Ibn 'Umar
Sa'īd b. al-Musayyib
al-Ḥasan
al-Sha'bī
Mujāhid
al-Rabī' b. Anīs
al-Kalbī
Muḥammad b. Ka'b al-Qurṭubī
Abū 'Abdallāh
Abū Ja'far

*al-Kisā'ī:*
Ibn 'Abbās
Mujāhid
al-Ḍaḥḥāk
The Prophet

*Ibn al-Athir:*
The following rely on Ibn 'Abbās saying that it was Ishmael:
Sa'īd b. Jubayr, Yūsuf b. Mihrān, al-Sha'bī, Mujāhid, 'Atā' b. Abī Rabāḥ.

*Ibn Kathir (Commentary):*
The following rely on Ibn 'Abbās saying that it was Ishmael:
Sa'īd b. Jubayr, 'Āmir al-Sha'bī, Yūsuf b. Mihrān, Mujāhid, 'Atā', "and others".
'Atā' b. Abī Rabāḥ. + Ibn 'Abbās
Mujāhid + Ibn 'Umar
Ibn Abī Najīḥ + Mujāhid
al-Ḥasan al-Baṣrī
Aḥmad b. Ḥanbal
The father of Ibn Abī Ḥātim
Ibn Abī Ḥātim said that the following said it was Ishmael:
'Alī, Ibn 'Umar, Abū Hurayra, Abū al-Ṭufayl, Sa'īd b. al-Musayyib, Sa'īd b. Jubayr, al-Ḥasan, Mujāhid, al-Sha'bī, Muḥammad b. Ka'b al-Quraẓī, Abū Ja'far Muḥammad b. 'Alī, Abū Ṣāliḥ.
al-Baghawī in his commentary said it was Ishmael, as did 'Abdallāh b. 'Umar, Sa'īd b. al-Musayyib, al-Suddī, al-Ḥasan al-Baṣrī, Mujāhid, al-Rabī' b. Anās, Muḥammad b. Ka'b al-Quraẓī, al-Kalbī + Ibn 'Abbās, al-Kalbī + 'Amr b. al-'Alā'.

*Ibn Kathir (History):*
Most sound authorities say it was Ishmael: The following were of the opinion that it was Ishmael on the authority of Ibn 'Abbās: Mujāhid, Sa'īd al-Sha'bī, Yūsuf b. Mihrān, 'Atā'.
al-Ṭabarī . . . Ibn 'Abbās
Aḥmad b. Ḥanbal
Father of Ibn Abī Ḥātim
Ibn Abī Ḥātim said that the following said it was Ishmael:
'Alī, Ibn 'Umar, Abū Hurayra, Abū al-Ṭufayl, Sa'īd b. al-Musayyib, Sa'id b. Jubayr, al-Ḥasan, Mujāhid, al-Sha'bī, Muḥammad b. Ka'b al-Quraẓī, Abū Ja'far Muḥammad b. 'Alī, Abū Ṣāliḥ.
al-Baghawī in his commentary said it was Ishmael, as did al-Rabī' b. Anās, al-Kalbī, and Abū 'Amr al-'Alā'.

*Mujīr al-Dīn:*
Ibn 'Abbās
Sa'īd b. al-Musayyib
al-Sha'bī
al-Ḥasan
Mujāhid

# OPINIONS OF THE TRADITIONISTS REGARDING WHO WAS THE INTENDED SACRIFICE[1] (LISTED ACCORDING TO THE TRADITIONISTS)

*Supporters of Isaac*

al-'Abbās b. 'Abd al-Muṭṭalib + the Prophet 3
al-'Abbās b. 'Abd al-Muṭṭalib 8
'Abdallāh b. Mas'ūd 2
'Abdallāh b. Shaqīq 2
'Abd al-Raḥmān b. Abī Sābiṭ 1
Abū Hudhayl 3
Abū Hurayra + Ka'b 3
Abū Mālik 1
Abū Maysara 3
'Alī b. Mas'ūd 1
Ḥusayn 1
Ibn Abī Burka 1
Ibn Abī al-Hudhayl 1
Ibn Mas'ūd 5
Ibn Sābiṭ 5
'Ikrima 7
al-Jabā'ī 1
Ka'b al-Aḥbar 10
Makḥūl 2
Masrūq 8
al-Qāsim 1
al-Qāsim b. Abī Barra 1
al-Qāsim b. Abī Yarza 1
Qatāda 7
'Ubayd b. 'Umayr 3
'Umar b. al-Khaṭṭāb 4
'Uthman b. Abī Ḥāḍir 1
'Uthman b. Ḥāḍir 1
al-Zuhrī 4
Total number of citations is 91

*Supporters of Ishmael*

'Āmir 2
'Āmir b. Wā'ila (see also 'Āmir)
'Abdallāh b. 'Umar 2 (see also "Ibn 'Umar")

Abū ʻAbdallāh 2 (al-ʻAbbās b. ʻAbd al-Muṭṭalib?)
Abu Jaʻfar 3 (including Abu Jaʻfar Muḥammad b. ʻAlī)
Abū Ṣāliḥ 2
Abū al-Ṭufayl 3
Aḥmad b. Ḥanbal 2
ʻAmru b. al-ʻŪlā' 1
al-Ḍaḥḥāk 1
Father of Ibn Abī Ḥātim 2
Ibn Isḥāq said that he heard Muḥammad b. Kaʻb al-Quraẓī say often that it was Ishmael 4
al-Kalbī 2
Muḥammad b. Kaʻb al-Qurṭubī 1
Mujāhid + Ibn ʻAbbās 2
al-Rabīʻ b. Anīs 3
Saʻīd b. al-Musayyib 6
al-Shaʻbī + Ibn ʻAbbās 5
Yūsuf b. Mihrān 6
Total number of citations is 49.

| *Supporters of both:* | *Isaac* | *Ishmael* |
|---|---|---|
| ʻAbdallāh | 1 | 1 |
| ʻAlī | 7 | 2 |
| ʻAṭā' | 4 | 4 |
| al-Ḥasan al-Baṣrī | 3 | 11 |
| Ibn ʻAbbās | 10 | 30 |
| Ibn ʻUmar | 1 | 10 |
| Mujāhid | 2 | 12 |
| Saʻīd b. Jubayr | 5 | 4 |
| al-Shaʻbī | 2 | 9 |
| al-Suddī | 5 | 1 |
| TOTALS: | 40 | 84 |
| GRAND TOTALS: | 131 | 133 |

# Notes

## INTRODUCTION

1. "Judeo-Christian" also tends to exclude what was eventually considered unorthodox or sectarian, but which remains firmly "Biblicist."

2. "The Forms of Folklore: Prose Narratives," in Alan Dundes (ed.), *Sacred Narrative: Readings in the Theory of Myth* (Berkeley: University of California Press, 1984), 5-29.

## CHAPTER 1

1. Classical Arabic genealogists agree with the basic thrust of the biblical anthropology, though this appears to have evolved sometime after the beginning of Islam. See Rene Dagorn, *La Geste d'Ismaël d'après l'onomastique et la tradition arabes* (Paris: Champion, 1981); Werner Caskel, *Ghamarat an-nasab ("The Abundance of Kinship"): The Genealogical Work of Hishām b. Muḥammad al-Kalbī* (Leiden: Brill, 1966); Carl Brockelmann, "Arabia" in EI1 (esp. the subheading, "Ethnology," Vol. 1, 372-74), and G. Rentz, "Djazīrat al-'Arab" in EI2 (esp. "Ethnography," Vol. 1, 543-47).

2. Cf. James A. Montgomery, *Arabia and the Bible* (New York: Ktav, 1934, reissued in 1969).

3. As in the biblical Joseph story (Gen. 37:27; 39:1). The (Babylonian) Talmud was redacted sometime around the year 600 C.E. See also, D.S. Margoliouth, *The Relations between Arabs and Israelites prior to the Rise of Islam* (London: Oxford University Press, 1924).

4. F.E. Peters, *Allah's Commonwealth: A History of Islam in the Near East* (New York: Simon & Schuster, 1973), 15; J. Spencer Trimingham, *Christianity Among the Arabs in Pre-Islamic Times* (London: Longman, 1979), 1-20; Michael Morony, *Iraq After the Muslim Conquest* (Princeton: Princeton University, 1984), 214-23.

5. See p. x for the meaning of this term.

6. Gordon Darnell Newby, *A History of the Jews of Arabia From Ancient Times to Their Eclipse Under Islam* (Columbia, S.C.: University of South Carolina Press, 1988), 14-23; Moshe Gil, "The Origin of the Jews of Yathrib," *Jerusalem Studies in Arabic and Islam* 4 (Jerusalem: Hebrew University, 1984), 203-23.

7. Trimingham, *Christianity*, 159-70, 248-311; Newby, *History*, 35-37.

8. Newby, *History*; Gil, "The Origin of the Jews of Yathrib," Ibid.; Trimingham, *Christianity*; Margoliouth, *Relations*; Delacy O'Leary, *Arabia Before Muhammad* (London: Kegan Paul, 1927). Indeed, both Jewish and Christian missionaries are said to have been active there (Newby, *History*, 38).

9. Newby, *History*, 33-77, and especially 40, 52.

10. Trimingham, 247-48.

11. Julian Obermann, "Islamic Origins: A Study in Background and Foundation," in N.A. Faris, *The Arab Heritage* (New York: Russell and Russell, 1963), 62; cf. Gil, "The Origin of the Jews of Yathrib," 205-6, 219. Some Jews may have known and even spoken Aramaic in their communities, but more likely, their language was a Jewish dialect of the local Arabic (Newby, "Observations About an Early Judaeo-Arabic," *Jewish Quarterly Review* 61 (1970), 212-21.

12. Newby, *History*, 49-53; Gil, "The Origin . . . ," 210ff; Trimingham, 249-50.

13. Fred M. Donner, *The Early Islamic Conquests* (Princeton: Princeton U., 1981), 25-26, 31-32; Newby, *History*, 51-55, 146 note 5.

14. Donner, *Conquests*, 96; Michel Hayek, *Le Mystere d'Ismael* (Paris: Mame, 1964), 105-6.

15. Hamilton A.R. Gibb, "Pre-Islamic Monotheism in Arabia," *Harvard Theological Review* 55 (1962), 271.

16. Trimmingham, 68, Newby, *History*, 125 note 5.

17. Newby, *History*, 57-64; David Halperin and Gordon Newby, "Two Castrated Bulls: A Study in the Haggadah of Ka'b al-Ahbar," *J.A.O.S.* 102 (1982), 631-38.

18. EI1 (new edition) VI, 745-6; VIII, 997, 1121-1122, 1194; Hamilton A.R. Gibb, "Pre-Islamic Monotheism in Arabia," *Harvard Theological Review* 55 (1962), 269-80; M.J. Kister, "Labbayka, Allāhumma, Labbayka . . . : On a Monotheistic Aspect of a Jāhiliyya Practice," *Jerusalem Studies in Arabic and Islam* II (1980), Jerusalem: Hebrew University, 33-57; Trimmingham, 249, 261-67.

19. Qur'ān 6:1, 137; 7:190-198; 8:35; 9:37; 37:149-58; 9:15-24; 53:19-23; etc.

20. The Qur'ān often refers to biblical personalities in groups as if its audience were quite familiar with them and their roles (3:84; 4:163; 6:84-90; etc.). Cf. Gibb, "Pre-Islamic Monotheism," 273.

21. One of the few sources is Hishām b. Muḥammad Abū al-Mundhir Ibn al-Kalbī, whose only extant works are his *Kitāb al-aṣnām* (Cairo, 1912; and translated into English by N.A. Faris, Princeton, 1952) and *Jamharat al-Nasab* (Leiden: Brill, 1966). For a brief overview of the historiographical controversy, see Fred Donner's introduction to A.A. Duri, *The Rise of Historical Writing Among the Arabs* (Princeton: Princeton University, 1960), vii-xvii.

22. Georgio Levi Della Vida, "Pre-Islamic Arabia," In N.A. Faris (ed.), *The Arab Heritage* (New York: Russell and Russell, 1963), 49.

23. Ibid., p. 53. See Toufic Fahd, *Le Panthéon de l'Arabie centrale à la veille De L'Hégire* (Paris: Paul Geuthner, 1968); A.F.L. Beeston, "The Religions of Pre-Islamic Yemen," and "Judaism and Christianity in Pre-Islamic Yemen," in Joseph Chelhod ed. *L'Arabie du Sud* Vol. I (Le Peuple yéménite et ses racines) (Paris, 1984), 259-69, 271-78.

24. Newby, *History*, 49-53.

25. Fazlur Rahman, "Review Essay," in Richard C. Martin (ed.), *Approaches to Islam in Religious Studies* (Tucson: University of Arizona, 1985), 201.

26. Paret, "Qur'ān as Literature," in *Arabic Literature to the End of the Umayyad Period*, Edited by A.F.L. Beeston et al., (Cambridge: Cambridge University Press, 1983), 209.

27. Alfred Guillaume, *The Life of Muhammad: A Translation of Ibn Ishaq's Sirat Rasul Allah* (Oxford: Oxford University, 1955), 87. See also Gibb, "Pre-Islamic Monotheism . . . ", 271.

28. See Chapter 2, below.

29. See, for example, Sidney H. Griffith, "The Prophet Muhammad, His Scripture and His Message According to the Christian Apologies in Arabic and Syriac from the First Abbasid Century," in *La Vie Du Prophète Mahomet* (*Colloque de Strasbourg*, 1980), Paris: Presses Universitaires, 1983, 99-146 and esp. 135-38.

30. See Qur'ān 2:175, 179; 4:46, etc., and Franz Buhl, *"Taḥrīf"* in EI1 (New Edition), 7:618-19.

31. W. Ahrends, *Muhammad als Religionsstifter* (Leipzig, 1935); Richard Bell, *The Origins of Islam in its Christian Environment* (London, 1926); Abraham Geiger, *Judaism and Islam* (Madras, 1898, repr.: New York: Ktav, 1970) (originally published as *Was hat Mohammed aus dem Judenthume aufgenommen* [Bonn, 1833]); Charles C. Torrey, *The Jewish Foundation of Islam* (New York: Bloch, 1933).

32. See the following chapter.

33. See previous note.

34. M.J. Kister, "*Ḥaddithū 'an banī isrā'īla wa-lā ḥaraja*: A Study of an early tradition," *Israel Oriental Studies* II (Tel Aviv: Tel Aviv University, 1972) reprint ed. M.J. Kister, *Studies in Jāhiliyya and Early Islam* (London, 1980), 215-39.

35. Ibid., 218-22.

36. See John Wansbrough, *Qur'ānic Studies* (Oxford: Oxford University Press, 1977), 20; Rudi Paret, "The Qur'ān as Literature," 209.

37. Nabia Abbott, *Studies in Arabic Literary Papyri II: Qur'ānic Commentary and Tradition* (Chicago: University of Chicago, 1967), 5-32.

38. The first of the two death dates provided is according to the Islamic calendar (A.H. = *Anno Hegirae*) and the second according to the Western system (C.E. = Common Era).

39. Nabia Abbott, *Studies in Arabic Literary Papyri I: Historical Texts* (Chicago: University of Chicago, 1957), 47, and *Studies II*, 9. Religious influence was apparently not restricted to the adoption of legends and stories. Specific religious practices may also have been learned through contacts with Jews and Christians (M.J. Kister, "On the Jews of Arabia: Some Notes" (Hebrew), in *Tarbiz* 48 (1979), 231-47.

40. W.R. Taylor, "Al-Bukhari and the Aggadah," *Moslem World* 33 (1943), 191-97.

41. Richard Bulliet, *Conversion to Islam in the Medieval Period* (Cambridge, MA: Harvard University, 1979), 16-32.

42. Marshall G.S. Hodgson, *The Venture of Islam*, Vol. I: "The Classical Age of Islam" (Chicago: University of Chicago, 1974), 315-26. The development and religious institutionalization of *sharī'a* was also affected by the interests of the religious leadership to counter caliphal power, which indeed began to weaken at about this time (Bulliet, *Conversion*, 128-29, 138).

43. See Moshe Zucker, "The Problem of 'iṣma—Prophetic Immunity to Sin and Error in Islamic and Jewish Literatures" (Hebrew), *Tarbiz* 35 (1966), 149-173; Harris Berkeland, *The Lord Guideth: Studies on Primitive Islam* (Oslo: I Kommisjon Hos H. Aschehoug & Co., 1956), 40.

44. This was a long process, beginning in the mid-eighth century and continuing through the ninth.

45. Hodgson, *Venture I*, 317.

## CHAPTER 2

1. From the Arabic root *f-s-r*, to explain or reveal. A second term, *ta'wīl* was used as a synonym for *tafsīr* during the earliest Islamic period, but eventually became associated with esoteric or symbolic interpretation of the Qur'an. The nuances of each term have undergone changes during various periods of Islamic history. The classic

Western study of qur'ānic exegesis is Ignaz Goldziher's *Die Richtungen Der Islamischen Koranauslegung* (1920; reprint ed., Leiden: E.J. Brill, 1970). More recent works include Nabia Abbott's *Studies in Arabic Litereary Papyri II: Qur'ānic Commentary* (Chicago: University of Chicago Press, 1967); M.O.A. Abdul, "The Historical Development of Tafsīr," *Islamic Culture* 50 (1976), 141-53; Rashid Ahmad (Jullandri), "Qur'ānic Exegesis and Classical Tafsīr," *Islamic Quarterly* 12 (1968), 71-119; Ilse Lichtenstadter, "Quran and Quran Exegesis," *Humaniora Islamica* II (1974), 3-28; Harris Birkeland, *Old Muslim Opposition Against Interpretation Of The Koran* (Oslo: I Kommisjon Hos Jacob Dybwad, 1955); J.J.G. Jansen, *The Interpretation of the Koran in Modern Egypt* (Leiden: E.J. Brill, 1980); Andrew Rippin, "The Exegetical Genre *Asbāb al-Nuzūl*: A Bibliographical and Terminological Survey," *BSOAS* 48 (1985), 1-15; Mujāhid Muḥammad al-Ṣawwāf, "Early Tafsīr—A Survey of Qur'ānic Commentary up to 150 A.H.," Aḥmad and Anṣārī (eds.), *Islamic Perspectives: Studies in Honor of Mawlānā Sayyid Abdul A'la Mawdūdī* (Saudi Arabia, 1979), 135-145; John Wansbrough, "*Majāz al-Qur'ān*: Periphrastic Exegesis," *BSOAS* 33 (1970), 247-256; Andrew Rippin, *Approaches to the History of the Interpretation of the Qur'an* (New York: Oxford University Press, 1988).

2. See J. Robson, "Ḥadīth," EI2 3:23-28; Alfred Guillaume, *The Traditions of Islam: An Introduction to the Study of the Hadith Literature* (Lahore: Universal, 1977); Mohammad Mustafa Azmi, *Studies in Early Ḥadīth Literature* (Indianapolis: American Trust, 1977).

3. A truly sound *ḥadīth* report has come to mean only those whose ultimate source of authority is the Prophet Muḥammad, though most reports in the vast tradition literature of Islam cannot be traced back to him through an acceptable chain of authorities. Many cannot be traced back to him at all (See Azmi, *Studies*, 302; G.H.A Juynboll, "On the Origins of Arabic Prose: Reflections on Authenticity," in Juynboll [ed.] *Studies on the First Century of Islamic Society* [Carbondale: S. Illinois University, 1982], 161-75).

4. The hagiographic "Tales of the Prophets" collections of popular literature are the least exacting on this issue and are the least authoritative.

5. William M. Brinner, "An Islamic Decalogue," in *Studies in Islamic and Judaic Traditions*, ed. W.M. Brinner and S.D. Ricks (Atlanta: Scholars Press, 1986), 82 note 3. *Isrā'īliyyāt* is a plural noun. The singular form is *isrā'īliyya*. The term tends to refer to legends set in what is assumed to be biblical history, the period of the Israelites, as opposed to Jewish tales set in later contexts (Arabic distinguishes between "Israelite" and "Jew" in the same way as does English). On Israelite Tales, see Goldziher, "Melanges Judeo-Arabes IX: *Isrā'īliyyāt*," *REJ* 44 (1902), 63-66; S.D. Goitein, "*Isrā'īliyyāt*," *Tarbiz* 6 (1934-5), 89-101, and 510-522; G. Vajda, "*Isrā'īliyyāt*" in EI2 4:211-212; and Gordon D. Newby, "Tafsīr Isrā'īlīyāt," *JAR* Thematic Issue 47 (December 1979), 685-697.

6. Abbott, *Studies* II, 7-10.

7. Newby, 686; Vajda, 212. The term does not appear in works prior to this period and may have been used only as a disqualifying label.

8. Ismā'īl b. 'Umar Ibn Kathīr, *Qiṣaṣ al-anbiyā'* (Beirut: 1402/1982), 232-233 (henceforth referred to as *History* because it is actually the first two volumes of his standard history, *Al-bidāya wal-nihāya*).

9. Today, some modern Islamic exegetes dismiss any kind of narrative exegesis as Israelite Tales or primitive and fantastic folk explanations that run counter to a modern sensibility (H.A.R. Gibb, *Modern Trends in Islam* [Chicago: University of Chicago Press, 1947], 73; and J. Jansen, *The Interpretation of the Koran in Modern Egypt* [Leiden, E.J. Brill, 1970], 27 note 34). This modern definition is influenced less by a suspicion of non-Islamic material than by a modernist apologetic for the imaginative but fantastic narrative material employed in traditional Islamic narrative exegesis.

10. Qur'ān 3:67.

11. As certain individuals came to be associated with transmitting Israelite Tales, all traditions given on their authority were considered suspect. Such important early figures as Ka'b al-Aḥbār and Wahb b. Munabbih were later considered unacceptable authorities largely for this reason.

12. A major argument against the Israelite Tales is that they consist of traditions without a "sound" record of authentication *(isnād)*. But by definition, any tradition attributed to the "People of the Book" or any traditionists accused of transmitting Israelite Tales came to be considered suspect at best. This circular argument clearly developed after the first few generations of Islam when the traditions later to be considered Israelite Tales were freely accepted.

13. Cf. Marshall G.S. Hodgson, "Two Pre-Modern Muslim Historians: Pitfalls and Opportunities in Presenting Them to Moderns", in John Nef (ed.), *Towards World Community* (The Hague: World Academy of Art and Science #5, 1968), 56.

14. Obermann, "Islamic Origins," 65-67 (Cf. Azmi, 1-5).

15. Michael Zwettler, *The Oral Tradition of Classical Arabic Poetry: Its Character and Implications* (Columbus: Ohio State University Press, 1978); J. Monroe, "Oral Composition in Pre-Islamic Poetry," *Journal of Arabic Literature* 3 (1972), 1-52, and A.K. Julius Germanus, "Legacy of Ancient Arabia," *Islamic Culture* 37 (1963), 261-69.

16. Hirschberg, "Stories of the Torah," 95.

17. The Qur'ān also provides legends that are most likely from native Arab sources, including those of the 'Ād (Q.7:65ff., 9:70, 11:50ff., 14:9, 22:42, 25:38, 26:123ff.), the Thamūd (Q.7:73, 9:70, 11:61, 14:9, 17:59, 27:45ff., 51:43ff.), etc., though biblical motifs clearly predominate.

18. Such as battles and raids, personal courage and memories of older days, peculiarly Arab concerns such as the ideal of manhood (*murū'a* or *murūwa*), etc. (Trimingham, 246-48). Cf. M.M. Bravmann, *The Spiritual Background of Early Islam* (Leiden: E.J. Brill, 1972); Nabia Abbott, *Studies in Arabic Literary Papyri* 2, 5.

19. Albert Lord, *Singer of Tales* (Cambridge: Harvard University Press, 1960), 130.

20. Lord, *Singer of Tales* (22 and throughout). On the differences between oral and literary cultures, see Walter Ong, *Orality and Literacy* (London: Methuen, 1982).

21. Dov Noy, "The Jewish Versions of the 'Animal Languages' Folktale (AT670): A Typological-Structural Study" in *Scripta Hierosolymitana* 22 (1971), ed. Joseph Heinemann and Dov Noy (Jerusalem: Hebrew University), 171-208.

22. Robert Georges, "Toward an Understanding of Storytelling Events," *Journal of American Folklore* 82 (1969), 313-329; Barbara Herrnstein Smith, "Narrative Versions, Narrative Theories" In W.J.T. Mitchell (ed.), *On Narrative* (Chicago: U. of Chicago, 1980), 209-232.

23. Noy, "The Jewish Versions of the 'Animal Languages' Folktale (AT670) . . . ," 173.

24. See pp. 63-64 below.

25. Hayek, *Le Mystère d'Ismaël* (Paris: Mame, 1964), 105-6.

26. Ibid., 108.

27. Lord, *Singer of Tales*, 137; Ong, *Orality and Literacy*, 42 and Ch. 4: "Writing restructures consciousness" (78-116).

28. Obermann, "Islamic Origins," 66. The religious and political leadership may have subscribed to a literate culture, but the majority of the common people remained a part of oral culture. In Macedonia, for example, despite the fact that it was the place in which the Cyrillic alphabet was invented, oral culture continued to thrive there to such an extent that it became the place in which the most famous researches in oral culture were conducted during this century (Lord, 134ff.).

29. Ignaz Goldziher, *Richtungen*; Joseph Schacht, *The Origins of Muhammadan Jurisprudence.* (Oxford: Oxford University Press, 1950); G.H.A Juynboll, *Muslim tradition: Studies in chronology, provenance and authorship of early hadith* (Cambridge: Cambridge University Press, 1983).

30. The same phenomenon applies in Judaism, where much more care is applied to reconciling different versions of legal materials *(halakha)* than to legendary lore *(aggadah)*.

31. Muḥammad b. Jarīr al-Ṭabarī, *Jāmi' al-bayān 'an ta'wīl āya al-Qur'ān* (Beirut: Dār al-Fikr, 1405/1984), henceforth designated as *Commentary*.

32. Idem. *Ta'rīkh al-rusul wal-mulūk*, ed. by M.J. Goeje and entitled "*Annales*" (Leiden: E.J. Brill, 1964), henceforth designated as *History*.

33. Jonathan Culler, "Presupposition and Intertextuality," *MLN* 91 (1976), 1380-96.

34. Thais E. Morgan, "Is There an Intertext in this Text? Literary and Interdisciplinary Approaches to Intertextuality," *American Journal of Semiotics* 3 (1985), 1-40.

35. Jonothan Culler, ibid.

36. Because this study is limited to the biblical characters of Abraham and Ishmael in Islamic exegetical literature, the probability of material deriving from Persian, Indian, or other religious traditions is remote. See William Brinner's foreword to his translation of volume 2 of Tabari's History, *The History of al-Ṭabarī vol. II: Prophets and Patriarchs* (Albany: State University of New York Press, 1987), vi-vii, and p. 1 note 1.

37. Because of the paucity of pre-Islamic literary materials, this criterion is difficult to measure. An Arab motif found in our sources might represent the *only* surviving example of a pre-Islamic motif, therefore rendering the possibility of comparing it with parallel pre-Islamic sources difficult.

38. The exegetes and their works are listed chronologically in Appendix I.

39. Like Jewish and Christian exegesis, Islamic exegesis cannot be reduced to a single type or approach. The variety of approaches exhibited by the sources of this study nevertheless represents the most basic Islamic views regarding the Abraham-Ishmael story. Some popular works such as the *Tafsīr Jalālayn* or that of al-Baydawī were not included, the former because it is a condensed reworking of fuller comments and traditions found in other sources. Al-Baydawī's work, which is largely a reworking of al-Zamakhsharī's *al-kashshāf*, was excluded in favor of the latter. Many other works, of course, could have been represented in the sample.

## PART TWO INTRODUCTION

1. These traditions can be found in Ibn Sa'd, 46ff.; al-Ya'qūbī, 21-22; al-Ṭabarī, *History*, 252-59; al-Mas'ūdī, 56-57; al-Tha'labī, 72-78; al-Kisā'ī, 128-39; Ibn al-Athīr, 94-100; Ibn Kathīr, *History*, 191-212; Mujīr al-Dīn, 23-34; and in the exegetical works on Qur'ān 2:124, 6:75-82, 19:41-50, 37:83-99, etc. Similar stories can be found in Jewish and Christian legends *(aggadah)* in Ginzberg, *Legends of the Jews* (Philadelphia: Jewish Publication Society, 1968), 186-203; and Budge, *The Book of the Cave of Treasures* (London: Religious Tract Society, 1927), 145-47.

2. *Hijra* in Arabic. The same word refers to the emigration of the Prophet Muḥammad from his idolatrous people in Mecca to Medina (Hegira in English). The prophetic paradigm linking Muḥammad to the earlier biblical prophets is a common phenomenon in the Qur'ān.

3. *Al-Sha'm* (generally written *al-Shām*), the most common medieval Arabic reference for the area roughly corresponsing to today's Syria, Lebanon, Israel, and Jordan. Because it is the term utilized by all the sources for what is generally refered to in Western circles as the Holy Land, we reproduce it in English when referring to the

same area. This area is occasionally refered to as the Holy Land *(Al-arḍ al-muqaddasa)* in the Arabic sources (Cf. Qur'ān 5:22f: REMEMBER MOSES SAID TO HIS PEOPLE . . . O MY PEOPLE, ENTER THE HOLY LAND (*AL-ARḌ AL-MUQADDASA*) WHICH GOD HAS ASSIGNED TO YOU . . .).

4. The names Sodom and Gemorrah are not mentioned in the Arabic stories except in glosses relating to Biblicist lore.

## CHAPTER 3

1. The setting in Syria for the narratives making up the Syrian Prologue, which is not specified in the Qur'ān, reflects a natural inclination in Islam to follow the biblical story line. More than that, however, the powerful precedence of Judaism and Christianity, with their connection to the "Holy Land," almost requred that Islam find its own connection there as well. Early Muslims may have assumed that this association would support the legitimacy of Islam in the eyes of Judaism and Christianity. The connection is also made through the "Night Journey" of Muḥammad (see Ibn Isḥāq, *Sīra*, 263-71 [181-87 in Guillaume's translation], and al-Ṭabarī and other exegetes on Qur'ān 17:1).

2. An ancient town in Iraq on a canal joining the Tigris and the Euphrates rivers, and the place of Abraham's birth according to Islamic Abraham legends (EI2 5:550). The Babylonian Talmud (*Baba Metzi'a* 91a) also associates Kūthā with Abraham's birthplace of "Ur of the Chaldees" in Genesis 11:28, 31. See also PRE, 61a.

3. As in Genesis 11:31.

4. This parallels Genesis 12:10-20. The Tyrant legend will be discussed in the following chapter.

5. Exegetes' names in parantheses (i.e., [al-Qummī]) refer to the opinions of the exegetes themselves rather than a citation of an authority from a report.

6. Al-Ya'qūbī also refers to it as the Holy Land and Palestine.

7. Haran is spelled in a variety of ways among the texts.

8. The exact location is then given as "Beersheba in Palestine."

9. Syria is not specified at this point in the narrative though it continues with the assumption eventually spelled out that Abraham was in Syria.

10. The Qur'ān verse is cited as support.

11. Ibn Kathīr defines this as meaning an area around Jerusalem *(bilād tayman ya'nī 'arḍ bayt al-maqdis wamā wālāha)*.

12. Or, he says, Baalbek *(Ba'labakka)* under Egyptian hegemony.

13. Some will simply have "So-and-so says . . .".

14. Cf. Genesis 12:5.

15. Ibn Kathīr, *History*, 213.

16. It cannot be demonstrated definitively with only one rendition that this is part of an Ibn 'Abbās school of traditions. Nevertheless, it is wholly consistent with the Ibn 'Abbās traditions examined below in The Meccan Sequence.

17. This is given by Ibn Qutayba (p. 31) on the authority of Wahb b. Munabbih. According to this legend, Sarah is the daughter of Haran, the brother of Abraham and Nahor. Milkah and Sarah are sisters. Compare with Genesis 11:26ff.:

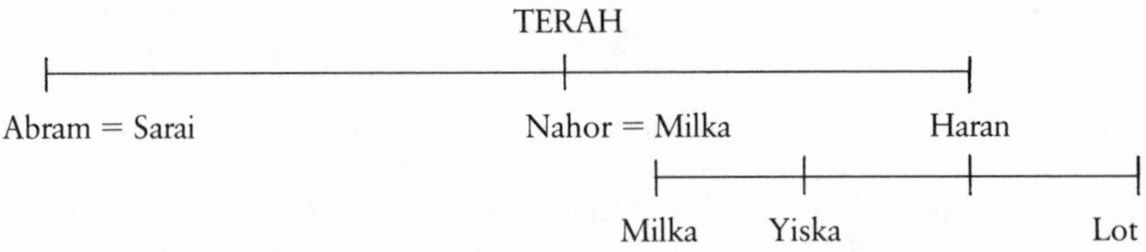


The other relevant biblical passages are Genesis 20:12: "She is my sister; she is the daughter of my father but not my mother" referring to Sarah in Abraham's explanation to Abimelekh. In I Chron. 23:9 a different Haran is a Levite and one of Shi'i's 3 sons (Shlomit, Hazi'el, and Haran) from the clan of Gershon.

18. *History*, 214.

19. Reuben Levy, *The Social Structure of Islam* (Cambridge: Cambridge University Press, 1969), 102f.; Safia Mohsen, "Aspects of the Legal Status of Women Among Awlad 'Ali", in Louise Sweet (Ed.), *Peoples and Cultures of the Middle East* Vol. 1, (New York, 1970), 231.

20. According to this view, which became widespread by the early ninth century but never universally accepted, the prophets were protected by God or innately immune to committing sin (E. Tyan, "'Iṣma" in *EI2*, 4, 182). For a comparative analysis between Judaism and Islam, see Moshe Zucker, "The problem of 'iṣma—prophetic immunity to sin and error in Islamic and Jewish literatures" (Hebrew), in *Tarbiz* 35 (1966), 149-173.

21. Milkah and Sarah are given as sisters.

22. The spelling of the name varies.

23. According to both renditions of Ibn Isḥāq, both Abraham's paternal uncle and his brother are named Haran.

24. The Palestinian Targum (TJ1) on Genesis 11:29 has: "And Abram and Nahor took wives. The name of the wife of Abram is Sarai and the name of the wife of Nahor is Milkah, the daughter of Haran, the father of Milkah and Yiskah who is Sarai *(va'avoi d'yiskah hi sarai)*. The Babylonian Talmud (*Megillah* 14a) provides an explanation: "R. Isaac said: Yiskah is Sarah. Why was she called Yiskah? Because she *saw* [*sakhtah* has

the same Hebrew root as Yiskah] by means of the holy spirit, as it is written: 'In all that Sarah says to you, hearken to her voice' (Genesis 21:12). Another explanation: because everyone *sees (sokhin)* her beauty" (cf. *Sanhedrin* 69b).

25. The "Oral and Written Torahs" (*Torah she-b'al peh* and *torah she-bikhtav*), the full compendium of Jewish law and lore including the Bible, Talmud, Midrash, etc.

26. Arthur Jeffery, *The Foreign Vocabulary of the Qur'ān* (Baroda: Oriental Institute, 1938), 95-96, but he notes that Hirschfeld considers the Qur'ānic *Tawrā* to include the Oral Law as well as written Scripture.

27. This understanding is indeed mathematically more plausible than the rabbinic one, for which Haran would have had to conceive his first child at age six according to the biblical chronology (Cf. *Bereshit Rabbah* 45:1).

28. They provide little additional information.

29. Q.6:75ff., 37:83ff., etc.

30. Q.11:69ff., 15:51ff., 51:24ff.

31. Q.2:125ff., 22:26ff., etc.

## CHAPTER 4

1. 'Abdallāh or 'Abd al-Raḥmān Abū Hurayra al-Dawsī al-Yamānī (d.58/678), a companion of the Prophet and noted for the great number of traditions given in his name, though he became a Muslim only four years before the death of Muḥammad. He is regarded with great respect among Muslim traditionists, but the authenticity of his traditions is regarded with scepticism by modern critical scholarship (J. Robson in EI2 1:129; Cf. Al-Dhahābī, *Tadhkirat al-ḥuffāẓ* 1:32-35).

Sixteen of the twenty-eight Tyrant traditions are attributed to Abū Hurayra. Numerical relationships such as this will henceforth be inserted in the body of the text in parentheses (16/28).

2. Ibn Sa'd, 49-50; Ibn Ḥanbal, 2:403; al-Bukhārī, 3:230-32, 4:368-69; al-Ṭabarī, *History*, 268-69; Ibn Kathīr, *History*, 214-15, 215-16, 216-17. The eight other reports attributed to Abū Hurayra are not full narratives.

3. "AND HE SAID: 'I AM SICK!' "

4. "NO! THE BIGGEST ONE DID IT!" Both this and the previous case concern Abraham's attempt to prove to his people that belief in idols is spurious. In the fuller narrative exegesis of this motif, it is explained that these two lies were done "on behalf of God"—i.e., for the cause of monotheism. Note the admission of sinfulness on the part of Abraham in light of the doctrine of the infallibility of prophets discussed in the previous chapter.

5. Abraham's third lie has no Qur'ānic proof text and is taken entirely from the tradition literature. Seven of the eight "Abū Hurayra" traditions include this motif (7/8).

6. Blank lines appearing in the paradigmatic sketches denote a motif not found in the version at hand, but appearing in another version. The reader will note that motif numbers 2 and 4, which do not appear here, are found in Version 2 (pp. 33-34 below).

7. Ibn Kathīr (*History,* 218) defines this as "what is the report?".

8. The pre-Islamic Lakhmid kings were known as the *Banū mā' al-samā'* or the "people of the water of heaven," perhaps because of the alleged purity or nobility of their descent (the water of the Zamzam well in Mecca is also occasionally referred to as "water of heaven"). The term is also used as a name for Arabs in general, and Abū Hurayra is referring here to this usage.

9. This is the recurring wife/sister legend found in Genesis 12:10-20; 20:1-18; and 26:6-16. See John Van Seters, *Abraham in History and Tradition* (New Haven: Yale University Press, 1975), 167-91; Robert Polzin, " 'The Ancestress of Israel in Danger' in Danger," *Semeia* 3 (1975), 81-97; David Petersen, "A Thrice-Told Tale: Genre, Theme, and Motif," *Biblical Research* 18 (1973), 30-43.

10. Ginzberg, *Legends* 1:221-25, 258-61, and 5:220-22, 243-44.

11. The Palestinian Targum and *Bereshit Rabbah* (BR) include motifs that are woven together in later Midrash to form a full narrative account (see BR 40:5, 41:2, 45:1; Targum Jonathan [TJ1] on Genesis 12:11 and 16:1, PRE Chpt. 25 [ 61a-62a] and *Sefer HaYashar,* 41-2). BR is generally assumed to have been compiled in the early fifth century C. E. or earlier (EJ 7:399-400; Hermann Strack, *Introduction to the Talmud and Midrash* [Philadelphia: Jewish Publication Society, 1931] 218). The Palestinian Targums (TJ1 and TJ2) are homiletical renderings of the Bible text in Aramaic. There is still a great deal of controversy regarding their dating, but acknowledging some later insertions, virtually all scholars in the field date them as being earlier than the late sixth century and definitely pre-Islamic. P. Kahle considers much of the Palestinian Targum to be pre-Christian (*The Cairo Geniza* [London, 1947 & repr. Oxford, 1959]). For a full discussion of the dating of the Palestinian Targums, see Anthony D. York, "The Dating of Targumic Literature," in Journal for the Study of Judaism 5 (1974), 49-62; and Martin McNamara, *The New Testament and the Palestinian Targum to the Pentateuch.* (Rome: Biblical Institute, 1978), pp. 5-66.

12. Note the qur'ānic parallel in Sūra 9:11: "[THEY ARE] YOUR BROTHERS IN RELIGION" *(fa-ikhwānukum fī al-dīn).*

13. Rene Dagorn, *La Geste d' Ismaël d'apres l'onomastique et la tradition arabes* (Paris: Champion, 1981), and see p. 179 note 1 above.

14. *History,* 269-70 and *Commentary,* 23:71.

15. p. 101.

16. Ibn Sa'd 1:48-9; al-Tha'labī 79-80.

17. Tabarī, *History*, 267-8.

18. Al-Kisā'ī 142.

19. Ibn Kathīr, *History*, 217f.

20. Al-Qummī 1:332-3; Ibn al-Athīr 100-101; Mujīr al-Dīn 34.

21. P. 32.

22. See p. 190 note 7 above.

23. 1:332f.

24. Also *Sefer HaYashar*, 24, *Tanhūma* (Buber) *Lekh lekha* 8(336), etc.

25. Biblical Gerar is a wadi about 12 miles northwest of Beersheba, located in a Philistine area that came within the territory of the tribe of Judah.

26. *Ṣādūq*. King Zadoq does not appear in the Pentateuch. The king of Gerar in Genesis 1:18 is Abimelekh. But see II Samuel 15:27, where Zadoq is the priest under King David and is whence the term Sadducees *(Tzeduqim)* is derived. In I Chronicles 18:16, Zadoq and Abimelekh are noted together as priests under the rule of King David. A likely cause for the confusion between Zadok and Abimelekh is the narrative in Genesis 14:18 where king Melki-Zedeq brings Abraham gifts. Al-Kisā'ī's introduction of King Zadok, *wakāna bihā malik yuqālu lahu sādūq*, is a likely misunderstanding of the Hebrew name Melkizedeq, where the Hebrew meaning, "My King is Righteousness (or King of Righteousness)," was taken into Arabic simply as "King Ṣādūq."

27. The editor notes on p. 32 that three manuscripts have *Ṣādūq*. The orthographic error of confusing a *qāf* with a *fā'* is common.

28. Both were Jewish converts to Islam and were accused of taking too freely from the Israelite Tales. See I. Wolfensohn, *Ka'b al-Aḥbār and seine Stellung in Hadit und in der islamischen Legendenliteratur* (Frankfurt a/M thesis) Gelnhausen, 1933; and R. G. Khoury, *Wahb b. Munabbih* (Wiesbaden, 1972), especially 203-317.

29. This may provide some explanation for the popularity of the rendition attributed to him.

30. It is quite possible that it did not, considering the massive number of traditions attributed to him. Many are considered spurious by scholars of Ḥadīth. But even if Abū Hurayra was not the source of the Islamic version we have before us, the version is indeed a single and coherent rendition that appears and reappears in the sources for centuries. For our purposes, it makes little difference whether or not we can prove that he is the earliest Islamic source.

31. He is known to have had extensive knowledge of the Torah (Abbott 2:9).

32. Rene Dagorn, *La Geste d'Ismaël* (Paris, 1981) Ch. 1 and throughout, but especially p. 377, strongly suggests that the genealogical connection between Ishmael and the Northern Arabs did not exist before the beginning of Islam.

33. The two comments attributed to Abū Hurayra frame the legend and do not alter its basic content.

34. T. Glick, Islamic and Christian Spain in the Early Middle Ages (Princeton, 1979), p. 285.

35. At least one Christian Syriac rendition is attributed to Ephrem and more may exist as well (Ginzberg 5:221 n. 74).

36. Q.3:67.

37. The origin of Hagar.

## CHAPTER 5

1. *Midrash Rabbah meforash perush mada'i ḥadash . . . me'et Moshe Arye Mirkin* (Tel Aviv: Yavneh, 1980), 2:162-163.

2. With the exception of some Shi'ite works which assign a special significance to the birth of all prophets. Ishmael, in this case, does not appear to be singled out.

3. See Chapter 4.

4. With virtually no exception, the Islamic histories and folk literature collections include no biblical material between the Tyrant story (Genesis 12:10-20) and the story of Sarah giving Hagar to Abraham (Genesis 16:1ff). Al-Ya'qūbī refers briefly to the battle between the kings of Genesis 14 (pp. 22-23), and some accounts mention simply that Lot settled in a different place than Abraham, but no details are given regarding either of these narratives. There is, of course, no logical reason for Arab or Islamic tales to include the enigmatic chapter of Genesis 15. The Islamic sequence therefore places the story of Hagar and Ishmael immediately after the Tyrant story.

5. Chapter 3 above.

6. This is the brief tradition given by al-Ṭabarī in his *History* (p. 270) on the authority of Ibn Isḥāq and given by al-Tha'labī (p. 80) without a record of authentication. A slightly different rendition is given by Ibn al-Athīr (p. 102). The translated texts are provided below.

7. Pp. 48-9.

8. *'an ghayri wāḥidin min ahli al-'ilm.*

9. The Hebrew name is *Yishma''el.*

10. And of course, the biblical story of 12:10-20 does not even mention Hagar, let alone imply that she was given to Sarah as a maidservant by Pharaoh. This element only appears in the exegetical accounts.

11. Pp. 32-3.

12. The editor of our edition of *al-Maʿārif* provides variant readings from manuscripts *ba', tā'*, and *lām* that have "we will become strengthened" rather than "consoled."

13. Pp. 22-3.

14. Compare Genesis 15:2-3.

15. Compare Genesis 15:5.

16. Compare Genesis 16:10.

17. See Rashi on Genesis 15:5, but also Ibn Ezra and Nachmanides, who raise the question as to how specific the text is regarding which son is intended.

18. *History*, p. 270.

19. 1:57.

20. Al-Thaʿlabī p. 80.

21. References in Shiʿite sources to al-Ṣādiq refer invariably to Abū ʿAbdallāh Jaʿfar al-Ṣādiq (d. 765 C.E.), the sixth Imam revered by Shiʿite Islam (Haim Schwarzbaum, *Biblical and Extra-Biblical Legends in Islamic Folk-Literature* [Walldorf-Hessen: Verlag fur Orientkunde Dr. H. Vorndran, 1982], 25).

22. 1:469.

23. P. 142.

24. *Nūr nabīyyina muḥammad.* This is most likely a reference to the Shi'ite concept of the *nūr muḥammadiyya*, a prophetic spiritual essence that was passed from generation to generation until it reached Muḥammad and, by implication, continued to be passed down to the Shiʿite Imams. See Uri Rubin, "Prophets and Progenitors in the Early Shiʿa Tradition", 61, in *Jerusalem Studies in Arabic and Islam* vol. 1 (1979) Jerusalem. This is also reminiscent of the Jewish concept of the *ruaḥ haqodesh* ("holy spirit", not to be confused with the different Christian concept of the same name), a God-given spirit of prophecy. This divinely given quality could be passed on to a disciple. Joshua, for example, receives it from Moses (*Tanhuma, Veʿethanan* 6 [pp. 858-859], though the act is there referred to as *masorot hokhmah* or "the passing on of wisdom").

25. In opposition to the account of Genesis 17:19-21, no covenant is specifically mentioned by al-Kisā'ī. The singling out of Muḥammad as the seal of the prophets represents a type of covenantal promise, which is extended further in Shiʿism to apply to certain members of his family through the person of ʿAlī and his descendants.

26. P. 102. This is the third rendition of the same basic tradition first presented by al-Ṭabarī on the authority of Ibn Isḥāq.

27. A special status given to the "People of Scripture" that would guarantee certain religious and personal rights so long as they recognize the hegemony of Islam through specific practices and a poll tax. A number of works have been written on the treatment of the "protected minorities" under Islam, some of them controversial. The most recent include Norman Stillman, *The Jews of Arab Lands* —Philadelphia: Jewish Publication Society, 1979); Bernard Lewis, *The Jews of Islam* (Princeton: Princeton University, 1984); and Bat Ye'or, *The Dhimmi* (Rutherford, NJ: Fairleigh Dickinson University, 1985).

28. *History*, 220f.

29. Ibn Kathīr interjects his own comments into the tradition he quotes on the authority of the People of the Book. Ibn Kathīr's comments are in brackets.

30. *Bilād al-maqdis.*

31. Cf. Genesis 16:3.

32. *Ama* (Lane, *Lexicon* 1:103, Penrice, *A Dictionary and Glossary of the Kor'an* [London: Curzon, 1970], 10). See Genesis 21:10, where Hagar is referred to as *amah*. Genesis 16:2 is the biblical parallel of this narrative section. Other renditions describe Hagar as a *jāriya*, the common Arabic term for handmaid or slave girl.

33. This is the only rendition we located that ascribes any blame to Hagar for Sarah's ill-treatment of her. (Cf. Genesis 16:4).

34. Cf. Genesis 16:6.

35. *Yaduhu 'ala l-kulli wa-yadu l-kulli bihi*, lit: "his hand over (or, against) everyone and the hand of everyone against him", a prophecy that aptly describes the future Islamic hegemony over most of the world in Abbasid times. Compare with the Hebrew of Genesis 16:12: *yado bakol v'yad kol bo.*

36. This line actually consists of the beginning of the exegesis on the previous line of prophecy, of which more follows in the next paragraph.

37. Compare Genesis 16:16, 17:24; but Cf. also Genesis 21:5.

38. I.e., your original request for a sound progeny.

39. Note the clear difference from the biblical intent of designating the genealogical line through Sarah. Here, God's great blessing is carried through Ishmael to the Arab people.

40. As in Genesis 15:12ff.

41. *Umma.*

42. *Quraysh* were the leading tribe of Mecca at the time of Muḥammad. Muḥammad came from a lesser clan from within that tribe. The Quraysh were Muḥammad's main opponents until his successful take-over of the city of Mecca in A.H. 8 (630 C.E.).

43. *Akhrajāhu fī' l-ṣaḥīḥayni.* This refers to al-Bukhārī (d. 256/869-70) and Muslim (d. 261/874-5), each of whom wrote a separate work entitled al-Jāmi' al-ṣaḥīḥ. Both are considered the collections of Prophetic Tradition of highest authority in Islam.

44. These first four are the first four Caliphs, often referred to as the "Rightly Guided."

45. The Umayyad caliph, who ruled from 717-720 and is known by Westerners as 'Umar II. He was considered a pious caliph and, as such, an exception to what has been traditionally considered the debaucherous rule of the Umayyad dynasty.

46. A dynasty of caliphs that ruled from 132/750 to 656/1258, taking its name from its ancestor, al-'Abbās b. 'Abd al-Muṭṭalib b. Hāshim, the uncle of the prophet Muḥammad.

47. Literally, "the renegades" or "dissenters", a Sunni term referring in this context to the "Twelver Shi'ites" who follow a line of twelve Masters (Imāms) who were direct descendants of 'Alī, the fourth caliph. According to tradition, the last of the twelve disappeared in 264/878 in the underground cistern of the great mosque at Sāmarrā without offspring, becoming therefore the "hidden" or awaited Imām who will return and redeem the people.

48. Mu'āwiya b. Abī Sufyān, who contested the caliphal authority of the fourth caliph, 'Alī, with an army of Syrians. Mu'āwiya's Syrians met 'Alī's Iraqi army on the plain of Siffin in 657. Although near the point of victory in battle, 'Alī agreed to arbitration, which resulted in the loss of the caliphate to Mu'āwiya, the first ruler of the Umayyad dynastic caliphate in Damascus.

49. The remaining supporters of 'Alī.

50. Especially verses 15-21.

51. The editor of the 1982 Beirut edition includes the insertion in the same paragraph as the prophecy, just as we have reproduced here, but separates all of Ibn Kathīr's comments by including them in separate paragraphs, marked here with brackets.

52. Most of the other sources refer to twelve biological sons of Ishmael in parallel with Genesis 25:12ff. Some of the Arabic names of Ishmael's sons are those given in Genesis 25:1ff as the names of Abraham's sons from his union with Qetura. See Ibn Sa'd 51 and note Ibn Sa'd's tradition on the authority of the father of Hishām b. Muḥammad b. al-Sā'ib: "Ishmael did not speak Arabic, for he would not think to be contrary to his father (who spoke Hebrew). The first of his sons to speak Arabic were the Banū Ri 'la bt. Yashjub b. Ya 'rub b. Lūzān b. Jurhum b. 'Āmir b. Sabā' b. Yaqtān b. 'Ābir b. Shālikh b. Arfakhshad b. Sām b. Nūḥ. Ishmael is nowhere mentioned in the genealogy, though he may have been assumed through the Jurhum (see chapter 9 below). On Ishmael's sons, see al-Azraqī 71ff, al-Ṭabarī, *History*, 351ff., al-Tha 'labī 100, al-Kisā'ī 144, etc.

53. This is not to say that the Qur'ān does not consider Ishmael a prophet. He certainly fits the role of prophet in verses such as Qur'ān 3:84, 4:163, 6:87, 21:86, and 38:49, which connect Ishmael directly to revelation, though only verse 19:54 explicitly names Ishmael as a messenger *(rasūl)* and a prophet *(nabī)*. Despite these references, the Qur'ān contains no allusions to any prophecy regarding the birth of Ishmael or his offspring as we find in the Bible, even though it does regarding Isaac, who is twice referred to in prophecy: Q.11:71, which parallels the story of the angels' visit in Genesis 18:10ff, and Q.37:112.

54. William Millward, "Al Ya'qūbī's sources and the question of Shi'a partiality", in *Abr-Nahrain* 12 (1971-2), 47-74.

55. Al-Kisā'ī does not provide a record of authentication but refers to Ka'b al-Aḥbār at the beginning of his section on Abraham's emigration. Ka'b is not considered an authoritative transmitter, though he apparently was considered so in the earliest period of Islam (Abbott 2:8-9; Ayoub, *The Qur'ān and its Interpreters*, 30-31). He is known for his extensive knowledge and use of biblical traditions. Ibn Kathīr's reliance on the People of the Book for the tradition he cites similarly disqualifies it, even according to his own opinion (*Commentary* 4:17), from generally being considered sound.

56. Newby, "Isrā'īlīyāt", 688-89.

57. Most exegetes understand this verse to be a call to rid the pagan Ka'ba of its idols.

58. On the various Western and Islamic views on the identity of this qur'ānic prophet, see G. Vajda's article, "Idrīs" in EI2: 3:1030-1.

59. Like Idrīs, Dhū al-Kifl is an enigmatic personality to Muslims as well as Western scholars. See Vajda's article "Dhū 'l-Kifl" in EI2: 2:242.

60. See below, pp. 72-75.

61. The Islamic legends nevertheless contain some Jewish material, as will be demonstrated below. Interestingly enough, some material seen as uncomplimentary in a Jewish context is actually taken as positive in the Arab world view. Schussman has pointed out how Ishmael's biblical traits of being a hunter (Genesis 21:20) and an aggressive fighter (Genesis 16:12) are seen by rabbinic Judaism as negative qualities, while Arab culture views them as being honorable and prestigious ("Abraham's visits to Ishmael—The Jewish Origin and Orientation," *Tarbiz* 49 (1980), 336. The rabbinic view of Ishmaelites is clearly portrayed in the description of the creation of all the nations of the world in *Midrash Esther Rabbah* 1:17: Of ten portions of stupidity in the world, nine were given to the Ishmaelites and one to the rest of the world. In the same manner, nine portions of robustness were alloted to the Ishmaelites and one to the rest of the world. Compare with their view that nine portions of vermin were given to the Persians (and one to the rest of the world, etc.) nine portions of witchcraft to the Egyptians, nine portions of beauty to Media, nine of courage to Judea, nine of wisdom to the Land of Israel, nine of Torah to the Land of Israel, and nine of hypocrisy to Jerusalem (based on Jeremia 23:15).

62. This would lend evidence to the view that Ishmael was a minor character in pre-Islamic Arabia and that his connection with Arab genealogy occurred after Muḥammad (Dagorn, 377ff.).

63. *Commentary* 16:95.

64. 2:51.

65. *Ismāʿīl b. Ḥisqīl.*

66. See chapters 14 and 16 below for the story of the Sacrifice and the claim that it was Ishmael who was the intended victim.

67. 16:45f.

68. Presumably rather than do an evil act himself.

69. ʿAlī b. Abī Ṭālib's son, who according to Shiʿite Islam, died a martyr's death at the hands of ʿUmar b. Saʿd b. Abī Waqqāṣ and his troops at Karbalāʾ, just north of Kūfa in today's Iraq. This occurred on the tenth day of the month of Muḥarram, which is commemorated to this day as an important holiday in Shiʿite Islam. We have not succeeded in identifying a historical Ishmael b. Ezekiel.

70. *Commentary* 3:125.

71. This is not to say that other prophets referred to in the Qurʾān have well developed characters. Most are simply referred to as if the listener was already familiar with their identities. Some, such as Dhū al-Qarnayn, Dhū al-Kifl, and Idrīs, who are not clearly identified with biblical characters, are quite enigmatic.

## CHAPTER 6

1. Ibn Saʿd 46-7; al-Ṭabarī *History*, 271; al-Thaʿlabī 80-81; Ibn al-Athīr 102; and Mujīr al-Dīn 35-6.

2. Ibid.

3. *Īlyā*, from the Hadrianic name, *Aelia Capitolina.*

4. This motif is reminiscent of Isaac's conflict with Abimelekh in Genesis 26:12-17. In fact, the biblical chronology of Genesis 26 is parallel to a section of the Islamic Syrian Prologue: the tyrant story of Genesis 26 (in contrast to the tyrant stories of Genesis 12 or 21) is followed by a Beersheba story. Notice the strikingly close parallel between the Beersheba renditions of Genesis 21:22-34 and 26:26-36. In both, Abimelekh and Phicol, his captain, come to Abraham or Isaac and state that since God is clearly the special benefactor of the Hebrew, they want to form a pact and elicit an oath for their own safety. In both rendtions, the oath is associated with a well of water. Both stories also provide an etymology for the name Beersheba based on the word, "oath" = *sh-b-ʿ* in Hebrew.

5. Mujīr al-Dīn, p. 35. A similar sequence is given by al-Qummī (1:332) in a different context. When Abraham tries to emigrate from the land of Nimrod, he is detained by agents of the king. His flocks are confiscated on the grounds that they were gained within the dominion of the king, so were not legally Abraham's to take out with him. A judge or wise man named Sadūm is called to mediate and is about to decide in favor of the king when Abraham says: " 'If you do not judge fairly, the last hour will have come!' Sadūm said: 'What is fairly?' He answered: 'Tell them to return to me [the years of] my life that I have passed in the gain of what I own and I will give it to them.' So Sadūm said: 'You [agents of the king] must return [the years of] his life.' So they refrained from [taking] his possessions."

6. The number seven has special significance for Islam as well as Judaism and Christianity, and other Semitic and non-Semitic peoples. See Wensinck, "Sabʿ" in EI1 7:2-3; *Encyclopedia of Religion* (Ed. Mircea Eliade), 11:13-16.

7. This etymology, however, conflicts with the etymology for the name given by the Bible, of which more below.

8. Josephus mentions a different Beersheba in Galilee (*Wars* Book III, Ch. 3 #1 [p. 503 in Whiston, William (translator), *Josephus: Complete Works* [Grand Rapids, Mich.: Kregel Publications, 1982]). Yāqūt lists two legends connected to a place called *Sabaʿ* in Palestine, one based upon our legend and a foreign story which nevertheless includes the motif of sheep (3:34). "Seven wells" may have been a relatively common place name.

9. It is not clear whether the versions of Genesis 21 and 26 describe a historical practice as well.

10. The motif of water in a well rising for Abraham's flock is found in BR 54:5 (on Genesis 21:30): "Abraham's shepherds were quarreling with Abimelekh's shepherds. Abimelekh's shepherds said: 'The well is ours!' Abraham's shepherds said to them: 'Let the well belong to whomever's flocks the water will rise to when it sees them.' When the water saw the flocks of Abraham, it immediately ascended . . ." L. Ginzberg has pointed out (5:247 note 220) that the motif of the rising water occurs in other Jewish legends as well. See especially the legends connected to Miriam's well in Ginzberg 3:52f and notes.

11. Genesis 21:1: *'al ken qara' lamaqom hahu be'er shavaʿ ki sham nishbʿu shneyhem*, meaning "They therefore call that place Be'er Shevaʿ because there both of them swore (to uphold the pact)."

12. Genesis 26:31-33: *Vayashkimu vaboqer vayishavʿu ish l'aḥiv . . . vayiqra' otah shivʿah, ʿal-ken shem haʿir be'er shevaʿ*, meaning "And they rose up early in the morning and made an oath (*vayishavʿu* from the root *sh-b-ʿ*) one to the other . . . And he called it (referring to a well of water) *Shivʿah*: therefore the name of the city is Be'er Shevaʿ."

13. That is, by binding oneself over seven things or through the act of giving seven objects as a type of "witness" of the act of swearing. See Francis Brown, et al., *A Hebrew and English Lexicon of the Old Testament* (Oxford: Clarendon, 1907), 989;

Solomon Mandelkern, *Veteris Testamenti Concordantiae (Qonqordantzia LaTanakh)* (Tel Aviv: Schocken, 1977, 1144; Ernest Klein, A Comprehensive Etymological Dictionary of Hebrew Language (New York: Macmillan, 1987).

14. The Benjaminite Sheva' ben Bikhri in 2 Samuel 20:1, 2, 6, etc., and Sheva', one of seven (!) Gadites listed in 1 Chron. 4:13, are probably derived also from the meaning, "seven".

15. If the characters were arabized as in the case of King Ṣādūq for Melkizedeq (confused with Abimelekh) discussed in the previous chapter, we would expect to find an Arabic or arabized name, which is also lacking.

16. They share a common root for making a vow, but it is the unrelated *n-d-r* (Hebrew)/*n-dh-r* (Arabic).

17. The process, then, resulted in a return to what is presumably the earlier etymology of the genesis 21 version. This would have been less likely among rabbinic Jews than among heterodox Bibilicists. The former are assumed to have had access to a biblical text virtually identical to today's masoretic version and would therefore have been less likely to allow the alternative etymology to take the place of the "official" biblical one. Nor would it be likely among Syriac Christians, who would be familiar with the identical meaning of swearing an oath in Hebrew and Aramaic/Syriac. It would also have been unlikely for pagan Arabs to be interested in retaining such a foreign tradition that had little to say to them. The legend perhaps evolved in the hands of heterodox Arabic-speaking Biblicists who may not have been as familiar with or as closely bound to the recensions of the Hebrew Bible we know today.

## CHAPTER 7

1. The qur'ānic term, "People of Lot" *(qawm lūt)* is used rather than the biblical idiom "Sodom and Gemorah" to refer to the object of God's destruction.

2. Both sections continue with the angels heading off to destroy the people of Lot on account of their evil sins. A third Qur'ān section (Sūra 15:51-59) treats the identical episode, though in a less detailed manner than our two sections here. Other sections (such as Sūra 29:31) only make reference to the angels' visit without recounting it. Most of the traditional exegesis centers on the two qur'ānic references quoted here.

3. *Rusul* in Q.11:69 and *mursalūn* in Q.51:31.

4. *Al-Mu'tafika* or *al-mu'tafikāt:* from the root *'-f-k*, "the overturned cities" that were destroyed by God for the sins of their inhabitants (Qur'ān 9:70, 53:53, 69:9). The Hebrew cognate *h-p-k* is used in the same way in Jonah 3:4: "In 40 days, Ninveh will be overturned" *('od arba'im yom v'ninveh nehepakhet)*. The Qur'ān refers to Lot and the destruction of these cities relatively frequently, particularly in those sections generally dated by Western scholars as belonging to the second and third Meccan periods. *Al-mu'tafika* refers to the biblical cities Sodom and Gemorrah, neither of which is named in the Qur'ān. Cf. Genesis 19:21, 25.

5. Because this episode has little direct bearing on the Abraham/Ishmael story, only a small sample of the many traditions referring to it are included here. All are taken from the histories and collections of popular literature, which tend to provide fuller accounts.

6. al-Ṭabarī, *History*, 272-4, al-Mas'ūdī 57, al-Tha'labī 81, al-Ya'qūbī 23-4, al-Kisā'ī 145-150.

7. P. 81.

8. Abraham's emigration is referred to briefly in both the Bible and the Qur'ān but does not have the narrative detail of the angels' visit. The Tyrant and Beersheba stories do not occur at all in the Qur'ān, while none of the sections in the Meccan Sequence can be found in the Bible.

9. Q.11:71.

10. Through the use of a standard formula such as *kamā qāla ta'āla* ("as the most High said") or *kamā qāla Allāhu 'azza wajalla* ("as God the Great and Exalted said"). All Qur'ān quotations given by these and other standard formulas are translated here simply as "as the Qur'ān says" or "as is written."

11. Some have considered this to be evidence for a late date for the Qur'ān. If verses now known to be qur'ānic are not noted as such in the commentaries, it is seen as an indication that they were not considered Scripture at the time of the compilation (Norman Calder, "From Midrash to Scripture: The Sacrifice of Abraham in Early Islamic Tradition", *Le Museon* 101 [1988] 375-402).

12. Rather than the presumably available qur'ānic term, *al-mu'tafika.*

13. Al-Ya'qūbī's ages for Abraham and Sarah represent a common misreading of the Bible. According to Genesis 17:1f, Abraham was 99 when God told him that he would have a son through Sarah. In verse 17 when Abraham says: "shall he who is 100 years old have a child? and shall Sarah, who is 90 years old, give birth?", he is speaking of the age he and Sarah will be one year hence. Genesis 21:1-8 confirms the birth of Isaac one year later and notes that Abraham was 100 years old at the time, making his age 99 at the time of the angels' visit.

14. Pp. 272-73.

15. *Kamā qāla Allāhu 'azza w'jalla.*

16. The editor's note mentions textual variants here as *hanīd* and *al-ihnād.*

17. *Ahlu al-'ilm.*

18. P. 81.

19. According to Jewish tradition which follows the simple chronology of the Bible text, Abraham was recovering from his own circumcision when the angels visited (Genesis 17:23-18:1). According to BT, *Baba Metzi'a* 86b: "R. Hama son of R. Ḥanina

said: It was the third day from Abraham's circumcision, and the Holy One, blessed be He, came to enquire after Abraham's health. He drew the sun out of its sheath [to cause great heat on earth] so that the righteous man [Abraham] would not be troubled with wayfarers. Abraham sent [his servant] Eliezer out [to seek travelers], but he found none. . . ." In the *Tanḥuma* version in *Vayera* 3 (p. 74): "What is 'in the heat of the day' (Genesis 18:1)? The Holy One Blessed be He made that day extremely hot so that no one would come by Abraham and he would not be upset over not being able to be hospitable to them [because of his circumcision]." *(Mahu kaḥom ha-yom? Hirtiaḥ ha-Qadosh Barukh Hu 'oto ha-yom k'dei she-lo y'hu 'ovrim v'shavim ba'im, vayelekh Avraham vayitzta'er l'hakhnisam l'khalk'lam.).*

20. Al-Tha'labī 81, al-Kisā'ī 144. In al-Kisā'ī's rendition, guests are withheld from him for three days rather than the 15 days of al-Tabarī and al-Tha'labī, a more direct relationship with the BT tradition.

21. It is true that according to the Islamic doctrine of 'iṣma, God does occasionally intervene in order to ensure that the behavior of His prophets is impeccable. But even so, Abraham was nowhere tempted in this narrative to be inhospitable. The parallel with the Jewish legend suggests a far more logical derivation from a Biblicist milieu.

The reason for the circumcision detail dropping out of the Islamic version is puzzling. The story may have entered Islam through a Christian source which would have found the circumcision motif irrelevant or perhaps even contrary to Christian dogma. Islamic sources tend to place Abraham's circumcision earlier in the Abraham cycle and refer to it in sections treating his emigration from the land of Nimrod (See Ibn Sa'd 47, Ibn Qutayba 33, Mujīr al-Dīn 1:47f, etc.). The Qur'ān itself does not refer to his circumcision.

22. *History*, 273-4.

23. 'Abdallāh b. Ghāfil, a famous companion of the Prophet and reader of the Qur'ān. A qur'ānic reading is attributed to him which is sometimes at variance with the established 'Uthmanic version.

24. Two phrases of praise and thanks traditionally recited at the beginning and end of the meal.

25. *Khalīl.* This is Abraham's *laqab* or honorific title in Arabic tradition: *Al-Khalīl*, the friend (of God). Qur'ān 4:125 refers directly to Abraham as the Friend of God: GOD TOOK ABRAHAM FOR A FRIEND. But note the Jewish sources: Isaiah 41:8: "but you, Israel, My servant, Jacob, whom I have chosen, Seed of Abraham My friend *(zera' avraham ohavi)*. . . ." BT Menahot 53b: "Rabbi Isaac said: At the time of the destruction of the Temple, the Holy One blessed be He, found Abraham standing in the Temple. He said: 'What is My friend doing in My house (*mah lididi b'veyti* . . . [Jer. 11:15]) . . .". Eastern Christian tradition also has legends about Abraham the Friend of God. Bar Hebraeus has: "It is said that God said to Abraham, 'Knowest thou why I have chosen thee to be My 'friend'?' And Abraham replied, 'Tell me O Lord.' And the Lord made answer to him saying, 'It is because thou has taken upon thyself to be injured and not to do injury; therefore let him that would increase friends do likewise.' " (E.A.W. Budge [transl.]

*Oriental Wit and Wisdom . . . Collected by Mar . . . Bar Hebreaus* [London: Luzac and Co., 1899], 136). See also p. 236 note 46 below.

26. This trait of Abraham is found repeatedly in early Jewish Tradition. In BR 34:14 and 84:4 (on Genesis 12:5), Abraham and Sarah make converts while they are in Haran (see Ginzberg *Legends* 1:203 and 219 for additional sources). The hesitation of the angels in the qur'ānic rendition probably reflected the (rabbinic) view that angels do not eat. They did not reach out their hands for the food simply because, as was already known, angels do not eat. In the Qur'ān rendition, Abraham did not know immediately that they were angels and feared that they might have ulterior motives. The extra-qur'ānic tradition about the blessings is repeated in al-Tha'labī, p. 81. compare BR 48:14, which explains the problem of the angels eating in Gen. 18:8. The *Targum* (TJ1) on Genesis 18:8 explains that they made as if they ate without actually eating *(v'damey ley k'ilu akhlin)*.

27. This is explained in the commentary *Yonatan* on Genesis 18:5: "the meaning of *odu* ('give thanks') is the blessing after the meal" *(v'odu perush birkat ha-mazon)*.

Ginzberg (5:248 n. 224) points out the closer parallel in *Tanhuma, lekh lekha* 12 (pp. 62-3): " '. . . and Abraham planted a tamarisk tree in Beersheba, and called there on the name of the Lord, the everlasting God' (Genesis 21:33). After giving [travelers] food and drink, they would bless him. He would say to them, 'You bless me? Bless the Master of the house who gives all creation food and drink and gives them life!' They would ask: 'Where is He?' and he would answer: 'He rules in heaven and earth. He causes death and gives life, causes wounds and [also] heals, he forms the embryo in the womb of the mother and causes it to enter into the air of this world. He causes plants and trees to grow. He brings down to Sheol and brings up.' When they would hear that, they would ask how to bless Him and show their gratitude. He would say to them: 'Say: Blessed is God for ever and ever. Blessed is He who gives bread and food to all flesh!' Thus would he teach them blessings and righteousness." Note, however, that the collection of *midrashim* generally called *Tanhuma* is assumed not to have been redacted in its present formats earlier than 800 C.E. though many of the traditions included therein are earlier.

28. P. 81.

29. By reciting the *"Basmalla"* before eating, and *"al-Ḥamdu li-llāhi"* afterwards (Cf. al-Ṭabarī's rendition above).

30. This is meant to explain the verse (11:71): AND HIS WIFE WAS STANDING AND LAUGHED . . .

31. Compare with the biblical explanation given in Genesis 21:3-7, which is closely connected with the passage in Genesis 18:12-15. Note also that the immediate reason provided by the Bible for Sarah's anger at Hagar is that her son Ishmael was laughing (*m'tzaḥeq*, the same root meaning as the name *Yitzḥaq* = Isaac), presumably at Sarah or Isaac.

32. This is the reason given here for God's command to Abraham to sacrifice his son. Once his public oath was made, he was obligated to fulfill it. See chapters 13, 14, and 16 below.

33. As odd as this tradition may seem at first sight, Sarah's sudden ability to give birth in old age is demonstrated here by the appearance of her menses.

34. Al-Suddī's comment about the miracle of the dry stick is given in al-Ṭabarī *Commentary* 12:75 and elsewhere; the tradition about Sarah menstruating is found in his *Commentary* 12:73 and elsewhere. Al-Ṭabarī also includes traditions that are ommitted here. All are brief and serve to explain particular aspects of the Qur'ān text.

35. Numbers 17:23, where Aaron's staff sprouts flowers and almonds as a sign of his divinely sanctioned authority (Cf. Genesis 30:37-43).

36. With the exception of the proof of the sprouting twig, which may represent a remnant of a Biblicist legend.

37. That is, without a record of authentication.

38. Cf. Genesis 21:6f.

39. With the possible exception of the comment that rabbits laugh when they menstruate, an observation rather than a narrative tradition.

## PART THREE INTRODUCTION

1. Qur'ān 5:23 unambiguously states that Moses brought his people to the Holy Land *(al-arḍ al-muqaddasa)*, but the term is not common in the sources. Syria *(al-sha'm)* is the term most common term to identify the area in which Jerusalem and the biblical sites are situated.

2. Islam does not consider the Israelites a religious community until they receive the Torah.

## CHAPTER 8

1. Qur'ān 2:125-129, 3:96-97, 14:37, 22:26.

2. Died in 68/687 in al-Ṭā'if. His full name is 'Abdullāh b. 'Abbās b. 'Abd al-Muṭṭalib, and he was called "al-baḥr" ("The Sea") for the vast number of traditions attributed to him. Born in Mecca before the Hegira, he was only about thirteen when Muḥammed died. Ibn 'Abbās is considered an excellent commentator and the originator of Islamic exegesis, having learned most of his reports from Companions of the Prophet, though he is said to have collected traditions from Jews and Christians and is the authority for many Biblicist traditions. He has also been referred to as "the rabbi of the community" *(ḥibr al-umma)* and "the interpreter of the Qur'ān" *(tarjumān al-Qur'ān)*. The validity of many of the attributions to Ibn 'Abbās may be questioned simply because of the sheer number transmitted on his authority. Some of his disciples include such important transmitters as 'Ikrima, Mujāhid, Sa'īd b. Jubayr, Qatāda, and al-Daḥḥāk. (Abbott 2:9; al-Dhahabī, *Tadhkirat al-Ḥuffāẓ* [Hyderabad, 1376/1956]:

1:40-41; Newby, "Isrāʾīlīyāt," 688f.; I. Goldfeld, "The Tafsir of ʿAbdallāh b. ʿAbbās"; *Der Islam* 58 (1981), 125-35.

3. ʿAlī b. Abī Ṭālib (died in 40/660), cousin and son-in-law of Muḥammad. He was one of the first to believe in Muḥammad's prophecy and ruled for a while as the fourth caliph. ʿAlī is a well-respected transmitter of Tradition. According to Shiʿite Islam, he was deprived of his rightful status as caliph by Muʿāwiya through arbitration after the Battle of Ṣiffīn in 37/657 (al-Dhāhabī 1:10-13; L. Veccia Vaglieri, "ʿAlī b. Abī Ṭālib" in EI2, 1:381-6.

4. Mujāhid b. Jabr al-Makhzūmī, also known as Abū al-Ḥajjāj, died in 104-722 in Mecca. He was a great authority of Qur'ān commentary and recitation and was a respected transmitter of tradition, though he has been criticized for taking traditions from the People of the Book. Much material related on his authority has a mythic character. He transmitted material from ʿAlī, Ubayy b. Kaʿb, ʿAbdallāh b. ʿUmar, and many others, and was a student of Ibn ʿAbbās. Al-Ṭabarī cites him liberally (Abbott 2:97; Ayoub 29f; al-Dhāhabī 1:92-3).

5. Al-Azraqī 22f., 279-80; al-Bukhārī 4:372-75, 379-80; al-Ṭabarī *History* 279-81, 282-83, *Commentary* 13:229, 230-31; Ibn Kathīr *Commentary* 1:176, 177, *History* 223-24, 227-28.

6. Ibn Ḥanbal 1:253, 347-48.

7. Ibn Saʿd 50; Ibn Ḥanbal 1:360, 5:121; al-Azraqī 22, 279.

8. *Al-bayt*, referring to the Kaʿba.

9. The famous well next to the Kaʿba in Mecca.

10. *Dawḥa*. Al-Ṭabarsī 1:470 and al-Kisāʾī 142 have Hagar hanging a piece of cloth on the tree to shade her son and herself from the sun. Al-Ṭabarsī's tradition is given on the authority of al-Ṣādiq, while al-Kisāʾī's is without a record of authentication. Al-Azraqī 22f and 279-80 (on the authority of Ibn ʿAbbās) has Hagar hang the water skin on the tree. Pre-Islamic Arabs sometimes hung garments or other objects on sacred trees as an offering or substitute for sacrifice (Noeldeke ["Arabs Ancient"] in EI1 1:666b).

11. A location just outside of Mecca.

12. *Al-Ṣafā* and *al-Marwa*, two hills in Mecca close to the location of the Kaʿba. Part of the Pilgrimage ritual in both the pre-Islamic and Islamic Ḥajj is to move between the two hills seven times at a brisk walking pace. This act is called *al-saʿī* or the "running." On the early significance of these locations and the running ritual associated with them, see Uri Rubin, "The Kaʿba: Aspects of its ritual functions . . . ," pp. 122-127.

13. Both are names used to refer to the Prophet, Muḥammad.

14. This is now considered the legendary origin of the famous Zamzam well next to the Kaʿba.

15. All three are names referring to the Prophet.

16. Michael Avi-Yonah, EJ 13:88.

17. The Ḥijāz could have been associated among Arabian Biblicists even with the "Desert of Beersheba" of Genesis 21:14, the location to which Ishmael and Hagar were first sent. Although under the control of the tribe of Judah during the Israelite monarchy, the Beersheba area was associated with Idumaea from the time of the restoration of Judah in the fifth century B.C.E. until well into the Roman period. Idumaea was ethnically Arab, as was its successor state Nabataea, which included part of the area around Beersheba during and after the reign of Herod. The entire area south of Beersheba, including the area known in the Bible as Paran, was considered "Arabia" from the second century C.E. onwards. The association of both Paran and Beersheba with Arabia and Arab peoples would be a natural function of the Jewish worldview during the centuries leading up to the beginning of Islam.

18. *Kitāb Mu'jam al-Buldān*, ed. Wuestenfeld (Leipzig, 1868): 3:834. Ibn Kathīr writes: "Abraham went to visit his son and his son's mother at all times in the land of *Farān*. . . . It is reported that he would ride there very quickly on (the magic horse) *al-burāq*, but God knows best." (*Commentary* 4:14). Wahb b. Munabbih offers an etymology for *Tal Farān* on the outskirts of Mecca in his *Kitāb al-Tijān* (F. Krenkow, "The two oldest books on Arabic Folklore," in *Islamic Culture* 2 (1928), 207).

19. *Yalqut Shim'oni*, Genesis 95 (1:424) has: "He took a veil *(radid)* and tied it around her waist to show that she was a bondwoman.

20. While Hagar is rebuked for damming up the well or drinking from it, no explanation for the rebuke is provided in the Islamic sources. The Islamic version may in fact blame Hagar for drinking from the well during her menses (or while still in an impure state from the recent birth of her still-suckling baby?). The word used in some of the renditions for damming up the flow of the water is *ḥāḍat* (al-Azraqī 23, 280; al-Bukhārī 4:374; Ibn Kathīr *Commentary* 1:176, *History* 204. Mujīr al-Dīn uses *ḥātat*). The verb *ḥāḍ (ḥā' / waw / ḍāḍ)* can mean either to collect water or to menstruate. This may have originated from a play on words between her own flow and the flow of the well. We already know from Chapter 6 that menstruating women are forbidden to drink, or in some cases, even approach magic wells. Menstruating women were also forbidden in pre-Islamic times from approaching idols or holy sites. A pre-Islamic poem reads: "Full of awe, they draw not nigh unto it, But stand afar off like the menstruating women before Isāf" (Nabih Amin Faris, *The Book of Idols* (*Kitāb al-Aṣnām* of Ibn al-Kalbī), 25, 27. Other restrictions apply to menstruating women taking part in the Islamic Pilgrimage and participating in other religious acts. Some have suggested a late Zoroastrian influence (Morony, *Iraq*, 445-46).

21. Faris, *The Book of Idols*, 8; Toufic Fahd, *Le Panthéon de l'Arabie centrale à la veille de l'Hégire* (Paris: Paul Geuthner, 1968), 103-9.

22. Western descriptions of Zamzam tend to describe a weak and brackish spring. From reports of recent pilgrims, however, it appears to be quite abundant and

fine today. In fact, it is unlikely that the "magic well" of Zamzam would have been considered so had it not in ancient days offered an abundant supply of water in such a desolate place as Mecca.

23. Cf. Genesis 21:14.

24. BT, *Pesaḥim* 54a and Rashi ibid. s.v. *be'er*; Rashi on BT, *Shabbat* 35a s.v. *zehu be'erah shel Miryam, Yalqut Shim'oni* 95, etc. The motif of objects created on the evening of the first Sabbath is a popular one in Jewish folklore, and the objects vary from rendition to rendition. In the *Mekhilta d'Rabbi Yishma'el*, for example, the well is not included in the list (Horowitz-Rabin, eds. Jerusalem, 1970 [*vayassa'* 6 (p. 171)].

25. "She went and sat to one side and took on a foreign religious worship . . ." (Palestinian Targum [TJ1] on Genesis 21:16; Cf. PRE 67b, *Yalqut* 95, etc.). The approach of PRE is probably polemical. Virtually all scholars are in agreement that TJ1 predates Islam, though it is also known that some sections were clearly inserted after, such as the well-known TJ1 passage on Genesis 21:21 where Ishmael ". . . dwells in the wilderness of Paran and takes 'Adisha to wife. But he divorced her, so his mother took him Fatima for a wife out of the land of Egypt." The obvious connection with Muḥammad's wife 'Ā'ishah and daughter Fāṭimah clearly date this particular passage after 600 C.E.).

26. Gaudefroy-Demombynes, *Le Pélerinage à la Mekke* [Paris: Paul Geuthner, 1923]), 192-234; or G.E. Von Grunebaum, *Muḥammadan Festivals* [(New York: Henry Schuman, 1951], 26-31).

27. Pp. 22-3.

28. P. 142.

29. On this supernatural light, see pp. 41, 193 note 24.

30. 1:103.

31. Pp. 36-7.

32. *History*, 277-78.

33. This parallels the complete Sarah/Hagar conflict portrayed in Genesis 16:5ff. and Genesis 21:9ff.

34. "She said: 'I will cut off her nose! I will cut off her ear! That will disfigure her!' Then she said: 'No, but I will humble her through circumcision!' [*kh-f-ḍ*]. So she did that. Hagar then took the edge of her dress *(dhayl)* to wipe off the blood. That is why women are circumcised and take up the ends of their dresses [to this day]."

35. Pp. 81-2.

36. She was obligated by her vow, but Abraham suggested a less drastic alternative to mutilation. Cf. Exodus 21:5 and Deuteronomy 15:16 where slaves are marked for life by having their ear pierced.

37. See below.

38. *Asma''īl* = "I hear God".

39. Gabriel is credited by most sources with being the angel that brought forth Zamzam to save Hagar and Ishmael.

40. Al-Ṭabarī, *History*, 275-76, 276, *Commentary* 1:548-49, 1:551; Ibn Kathīr *Commentary* 1:178. A co-variant of this version is repeated in the sources when describing Abraham's journey to Mecca to build the Ka'ba with Ishmael (chapter 11 below).

41. Al-Ṭabarī, *History*, 276, and *Commentary* 1:548-9.

42. The *sakīna* is defined in al-Ṭabarī, *History*, 276 as "a wind that has a tongue for speaking with him." Many descriptions are provided in the sources (see chapter 11 below). The name is clearly derived from the rabbinic concept of the *shekhina*, or "Divine Presence," but it became confused with the pure Arabic root *s-k-n*, which denotes quiet rest or tranquility (compare Qur'ān 2:48 with Q.9:26, 9:40; 48:4, etc.). The original rabbinic notion dropped out and it became a term for a benevolent supernatural being. In all our sources, the *sakina* acts a a kind of divinely commissioned guide for Abraham (Cf. I. Goldziher, "La Notion De La Sakina Chez Les Mohametans" in *Revue de l'Histoire des Religions*, XXVII [1893], 296-308; A.J. Wensinck, "The Ideas of the Western Semites Concerning the Navel of the Earth," in *Studies of A.J. Wensinck* [New York, 1978], 60-65).

43. The editor of al-Ṭabarī's *Commentary* provides a footnote quoting another source: "It showed him the site of the House just as the spider builds its home, so he dug underneath the *sakīna* and revealed the foundations of the House. He could not move any of the foundation without 30 men." According to this legend, God brought down the original Ka'ba from heaven and established it for Adam as a solace for him being denied the pleasures of hearing the heavenly angels praise God. Adam was therefore the first human to circumambulate the Ka'ba. In order to protect it from the Flood during the days of Noah, however, God raised up all but its foundations to heaven. The *sakīna* therefore actually revealed to Abraham the ancient foundations which dated from the epoch of Adam (Ibn Sa'd 38, 41; al-Azraqī 6-12, 28).

44. Al-Ṭabarī, *History*, 275-6, *Commentary* 1:551, and Ibn Kathīr *Commentary* 1:178.

45. *Ghamāma*. Note the parallel with the cloud that guided the Israelites through their journeys in the desert (Ex. 13:21, Nu. 14:14). A closer parallel is found in God's practice of descending over the Tabernacle in the desert in a cloud (Ex. 16:10, 34:5, Lev. 16:2, Nu. 11:25, Deut. 31:15, etc.). In Syriac Christian writings dating from the eighth century C.E., a cloud floating over a man's head signified greatness (Griffith, "The Prophet Muḥammad, His Scripture and His Message According to the Christian Apologies ... ", p. 137). In the Arabic version here, however, the cloud is its own strange being and has largely parted ways with any biblical role.

46. Cf. Ibn 'Abbās version above.

47. Ursula Nowak, *Beiträge zur Typologie des arabischen Volksmärchens.* Freiburg im Breisgau: Albert-Ludwigs-Universität Doctoral Dissertation, 1969: pp. 210-49.

48. Al-Azraqī 21, al-Ṭabarī, *History*, 278-9, al-Ṭabarī, *Commentary*, 1:548, and Ibn Kathīr, *Commentary*, 1:179.

49. Al-Azraqī 21-2.

50. Al-Ṭabarsī 1:470.

51. Based on Q.22:26: WE SHOWED ABRAHAM THE SITE OF THE HOUSE *(wa'idh bawwa'nā li'ibrāhīm makān al-bayt).*

52. The narrative fragment ends here. Buraq *(al-burāq)* is the supernatural steed upon which some of the early prophets and Muḥammad rode. Muḥammad rode upon it during his famous "Night Journey" *(isrā')* from Mecca to Jerusalem and back in one night (the legend is connected to Qur'ān 17:1). According to tradition, Buraq could gallop in one pace as far as its eye could see, thus covering immense distances. The earliest datable mention of Buraq is by the poet 'Ajjāj (d. 97/715), who mentions it in connection with Abraham. The motif of this magic steed may have originated in pre-Islamic Arabia, though Noy mentions a magic cow that "covers the distance from Palestine to Babylonia in short time" (Motif Index 1:220).

53. Not in al-Ṣādiq rendition.

54. Not in al-Ṣādiq rendition.

55. Not in al-Ṣādiq rendition.

56. This motif is found often in Chapter 10 below.

57. It may have developed from a strongly equestrian culture such as pre-Islamic Arabia, where swift horses were considered extemely valuable prizes.

58. In addition to the complete narratives listed above, a number of short authoritative comments may be found in the sources. These tend to function as glosses clarifying particulars within the narratives, such as how old Ishmael was when he was taken to Mecca or who was the agent that made the water flow for Hagar, etc.

59. Including the Ka'ba, Zamzam, and Kadā.

## CHAPTER 9

1. G. Rentz, "Djazīrat al-'Arab", EI2 1:543-546.

2. Al-Azraqī pp. 44-56; Faris, *Book of Idols*, 6-71; Guillaume, *Life*, 45-48; Montgomery Watt, "Djurhum", EI2 2:603-4. Cf. Dagorn, *La Geste*, 314ff.

3. Al-Azraqī 24, 280; al-Bukhārī 4:375-77, 381-82; al-Ṭabarī, *History*, 281, 283; *Commentary*, 13:230, 231; Ibn Kathīr, *Commentary*, 1:176, 177; *History*, 224-25.

4. Al-Tha'labī 82-3, al-Kisā'ī 143, Ibn al-Athīr 103.

5. Mujīr al-Dīn 37-8.

6. Al-Ṭabarī *Commentary* 13:232.

7. Ibn Qutayba 34.

8. Al-Ṭabarsī 1:471.

9. *'Ā'if.* The root also means "to auger" and carries the meaning of an omen or Fortune, and a theophoric name 'Abd 'Awf ("servant of the god 'Awf") is attested in pre-Islamic Arabia (Noeldeke, "Arabs [Ancient]" in Hastings, ed., *Encyclopaedia of Religion and Ethics*, 663a).

10. Chapter 10 below.

11. Ibn Qutayba, 34; al-Tha'labī, 83; Ibn al-Athīr, 144.

12. Cf. Genesis 21:20.

13. Genesis 21:21b: "and his mother got a wife for him from the land of Egypt" is problematic and is not informed by the Jurhum sequence, which contradicts it in Motif #8.

14. P. 34.

15. The connection between the seven sheep and the water of Zamzam appears to be a reiteration of the motif found in the Beersheba legend, where Abraham gives the inhabitants of Beersheba seven goats to ensure that their water will continue to flow (see Chapter 6).

16. 1:471.

17. A deserted area near Mecca and the most important site of the pre-Islamic Pilgrimage (see Chapter 12 below).

18. Ibid.

19. Muslims partaking of the Islamic pilgrimage today also recite liturgical response known as *talbiya*, though different from that quoted here (see p. 219 note 23 below).

20. Al-Azraqī, 281-282; al-Ṭabarī, *Commentary*, 13:233.

21. Rene Dagorn, *La Geste*, 22, 33, 100f., 124, 177, 330f., etc.; Mishal Hayek, *Le Mystere d'Ismael*, 82f. It is clear, however, that Ishmael's connection with the Arab peoples is well attested in the Bible and would have been known in early Biblicist communities (Cf. James Montgomery, *Arabia and the Bible*. [1934 reprint. New York, 1969], 45f.; D.S. Margoliouth, *The Relations between Arabs and Israelites prior to the Rise of Islam* [London, 1924], 28-55).

22. See note 9 above.

23. See page 66 above.

## CHAPTER 10

1. These are the Jewish PRE Chapter 30 (68a-b), *Sefer HaYashar* Vayera, 55-7, *Yalqut Shim*'oni, Genesis 95 *(Vayera)* 1:424-425, etc. (see also the Palestinian Targum on Genesis 21:21). Bernhard Heller ("*Muhammedanisches und Antimuhammedanisches in den Pirke Rabbi Eliezer*," MGWJ 1925, 47-54) and Joseph Heinemann (*Aggadot Ve-Toldoteihen* [Jerusalem, 1974] 189ff.) consider the Jewish version to be a response to Islam. Aviva Schussman ("Abraham's Visits to Ishmael—The Jewish Origin and Orientation" [Hebrew], *Tarbiz* 49 [1980], 325-345), however, suggests that the Jewish legend is earlier and served an originally Jewish role of providing narrative exegesis to Genesis 21:21. A second purpose, she claims, was to serve as a Jewish apologetic for Abraham's harsh behavior in Genesis 21:9ff., though it later evolved into a polemic in response to Islam as well.

2. Al-Azraqī 25; al-Bukhārī 4:375-7, 4:381-2, al-Ṭabarī, *History*, 281-82, 283-85, *Commentary*, 13:230, 13:231; al-Ṭabarsī 1:461; Ibn Kathīr, *Commentary*, 1:176, 1:177 (incomplete narrative), *History*, 225.

3. Al-Ya'qūbī 24-5, al-Mas'ūdī 2:19-20; al-Tha'labī 83, al-Kisā'ī 144, Ibn al-Athīr 104, and Mujīr al-Dīn 37-8.

4. According to al-Mas'ūdī's rendition, which parallels Jewish tellings, Ishmael is out pasturing the flocks or hunting with his mother Hagar. This is the only Islamic rendition in which Hagar is mentioned after Ishmael takes his first wife, who according to al-Mas'ūdī is an Amalekite. When Ishmael divorces her, he marries a woman from the Jurhum tribe, which settled in Mecca after the Amalekites.

5. All are names for Muḥammad.

6. This motif is the only significant variant of a surprisingly consistent story among all of its renditions. In three renditions, Abraham stands on a stone block to facilitate the hair washing, while in two he stands upon a water jug. In four of these renditions, Abraham's footprint remains on the stone or jug. This section provides an origin for the Maqām Ibrāhīm, though it is different from the common explanation for its origin given later in the "Ibn 'Abbās" legend about the building of the Ka'ba (See p. 212 note 8 below). The traditions specifically naming it the Maqām Ibrāhīm are al-Ṭabarī *Commentary* 13:321, al-Mas'ūdī 2:21, al-Ṭabarsī 1:461, and al-Tha'labī 83.

7. As in the case of his mother, Hagar, Ishmael's wife must be exceptional.

8. Pp. 51-52.

9. Muḍāḍ b. 'Amrū is often listed in Islamic legends as the leader of the Jurhum who took control of the Ka'ba in pre-Islamic times (al-Azraqī 44ff.).

10. Pp. 24-25.

11. P. 21.

12. P. 144.

13. Ibid. (on the authority of al-Kalbī).

14. 2:19.

15. PRE 68b and *Yalqut* 424.

16. P. 20.

17. *Sefer HaYashar* has Hagar take a wife for Ishmael from Egypt named Merivah. Merivah means "strife," as in Numbers 20:13. Compare these names with 'Adisha (TJ1 s.v. 21:21), 'Ayefa (PRE 68a) or 'Ayyisha (*Yalqut Shim'oni* 94 [1:424]) and Fatima, names given in the Jewish sources. The Islamic influence upon these names has often been noted (Heller, 49f.; Ginzberg, 5:247 n. 218; PRE2, 219 n. 2).

18. The collections of popular literature *(Qiṣaṣ al-Anbiyā')* are made up largely of imaginative anonymous traditions. It becomes clear from the more fantastic renditions found in these works why they are suspect among traditionalists yet popular among the common folk.

19. *Al-janna* (literally, "the Garden"). Al-Mas'ūdī (ibid.) mentions a dispute among the authorities about whether Abraham rode on Buraq, on a she-ass, or on other animals.

20. It may have been inserted to answer a possible question about how Ishmael the hunter (Genesis 21:20) could live in the Sacred Precinct of Mecca where the taking of any life is forbidden.

21. Al-Bukhārī 4:376; Ibn Kathīr, *Commentary*, 1:176, *History*, 225 (all on the authority of Ibn 'Abbās).

22. The renditions vary slightly in their wording (al-Azraqī 25, al-Ṭabarī, *History*, 284, *Commentary*, 13:231, al-Ṭabarsī, 1:461 [all on authority of Ibn 'Abbās], al-Tha'labī 83 [anonymous], Ibn al-Athīr 104 [anonymous]).

23. The content of either of these could reflect a pre-Islamic Arab as well as Islamic outlook.

24. This is in opposition to the Jewish exegetical narrative which serves as an apologetic for Abraham, a good father despite the fact that he expelled Ishmael (with God's indirect permission—Genesis 21:12).

25. PRE chapter 30 (68a-b), *Yalqut Shim'oni*, 425, and elsewhere.

26. But in *Sefer HaYashar*, Ishmael gets his second wife from the land of Canaan (p. 56).

27. This is Schussman's major argument in favor of the legend originating in a Jewish rather than Islamic environment *(op. cit.)*.

28. The contradiction is anticipated in the Jurhum story as well, where Ishmael's mother dies before or soon after he takes his first wife (p. 73 above). She cannot therefore fulfill her biblical role of taking a wife for him out of the land of Egypt.

## CHAPTER 11

1. See Chapter 12 below.

2. On Ibn ʻAbbās and ʻAli b. Abī Ṭālib, see pp. 203 note 2 and 204 note 3 above. Ismāʻīl b. ʻAbd al-Raḥmān b. Abī Karīma al-Hāshimī al-Suddī (d. 127/744) was from the Ḥijāz and was under the patronage of Zaynab bt. Qays b. Makhrama from the tribe of Abū al-Muṭṭalib b. ʻAbd al-Manāf. He was a well-known Qur'ān commentator and is credited with a Qur'ān commentary that was purported to have included legendary tradition material as well as linguistic explanations. That work is not extant (al-Dawūdī 1:110 and Abbot 2:95, 99).

3. Al-Azraqī 25-26; al-Bukhārī 4:377-78, 381; al-Ṭabarī, *History*, 285-86, *Commentary* 1:550, 550-51, 13:231; Ibn Kathīr *Commentary* 1:177, 177, 177-78, *History* 226-27, 227.

4. Al-Azraqī 26; al-Ṭabarsī 1:469.

5. Mujīr al-Dīn 38-9.

6. Al-Azraqī 26: "Saʻīd said: Then he said: 'O Ishmael, God has commanded something of me.' He said: 'So obey the command of your Lord!' He said: 'You will help me?' Ishmael answered: 'I will help you!' Abraham continued: 'God commanded me to build Him a House here.' And with that, Abraham raised up the foundation of the House."

7. See pp. 63, 64, and 204 note 10 above.

8. In al-Azraqī, 26, the comment is an obvious insert: "Ibn ʻAbbās says: It is named Maqām Ibrāhīm because of his standing upright upon it *(yaqūlu Ibn ʻAbbās falidhālika summiya maqām ibrāhīm liqiyāmihi ʻalayhi)*." In al-Bukharī (4:381), Abraham stands upon the stone of the Maqām *(ḥajar al-maqām)*. Al-Ṭabarī (*Commentary*, 286) has: "... he stood upon a stone which was the Maqām Ibrāhīm." According to a second telling found in al-Azraqī, "When the building was raised up [Ishmael] brought the *Maqām* near to him. He would stand upon it and build as Ishmael would move it around the sides of the House ..." (p. 31). Mujīr al-Dīn has: "Abraham stood upon a stone while he built, and that place is the Maqām Ibrāhīm" (p. 39). The motif of the stone upon which Abraham stood is included in all renditions attributed specifically to Ibn ʻAbbās, but most do not identify it specifically as the Maqām Ibrāhīm. Whether or not the connection was already made in the minds of the listener is difficult to say; it cannot be determined from this legend whether the association is pre-Islamic. For a synopsis of most extant traditions on the Maqām Ibrāhīm, see M.J. Kister, "Maqām Ibrāhīm: A Stone with an Inscription," in *Le Museon* 84 (1971), 477-91; Cf. G. Hawting, "The Origins of the Muslim Sanctuary at Mecca," in G.H.A. Juynboll (ed.), *Studies on the First Century of Islamic Society* (Carbondale, Ill: Southern Illinois University, 1982), 40-41.

9. Guillaume, *Life*, 84-85, and the ʻAlī and Suddī versions below, etc.

10. Establishing God's House in Mecca contradicted later biblical books, which set the Temple in Jerusalem, but nowhere in Genesis is the latter connection explicitly made.

11. Most renditions place this connection in the order given in the paradigmatic version. Some, however, place it before motif (5) (al-Azraqī 26, al-Bukhārī 4:381, al-Ṭabarī *Commentary* 286, Ibn Kathīr *Commentary* 1:177).

12. Cf. Hawting, "Origins," 23-28. Despite a few tenuous parallels, Hawting makes a strong case for connecting the pre-Islamic Meccan sanctuary tradition with Biblical and post-biblical Jewish lore.

13. As opposed to the version attributed to Ibn 'Abbās, which had Abraham journey to Mecca to establish Ishmael there.

14. Al-Azraqī 28-9; al-Ṭabarī, *History*, 275, *Commentary*, 1:555, ibid., ibid.; al-Tha'labī 87-8; Ibn Kathīr, *Commentary*, 1:178.

15. The Ka'ba.

16. The question is based on Qur'ān 3:96f.: THE FIRST HOUSE APPOINTED FOR MANKIND WAS THAT AT *BAKKA*, FULL OF BLESSING AND GUIDANCE FOR ALL. THERE ARE CLEAR SIGNS IN IT, [AMONG THEM] THE MAQĀM IBRĀHĪM. WHOEVER ENTERS IT IS SAFE.

17. Ibid.

18. One rendition ends here.

19. It is not clear from the narrative whether he brought a stone or not.

20. *(Al-ḥajar al-aswad)*, a stone of probable meteoric origin that has been a part of the structure of the Ka'ba and associated with it from earliest Arab memory (Gaudefroy-Demombynes, 41ff.; Guillaume, 84-7; Wensinck, "Ka'ba" in EI2 4:317, 321f.

21. Al-Ṭabarī, *History*, 277.

22. The presence of the *sakīna* again raises the question of its connection with the rabbinic notion of the *shekhina*. As we mentioned above, the name is used in pre-Islamic rabbinic sources, but the Arab *sakīna* portrayed in our sources has little in common with the rabbinic motif. The fantastic and almost demonic depiction in the Arabic exegetical sources is far different from the portrayal of the "Divine Presence" found in the rabbinic sources. It is also at variance with the use of the word *sakīna* in the Qur'ān itself, which means "quiet" or "tranquility" in most places, but has a similar meaning to the rabbinic *shekhina* in Qur'ān 2:248 (See p. 207 note 42 above.)

23. And Qur'ān 2:125. This interpretation is given also in the name of Mujāhid, and Ibn 'Abbās is quoted as considering the entire Pilgrimage the Maqām Ibrāhīm (al-Ṭabarsī 1:460, s.v. Qur'ān 2:125).

24. This tradition was examined briefly in Chapter 8 above.

25. Al-Ṭabarī *Commentary* 1:551, *History* 275-6; Ibn Kathīr *Commentary* 1:178. Ibn al-Athīr credits ʿAlī with fragmentary renditions of the Maqām Tradition and the Cloud Tradition (p. 106), and al-Azraqī also refers to the Cloud Tradition (p. 27). Ibn Kathīr, who received his tradition from al-Ṭabarī, criticizes its record of authentication and notes that it appears to contradict Qur'ān 2:217 and those traditions stating that Abraham built the Kaba along with Ishmael. He resolves the conflict by assuming that Abraham built a low wall or enclosure when he first brought Ishmael and Hagar to Mecca and completed the structure after Ishmael had grown up. The three complete renditions are virtually identical.

26. See p. 68 above.

27. See Exodus 40:34, Numbers 9:15ff, etc. In Exodus 24:16 God calls to Moses from the midst of the cloud, and in Deuteronomy 31:15 God appears in a pillar of cloud at the Tent of Meeting. The most obvious source for the Arab tradition is the Bible, though the cloud *(ghamāma)* in our legend is a being in and of itself more along the lines of a jinni.

28. Al-Azraqī 27, 29; al-Ṭabarī, *Commentary*, 1:548-9; Ibn Kathīr, *Commentary*, 1:178.

29. A kind of bird of prey larger than a sparrow and dark in coloring, perhaps related to the crow, which is native to the Arabian Najd. It is sometimes regarded as an evil omen.

30. It is not clear from the sources who this is referring to.

31. On *al-ḥijr*, see Uri Rubin, "The Kaʿba: Aspects of its ritual functions and position in pre-Islamic and early Islamic times," in *Jerusalem Studies in Arabic and Islam* 8 (1986), 97-131.

32. Al-Azraqī 27.

33. Al-Azraqī 27.

34. Ibid. 29.

35. *Falidhālika la yaṭūfu bil-bayt mālik min hādhihi al-mulūk wala aʿrabiyyun nāfirun illa ru'iyat ʿalayhi al-sakīna.* This tradition equates the sakīna with the Arabic meaning of tranquility as well as the magic being. In other words, because Abraham built the Kaʿba with the help of a kind of personified tranquility, the best pilgrims also circle it in a state of personal religious calm.

36. Qur'ān 29:41, from which the name of the Sūra "The Spider" *(al-ʿankabūt)* comes, equates the feebleness of pagan worship to a spider's web. Neither al-Ṭabarī's comments and the traditions he cites (*Commentary* 20:152f.) nor Ibn Kathīr's (*Commentary* 5:324f.) offers any particular insight regarding this problem. There may be a special connection between the *sakīna* and the Bedouin, a subject which is, unfortunately, beyond the scope of this study.

37. Al-Ṭabarī, *Commentary*, 1:550; Ibn Kathīr, *Commentary*, 1:178-79, *History*, 245-46.

38. Al-Ṭabarī, *History*, 276, *Commentary*, 17:143.

39. Al-Ṭabarsī 4:97.

40. Based on Q.2:125: . . . WE ENJOINED UPON ABRAHAM AND ISHMAEL TO PURIFY MY HOUSE FOR THOSE WHO CIRCUMAMBULATE IT, ITS DEVOTED INHABITANTS, AND THOSE WHO KNEEL AND PROSTRATE THEMSELVES [THEREIN].

41. That is, the foundations of the Ka'ba that God established in the days of Adam (see below note 47, and p. 220 note 29).

42. The two incomplete renditions end here.

43. A plant found in the Ḥijāz with totally white flowers and fruit.

44. Al-Azraqī 28 defines the *sakīna* as *wahiyya rīḥ khajūj lahā ra's* ("it is a gale wind with a head"). We find the same definition in al-Ṭabarī, *History*, 275, al-Tha'labī 87, Ibn al-Athīr 106, etc. The oldest Arab legends probably described a magic wind which later became associated with the concept of the *shekhina/sakina* as the latter became integrated into Arab culture (Cf. the magic wind in Wahb's *Kitāb al-Tijān*, in Krenkow, 82-83.

45. They first establish the foundations with their pick axes and then build enough of the structure to reach the height of the Black Stone.

46. The emphasis on the corner *(rukn)* and the fact that Ishmael brings a stone that is rejected by Abraham may have significance. Does Ishmael's stone become the *Maqām Ibrāhīm*, which is otherwise unaccounted for in this version? If so, then this would be as complete as the Maqām Tradition, with explanations of the sanctity of the Ka'ba and its major constituent parts, the Black Stone and the Maqām Ibrāhīm. Most likely, Ishmael's rejected stone was not originally associated with the Maqām Ibrāhīm and failed to evolve into that role by the time this version of the legend was transcribed and fixed. The original significance of Ishmael's failure to find a suitable stone was lost but no new significance assigned to it, yet it remained in the sources because it had become fixed in its written form.

47. Many traditions treat the legend of the descent of Adam and the original Ka'ba being established on earth under the very spot of God's eternal Throne. This Ka'ba was to be circumambulated by humans in the same way that God's Throne or the heavenly Ka'ba was circumambulated by the angels. The earthly Ka'ba was raised up to heaven during the Noahide Flood and became the *Bayt al-ma'mūr* (see al-Azraqī 1-20, Ibn Sa'd 35ff, al-Ṭabarī, *History*, 130ff., al-Tha'labī 85ff., etc).

48. See Chapters 13-16 below.

49. Al-Kisā'ī 144f.

50. Ibn al-Athīr 106. According to legend, the original Ka'ba established for Adam and his offspring remained until the days of the great Flood of Noah's generation. In order to protect the sacred Ka'ba and Black Stone from damage, the former was raised to heaven and the latter was kept in a vault in the Meccan mountain known as Abū Qubays.

51. P. 25. See Chapter 11 below. Al-Ya'qūbī also mentions that Mt. Abū Qubays contained the Black Stone without specifying its special role of keeping it safe during the Flood.

52. Pp. 30-32.

53. The traditional site of Hagar and Ishmael's burial adjacent to the Ka'ba, and associated with other pre-Islamic prophets as well (Rubin, "The Ka'ba: Aspects of its ritual functions . . .", 109-111.

54. *Adam al-awwal.*

55. Cf. Rubin, "The Ka'ba:" 106-7.

56. Ibid. 118-121.

57. 1:161f.

58. 1:471.

59. Perhaps associated with the location of Moses' encounter with the Burning Bush (*al-wādi al-muqaddas tuwan* in Qur'ān 20:12 and 79:16). Al-Ṭabarsī defines the location of Kadā as being a hill in *dhū al-Tuwwin*, which is just outside of Mecca (1:470).

60. Al-Azraqī 27f.

61. See page 91 and note 64 below.

62. *Commentary* 1:179. He gives a similar though not identical rendition in his *History* 246. On Dhū al-Qarnayn, see Montgomery Watt, "Iskandar" in EI2 4:127.

63. Most of these are found in Al-Azraqī, 27, 32.

64. Ibid 29. Ibn Kathīr, *History*, 246. The religious significance of most of these mountains is clear: Mt. Sinai is associated with the biblical revelation; the Mount of Olives with the ascension of Jesus; Lebanon occurs in Hebrew Scriptures no less than 65 times; Jūdī is where Noah's ark came to rest according to Islamic tradition; Ḥirā' is the hill slightly northeast of Mecca where Muḥammad spent a great deal of time in religious devotion and where he was said to have been visited by an angel; Thabīr is opposite Ḥirā' and associated with the sacrifice of Abraham's son.

65. Al-Ṭabarī, *Commentary*, 1:550, 552; 13:231-2; al-Ṭabarsī 1:469; Ibn Kathīr, *Commentary*, 1:175.

66. Ibn Kathīr, *History*, 241-2.

67. Note the term "The Ancient House" *al-bayt al-'atīq* in Qur'ān 22:29 and 22:33. The first reference appears as a statement made to Abraham. The exegetes base their reasoning on Qur'ān 22:26 "the site of the House" *(makān al-Bayt)* which assumes that a structure once had stood on that site (see Ibn Kathīr, *History*, 242-3 for a summary of this view).

68. *History* 241-2, where he quotes Qur'ān 22:26ff., 3:96ff., and 2:125ff.

69. *History* 242-3.

70. The Suddī version also may have begun to develop a comprehensive approach similar to that of the Ibn 'Abbās Abraham-Ishmael cycle (note the three traditions providing a transition from Syria to Mecca on the authority of al-Suddī found in al-Ṭabarī's *History*, 274, 277-78, and in al-Tha'labī 81-82. The two full narratives are outlined above in this chapter).

71. Ch. 49 #667 (2:390-1).

72. Ch. 56 #675 (2:394-5).

73. Al-Ṭabarī, *History*, 258f.

74. Ibid., 264.

75. Ibn Sa'd 46. But the emigration is not complete until he arrives in Mecca (Ibn Kathīr, *History*, 213).

76. And their reward of the slave-girl Hagar who would give birth to the forefather of the Northern Arabs and the Quraysh.

77. See Part Four, The Sacrifice below.

78. All the legends taking place during or after Abraham's emigration are provided in the chapters above.

79. And in other Jewish sources as well. The trials of Abraham occur as early as Jubilies (17:17) and are found in Christian Syriac literature as well (Sebastian Brock, "Two Syriac Verse Homilies on the Binding of Isaac," in *Le Musēon* 99 (1986), 112.

80. Qur'ān 22:27.

81. Some claim that the *kalimāt* are the canonical laws of Islam and that there are thirty groups. Others assume that they are ten qualities or characteristics of Islamic custom *(hiyya khisal 'ashara min sunan al-islām)*. Still others connect them with ten aspects of bodily purity or ritual stations of the pilgrimage.

82. Al-Ṭabarī, *Commentary*, 1:523ff., *History*, 310ff. This rendition is closest to that of PRE.

# CHAPTER 12

1. See also Qur'ān 2:158, 189, 196-202; 3:95-97; 22:27-33; Muḥammad Labīb al-Batanūnī, *Al-riḥla al-ḥijāzīya*, Cairo 1329/1911: pp. 150-208; Gaudefroy-Demombynes, *Le Pelerinage à la Mekke*, Paul Geuthner, Paris 1923; G.E. Von Grunebaum, *Muḥammadan Festivals*, Henry Schuman, New York 1951, 15-50. The lesser pilgrimage or *'umra* is localized only around the Ka'ba in Mecca and can take place at any time.

2. PROCLAIM THE PILGRIMAGE AMONG THE PEOPLE . . .

3. Al-Ṭabarī, *History*, 286-87, 287, *Commentary* 17:144, ibid, ibid, 17:145, ibid; al-Ṭabarsī 4:97, ibid; Ibn Kathīr, *Commentary*, 1:184.

4. Al-Ṭabarī, *History*, 287; *Commentary*, 17:144, 17:145, ibid, ibid, Ibn Kathīr *Commentary*, 1:183-4.

5. Each is found in Ibn Kathīr's *Commentary* 1:183-4 *sub verse* Q2:128.

6. Al-Azraqī 33-34 (Muḥammad b. Isḥāq); al-Ya'qūbī 25-26 (anonymous); al-Ṭabarī, *History*, 287-88 ('Ubayd b. 'Umayr al-Laythī), 289 (the Prophet); *Commentary* 1:554 (al-Suddī); al-Qummī 1:62 (anonymous), 2:83 (anonymous), al-Tha'labī 88 (anonymous); al-Ṭabarsī 1:471-2 (al-Sādiq); al-Kisā'ī 145 (anonymous); Ibn al-Athīr 107 (anonymous); Ibn Kathīr 3:216 (associated with Ibn 'Abbās, Mujāhid, 'Ikrima, Sa'īd b. Jubayr, and others).

7. Ibn Sa'd 1:48 (the father of Hishām b. Muḥammad); al-Ṭabarī, *Commentary*, 1:553 (Qatāda), 17:144 (Ibn Jubayr), ibid. (Sa'īd b. Jubary), 17:145 ('Ikrima); al-Tha'labī 89 ('Ubayd b. 'Āmir); al-Ṭabarsī 1:474 (Qatāda). This list of comments excludes those consisting of exegesis on individual words of Qur'ān verses.

8. The root meaning of *mansik* (singular of *manāsik*) originated as "outpouring" (n-s-k). The Hebrew cognate *n-s-k*, "to pour out," is used in the Israelite cult as *nesekh*, "drink-offering" (Ex. 29:40, 30:9 etc.), among other usages. The Semitic root is probably connected to the pouring of blood onto altars (Noeldeke, "Arabs [Ancient]," 666). The Arabic *mansik* or "place of the pouring out" later came to refer to any place of religious ritual.

9. Only al-Ṭabarsī (4:97) mentions a second opinion, that the person spoken to is the Prophet Muḥammad.

10. A third qur'ānic section is occasionally connected to the Pilgrimage traditions: THE FIRST HOUSE APPOINTED FOR THE PEOPLE WAS THAT AT *BAKKA*, FULL OF BLESSING AND GUIDANCE FOR ALL. IN IT ARE CLEAR SIGNS: [FOR EXAMPLE] THE *MAQĀM IBRĀHĪM*. WHOEVER ENTERS IT IS SECURE. PILGRIMAGE TO IT IS A DUTY PEOPLE OWE TO GOD FOR THOSE WHO CAN AFFORD THE JOURNEY. AS FOR THOSE WHO DISBELIEVE, GOD IS NOT IN NEED OF ANYONE. (3:96-7).

11. Four on the authority of Ibn 'Abbās, one each on the authority of Ibn Jubayr and 'Ikrima, and one lacking a record of authentication.

12. One on the authority of 'Alī, one according to al-Ṣādiq, one attributed to Mujāhid, and one anonymous.

13. One on the authority of Ibn Isḥāq and two anonymous.

14. One on the authority of al-Suddī and one anonymous.

15. Attributed to 'Ubayd b. 'Umayr al-Laythī.

16. 'Ikrima b. 'Abdallāh Abū Abdallāh al-Barbarī al-Hāshimī (d. 105/723) was a client *(mawla)* of Ibn 'Abbās and one of the main transmitters of traditional interpretation of the Qur'ān among the Successors. He transmitted traditions from Ibn 'Abbās, 'Ā'isha, Abū Hurayra, and other famous Companions. He was very well respected in the early period of *ḥadīth* collection (al-Bukhārī, Muslim, Abū Dāwūd, and al-Nasā'ī include his traditions in their collections) but was later considered suspect because of his Kharijite views. He is generally credited with being the first to write a work of Qur'ān commentary of the *genre 'ilm al-wujūh wal-naẓā'ir* (al-Dawūdī 1:389f., Dhahabī 1:95, Abbott 2:100).

17. 'Ubayd b. 'Umayr al-Laythī (d. 74/693).

18. The four Ibn 'Abbās traditions here are given only by al-Ṭabarī in his two works.

19. Wensinck, "Hadjdj," EI2 3:31.

20. If the Minor Pilgrimage ('umra) consisting of the rites associated with the Ka'ba was connected with the Hajj by the early Muslims, it may have been influenced by their knowledge of Muḥammad's special regard for the 'umra ritual. Muḥammad undertook the 'umra a number of times, but completed the Islamic Hajj only once at the very end of his life. Rodinson suggests that his hesitation was a result of the obvious pagan associations with the Ḥajj, whereas the 'umra was associated more closely to the supreme pre-Islamic god, Allāh (Rodinson, *Mohammed* [New York: Random House, 1974], 283-5). Combining the Hajj with the 'umra may have been an attempt to associate the entire rite with monotheism.

21. Al-Ṭabarī, *History*, 286, 286-7, 287, *Commentary*, 17:144, ibid., ibid., 17:145, ibid.; al-Ṭabarsī 4:97, ibid.

22. Al-Ṭabarī, *History*, 287, *Commentary*, 17:144, 17:145, ibid., ibid.

23. *Labbayka Allāhumma Labbayka!* This phrase, meaning essentialy "I am ready and at Your service!" is repeated throughout the Ḥajj ritual from the moment of assuming the state of consecration for the ritual *(iḥrām)*. It is a religious statement of intent that was commonly recited in the pre-Islamic period at religious shrines as well (A.S. Tritton, "Notes on Religion in Early Arabia," *Le Muséon* #72 (1959), 193-95; Faris, *The Book of Idols*: p. 5 and n. 16; M.J. Kister, "Labbayka, Allāhumma Labbayka . . . : On a Monotheistic Aspect of a Jāhiliyya Practice," *Jerusalem Studies in Arabic and Islam* 2 (1980), 33-57; "Gaudefroy-Demombynes, 169; Von Grunebaum, 28f.; Wensinck, "Talbiya", EI1 8:640.

24. The space between the Ka'ba and the semi-circular wall *(al-ḥaṭīm)* running opposite the northwest wall of the Ka'ba. The space is also called *ḥijr Ismāʿīl* because of its association with his burial place. Because the texts are unvocalized, the word could be *al-ḥajar* and simply refer to a stone upon which Abraham stood. This rendering would associate the *ḥajar* with the Maqām Ibrāhīm, since *ḥajar* is often used to describe the stone upon which Abraham stood when building the Ka'ba (see Chapter 11).

25. A variety of messages are employed in the traditions for his call. The most common is, "O People, you are obligated to make the Pilgrimage to the Ancient House!" Other renditions include, "Your Lord has taken a House and commanded you to make Pilgrimage to it!", "O People, God has called you to the Pilgrimage!", "O people! Answer your Lord!", etc.

26. This is the third explanation for the Maqām Ibrāhīm, most clearly rendered in Ibn Kathīr's *Commentary* 3:216: *faqāma 'ala maqāmihi*: "He stood upon his *maqām*." The first explanation is that the *maqām* is the stone or water jug upon which Abraham stood when Ishmael's second wife washed his head (Ch. 10). The second is that it was the stone upon which Abraham stood to reach the upper parts of the walls of the Ka'ba when he and Ishmael built it (Ch. 11).

27. The more complete renditions are found in al-Azraqī 33-34 (Ibn Isḥāq); al-Qummī 2:83 (anonymous); al-Tha'labī 88 (anonymous); and Ibn Kathīr *Commentary* 3:216 (a composite rendition attributed to ". . . Ibn 'Abbās, Mujāhid, 'Ikrima, Sa'id b. Jubayr, and others of our ancestors").

28. The pre-Islamic *talbiya* varied from sacred site to sacred site and was not identical with the litany recited today. Ibn al-Kalbī reproduces a polytheistic *talbiya*: "Here I am O Lord! Here I am! Here I am! Here I am! You have no associate except one who is Yours. You have dominion over him and over what he possesses" (*labbayka Allāhumma labbayka labbayka labbayka lā sharīka laka illa sharīkun huwa laka tamlikuhu wa-mā malaka*. Faris, ibid.).

29. Abraham is not considered by all to be the first person making the Pilgrimage. Angels circumambulated the Ka'ba even before the creation of the world, but Adam is considered by some to be the first human to circumambulate it: "It is said that it [the Ka'ba] was the first house built by Adam on earth. It is said that when Adam was brought down [from Heaven], the angels said to him: 'Circumambulate this house, for we have circumambulated it for two thousand years before you.' Before Adam, there was a house on its site called *al-Ḍurāḥ* [another name for *al-Bayt al-Ma'mūr*]. It was raised up to the fourth heaven where the angels of heaven circumambulated it." (al-Zamakhsharī 1:446, and see p. 215 note 47 above).

30. Al-Azraqī 33-4 (Ibn Isḥāq); al-Ya'qūbī (anonymous); al-Ṭabarī, *History*, 287-8 ('Ubayd b. 'Umayr al-Laythī), 289 (the Prophet), *Commentary* 1:553 (Qatāda), 1:554 (al-Suddī); al-Qummī 1:62 (anonymous); al-Tha'labī 88 (anonymous); al-Ṭabarsī 1:471-2 (al-Ṣādiq), 1:474 (Qatāda): al-Kisā'ī 145 (anonymous); Ibn al-Athīr 107 (anonymous); Ibn Kathīr *Commentary* 1:183-4 (Mujāhid), 1:184 (Ibn 'Abbās).

31. Minor Pilgrimage consists essentially of the circumambulations of the Ka'ba and the ritual running between Ṣafā and Marwa *(al-sa'i)* and is performed independently of the Ḥajj (the Great Pilgrimage), though the Islamic Ḥajj ritual now also includes the rituals of the 'umra. Traditions referring to the 'umra may be found in al-Azraqī 33-34 (Ibn Isḥāq); al-Ṭabarī, *Commentary*, 1:553 (Qatāda); and al-Ṭabarsī 1:474 (Qatāda), and renditions referring to the sa'i may be found in Ibn Kathīr, *Commentary*, 1:183-4 (Mujāhid) and ibid. 1:184 (Ibn 'Abbās). On the Minor Pilgrimage, see Gaudefroy-Demombynes, 192-204, Von Grunebaum, 36. On the sa'i, see Gaudefroy-Demombynes, 225-234, Von Grunebaum, 30, and Calder, "The Sa'y and the Jabīn: Some Notes on Qur'ān 37:102-3," JSS 31 (1986), 17-22.

32. Pre-Islamic accounts describe the procession to 'Arafāt from 'Ukāẓ or other locations.

33. For the names and rituals associated with the various stations of the Pilgrimage, see Gaudefroy-Demombynes, Von Grunebaum, and EI2: "Hadjdj."

34. After the Minā station, there is some confusion as to the order of his activities.

35. The words *'arafa* and *'arafāt* are used almost interchangeably within the sources to refer to a plain about seven miles in length and four in breadth, situated roughly thirteen miles east of Mecca. It is the location where the central ceremonies of the Ḥajj take place. Noeldeke surmises that 'Arafāt may have originally referred to the entire area, whereas the singular 'Arafa may have originally referred to a specific location within it ("Arabs [Ancient]," 668a).

36. Sometimes Abraham throws the stones with Gabriel's instruction. This is one of the explanations for the lapidation or *rajm*, the "stoning," which consists in the Pilgrimage ritual of throwing pebbles at three pillars located in the plain of Minā in a particular order.

37. A standard liturgical phrase.

38. It is unclear whether this is his first or a later appearance at Minā.

39. Rapid pace walking or "running" from a ritual station.

40. "To combine," or "put together."

41. Various traditions explain that these are names for the same place.

42. Al-Ya'qūbī 25-6 only (see Chapter 14 below).

43. *Ḥalaqa.*

44. *Ramā al-jimār* ("threw the pebbles") in al-Ṭabarī *History* 288. There is no mention of the Devil during these lapidations.

45. It is not clear whether this is independent of the second visit to Minā after his stay at al-Muzdalifa/Jam'/al-Mash'ar.

46. See note 41 above.

47. Although the Pilgrimage legends are far more closely connected with pre-Islamic Arab legends than with Biblicist material, Abraham's association with the ultimate religious rite of Islam may also reflect a Jewish outlook. Rabbinic tradition credits Abraham with instituting the morning prayer, the most substantial of daily prayers (BT, *Berakhot* 26b. Cf. Samuel Rosenblatt, "Rabbinic Legends in Ḥadīth," *Moslem World* 35 [1945], 245).

48. The three pillars may be called (1) al-Jamra al-ʻAqaba, Jamrat al-Aqaba, al-Jamra al-Kubrā, or al-Jamra al-Quṣwā; (2) al-Jamra al-Wusṭā or al-Jamra al-Thāniya; (3) al-Jamra al-ʻŪlā, al-Jamra al-Dunyā, or al-Jamra al-Suflā. All three may be referred to collectively as *al-Muḥassab*.

49. Al-Ṭabarī, *Commentary*, 1:553 and al-Ṭabarsī 1:474.

50. Al-Qummī 1:62 (anonymous) and al-Ṭabarsī 1:471f (al-Ṣādiq).

51. Charts listing the Ḥajj requirements according to the four surviving schools of Islamic law may be found in al-Batanūnī, 178, and in *Aḥkām al-zakā wal-ṣiyām wal-ḥajj ʻalā madhhab al-imām abī ḥanīfa al-nuʻmān* (nd:nd), 186-87. A briefer list including the Imāmī and Zaydī Shiʻite schools can be found in al-Sayyid Sābiq, *Al-ḥajj wamanāsikuh* (Cairo, 1961).

52. Uri Rubin notes the quarrels between different early Islamic factions, each claiming that their specific rite was the proper Pilgrimage ("The Great Pilgrimage of Muḥammad: Some notes on Sūra IX," in *Journal of Semitic Studies* 27 (1982), 255.

53. We have noted that Abraham was associated with Mecca in Arabian Biblicist and non-Biblicist lore, but he was not seen as the quintessential Meccan pilgrim until after the first generations of Islam.

54. The change from the pre-Islamic intercalated lunar-solar calendar to the purely lunar calendar may have had a profound effect in erasing the Arabs' pre-Islamic associations with the Ḥajj. If Wellhausen is correct that the pre-Islamic Ḥajj occured in the autumn, or Hurgronje and Houtsma are correct in their theory that it was connected to the triumph over the dying sun, then the original significance of much of the ritual process would be lost as the month of the Ḥajj moved throughout the year cycle. Others have pointed out that the slight alterations of the ritual in Muḥammad's "Farewell Pilgrimage" were designed to make worship of the original pagan deities impossible (Cf. Rubin, ibid., 241-60).

55. Had Muḥammad performed the Ḥajj for some years, or had a Companion or Successor recorded his actions in a more complete manner than they are recorded in the Ḥadīth, we would undoubtedly see greater consistency (Cf. Rubin, ibid., 254-55).

56. The other two are found in al-Ṭabarsī.

57. Al-Dhahabī, 40f.; al-Ṣawwāf, 139. Goldziher was probably the first Western scholar to draw attention to the practice of attributing late traditions to famous early traditionists. Because of the large number assumed even by Islamic sources to be falsely attributed to Ibn 'Abbās, Goldziher considered virtually any tradition with Ibn 'Abbās the ultimate member of the record of authentication to be spurious (*Richtungen*: p. 74).

58. This would not have been the case if he had indeed produced his own *Commentary* (al-Dawūdī, 239; Smith, *Islam*, 41. Cf. Abbott 2:99, who disagrees with the view that Ibn 'Abbās organized his own comments into a written commentary).

59. *Commentary* 1:183-84.

60. Wensinck, "Ḥadjdj," EI2 3:31.

61. Al-Bukhārī, #780 (2:453).

62. Bukhari, #793 (2:459).

## PART FOUR INTRODUCTION

1. Qur'ān 37:102-111.

2. Western scholars have also been divided over whom they believe was intended in the qur'ānic narrative. Geiger (pp. 103ff.) was convinced that it was Ishmael, while Bell ("The Sacrifice of Ishmael," in *Transactions of the Glasgow University Oriental* Society #10) believed Muḥammad originally intended Isaac (Cf. Grunbaum, *Neue Beiträge Zur Semitischen Sagenkunde* [Leiden, 1893], 113ff.; Goldziher, *Richtungen*, 79-80; and Firestone, "Abraham's Son as the Intended Sacrifice (al-dhabīḥ, Qur'ān 37:99-113): Issues in Qur'ānic Exegesis" (*JSS* 34 [1989], 95-131).

## CHAPTER 13

1. That Abraham tells his son he will sacrifice him and that his son willingly consents is nowhere hinted in the Bible text but parallels the account of the Targum (TJ2 on Genesis 22:8 and TJ1 and TJ2 on Genesis 22:10. Cf. Robert Hayward, "The Present State of Research into the Targumic Account of the Sacrifice of Isaac," *Journal of Jewish Studies* 32 [1981], 127).

2. The last line refers to the assumption from the word *linafsih* that all reap the rewards or the punishments for their own deeds, understood by *wamin dhurriyyatihimā muḥsinun waẓālimun linafsih mubīn*.

3. Cf. BR 38:13; BT, *Pesaḥim* 118a, *Sefer HaYashar*, *Noaḥ* 29-30.

4. Most exegetes understood the word *kalimat* (literally "words") to refer to other things (see p. 217 note 81 above).

5. Al-Ṭabarī, *History*, 260ff., al-Tha'labī 77ff., al-Kisā'ī 138ff.

6. Al-Ṭabarī, *History*, 309.

7. Mishnah *Avot* 5:3, *Avot d'Rabbi Natan* 33:2, PRE Chs. 26-31 (pp. 60b-72a), and pp. 92-93 above.

8. Al-Ḥasan al-Baṣrī (d. 110/728), one of the best known teachers, dogmatists, and preachers, known for his great piety.

9. Al-Ṭabarsī 1:453. Al-Ḥasan's opinion is referred to also by Ibn al-Athīr (p. 114).

10. The feminine form, *dhabīḥa* regularly refers to a victim destined for sacrifice in fulfillment of a vow.

11. Qur'ān 11:69-74, 51:24-30, 15:51-59, etc. (see above, pp. 57, 202 note 32).

12. *Commentary* 23:78.

13. Ibid. and al-Tha'labī 93.

14. *History* 302.

15. Ibid. 295.

16. Al-Ṭabarī refers to it in his introduction to the tradition itself (see his *Commentary* 23:77-8 and *History* 301).

17. 23:768.

18. P. 111.

19. 3:348.

20. Jephthah's daughter is an only child just as Isaac is an only child in terms of covenant genealogy.

21. A possibly related motif may be found in Genesis 30:37ff. with Jacob's streaked rods which, though not themselves fertile, cause abundant fertility when looked upon.

22. Guillaume, *Life*, 66-68. The legend reflects other pre-Islamic motifs such as the ways in which Hubal and other gods of the Ka'ba were invoked by pre-Islamic Arabs to assist them in decision-making through the casting of lots.

23. M.J. Kister, "Mecca and Tamīm (Aspects of their Relations)," *Journal of the Economic and Social History of the Orient* 8 (1965), 152.

24. Q.37:83-99.

25. Some exegetes argue that this notion is contradicted by Q.37:12 occurring after the episode of the Sacrifice: AND WE GAVE HIM THE GOOD NEWS OF ISAAC—A PIOUS PROPHET (the traditional arguments supporting each brother as the intended sacrifice are given below in Chapter 16).

26. But to my knowledge, never connected with the character of Abraham or Isaac.

27. See below, pp. 144-151.

28. Al-Ṭabarsī 23:78 mentions that its record of authentication can be found in the books of al-ʻAyāshī and ʻAlī b. Ibrāhīm.

29. Al-Ṭabarī, *Commentary*, 23:82, *History*, 292-4, al-Thaʻlabī 94-5, Ibn al-Athīr 109-10, and Ibn Kathīr 4:15. The two renditions given by al-Ṭabarī in his two sources are virtually identical.

30. A slightly different rendition in al-Thaʻlabī has Satan reply to Abraham's comment that he went to do an errand by saying: "By God, I see that Satan came to you in your sleep and commanded you to sacrifice your own son!" But Abraham recognized him as Satan and said: "Away, O cursed one! It was God, and I will obey His command!" Al-Thaʻlabī's (pp. 94-95) rendition of the Kaʻb version is actually influenced by the Ibn Isḥāq version (see below), as al-Thaʻlabī points out himself when he prefaces the story with: "Abū Hurayra related on the authority of Kaʻb al-Aḥbār, and Ibn Isḥāq related on the authority of others who said: . . ."

31. Al-Ṭabarī, *History*, 303-4, in which Ibn Isḥāq relates the tradition on the authority of some scholars, and Ibn al-Athīr 111-2. A third reference is found in al-Thaʻlabī 94-5 (see previous note) and is essentially the Kaʻb version, though it includes some minor influence from the Ibn Isḥāq version as well.

32. *Samʻan waṭāʻatan.*

33. Al-Qummī 2:225, al-Ṭabarsī 23:77.

34. *Iblīs.* The old man in the preceeding paragraph is not named as the devil.

35. In the full rendition given by al-Ṭabarsī below, Abraham actually brings the knife down onto the boy's throat, but Gabriel turns the knife over onto its dull side.

36. P. 150.

37. It is not attributed to anyone earlier than Muḥammad b. Isḥāq (d. 150/767), a controversial figure assumed to have been forced to leave his birthplace of Medina, either because of his Shiʻite leanings or because he freely transmitted traditions that were opposed by others. One of the objections raised was that he was too free in transmitting traditions treating the military expeditions of the Prophet on the authority of sons of Jewish converts to Islam who remembered the story of Khaybar (Guillaume, *Life* p. xiiif and J.M. Jones, "Ibn Isḥāq," EI2 3:810-11).

38. Uri Rubin, "Prophets and Progenitors in the Early Shiʻa Tradition," *Jerusalem Studies in Arabic and Islam* 1 (1979), Jerusalem: Magnes Press, 51, 55.

39. If it is a standard Shiʻite view that the intended sacrifice was Isaac, then Ibn Isḥāq's position would lend credence to the view that he was not a Shiʻite. The opinion

that the intended sacrifice was Isaac fits into the Shi'ite concept of the *nūr Allāh* ("divine light"), a spiritual possession given to every prophet and to other carriers in the generations lacking prophets, passing ultimately to Muḥammad from Adam through the Jewish prophets, Jesus, Peter, and so forth. This is not a genetic trait (as is the *nūr Muḥammad*) but rather a *waṣīya* or bequest that is passed down through the generations. It is therefore possible for the *nūr Allāh* to pass from Abraham through Isaac, Jacob, etc. (and not through the genetic line of the Arabs from Ishmael) and still reach Muḥammad (Rubin, ibid., 41-65).

40. As is Goldziher's opinion (ibid.).

41. *Tanhuma Vayera* 22 (1:92), *Sefer HaYashar* 61, and *Midrash Vayosha'* in Eisenstein, *Ozar Midrashim* (New York, 1915), 147. The *Sefer HaYashar* rendition is closest to the Islamic renditions and parallels the Ibn Isḥāq rendition closely. The *Tanhuma* and *Midrash Vayosha'* renditions are also closer to the Ibn Isḥāq rendition than the other Islamic renditions, though not as close as *Sefer HaYashar. Tanhuma* may have been redacted as early as the ninth or tenth centuries (on the problem of *Tanhuma*'s origin and sources, see EJ 15:794). *Midrash Vayosha'* may have been redacted in the late eleventh century C.E., though its origin is unknown. *Sefer HaYashar* is assumed to have been redacted also in the late eleventh century, perhaps in southern Spain under Muslim hegemony (Strack, 213, 227, EJ 16:1516f; Cf. *Pesikta Rabbati* 40 [p. 170b], which is assumed to have been composed in the late ninth century).

42. 56:4. Here, the "tempter" is *Sama'el*, the name of a wicked angel later identified in Jewish tradition as Satan. Rashi identifies Samael in BT, *Sotah* 10b as the prince of Edom *(sar shel Edom)*, connoting in rabbinic tradition the evil associated with Edom, Rome, and the Church.

43. *Sanhedrin* 89b, but in this version, Satan convinced God to test Abraham in the first place (Cf. BR 55:4).

44. Guillaume, *Life*, 66-68.

45. Ibid. 67.

46. The fact that some Muslim exegetes trace the origin of the devil *(iblīs)* to a jinni points to a parallel pre-Islamic association as well. The Qur'ān also considers the devil to be a jinni in 18:50 but an angel in 2:34, and may be presenting both Biblicist and native views in its two representations. It is quite possible that Jewish or Christian concepts of Satan became part of the pre-Islamic Arabian religious world view. Pre-Islamic jinnis, while exhibiting both good and evil traits, appear to have the ability to serve the same function as Satan with regard to evil temptation or inclination. See Gordon Newby, *The Making of the Last Prophet: A Reconstruction of the Earliest Biography of Muḥammad* (Columbia, South Carolina: University of South Carolina, 1989) 34-35.

47. *Tanhuma, Vayera* 22 (p. 91), *Pesikta Rabbati* 40 (p. 170a-b).

48. Syria is the location in most renditions assuming Isaac as the intended victim. One tradition identifies the location as being two miles from Jerusalem (al-Ṭabarī,

*History*, 273, al-Tha'labī 78). Those supporting Ishmael consider the location to be in the vicinity of Mecca.

49. 'Abd al-Muṭṭalib and his sacrificial vow (Guillaume, *Life*, 67).

50. It may have been carried out occasionally, but was apparently not a custom, as the condemning remark of 'Abd al-Muṭṭalib's critics attests. Mention of Abraham's vow is also given in some Syriac Christian sources, but the meaning of the vow is not specified (Brock, 72, 109).

51. With the possible exception of the last line of Version 3, which refers to Sarah's fear of being punished for expelling Hagar and Ishmael from the household.

52. Ibn Ḥanbal 1:306-7; al-Ṭabarī, *Commentary*, 23:80-1, *History*, 306-7; al-Tha'labī 95; and Ibn Kathīr, *Commentary*, 4:15. A sixth reference is given by al-Zamakhsharī (3:349) in very brief form: "It is related that he threw stones at Satan when he tried to tempt him from sacrificing his son."

53. One of three pillars at which the ritual of the Lapidation takes place during the Pilgrimage (see pp. 98f, 222 note 48 above).

54. Only Ibn Ḥanbal assumes it is Isaac. Al-Tha'labī's rendition ends here with: "Then Abraham proceeded to fulfill the command of God, and that is the story of the Sacrifice".

55. This tradition is probably made up of two slightly different covariants, though the small number of renditions makes it impossible to confirm. One, where Satan appears only at the first two Jamras, places Ishmael in the role of the intended sacrifice (al-Ṭabarī, *Commentary*, 23:80-1, *History*, 306-7, Ibn Kathīr 4:15.). The other either names the intended victim as Isaac or remains silent and has Satan appearing to Abraham three times (Ibn Ḥanbal ibid., al-Kisā'ī 95).

## CHAPTER 14

1. Al-Ṭabarī, *Commentary*, 23:78, *History* 302-3; al-Tha'labī 21; al-Ṭabarsī 23:76-77, and Mujīr al-Dīn 40. Al-Ṭabarī's *history* rendition has a chain of authorities that continues beyond al-Suddī to Abū Mālik and Abū Ṣaliḥ + Ibn 'Abbās and Murra al-Hamdānī + 'Abdallāh and some Companions of the Prophet.

2. *Qurbān.*

3. Al-Tha'labī's and al-Ṭabarsī's renditions end here.

4. Blank lines represent motifs not found in this version but included in other versions provided below.

5. *Ḍaraba bihi 'ala jabīnihi waḥazza min qafāhi.*

6. See N. Calder, "The Sa'y and the Jabīn: Some Notes on Qur'ān 37:102-3," *JSS* 31 (1986), 22-26.

7. This motif is explained in more detail in other versions. By laying his son on his forehead, Abraham would not be able to see his face. Otherwise, looking at his son's face might have caused him such sadness he would be tempted to desist from the sacrificial act.

8. *Allāhu akbar.*

9. Al-Ṭabarī, *History*, 304-5; al-Thaʿlabī 93-4; al-Ṭabarsī 23:78; Ibn al-Athīr 112.

10. A mountain outside of Mecca.

11. As is proper for most sacrifices.

12. See note 7 above.

13. Al-Ṭabarsī's rendition ends here, though he mentions that the story continues as other versions given previously.

14. Al-Zamakhsharī provides an anonymous hybrid rendition of these two versions as well (3:349-50).

15. See pp. 108-109 above.

16. The tears of Abraham and Isaac.

17. PRE 31 (p. 70b) contains motifs 3, 4, and 5a. *Tanhuma, Vayera* 22 (1:93-4) includes motifs 3, 4, 5a, 11, 12; *Pesikta Rabati* 40 (p. 171a) has 5a; *Midrash Vayosha'* 147-8 contains motifs 5a, 5b, 5c, 7, 11; *Sefer Hayashar* 62-3 has motifs 3, 4, 5a, 5e, 7, 11, 12; *Yalqut Shim'oni, Vayera* 101 (1:445-451) contains 5a, 5c, 5e, 7, 11, 12. 5e is also found in a Syriac verse homily on the binding of Isaac (Brock, 125).

18. *Bereshit Rabbah* 56:8 and both TJ1 and TJ2 on Genesis 22:10.

19. See p. 208 note 52 above.

20. Aside from camels, Islamic sacrifice requires that the animal be laid on its side facing Mecca. In contrast, Qur'ān 37:103 describes laying Abraham's son onto his forehead. Compare with N. Calder's view that the word *jabīn* refers to a geographic location (ibid.).

21. According to some Jewish exegetical renditions, everything about the Sacrifice was to be done according to Jewish law *(halakha)*. See Robert Hayward, "The Present State of Research into the Targumic Account of the Sacrifice of Isaac," in *Journal of Jewish Studies* 32 (1981), 137.

22. This aspect was probably not lost on Jewish readers either but remained a secondary issue.

Foreign origins of specific motifs in any art form, whether it be literature, music, or the visual arts, do not invalidate the native authenticity of that art form as it is created and develops in its native environment. Playing American jazz, for example, on an instrument originally designed for chamber music does not make the music "European."

23. Al-Ya'qūbī 25-6 (anonymous); al-Qummī 2:224-5 (on the authority of Abū 'Abdallāh); al-Ṭabarsī #1, 23:77 (anonymous), and al-Ṭabarsī #2, 23:78-9 (on the authority of Barīd b. Mu'āwiya al-'Ajalī).

24. For explanations of the various components of the Pilgrimage sequence, see Ch. 12 above.

25. See pp. 112-113 above.

26. See pp. 112-113 above.

27. *B'mawsim makka.*

28. The tenth of the month of *Dhū al-ḥijja*, when it is customary for those making the Islamic Ḥajj to sacrifice an animal.

29. *Wataṣaddaqa bilaḥmihi 'ala al-maskīn.*

30. The Qummī & Ṭabarsī #1 renditions.

31. Ibn Ḥanbal 1:306-7 (Ibn 'Abbās + the Prophet).

32. *Commentary* 23:79 and *History* 309 ('Ikrima).

33. Cf. BR 56:3.

34. *Commentary* 23:80 and *History* 307.

35. P. 78.

36. *Bayt al-maqdis.*

37. Cf. TJ1 on Genesis 22:20; *Tanhuma, Vayera* 23 (p. 74); PRE 32 (p. 72b-73a); *Sefer HaYashar, Vayera* (63-4). All provide renditions of the same motif that blames Satan for Sarah's death, for Satan came to her and told her that her husband had completed the sacrifice. When she heard the news, her soul left her. Another version has Sarah die when she hears that her son was almost sacrificed (Cf. *Vayikra Rabba* 20:2, *Kohelet Rabbah* 9:7; and *Pesikta D'Rav Kahana* [Solomon Buber edition, Lyck 1860], 26 *(Aharei Mot)* p. 170b [all of which are nearly identical with the *Yayikra Rabbah* rendition]. A similar motif is found in Syriac Christian sources (Brock, 75-6, 111, 125).

38. Pp. 150-52.

39. Al-Kisā'ī *uses the word, 'ashūra*, which is the name of the fast day adopted from the Jewish Yom Kippur fast (*'asora d'tishri* in Aramaic) but subsequently abolished in favor of Ramadan as a required time of fasting. Among Shi'ites, *'ashūra* is the commemoration of the day of Ḥusayn's martyrdom at Karbala. A number of miraculous or significant events are said to have occurred on this day: Noah's ark came to rest on Mt. Jūdī, and it is said to be the birthday of Abraham, the pre-Islamic Arab prophet Ṣāliḥ, Moses, and Jesus.

40. Compare with al-Kisā'ī's fantastic description of Ishmael's birth (p. 142).

41. Cf. Genesis 21:8.

42. *Al-bayt al-muqaddas.*

43. *Iblis.*

44. Cf. Genesis 22:2.

45. Note that the middle sentence, NOW SEE, WHAT IS YOUR VIEW? is missing from the verse.

46. Compare with *Tanhuma*, *Vayera* 23 (p. 95), *Pesikta Rabbati* 40 (p. 171a); *Yalqut Shim'oni* 101 (pp. 448-49); and *Midrash Vayosha* (p. 148), where God tells an angel to stop Abraham from completing the sacrifice. Abraham will not be swayed even by an angel, since God Himself gave the original command. Finally, God must command Abraham to cease. The Jewish exegesis is meant to explain either the repetition of "Abraham Abraham!" in Genesis 22:11, or the second revelation given in God's name in Genesis 22:15-16.

47. One would assume this refers to the feast known as *'īd al-aḍḥā* (the "Sacrificial Feast") or *'īd al-kabīr* ("Greater Festival"). It lasts three days of the Ḥajj from the tenth of *Dhū al-ḥijja* onward, also known as the *ayyām al-tashrīk*. Yet this vague reference to a festival is the only reference in the entire rendition that might be connected to Meccan or Arabian geography. Could the festival referred to here by Ka'b be the Jewish New Year (Rosh HaShanah) festival? The Binding of Isaac in Jewish tradition is closely connected with the ritual and liturgy of the Jewish New Year festival, wherein the important *zikhronot* (remembrance) prayers of the holiday include an appeal to God to remember the binding of Isaac and to count it as meritorious for the Jewish people. The blowing of the ram's horn on that day is connected with the ram that was sacrificed in place of Isaac (BT, *Rosh HaShanah* 16a), and the entire biblical rendition of the Sacrifice is read solemnly in synagogues on that holiday (BT *Meggilah* 31a). Some Jewish traditions assume that the binding took place on Rosh HaShanah, and some connect it to Passover (Ginzberg 5:252 n. 248).

48. See Ch. 15 below.

49. Compare Lev. 10:2 and the legends about the fire that consumed Nadab and Abihu, the sons of Aaron (Ginzberg 1:187 and 6:74-5 note 382).

50. 'Umayya was born in al-Ṭā'if, situated in the Ḥijāz southeast of Mecca. Many Jews are said to have fled there from wars in Yemen between Jews and Christians during the second half of the sixth century (H.Z. Hirshberg, "Stories of the Torah in Ancient Arabia" [Hebrew], in *Sinai* 18 [1946], (p. 92 n. 1).

51. *History* 308-9.

52. *Fadan laka ḥālī.*

53. Pp. 23-4. A third rendition is given by Hirschberg. Unfortunately, he does not provide the Arabic, but only a Hebrew translation (ibid., 171-75).

54. If the poem is authentic, it would demonstrate that at least some early sources considered the intended victim to be Ishmael.

55. We do not reproduce these technical comments here.

56. *Fanā'*.

57. Pp. 342-45.

## CHAPTER 15

1. Qur'ān 37:107: *wafadaynāhu bidhibḥin 'aẓīm.*

2. Genesis 22:13.

3. Sometimes the ram is described as being dark-eyed and salt-and-pepper in color *(amlaḥ)*.

4. Wa'*il.*

5. Al-Ṭabarī *Commentary* 23:307.

6. Tha'labī 94. See also Ibn Sa'd 32-3, al-Ṭabarī, *Commentary,* 23:86, and al-Ṭabarsī 23:76.

7. Ibn Sa'd 32-3.

8. *Al-janna,* literally, "the Garden."

9. But some later Jewish commentators claim that the ram came back to life again after being sacrificed and burnt to ashes (Ginzberg 5:252 note #246).

10. *Sefer HaYashar Vayera,* 63. PRE Ch. 31 (p. 71b) and Ch. 19 (p. 44a) has the ram created at the evening just before the first Sabbath *(beyn hashmashot)*, as does the Babylonian Talmud (*Pesaḥim* 54a), which is the earliest pre-Islamic source for this motif. The ram, like the well mentioned with regard to the legends about the Zamzam well (pp. 65-66 above), is included in a list of ten things created for specific purposes at the last moment of Creation. The blast of the ram's horn at the Sinaitic Revelation was blown on a horn from this ram, as will be the final blast of the horn on the day of redemption. The tendons of that ram were the strings for King David's harp and its skin became the prophet Elijah's loin-cloth, etc. (PRE ibid. 72a).

11. Al-Tabarī, *Commentary,* 23:86, Ibn Kathīr, *Commentary,* 4:16.

12. *'An yanḥar nafsahu.*

13. See pp. 142-143 above. The motif of redeeming a life for 100 camels is also found in Yemen, where the kings of Yemen and Hayrah accepted 100 camels as blood-money for a murdered man (M. Ajmal Khan, "Jāhilīya: A description of the state and mode of living," in *Studies in Islam* 3 (1966): 179.

14. *Commentary* 4:16.

15. Al-Azraqī 32; Ibn ʻArabī 2:87.

16. The Qur'ān renditions do not mention how the camel was brought forth (7:73-9; 11:61-68; 26:142-159; 27:45-53.), but the exegetical literature cites a miracle where the camel appears out of a rock that had split open (al-Ṭabarī, *History,* 245, al-Thaʻlabī 67, al-Kisā'ī 116, and Ibn Kathīr, *History,* 178).

17. A*ʻyan, Commentary,* 23:87.

18. Wa*'il* or *tays.*

19. *History* 231-2: *Thumma ghālib ma hahuna min al-athar ma'khūdh min Isrā'īliyyāt* ("Now that conflicts with the evidence taken from Israelite Tales"). He also uses the argument to demonstrate that Ibn ʻAbbās could not have said that the redemptive animal was a goat. In these cases, Ibn Kathīr appears to give credence to Israelite Tales as a kind of authentic though non-canonic authority regarding traditions. He is actually employing a kind of modern scholarly methodology with regard to the *content* of the Israelite traditions despite the fact that he deems them hopelessly unsound according to the traditional Islamic methodoloyg critical of records of authentication.

20. See pp. 142-143 below.

21. P. 150 (see pp. 124-125 above).

22. Sheep and goats and even occasional cattle were sacrificed regularly in pre-Islamic Arabia, and were slaughtered more often than camels. The camel is clearly the most likely contender for being a "magnificent sacrifice" in the pre-Islamic context. (Noeldeke, "Arabs [Ancient]" 665).

23. Cf. al-Kisā'ī 72-73.

24. Al-Ṭabarī repeats the exact tradition in his two major sources: *Commentary* 23:87 and *History* 306. Al-Ṭabarsī 23:15, al-Zamakhsharī 3:349.

25. He is referring to the lapidation ritual of the Ḥajj. The lapidation would serve to recall Ishmael's pastoral efforts to recapture the ram through the common practice still seen among Arab shepherds and goatherds in the Middle East today. They can be seen throwing pebbles at lead animals or straying animals in order to direct them on their course.

26. P. 115 above.

27. See pp. 98-99 above. All three tales are clearly related in providing a context for the lapidation ritual of the Ḥajj. The two Satan lapidations must have originated from the same tradition. Because one was used to stress the ritual of the Ḥajj while the other stressed the meaning of the Sacrifice, they grew apart and even became physically separated in their contexts within the sources—one being associated with Pilgrimage traditions and the other with the Sacrifice.

28. Al-Ṭabarī, *Commentary,* 23:82-3 (Ka'b al-Aḥbār), *History,* 294 (Ka'b tells Abū Hurayra); Ibn al-Athīr 110 (anonymous); and Ibn Kathīr, *Commentary,* 4:15 (Ka'b tells Abū Hurayra).

29. Al-Tha'labī 92 and Ibn Kathīr 4:16.

30. Ibid.

31. See pp. 138-140.

32. *Vayera'* 23 (p. 75).

33. Parallels to this legend are found in other Jewish sources as well. In the Palestinian Targum (TJ1 and TJ2) on Genesis 22:14 and in *Pesikta Rabbati* 40 (p. 171b), Abraham prays to God to forgive his son's descendants only on the basis of his merit for not speaking out against God's command, despite its contradiction of God's earlier promises. Merit for the act is generally credited to Abraham alone in Jewish tradition. In the traditional liturgy of the daily morning service, the following prayer is said: "Lord of the world, just as Abraham our father withheld his own compassion in order to do Your will with a perfect heart, so may Your compassion overpower your anger toward us. . ."

34. *Shabbat* 89b.

35. Hans Joachim Schoeps, "The Sacrifice of Isaac in Paul's Theology", in JBL 65 (1946), 385-92.

36. Israel Levi, *"Le sacrifice d'Isaac et la mort de Jésus,"* in *REJ* 64 (1912), 161-184, and Geza Vermes, "Redemption and Genesis XXII: The Binding of Isaac and the Sacrifice of Jesus," in his *Scripture and Tradition in Judaism* (chapter eight), Leiden: Brill, 1973.

37. See TJ1 on 22:1, BR 55:4, 56:8, but also *Tanhuma, Vayera'* 18 (p. 88) and 23 (p. 94), and the many citations given by Levi and Vermes.

38. The honorific *al-aḥbār* is an arabization of the Hebrew, *ḥaver,* which was a title of scholarship both among Palestinian Jews of the Tannaitic period and later among Babylonian Jews as well. Ka'b was a Jewish "learned fellow" before his conversion to Islam and was undoubtedly familiar with a great deal of Jewish narrative exegesis.

39. The Jewish version would have Isaac atone for the future sins of the Jewish people. In the Christian view, Jesus' atonement officially impacts upon all humanity, though the efficacy of the crucifixion really affects only those who believe in Jesus as Christ. Likewise, the Islamic version would allow salvation only for believers. The theme of vicarious atonement expressed by each religious system affects only those who are already adherents of the religious system for which the dogma has been developed. Whether Judaism or Christianity first developed the concept of vicarious atonement will rest on the dating of the Palestinian Targum, which currently appears to represent the earliest source for the concept.

# CHAPTER 16

1. Ibn Qutayba is the first to line up the supporters of each son (1:37-8). He is followed by al-Ṭabarī, al-Tha'labī, al-Zamakhsharī, al-Ṭabarsī, al-Kisā'ī, Ibn al-Athīr, Ibn Kathīr, and Mujīr al-Dīn.

2. A full accounting of the traditionists supporting each candidate is provided in the appendices.

3. P. 25.

4. *Commentary* 23:85f., *History* 299-301.

5. 23:85: *wa-ma'lūm annahu lam yas'alhu dhālika illā fī ḥālin lam yakun lahu fīhi walad min al-ṣāliḥīn.*

6. Al-Ṭabarī supports this view in his *Commentary* 23:289 by citing six reports on the authority of Qatāda, al-Suddī, and Ibn 'Abbās (four renditions on Ibn 'Abbās' authority) claiming that the intended victim was indeed Isaac.

7. Pp. 289-90.

8. Ibid., 299-300.

9. P. 58.

10. P. 354. For this tradition see pp. 142-143 below.

11. Al-Tha'labī p. 91.

12. P. 93.

13. 3:351.

14. 3:347.

15. As in Q.37:101: SO WE GAVE HIM THE GOOD NEWS OF A PATIENT AND FORBEARING SON *(wa-basharnāhu bi-ghulām ḥalīm).*

16. *Min al-ṣābirīn.*

17. 3:350.

18. *Wasafahu bil-ṣabr.*

19. *Kullun min al-ṣābirīn.* This quotation is actually a mixing together of two Qur'ān verses: 21:85: ISHMAEL, IDRIS, AND DHŪ AL-KIFL, ALL OF THEM PATIENTLY ENDURING, and 38:48: AND REMEMBER ISHMAEL, ELISHA AND DHŪ AL-KIFL, ALL OF THEM OUTSTANDING *(kullun min al-akhyār).*

20. 23:74-5.

21. *Ahl al-kitābayn.*

22. 23:75.

23. 110-11.

24. *History* 234.

25. Al-Suhaylī would therefore break up the verse as follows: *Fabashsharnāha bi'isḥāq. Wamin warā'i isḥāq ya'qūb.*

26. Ibid.

27. *Commentary* 4:14.

28. This refers to the Q.37:101 verse just given. The fact that the announcement regarding Isaac in 11:71 is closer to the beginning of the Qur'ān makes no difference because of the lack of chronological ordering of the Qur'ān.

29. I.e., Ishmael is still Abraham's son, even though he is living in Mecca rather than with Abraham's family in Syria.

30. *Ta'wīl wa-taḥrīf.*

31. *Walaysa dhālika fī kitābin walā sunna.*

32. Note here and in other instances that despite the public disregard for the traditions of the People of the Book, Muslims even in Ibn Kathīr's day felt the need to provide an answer to the claims of the Israelite Tales.

33. 4:17.

34. Pp. 232-33.

35. *Al-nuskha min al-mu'arraba.* Did Ibn Kathīr have in his possession an Arabic Bible in which it was written that Isaac was the first-born, or was this a Biblicist legend?

36. P. 41.

37. Al-Ṭabarī, *Commentary*, 23:83, *History*, 295; al-Tha'labī 91; Ibn Kathīr, *Commentary*, 4:17.

38. Al-Ṭabarī, *History*, 295; Ibn Kathīr, *Commentary*, 4:17. These renditions are cited after the Abū Maysara renditions are given in full, and their literary content *(matn)* is not provided. They simply have: "Joseph said the same thing to the king," or "the same thing was said."

39. The king is never referred to as Pharaoh *(far'ūn)*.

40. Al-Ṭabari, *Commentary*, 23:82 ('Abdallāh b. 'Umayr), ibid. ('Abdallāh b. 'Ubayd b. 'Umayr), *History*, 294 (the father of 'Abdallāh b. 'Ubayd b. 'Umayr), ibid. (idem.); al-Tha'labī 91 (the great grandfather of 'Ubayd Allāh b. 'Ubayd b. 'Umayr); Ibn al-Athīr 110 ('Ubayd b. 'Umayr); Ibn Kathīr 4:17 (the father of 'Abdallāh b. 'Ubayd b. 'Umayr). On the issue of family chains in records of authentication, see Abbott 2:36-39.

41. A parallel can be found in BT, *Shabbat* 30a: "When Israel sinned in the wilderness, Moses stood before the Holy One Blessed be He and gave prayers and supplications before Him but was not answered. Yet when he said: 'Remember Abraham, Isaac, and Jacob your servants' (Exodus 32:13), he was answered immediately." Cf. BT, *Sanhedrin* 107a: "Rav Judah said in the name of Rav: One should never bring oneself to a trial, for David, king of Israel brought himself to a trial and failed. He said: 'O Lord of the Universe! Why do we say 'God of Abraham, God of Isaac, and God of Jacob' but not 'God of David'? [God] replied: 'They were tried by Me, but you were not.' [David] said: 'Lord of the Universe, try me, test me!', as it is written, 'Examine me, O Lord, and test me' (Psalm 26:1).

42. Al-Zamakhsharī 3:350. Muḥammad b. Ka'b al-Quraẓī is a well-known traditionist of the school of Ibn 'Abbās, lived in the first Islamic century (d. 735) and was of Jewish origin (Helmut Gatje, *The Qur'ān and its Exegesis* [Berkeley: U. of California Press, 1976], 33).

43. *Mujtahid banī Isrā'īl.*

44. Al-Ṭabarī, *Commentary*, 23:81, *History* 292; al-Tha'labī 91; Ibn Kathīr *Commentary*, 4:17.

45. This is based upon the repeating biblical motif of God recognizing the three patriarchs Abraham, Isaac, and Jacob (Ex.3:6, 15; 4:5; 6:31; 1 Kings 18:36; 2 Kings 13:33, etc.).

46. The Bible is the logical source for the Arabic honorific for Abraham: *al-Khalīl*, "the friend (of God)." Clear parallels can be found in 2 Chronicles 20:7: "O our God, You dispossessed the inhabitants of this land before Your people Israel, and You gave it to the descendants of Your friend *(ohavkha)* Abraham for ever."; and Isaiah 41:8: "But you, Israel, My servant *('avdī)*, Jacob, whom I have chosen *(asher baḥartikha)*, Seed of Abraham My friend *(ohavī)*. . . ." Isaac is not mentioned. Rabbinic tradition does not refer to Isaac with a special honorific title, though he is referred to in the Midrash as the one bound up for slaughter: " 'And the two of them walked on together' (Genesis 22:6): one to bind and the other to be bound *(zeh la'aqod v'zeh le'aqed)*, one to slaughter and the other to be slaughtered *(zeh lishḥot v'zeh leshaḥet)*" (BR 56:3). A Jewish poem found in the Cairo Geniza, however, refers to Abraham as "friend," Isaac as "sacrifice," and Jacob as "prince" and "Israel" (Newby, *History*, 56 and 139 note 33. See also p. 201 note 25 above.

47. Al-Ṭabarī, *Commentary*, 23:84 ('Āmir), ibid (al-Sha'bī), *History* 297-8 ('Āmir), 298 (al-Sha'bī), 306 (Ibn 'Abbās); Al-Tha'labī (Ibn 'Abbās); al-Zamakhsharī (anonymous); Ibn al-Athīr 110 (Abū Ṭufayl and al-Sha'bī); Ibn Kathīr, *Commentary*, 4:15 (Ibn 'Abbās), 4:17 (Ṣafya bt. Shayba), ibid. (Sufyān), *History* 232 (Ṣafya bt. Shayba, ibid. (Sufyān), ibid. (Ibn 'Abbās).

48. *Mizāb.*

49. According to al-Tha'labī 93. The Sufyān renditions also refer to the burning of the Ka'ba, but they do not give the time of the incident. Al-Tha'labī is referring to

the act of al-Ḥuṣayn b. Numayr al-Sakūnī, who set siege to Mecca and pelted the Ka'ba with catapults in 683 C.E. The Ka'ba caught fire at this time and was burnt to the ground. Al-Ḥajjāj put Mecca to siege in 692 and eventually killed Ibn al-Zubayr, the counter-caliph to the Umayyad 'Abd al-Mālik, but the destruction of the Ka'ba took place nine years earlier under the Caliphate of Yazīd (Kharbūtlī, 158-61; Hitti, 189-93).

50. Ibn Kathīr, *Commentary*, 4:17, *History*, 232.

51. The full tradition is found in al-Ṭabarī, *Commentary*, 23:85 (al-Ṣunābiḥī), *History*, 290-1 (al-Ṣunābihī); al-Tha'labī 93 (al-Ṣabāḥī); Ibn al-Athīr 108 (al-Ṣunābiḥī); Ibn Kathīr, *Commentary*, 4:18 (al-Ṣunābiḥī); and Mujīr al-Dīn 41 (al-Ṣahājī). Al-Zamakhsharī 3:350 gives a slightly shorter anonymous tradition, and the references are found in al-Qummī 2:226; al-Ṭabarsī 23:75; al-Kisā'ī 152; and Ibn Kathīr *History* 235.

52. A companion of the Prophet who eventually became Caliph, and was proclaimed as such in Jerusalem in 660 C.E.

53. *Anā ibn dhabīḥayn.*

54. Pp. 97-100 (Guillaume, *Life*, 66-68).

55. Al-Ṭabarī identifies them as the two idols of Quraysh at which the people slaughtered their sacrifices. Ibn al-Kalbī locates them near the Ka'ba (Faris, *Idols*, 8, 24-5).

56. This parallels the *dhibḥ 'aẓīm* of Q.37:107.

57. Guillaume, p. 67.

58. Also known as 'Umar II, who ruled from 717-720 C.E., and is considered the most (or only) pious Umayyad caliph by later Islamic tradition.

59. Al-Ṭabarī, *Commentary*, 23:84-5, *History* 299; al-Tha'labī 92; al-Zamakhsharī 3:350; al-Tabarsī 23:75; Ibn Kathīr, *Commentary*, 4:18, *History*, 235-6; Mujīr al-Dīn 40-1.

60. *'Ulamā'.*

61. Hayek (p. 116) cites Goldziher (*Richtungen* p. 79) as stating that this tradition marks the transition from Isaac to Ishmael being considered the intended sacrifice among Muslims. This turning point occurred, according to Hayek's reading of Goldziher, during the caliphate of Umar II, although Goldziher does not consider the change so abrupt.

62. Ibn 'Abbās is quite early, of course. If 'Āmir is 'Āmir b. Sa'd b. Abī al-Waqqās, his death date is 104/722-3. Al-Sha'bī died around 110/728, and Sufyān al-Thawrī is half a century later (d. 161/778).

63. Al-Ṭabarī, *History*, 349; al-Tha'labī 97f., al-Kisā'ī 152f., etc. For Biblicist parallels, see Haim Schwarzbaum, "The Death of Abraham in the Apocryphal 'Testament of Abraham' and in Muslim Folklore," *Yeda-'Am* 9 (1963), 38-46; Ginzberg, 1:299ff.

64. P. 26: *barriyyatu al-amūriyīn.* Although possibly connected to the "land of Moriah" *(eretz hamoriyah)* in Genesis 22:2 (compare the Hebrew *hamoriyah* with the Arabic *amūriyīn*), Professor William Brinner suggests that the name may represent an arabization of the Hebrew *emori,* rendering "the Desert of the Amorites." The name is not listed in Yāqūt's geographical dictionary.

65. *Commentary* 23:78.

66. *History* 301-2. Ibn 'Abbās is the penultimate member of this record of authentication, which would contradict the view attributed to him below.

67. Ibid., 308.

68. Ibid., 273.

69. *Commentary* 23:80, *History* 306f. In *Commentary* 23:87 and with a second tradition in his *History* 306, Ibn 'Abbās connects it to Minā, but it is not clear from the incomplete tradition whether or not the context is Abraham's Pilgrimage.

70. *History* 307.

71. *Al-manḥar.*

72. Ibid.

73. Ibid., 303f.

74. Ibid., 287-8.

75. The lack of reference to the Sacrifice in traditions treating Abraham's first Pilgrimage is not uncommon and typifies traditions that pre-date the connection. Yet even Burkhardt only 150 years ago writes that the sacrifice during his Pilgrimage was not connected in any way to the near sacrifice of Abraham's son. Only after the completion of the Pilgrimage did some of the faithful return to Minā and make another sacrifice in commemoration of the attempted Sacrifice (*Travels in Arabia* [London, 1829], 2:65).

76. 2:224-6.

77. As we have suggested in Chapter 14, equating Isaac with the Sacrifice at Mecca appears to represent a specifically Shi'ite view.

78. *Al-mu'tafika* (See above chapter 7).

79. 1:57-8.

80. Ibid., 1:74.

81. See p. 136 above.

82. Al-Tha'labī, 78. Al-Ṭabarī, *History*, 273. The only difference between them is that al-Jabā'ī refers to Jerusalem as *bayt īlyā* while al-Sha'bī uses the more common

*bayt al-maqdis*; al-Jabā'ī has Sarah being sick *(maraḍat)* for two days and then dying after hearing of the Sacrifice while al-Sha'bī has her "linger" *(baqiyat)* for that period before dying.

83. Al-Tha'labī 93; al-Ṭabarī, *Commentary*, 23:78.

84. Al-Tha'labī 93-4; al-Ṭabarī, *History*, 303f.

85. Al-Tha'labī 94 and 95; al-Ṭabarī, *Commentary*, 23:87, *History*, 306, and *Commentary*, 23:80, *History*, 306f.

86. 3:348.

87. 3:349.

88. 23:73.

89. 23:75

90. 23:76-7.

91. 23:77.

92. 23:78.

93. Ibid.

94. 150-1.

95. 111.

96. Ibid., 112f.

97. *Commentary* 4:15.

98. Ibid., 4:15f., *History* 231.

99. 40.

100. Ibid., 41.

101. Qur'ān 37:100.

102. Qur'ān 11:71; 51:28, etc.

103. Qur'ān 37:102.

104. *History* 309.

105. The sources for this schema are al-Ṭabarī, *Commentary*, 23:78 (al-Suddī), *History*, 301-2 ('Abdallāh & Companions of the Apostle), 309 (al-Ṭabarī's own view), 273 (Shu'ayb b. al-Jabā'ī)' al-Tha'labī 78 (al-Sha'bī), 93 (al-Suddī); al-Ṭabarsī 23:76-7 (al-Ṭabarsī's own comment); al-Kisā'ī 150-1 (Ka'b); Ibn al-Athīr (anonymous); Mujīr al-Dīn (al-Suddī, though the last line is changed to place the location in Mecca).

106. At least one Christian Syriac rendition mentions a vow for Abraham: "I have vowed a vow that is for ever. Unto eternity will I fulfil it. And everything that the Lord tells me, that will I perform without hesitation." (Brock, 109).

107. Ishmael is the intended sacrifice in al-Ṭabarī, *Commentary*, 23:80 (Abū Ṭufayl + Ibn 'Abbās), *History*, 306-7 (Abū Ṭufayl + Ibn 'Abbās); al-Tha'labī 95 (Abū Ṭufayl + Ibn 'Abbās, but the name of the intended victim is not mentioned); Ibn Kathīr, *Commentary*, 4:15 (Ibn 'Abbās). Ibn Kathīr provides a second tradition in which he says: "The same except that he said it was Isaac" (ibid.). This most likely reflects an error since it contradicts all the other Ibn 'Abbās renditions. But al-Qummī (2:223f) gives a very different version with the intended victim being Isaac, who makes the Pilgrimage with his mother Sarah and father Abraham. The setting and chronology is nevertheless virtually identical. Al-Ṭabarsī's rendition (23:77) probably follows al-Qummī's. I have suggested above (p. 102) that these constitute a Shi'ite version.

108. Al-Ṭabarī, *Commentary*, 23:87 (Ibn 'Abbās), *History* (Ibn 'Abbās), al-Zamakhsharī 3:349 (anonymous), Ibn Kathīr *Commentary* 4:15 (Ibn 'Abbās). Ibn 'Abbās may perhaps be credited with connecting the lapidation of the pre-Islamic pilgrimage to the Sacrifice as represented in the Qur'ān.

109. *Al-jimār.*

110. Al-Ṭabarī, *History*, 303 (Salama + Ibn Isḥāq); al-Tha'labī 93-94 (Ibn Isḥāq); al-Ṭabarsī 37:78 (Ibn Isḥāq b. Yasār).

111. In the Islamic calendar, the day begins after sunset.

112. Al-Zamakhsharī 3:348.

113. 23:78f (Barīd b. Mu'āwiya al-'Ajalī).

114. This account ties in the biblical story with Mecca and the Pilgrimage but still does not account for Abraham and Ishmael's building of the Ka'ba.

115. Pp. 22-25 (anonymous).

116. Goldziher, *History*, 124; William G. Millward, "al-Ya'qūbī's Sources and the Question of Shi'a Partiality," *Abr-Nahrain* 12 (1971-2), 47-74.

117. Schwarzbaum, "Biblical Legends," 58.

118. As we have mentioned above, however, the character of Ishmael appears to be virtually unknown in pre-Islamic pagan Arabia. It is therefore doubtful whether pre-Islamic legends ever considered Ishmael to have been the intended victim of the Sacrifice.

119. Ibn Sa'd, Ibn Ḥanbal, al-Azraqī, and al-Bukhārī do not provide any chronology.

120. This aspect, however, does not enjoy the consistent repetition that is so pronounced in other sections of the Ibn 'Abbās Abraham-Ishmael cycle.

121. One cannot say that the less standardized Sacrifice traditions attributed to Ibn 'Abbās necessarily belong to the same coherent set of traditions. They are less consistent and may have originated differently.

122. Dagorn, p. 22f.

123. A half a century ago, Westermarck noted that some Morrocan Muslims still held the view that it was Isaac (Edward Westermarck, *Pagan Survivals in Mohammedan Civilisation.* [London: Macmillan, 1933], 162).

## CONCLUSION

1. H. A. R. Gibb, *Modern Trends in Islam,* 73, and J. Jansen, *The Interpretation of the Koran in Modern Egypt,* 27 note 34.

2. See Walter Ong, *Orality and Literacy,* 132-35.

3. Abraham's visits to Ishmael (Ch. 10 above).

4. Barbara Herrnstein Smith, "Narrative Versions, Narrative Theories," in W. J. T. Mitchel, *On Narrative* (U. of Chicago Press, 1981), 209-232.

5. Ibid., 214.

6. See James B. Pritchard, *Ancient Near Eastern Texts Relating to the Old Testament* (Princeton: Princeton University, 1955); Marilyn Robinson Waldman, "New Approaches to 'Biblical' Materials in the Qur'ān," in Brinner & Ricks (eds.) *Studies in Islamic and Judaic Traditions* (Atlanta: Scholars Press, 1986), 47-64.

7. Cf. G. Shaffer, "Origins of Islam: A Generative Model," in *The Eastern Anthropologist* 31 (1978), 355-63.

8. Julian Obermann, "Koran and Agada," in *The American Journal of Semitic Languages* 58 (1941), 25.

9. Such as the Arabian legends of the 'Ād, Thamūd, etc. (Qur'ān 7:65ff; 11:50 ff; 26:123ff, 141ff; 27:45ff; 41:13ff; 51:43ff, etc.).

10. A. J. Wensinck, *Muḥammad and the Jews of Medina* (First published as: Mohammed en de Joden te Medina. Leiden, 1908), trans. Wolfgang H. Behn (Berlin: Adiyok, 1982) 47ff.; Watt, *Muḥammad,* 99.

11. H. G. Reissner suggests that as the "illiterate" *(ummī)* prophet, Muḥammad was trying to appeal to the nonintellectual Jews (i. e., illiterate members of the Jewish masses) whose folklore probably had much more in common with Muḥammad's Arab monotheism than did the traditional lore of the literate Rabbinite Jews ("The Ummī Prophet and the Banū Israil of the Qur'ān," in *Muslim World* 39 [1949]: 276-281). On Muḥammad and his religious confrontation with Jews, see H. Hirschfeld, "Historical and Legendary Controversies Between Muhammed and the Rabbis," in *The Jewish Quarterly Review* 10 (1898), 100-16.

12. There is, of course, the theoretical possibility that the qur'ānic stories circulated in their semi-poetic form rather than in simple prose. This would place them in a similar category to epic poetry in terms of formulaic structure. There does not, however, appear to be any evidence to support this.

13. The Age of Ignorance (Cf. Amin Faris [transl.] *The Book of Idols,* p. vii).

14. See M. J. Kister, "Labbayka, Allāhumma, Labbayka . . . : On a Monotheistic Aspect of a Jāhiliyya Practice," *Jerusalem Studies in Arabic and Islam* II (1980), 33-57; Dale Eickelman, "Musaylima: An Approach to the Social Anthropology of Seventh Century Arabia," *Journal of the Economic and Social History of the Orient* 10 (1967), 17-52; H. A. R. Gibb, "Pre-Islamic Monotheism in Arabia," *Harvard Theological Review,* 55 (1962), 268-280; Uri Rubin, "The Ka'ba: Aspects of its Ritual Functions and Position in pre-Islamic and Early Islamic Times," *Jerusalem Studies in Arabic and Islam* 8 (1986), 97-131, etc. For pre-Islamic influence from non-Arabian environments, see Michael Morony, *Iraq After the Muslim Conquest* (Princeton: Princeton University, 1984).

## APPENDIX 1

1. Also known as *Al-Tabaqāt al-kubrā* (Beirut: 1380/1970). It has been translated into English by S.M. Haq (Karachi: Pakistan Historical Society, 1967-1972).

2. J. W. Fueck, "Ibn Sa'd" in EI2 3:922-3; Ignaz Goldziher, *A Short History of Classical Arabic Literature* (Hildesheim: Georg Olms Verlagsbuchlandlung, 1966), 121-2. Many of the exegetes listed here are the subjects of studies in Arabic and Western languages which, for the purposes of this study, need not be included here.

3. Beirut, 1389/1969.

4. The term "traditionist," not to be confused with traditionalist, refers to Muslims who collected and transmitted *ḥadīth* reports.

5. Goldziher, *History*, 43-4; H. Laoust, "Aḥmad b. Ḥanbal" in EI2 1:272-277.

6. Ed. Wustenfeld as *Chroniken der Stadt Mecca* (Leipzig, 1858; reprint ed., *Akhbār makka al-musharrifa*, Beirut, n.d.) The work is also known as *Ta'rīkh Makka.*

7. J. W. Fueck, "al-Azraqī" in EI2 1:826; Goldziher, *History*, 125.

8. Lahore, 1979.

9. Goldziher, *History*, 43-4; J. Robson, "al-Bukhārī" in EI2 1:1296-97.

10. Cairo, n.d.

11. Goldziher, *History*, 35, 83, 122; Isḥāq Mūsā Ḥuseinī, *The Life and Works of Ibn Qutayba* (Beirut, 1950), 11-46; G. Lecomte, "Ibn Kutayba" in EI2 3:844-47.

12. Ed. M. T. Houtsma (and titled *Historiae*) (Leiden: E. J. Brill, 1969).

13. C. Brockelmann, "Ya'qūbī" in EI1 4:736; Goldziher, ibid., 113, 124; Hitti, *History*, 385; Uri Rubin, "Prophets and Progenitors in the Early Shi'a Tradition," in *Jerusalem Studies in Arabic and Islam* 1 (1979) Jerusalem: Hebrew University.

14. Beirut, 1405/1984.

15. Ed. M. J. De Goeje as *Annales* and referred to in this study as *History* (Leiden: E. J. Brill, 1964).

16. Goldziher, ibid., 46, 122; Rudi Paret, "Ṭabarī" in EI1 5:578-79; Smith, *Islam*, 58-62.

17. Najaf, 1385/1966 (two volumes; also known as *Tafsīr al-Qur'ān*).

18. Goldziher, ibid., 61; Smith, *Islam*, 77-82.

19. Beirut, 1385/1965.

20. Brockelmann, "Mas'ūdī" in EI1 3:403-4; Goldziher, ibid., 124-5; Hitti, *History*, 391.

21. Beirut, n.d.

22. S. M. Stern, "'Abd al-Djabbār b. Aḥmad" in EI2 1:59-60; Rashid Ahmad, "Qur'ānic Exegesis and Classical Tafsīr," IQ 12 (1968), 91-92.

23. Cairo, 1374/1954, also known as *'Arā'is al-majālis fī qiṣaṣ al-anbiyā'* or simply as *Qiṣaṣ al-anbiyā'*.

24. C. Brockelmann, "Tha'labi" in EI1 4:735-36; W. Thackston, Jr., *The Tales of the Prophets of al-Kisa'i* (Boston: Twayne, 1978), p. xvi.

25. Cairo, 1385/1966 (four volumes), and known commonly as *Al-Kashshāf.*

26. Ahmad, 92-6; Goldziher, *History*, 46, 70, 84; Richard Bell and Montgomery Watt, *Introduction to the Qur'an* (Edinburgh: Edinburgh University Press, 1970), 169.

27. Beirut, n.d. (thirty volumes bound into six).

28. Ayoub, 6-7, Musa Abdul, "The Unnoticed Mufassir Shaykh Ṭabarsī," Islamic Quarterly 15 (1971), 96-105, and idem., "The Majma' al-bayān of Ṭabarsī," ibid., 106-20.

29. Ed. Isaac Eisenberg and titled, *Vita Prophetarum* (Leiden: E. J. Brill, 1922). An English translation was made by wheeler Thackston, *The Tales of the Prophets of al-Kisā'ī* (Boston: Twayne, 1978).

30. T. Nagel, "al-Kisā'ī" in EI2 5:176.

31. Beirut, 1385/1965.

32. Goldziher, *History*, 128; Nicholson, *A Literary History of the Arabs* (Cambridge: Cambridge University Press, 1930); Franz Rosenthal, "Ibn al-Athīr" in EI2 3:723-24.

33. Beirut, 1388/1968.

34. A. Ates, "Ibn al-'Arabī" in EI2 3:707-711; Ayoub 6.

35. Cairo, n.d.

36. Beirut, 1402/1982. This work is actually the first two volumes of Ibn Kathīr's history, *al-Bidāya wal-nihāya*, as the editor explains on p. 28 of the 1982 Beirut edition.

37. Ayoub, 4; H. Laoust, "Ibn Kathīr" in EI2 3:817-8.

38. Beirut, 1973.

39. *Al-Uns al-jalīl:* introductory pages (unnumbered).

## APPENDIX 2

1. The number following each name represents the number of times that authority is cited as holding that view among the sources.

# Selected Bibliography

## ARABIC EXEGETICAL SOURCES


al-Asadābādī, Abū al-Ḥasan al-Qāḍī 'Abd al-Jabbār b. Aḥmad b. 'Abd al-Jabbār al-Hamadhānī. *Tanzīh al-Qur'ān*. Beirut: n.d.

al-Azraqī, Abū al-Walīd Muḥammad b. 'Abdallāh b. Aḥmad. *Akhbār Makka* 2 vols. ed. F. Wustenfeld as *Chroniken der Stadt Mecca*. Leipzig, 1858; reprint ed., *Akhbār Makka al-Musharrifa* Beirut, n.d. Volume 1.

al-Bukhārī, Abū 'Abdallāh Muḥammad b. Ismā'īl b. Ibrāhīm b. al-Mughīra b. Bardizbah Abū 'Abdallāh al-Ju'fī. *Al-Jāmi' al-Ṣaḥīḥ*. Lahore, 1979.

Ibn al-'Arabī, Muḥyi al-Dīn Abū 'Abdallāh Muḥammad b. 'Alī b. Muḥammad al-Ḥātimī al-Ṭā'ī. *Tafsīr al-Qur'ān al-Karīm* 2 vols. Beirut: Dār al-Yaqza al-'Arabiyya, 1388/1968.

Ibn al-Athīr, 'Izz al-Dīn Abū al-Ḥasan 'Alī. *Al-Kāmil fī al-Ta'rīkh* 5 vols. Beirut: Dar Ṣādir lil-tibā'ati wal-nashir, 1385/1965 (photocopy of edition published by Tornberg and titled: *Ibn-el-Athiri Chronocon quod Perfectissimum Inscribitur* (Leiden: Brill, 1867-77). Vol. 1 *(Historia Anteislamica)* cited only.

Ibn Ḥanbal, Aḥmad b. Muḥammad. *al-Musnad.* Beirut: al-Maktab al-Islāmī, 1389/1969.

Ibn Kathīr, 'Imād al-Dīn Ismā'īl b. 'Umar. *Tafsīr al-Qur'ān al-'Aẓīm* 4 vols. Cairo: 'Isa al-Bābī al-Ḥalabī, n.d. and *Qiṣaṣ al-Anbiyā'*. Beirut:, 1402/1982.

Ibn Qutayba, Abū Muḥammad 'Abdallāh b. Muslim al-Dīnawarī. *Kitāb al-Ma'ārif.* Cairo: Dār al-Ma'ārif, n.d.

Ibn Sa'd, Abū 'Abdallāh Muḥammad b. Manī' al-Baṣrī al-Hāshimī *Kitāb al-Tabaqāt al-Kabīr* 9 vols. Beirut: Dār Ṣādir lil-tibā'ati wal-nashir, 1380/1970.

al-Kisā'ī, Muḥammad b. 'Abdallāh. *Qiṣaṣ al-Anbiyā'.* ed. Isaac Eisenberg and titled, *Vita Prophetarum.* Leiden: E.J. Brill, 1922.

al-Mas'ūdī, Abū al-Ḥasan 'Alī b. al-Ḥusayn *Murūj al-Dhahab wa-Ma'ādin al-Jawāhir* 4 vols. Beirut: Dār al-Andalūs, 1385/1965.

Mujīr al-Dīn, 'Abd al-Raḥmān b. Muḥammad Abū al-Yaman al-Ḥanbalī. *al-Uns al-Jalīl Bita'rīkh al-Quds wal-Khalīl* 2 vols. Amman: Maktabat al-Muḥtasab, 1973.

al-Qummī, Abū al-Ḥasan 'Alī b. Ibrāhīm b. Hāshim b. Mūsā b. Bābawayhī. *Tafsīr al-Qummī* 2 vols. Najaf, 1385/1966.

al-Ṭabarī, Abū Ja'far Muḥammad b. Jarīr. *Jāmi' al-Bayān 'an Ta'wīl Āy al-Qur'ān* 30 volumes in 15. Beirut: Dār al-Fikr, 1405/1984. and *Ta'rīkh al-Rusul wal-Mulūk.* ed. M.J. DeGoeje as *Annales* and Leiden: E.J. Brill, 1964. Vol. 1.

al-Ṭabarsī, Radī al-Dīn Abū 'Alī al-Fadl b. al-Ḥasan Amīn al-Dīn. *Majma' al-Bayān fī 'Ulūm al-Qur'ān* 30 parts in 6 volumes. Beirut: Dār al-Maktaba, n.d.

al-Tha'labī, Abū Ishāq Aḥmad b. Muḥammad b. Ibrāhīm al-Nīsābūrī. *'Arā'is al-Majālis.* Cairo: Muṣṭafā al-Bābī al-Ḥalabi, 1374/1954.

al-Ya'qūbī, Aḥmad b. Abī Ya'qūb b. Wāḍiḥ. *Ta'rīkh.* ed. M.T. Houtsma (and titled *Historiae*) Leiden: E.J. Brill, 1969.

al-Zamakhsharī, Abū al-Qāsim Maḥmūd b. 'Umar b. Aḥmad "Jār Allāh." *Al-Kashshāf 'an Ḥaqā'iq al-Tanzīl wa'Uyūn al-Aqāwīl fī Wujūh al-Ta'wīl* 4 vols. Cairo: Muṣṭafā al-Bābī al-Ḥalabī, 1385/1966.

## OTHER WORKS

Ahrends, W. *Muḥammad als Religionsstifter.* Leipzig, 1935.

Ali, Yusif, trans. *The Meaning of the Glorious Qur'ān.* Cairo and Beirut: 1938.

Arberry, A.J., trans. *The Koran Interpreted.* New York: Macmillan, 1969.

Asad, Muḥammad, trans. *The Message of the Qur'ān.* Gibralter: Dār al-Andalūs, 1980.

Ayoub, Mahmoud. *The Qur'ān and Its Interpreters.* Albany: State University of New York Press, 1984.

Azmi, Mohammad Mustafa. *Studies in Early Ḥadīth Literature.* Indianapolis: American Trust Publications, 1978.

Baljon, J.M.S. *Modern Muslim Koran Interpretation (1880-1960).* Leiden: Brill, 1961.

Bat Ye'or. *The Dhimmi.* Rutherford, NJ: Fairleigh Dickinson University Press, 1985.

al-Batanūnī, Muḥammad Labīb. *al-Riḥla al-Ḥijāzīya.* Cairo, 1329/1911.

Bell, Richard. *The Origin of Islam in its Christian Environment.* London, 1926.

Birkeland, Harris. *Old Muslim Opposition Against Interpretation of the Koran.* Oslo: I Kommisjon Hos Jacob Dybwad, 1955.

———. *The Lord Guideth: Studies in Primitive Islam*. Oslo: I Kommisjon Hos H. Aschehoug & Co., 1956.

Bravmann, M.M. *The Spiritual Background of Early Islam: Studies in Arab Concepts*. Leiden: Brill, 1972.

Brinner, William M. and Ricks, Stephen D. *Studies in Islamic and Judaic Traditions*. Atlanta: Scholars Press, 1986.

Brinner, William. *The History of al-Ṭabarī. Volume 2: Prophets and Patriarchs* (A translation of Ṭabarī's Ta*'rīkh al-rusul wa'l-mulūk*). Albany: State University of New York Press, 1987.

Brockelmann, Carl. *History of the Islamic Peoples* (Translated by Joel Carmichael & Moshe Perlmann) London: Routledge & Kegan Paul, 1980.

Brown, Francis, Driver, S.R., and Briggs, Charles A. *A Hebrew and English Lexicon of the Old Testament*. Oxford: Clarendon, 1907 (reprinted with corrections, 1957, 1977).

Budge, Ernest A. Wallis. *The Book of the Bee: The Syriac Text*. Oxford: Clarendon, 1886.

———. *Oriental Wit and Wisdom ... Collected By Mar ... Bar Hebreaus* (translated from the Syriac). London: Luzac, 1899.

———. *The Book of the Cave of Treasures* (translated from the Syriac). London: Religious Tract Society, 1927.

Bulliet, Richard. *Conversion to Islam in the Medieval Period*. Harvard University Press, 1979.

Burkhardt, John Lewis. *Travels in Arabia*. 2 vols. London: Henry Colburn, 1829.

Caskel, Werner. *Ghamarāt an-nasab ("The Abundance of Kinship"): The Genealogical work of Hishām b. Muḥammad al-Kalbī*. Leiden: E.J. Brill, 1966.

Crone, Patricia, and Cook, Michael. *Hagarism: The Making of the Islamic World*. Cambridge: Cambridge University Press, 1977.

Dagorn, Rene. *La Geste d'Ismaël d'après l'onomastique et la tradition arabes*. Paris: Champion, 1981.

Dawood, N.J., trans. *The Koran*. Suffolk: Penguin, 1974.

Dawūdī, Shams al-Dīn Muḥammad b. 'Alī b. Aḥmad. *Tabaqāt al-Mufassirīn*. Beirut, 1403/1983.

al-Dhahabī, Abū 'Abdallāh Shams al-Dīn. *Tadhkirat al-Ḥuffāẓ* 4 volumes. Hyderabad: Osmania University, 1377/1958.

Donner, Fred M. *The Early Islamic Conquests* Princeton: Princeton University Press, 1981.

Duri, A.A. *The Rise of Historical Writing Among the Arabs* Princeton University Press, 1983.

Eisenstein, J.D. *Ozar Midrashim.* New York: Eisenstein, 1915.

Emil, Esin. *Mecca and Medina.* London, 1963.

Fahd, Toufic. *Le Panthéon de l'Arabic centrale à la veille de l'Hēgire.* Paris: Paul Geuthner, 1968.

Faris, Nabih Amin (translator). *The Book of Idols. Being a Translation from the Arabic of the Kitāb al-Aṣnām by Hishām Ibn-Al-Kalbī.* Princeton: Princeton University Press, 1952.

Foley, John Miles, ed. *Oral Tradition in Literature.* Columbia, Missouri: University of Missouri Press, 1986.

Friedlander, Gerald. *Pirke De Rabbi Eliezer* (English). New York: Sefer Hermon, 1981.

Gatje, Helmut. *The Qur'ān and its Exegesis.* Berkeley: University of California Press, 1976.

Gaudefroy-Demombynes, M. *Le Pèlerinage à la Mekke: Etude d'histoire religieuse.* Paris: Geuthner, 1923.

Geiger, Abraham. *Judaism and Islam.* Madras, 1898 (repr. New York: Ktav, 1970, and originally published as *Was Hat Mohammad aus dem Judenthum aufgenommen?* Bonn, 1833).

Gibb, H.A.R. *Modern Trends in Islam.* Chicago: University of Chicago Press, 1947.

Ginzberg, Louis. *Legends of the Jews* (7 volumes). Philadelphia: Jewish Publication Society, 1968.

Goldziher, Ignaz. *Die Richtungen Der Islamischen Koranauslegung.* Leiden: E.J. Brill, 1970.

Grunbaum, M. *Neue Beiträge Zur Semitischen Sagenkunde.* Leiden: E.J. Brill, 1893.

Guillaume, A. *The Life of Muḥammad: A translation of Ibn Ishaq's Sirat Rasul Allah.* Oxford: Oxford University Press, 1955.

Guillaume, Alfred. *The Traditions of Islam: An Introduction to the study of the Hadith Literature.* Lahore: Universal, 1977.

Hayek, Michel. *Le Mystère D'Ismaël.* Paris: Mame, 1964.

Heinemann, Joseph. *Aggadah and Its Development* (Hebrew: *Aggadot vetoldoteihen*). Jerusalem: Keter, 1974.

Henninger, Joseph. *Arabica Sacra.* Freiburg, Switzerland: Universitatsverlag, 1981.

Hitti, Philip. *History of the Arabs.* New York: St. Martin's Press, 1970.

Hodgson, Marshall. *The Venture of Islam* (3 volumes). Chicago: University of Chicago Press, 1974.

Hurgronje, Snouck. *Het Mekkaansche Feest.* Leiden: E.J. Brill, 1880.

Huseini, Ishaq Musa. *The Life and Works of Ibn Qutayba.* Beirut: American University Press, 1950.

Jansen, J.J.G. *The Interpretation of the Koran in Modern Egypt.* Leiden: Brill, 1947.

Jason, Heda, and Segal, Dimitri. *Patterns in Oral Literature.* The Hague: Mouton, 1977.

Jeffery, Arthur. *The Foreign Vocabulary of the Qur'ān.* Baroda: Oriental Institute, 1938.

Juynboll, G.H.A. *The Authenticity of the Tradition Literature: Discussions in Modern Egypt.* Leiden: Brill, 1969.

Juynboll, G.H.A., ed. *Studies on the First Century of Islamic Society.* Carbondale, Illinois: Southern Illinois University Press, 1982.

al-Kalbī, Hishām b. Muḥammad. *Jamharat al-nasab.* Beirut, 1407/1986.

al-Kharbūtlī, 'Alī Ḥusnī. *Ta'rīkh al-Ka'ba.* Beirut, 1396/1976.

Khoury, Raif Georges. *Wahb b. Munabbih.* Wiesbaden: Otto Harrassowitz, 1972.

Kister, M.J. *Studies on Jāhilīya and early Islam.* London, 1980: Variorum Reprints, 1980.

Klein, Ernest. *A Comprehensive Etymological Dictionary of the Hebrew Language.* New York: Macmillan, 1987.

Knappert, Jan. *Islamic Legends.* Leiden: Brill, 1985.

Knauf, Ernst Axel. *Ismael: Untersuchungen zur Geschichte Palastinas und Nordarabiens im 1. Jahrtausend v. Chr.*. Wiesbaden: Otto Harrassowitz, 1985.

Lane, E.W. *An Arabic Lexicon* (Parts 6-8 edited by Stanley Lane-Poole). London: Williams and Norgate, 1863-93.

Levi, Reuben. *The Social Structure of Islam.* Cambridge: Cambridge University Press, 1969.

Lewis, Bernard. *The Jews of Islam.* Princeton: Princeton University Press, 1984.

Lord, Albert B. *Singer of Tales.* Cambridge, Mass.: Harvard University Press, 1960.

Mandelkern, Solomon. *Veteris Testamenti Concordantiae (Qonqordantzia LaTanakh),* Tel Aviv: Schocken, 1977.

McNamara, Martin. *The New Testament and the Palestinian Targum to the Pentateuch.* Rome: Biblical Institute Press, 1978.

Margoliouth, D.S. *The Relations between Arabs and Israelites prior to the Rise of Islam.* London: Oxford University Press, 1924.

Montgomery, James, A. *Arabia and the Bible.* New York: Ktav, 1969.

*Mekhilta de'Rabbi Ishmael,* H. Horowitz and I. Rabin, eds. Jerusalem, 1970.

*Midrash Pesikta Rabbati* (with traditional commentaries). Tel Aviv: n.p., 1963.

*Midrash Rabbah meforash perush mada'i ḥadash . . . me'et Moshe Arye Mirkin* (11 volumes). Tel Aviv: Yavneh, 1980.

*Midrash Rabbah* (with traditional commentaries, 2 volumes). Jerusalem: Pe'er Torah, 1970.

*Midrash Tanhuma* (2 volumes). Jerusalem: Eshkol, 1975.

*Miqra'ot Gedolot* (including the Targums and major medieval commentaries on the Hebrew Bible, in Hebrew). Jerusalem: Eshkol, 1976.

Montgomery, James A. *Arabia and the Bible.* New York: Ktav, 1969.

Morony, Michael G. *Iraq After the Muslim Conquest* (Princeton University Press, 1984).

Moubarac, Y. *Abraham Dans Le Coran.* Paris: J. Vrin, 1958.

al-Najjār, Muḥammad Wahhāb. *Qiṣaṣ al-Anbiyā'.* Beirut: Dār al-Fikr, n.d.

Newby, Gordon Darnell. *A History of the Jews of Arabia: From Ancient Times to Their Eclipse Under Islam* (Columbia: University of South Carolina Press, 1988).

______. *The Making of the Last Prophet: A Reconstruction of the Earliest Biography of Muḥammad.* Columbia, South Carolina: University of South Carolina Press, 1989.

Nicholson, R.A. *A Literary History of the Arabs.* Cambridge: Cambridge University Press, 1930.

Nowak, Ursula. *Beiträge zur Typologie des arabischen Volksmärchens.* Freiburg im Breisgau: Albert-Ludwigs-Univeresität Doctoral Dissertation, 1969.

Noy (Neuman), Dov. *Motif-Index of Talmudic-Midrashic Literature.* Bloomington: Indiana University Doctoral Dissertation, 1954.

O'Leary, DeLacy. *Arabia Before Muhammad.* London: Kegan Paul, 1927.

Ong, Walter. *Orality and Literacy.* London: Methuen, 1982.

Pedersen, Johannes. *The Scientific Work of Snouck Hurgronje.* Leiden: Brill, 1957.

*Pesikta d'Rav Kahana.* Solomon Buber, ed. Lyck, 1860.

Peters, Francis E. *Allah's Commonwealth.* New York: Simon and Schuster, 1973.

Philby, Harry St. John Bridger. *A Pilgrim in Arabia.* London: Robert Hale Limited, 1946.

Pickthall, Mohammad Marmaduke, trans. *The Meaning of the Glorious Koran.* New York: Mentor, n.d.

Prince, Gerald. *Narratology: The Form and Function of Narrative*, Berlin: Mouton, 1982.

Pritchard, James B. *Ancient Near Eastern Texts Relating to the Old Testament.* Princeton: Princeton University, 1955.

Robson, James (translator). *An Introduction to the Science of Tradition by Al-Hakim abu Abdallah Muhammad b. Abdallah al-Naisaburi*. London: Luzac, 1953.

Rodinson, Maxime. *Mohammed*. New York: Random House, 1974.

Ṣābiq, al-Sayyid. *Al-ḥajj wa-manāsikuhu*. Cairo, 1961.

Schacht, Joseph. *The Origins of Muhammadan Jurisprudence*. Oxford: Clarendon, 1950.

Schwarzbaum, Haim. *Biblical and Extra-Biblical Legends in Islamic Folk-Literature*. Walldorf-Hesen: Verlag fur Orientkunde Dr. H. Vorndran, 1982.

*Sefer HaYashar*. Tel Aviv: Alter-Bergmann, 1980.

*Sefer Pirqei Rabbi Eli'ezer* (with traditional commentaries, Warsaw Edition). Jerusalem: n.p., n.d.

Sidersky, D. *Les Origines des Légends Musulmanes Dans le Coran it Dans les Vies des Prophetes*. Paris: Paul Geuthner, 1933.

*Siddur Rinat Yisra'el* (Traditional Jewish prayers [Hebrew]). Third edition. Jerusalem, 1976.

*Sifre 'al Bamidbar*, critical edition with notes; ed. H.S. Horovitz. Jerusalem: Wahrmann, 1966.

Smith, Jane. *An Historical and Semantic Study of the Term Islām As Seen in a Sequence of Qur'ān Commentaries*. Missoula: Scholars Press, 1975.

Speyer, Heinrich. *Die Biblischen Erzählungen Im Qoran*. Hildesheim: Georg Olms Verlag, 1977.

Spiegel, Shalom. *The Last Trial*. Philadelphia: Jewish Publication Society, 1967.

Stillman, Norman. *The Jews of Arab Lands*. Philadelphia: Jewish Publication Society, 1979.

Strack, Hermann. *Introduction to the Talmud and Midrash*. Philadelphia: Jewish Publication Society, 1931.

Swartz, Merlin. *Ibn al-Jawzi's Kitāb al-Quṣṣās Wa'l-Mudhakkirīn* (Critical Edition and annotated translation). Beirut: Dar El-Machreq nd (Distribution: Librairie Orientale, 1986).

Sweet, Louise. *Peoples and Cultures of the Middle East* (2 volumes). New York: Natural History Press, 1970.

Thackston, Wheeler M. *The Tales of the Prophets of al-Kisa'i* (Translated from the Arabic). Boston: Twayne, 1978.

Torrey, Charles Cutler. *The Jewish Foundation of Islam*. New York: Bloch, 1933.

Trimingham, J. Spencer. *Christianity Among the Arabs in Pre-Islamic Times*. London: Longman, 1979.

Van Seters, John. *Abraham in History and Tradition*. New Haven: Yale University Press, 1975.

Vermes, Geza. *Scripture and Tradition in Judaism*. Chpt. Eight: Redemption and Genesis XXII: The Binding of Isaac and Sacrifice of Jesus. Leiden: Brill, 1973.

Von Grunebaum, G.E. *Muḥammadan Festivals*. New York: Henry Schuman, 1951.

Waldman, Marilyn Robinson. *Toward a Theory of Historical Narrative: A Case Study in Perso-Islamicate Historiography*. Columbus, OH: Ohio State, 1980.

Wansbrough, John. *Quranic Studies: Sources and Methods of Scriptural Interpretation*. Oxford: Oxford University Press, 1977.

Watt, W. Montgomery. *Muḥammad: Prophet and Statesman*. Oxford: Oxford University Press, 1961.

Wensinck, A.J. *A Handbook of Early Muhammadan Tradition*. Leiden: E.J. Brill, 1971.

______. *Studies of A.J. Wensinck* (New York, Arno, 1978).

Westermarck, Edward. *Pagan Survivals in Mohammedan Civilisation*. London: Macmillan & Co., 1933.

Whiston, William (trans.). *Josephus: Complete Works*. Grand Rapids, Michigan: Kregel Publications, 1960.

Wolfensohn, I. *Ka'b al-Aḥbār and seine Stellung in Hadit und in der islamischen Legendenliteratur* (Frankfurt a/M thesis) Gelnhausen, 1933.

*Yalqut Shim'oni* (critical edition). Jerusalem: Mosad HaRav Kook, 1973.

Zwettler, Michael. *The Oral Tradition of Classical Arabic Poetry*. Columbus: Ohio State University Press, 1978.

## ARTICLES

Abdul, Musa O.A. "The Unnoticed *Mufassir* Shaykh Ṭabarsī." *Islamic Quarterly* 15 (1971): 96-105.

______. "The *Majma' al-Bayān* of Ṭabarsī." *Islamic Quarterly* 15 (1971): 106-120.

______. "The Historical Development of Tafsīr." *Islamic Culture* 50 (1976): 141-53.

Ahmad (Jullandri), Rashid. "Qur'ānic Exegesis and Classical Tafsīr." *Islamic Quarterly* 12 (1968): 71-119.

Bascom, William. "The Forms of Folklore: Prose Narratives," in Alan Dundes (ed.), *Sacred Narrative: Readings in the Theory of Myth*. Berkeley: U.C. Press, 1984.

Beck, Edmund. "Die Gestalt Des Abraham Am Wendepunkt Der Entwicklung Muhammads." *Le Muséon* 65 (1952): 73-94.

Beeston, Alfred F.L. "The Religions of Pre-Islamic Yemen." Joseph Chelhod, ed. *L'Arabie du Sud.* Vol. I (Le Peuple Yemenite et ses Racines). Paris, 1984: 259-69.

______. "Judaism and Christianity in Pre-Islamic Yemen." Joseph Chelhod, ed. *L'Arabie du Sud.* Vol. I (Le Peuple Yemenite et ses Racines). Paris, 1984: 271-78.

Bell, Richard. "The Sacrifice of Ishmael." *Transactions of the Glasgow University Oriental Society* 10: 29-31.

Ben-Amos, Dan. "The Concept of Genre in Folklore", *Studia Fennica* 20 (1976): 30-43.

Ben Zvi, Yitzḥaq. "On the Antiquity of the Arabian Settlements of the Tribes of Israel (Hebrew)." *Eretz Yisra'el.* Vol. 6: 130-48.

Brinner, W.M. "An Islamic Decalogue." William M. Brinner and Stephen D. Ricks, eds., *Studies in Islamic and Judaic Traditions.* Brown Judaic Studies 110. Atlanta: Scholars Press, 1986: 67-84.

Brock, Sebastian. "Two Syriac Verse Homilies on the Binding of Isaac." *Le Muséon* 99 (1986): 61-129.

Caskel, Werner. "The Bedouinization of Arabia." *American Anthropologist* 56 (1954): 36-46.

Culler, Jonathan. "Presupposition and Intertextuality," in *MLN* 91 (1976): 1372-96.

Della Vida, Georgio Levi. "Pre-Islamic Arabia." Nabih Amin Faris, ed., *The Arab Heritage.* New York: Russell and Russell, 1963: 25-57.

Eickelman, Dale. "An Approach to the Social Anthropology of Seventh Century Arabia." *Journal of the Economic and Social History of the Orient* 10 (1967): 17-52.

Firestone, Reuven. "Abraham's Son as the Intended Sacrifice (Al-Dhabīḥi, Qur'ān 37:99-113): Issues in Qur'ānic Exegesis." *Journal of Semitic Studies* 34 (1989): 95-131.

Fueck, J. "The Originality of the Arabian Prophet." Merlin Swartz, ed. and translator, *Studies on Islam.* New York, 1981: 86-98.

Gibb, Hamilton A.R. "Pre-Islamic Monotheism in Arabia." *Harvard Theological Review* 55 (1962): 268-80.

Gil, Moshe. "The Origin of the Jews of Yathrib." *Jerusalem Studies in Arabic and Islam* 4 (1984). Jerusalem: Hebrew University, 1984.

Georges, Robert A. "Toward an Understanding of Storytelling Events," *Journal of American Folklore* 82 (1969): 313-29.

Goitein, S.D. "Isrā'īliyyāt." *Tarbiz* VI (1934-5): 89-101, 510-22.

Goldfeld, Isaiah. "The Tafsir or 'Abdallāh b. 'Abbās," *Der Islam* 58 (1981): 125-35.

Goldziher, Ingaz. "Melanges Judeo-Arabes (IX: Isra'iliyyat)." *REJ* 44 (1902): 63-66.

Griffith, Sidney H. "Comparative Religion in the Apologetics of the First Christian Arabic Theologians," in *Proceedings of the PMR (Patristic, Mediaeval and Renaissance) Conference* 4 (1979): 63-87.

______. "The Prophet Muḥammad, His Scripture and His Message According to the Christian Apologies in Arabic and Syriac From the First Abbasid Century," in *La Vie Du Prophete Mahomet* (Colloque de Strasbourg, 1983): 99-146.

Halperin, David, and Newby, Gordon. "Two Castrated Bulls: A Study in the Haggadah of Ka'b al-Ahbar." *American Oriental Society*. 102 (1982): 631-38.

Hayward, Robert. "The Present State of Research into the Targumic Account of the Sacrifice of Isaac." *Journal of Jewish Studies* 32 (1981): 127-50.

Heller, Bernhard. "Muhammedanisches und Antimuhammedanisches in den Pirke Rabbi Eliezer." *Monatsschrift fur die Geschichte and Wissenschaft des Judentums* 1925: 47-54.

Henninger, Joseph. "Pre-Islamic Bedouin Religion." Merlin Swartz, ed. and translator, *Studies on Islam*. New York, 1981: 3-22.

Hirschberg, H. "Stories of the Torah in Ancient Arabia" (Hebrew). *Sinai* 18 (1946): 92-107, 163-81.

Hirschfeld, H. "Historical and Legendary Controversies between Mohammed and the Rabbis." *Jewish Quarterly Review* 10 (1898): 100-116.

Hodgson, Marshall G.S. "Two Pre-Modern Muslim Historians: Pitfalls and Opportunities in Presenting them to Moderns," in John Nef (ed.) *Towards World Community* (The Hague: W. Junk, 1968) 53-68.

Horovitz, Joseph. "Judaeo-Arabic Relations in Pre-Islamic Times." *Islamic Culture* 3 (1929): 161-99.

Juynboll, G.H.A. "On the Origins of Arabic Prose: Reflections on Authenticity," in Juynboll, G.H.A. (editor), *Studies on the First Century of Islamic Society*. Carbondale, Illinois: Southern Illinois University Press, 1982.

Khan, M. Ajmal. "Jahiliya: A description of the state and mode of living." *Studies in Islam* 3 (1966): 175-84.

Kister, M.J. "Mecca and Tamīm (Aspects of their Relations)," *Journal of the Economic and Social History of the Orient* VIII (1965): 113-63.

______. "Maqām Ibrāhīm: A Stone with an Inscription." *Le Muséon* 84 (1971): 477-91.

______. "Some Reports concerning Mecca. From Jāhiliyya to Islam," *Journal of the Economic and Social History of the Orient* XV (1972): 61-93.

———. "Ḥaddithū 'an banī isrā'īla wa-lā ḥaraja: A Study of an early tradition." *Israel Oriental Studies* I (1972). Tel Aviv University: 215-39.

———. "On the Jews of Arabia—Some Notes" (Hebrew) *Tarbiz* 48 (1979): 231-47.

———. "Labbayka, Allāhumma, Labbayka . . .: On a Monotheistic Aspect of a Jāhiliyya Practice." *Jerusalem Studies in Arabic and Islam* II (1980). Jerusalem: Hebrew University.

Krenkow, F. "The Two Oldest Books on Arabic Folklore." *Islamic Culture* 2 (1928): 55-89, 204-286.

Lapidus, I.M. "The Arab Conquests and the Formation of Islamic Society," in G.H.A. Juynboll (ed.), *Studies on the First Century of Islamic Society*. Carbondale, Ill: Southern Illinois University, 1982.

Levi, Israel. "Le Sacrifice d'Isaac et la mort de Jesus," *REJ* 64 (1912): 161-84.

Lecomte, Gerard. "Les Citations De l'ancien et du Nouveau Testament dans l'oeuvre d'Ibn Qutayba." *Arabica* 5 (1958): 34-46.

Lichtenstadter, Ilse. "Quran and Quran exegesis." *Humaniora Islamica* 2 (1974): 3-28.

Lord, Albert B. "The Merging of Two Worlds: Oral and Written Poetry as Carriers of Ancient Values," in Foley, John Miles, ed., *Oral Tradition in Literature*. Columbia, Missouri: University of Missouri Press, 1986.

Millward, William G. "Al-Ya'qūbī's Sources and the Question of Shi'a Partiality." *Abr-Nahrain* 12 (1971-2): 47-74.

Morgan, Thais E. "Is There an Intertext in this Text? Literary and Interdisciplinary Approaches to Intertextuality," in *American Journal of Semiotics* 3 (1985): 1-40.

Naude, J.A. "Isaac Typology in the Koran." I.H. Eybers, ed., *De Fructu Oris Sui: Essays in honour of Adrianus Van Selms*. Leiden: Brill, 1971: 121-29.

Nettler, Ronald. "Islam as a Religion." *Humaniora Islamica* 2 (1974): 209-214.

Newby, Gordon. "Observations About an Early Judaeo-Arabic." *Jewish Quarterly Review* 61 (1970): 212-21.

———. "Tafsīr Isrā'īlīyāt." *Journal of the American Academy of Religion* 47 (1979 Thematic Issue): 685-97.

Noeldeke, Theodore. "Arabs (Ancient)." Hastings, ed., *Encyclopaedia of Religion and Ethics*. Edinburgh, 1908: 659-73.

Norris, H.T. "Fables and Legends in Pre-Islamic and Early Islamic Times." A.F.L. Beeston, et al., eds., *Arabic Literature to the End of the Umayyad Period*: 374-86.

Noy, Dov. "The Jewish Versions of the 'Animal Languages' Folktale (AT670): A Typological-Structural Study." *Scripta Hierosolymitana* Vol. 22. Jerusalem: Hebrew University Press, 1971: 171-208.

Obermann, Julian. "Koran and Agada: The Events at Mount Sinai." *The American Journal of Semitic Languages* 58 (1941): 23-48.

______. "Islamic Origins: A Study in Background and Formation." in Nabih Amin Faris, ed., *The Arab Heritage.* New York: Russel and Russel, 1963. 58-80.

Ong, Walter J. "Text as Interpretation: Mark and After," in Foley, John Miles, ed., *Oral Tradition in Literature.* Columbia, Missouri: University of Missouri Press, 1986.

Paret, Rudi. "The Qur'ān as Literature." A.F.L. Beeston, et al., eds., *Arabic Literature to the End of the Umayyad Period.* Cambridge: Cambridge University Press, 1983: 206-217.

Petersen, David. "A Thrice-Told Tale: Genre, Theme, and Motif," *Biblical Research* 18 (1973): 30-43.

Polzin, Robert. " 'The Ancestress of Israel in Danger' in Danger", *Semeia* 3 (1975): 81-97.

Rahbar, Daud. "Reflections on the Tradition of Qur'ānic Exegesis." *Muslim World* 52 (1962): 296-307.

Rahman, Fazlur. "Pre-Foundations of the Muslim Community in Mecca." *Studia Islamica.* 43 (1976): 5-24.

Reissner, H.G. "The Ummi Prophet and the Banu Israil of the Qur'ān." *Muslim World* 39 (1949): 276-81.

Renoir, Alain. "Oral-Formulaic Rhetoric and the Interpretation of Written Texts," in Foley, John Miles, ed., *Oral Tradition in Literature.* Columbia, Missouri: University of Missouri Press, 1986.

Rippin, Andrew. "The Present Status of Tafsīr Studies." *Muslim World* 72 (1982): 224-38.

______. "Al-Zuhrī, Naskh al-Qur'ān and the Problem of Early Tafsīr Texts." *Bulletin of the School of Oriental and African Studies.* 47 (1984): 22-43.

______. "The Exegetical Genre Asbāb al-Nuzūl: A Bibliographical and Terminological Survey." *BSOAS* 48 (1985): 1-15.

Rosenblatt, Samuel. "Rabbinic Legends in Hadith." *Moslem World* 35 (1945): 237-52.

Rosenthal, Franz. "The Influence of the Biblical Tradition of Muslim Historiography." Bernard Lewis, ed., *Historians of the Middle East.* Oxford: Oxford University Press, 1962: 35-45.

Rubin, Uri. "Prophets and Progenitors in the Early Shi'a Tradition." *Jerusalem Studies in Arabic and Islam.* Vol. 1 (1979). Jerusalem: Hebrew University, 1979.

______. "The Great Pilgrimage of Muḥammad: Some Notes on Sura IX." *Journal of Semitic Studies* 27 (1982): 241-60.

______. "The Ka'ba: Aspects of its ritual functions and position in pre-Islamic and early Islamic times." *Jerusalem Studies in Arabic and Islam*. Vol. 8 (1986). Jerusalem: Hebrew University, 1986.

al-Ṣawwāf, Mujāhid Muḥammad. "Early Tafsīr—A Survey of Qur'ānic Commentary up to 150 AH." Aḥmad and Anṣārī, eds., *Islamic Perspectives: Studies in Honor of Mawlānā Sayyid Abul A'la Mawdūdī*. Riyadh, 1979: 135-45.

Schoeps, Hans Joachim. "The Sacrifice of Isaac in Paul's Theology." *Journal of Biblical Literature* 65 (1946) 385-92.

Schwarzbaum, Haim. "The Death of Abraham in the Apocryphal 'Testament of Abraham' and in Muslim Folklore." *Yeda-'Am* 9 (1963): 38-46.

Schussman, Aviva. "Abraham's visits to Ishmael—the Jewish origin and orientation" (Hebrew: Mekoro hayehudi umegamato shel sippur bikkurei avraham atzel yishma'el). *Tarbiz* 49 (1980): 325-45.

Shaban, M. "Conversion to Early Islam," in Levtzion, N., *Conversion to Islam*. New York: Holmes & Meier, 1979.

Shafer, J.G. "Origins of Islam: A Generative Model." *Eastern Anthropologist* 31 (1978): 355-63.

Shahid, Irfan. "A Contribution to Koranic Exegesis." G. Makdisi, ed., *Studies in Honor of Hamilton A.R. Gibb*. Leiden: E.J. Brill, 1965: 563-80.

Smith, Barbara Herrnstein. "Narrative Versions, Narrative Theories," in W.J.T. Mitchel, *On Narrative* (University of Chicago Press, 1981): 209-232.

Stillman, Norman. "The Story of Cain And Abel in the Qur'ān and in the Muslim Commentators: Some Observations." *Journal of Semitic Studies* 19 (1974): 231-239.

Taylor, W.R. "Al-Bukhari and the Aggada." *Moslem World*. (1943): 191-202.

Tritton, A.S. "Notes on Religion in Early Arabia." *Le Museon* 72 (1959): 191-95.

Waardenburg, Jacques. "Towards a Periodization of Earliest Islam According to Its Relations with other Religions." R. Peters, ed., *Proceedings of the Ninth Congress of the Union Europeene Des Arabisants Et Islamisants 1978*. Leiden: Brill, 1978: 304-326.

Waldman, Marilyn Robinson. "New Approaches to 'Biblical' Material in the Qur'ān." William Brinner and Stephen Ricks (eds.), *Studies in Islamic and Judaic Traditions*. Atlanta: Scholars Press, 1986: 47-64.

Wansbrough, John. "Majāz al-Qur'ān: Periphrastic Exegesis." *BSOAS* 33 (1970): 247-266.

Watt, W. Montgomery. "The Materials Used by Ibn Ishaq." Bernard Lewis, ed., *Historians of the Middle East*. Oxford: Oxford University Press, 1962: 23-34.

Wensinck, A.J. "The Ideas of the Western Semites Concerning the Navel of the Earth." *Verhandelingen der Koninklijke Academie von Wetenschapen te Amsterdam.* Afdeeling Letterkunde, N.R., XVII/i (1916) and IVIII/i (1918). Reprinted in *Studies of A.J. Wensinck.* New York: Arno Press, 1978: 1-65.

Widengren, George. "Oral Tradition and Written Literature Among the Hebrews in the Light of Arabic Evidence, with Special Regard to Prose Narratives." *Acta Orientalia* 23 (1959): 201-262.

York, Anthony D. "The Dating of Targumic Literature." *Journal for the Study of Judaism* 5 (1974): 49-62.

Zucker, Moshe. "The Problem of 'iṣma—Prophetic Immunity to Sin and Error in Islamic and Jewish Literatures" (Hebrew). *Tarbiz* 35 (1966): 149-173.

# Index


A

Aaron, 45, 107, 110, 203n.3, 230n.49
al-'Abbās b. 'Abd al-Muṭṭalib, 170, 171, 172, 173, 177, 178 195n.46, 203
Abbasid Caliphate, 9, 72, 151, 163, 194n.35
'Abd al-Mālik, 43, 237n.49
'Abd al-Raḥmān b. Abī Sābiṭ, 171, 177
'Abdallāh b. 'Umar, 175, 176, 177, 204n.4
'Abdallāh b. Mas'ūd, 172, 177
'Abdallāh b. Shaqīq, 172, 173, 177
Abimelekh, 37, 50, 188n.17, 191n.26, 197n.4, 198n.10, 199n.15
'Ābis b. Rabī'a, 92
Abū al-Aḥwaṣ, 141
Abū al-Hajjāj, 204n.4
Abū al-Muṭṭalib, 212n.2
Abū al-Qāsim, 64, 73, 77. *See also* Muḥammad
Abū al-Tufayl, 175, 176, 178
Abū Dāwūd, 219n.16
Abū Hudhayl, 171, 172, 173, 177
Abū Hurayra, 9, 30, 32, 33, 34, 35, 36, 37, 39, 40, 111, 132, 170, 173, 174, 176, 177, 189n.1, 190n.5, 191n.30, 192n.33, 219n.16, 225n.30, 233n.28
Abū Ja'far, 175, 176, 178
Abū Mālik, 170, 177, 227n.1
Abū Maysara, 140, 172, 173, 177, 235n.38
Abū Qubays (Mt.), 90, 97, 130, 216n.50
Abū Sa'īd, 33
Abū Ṣāliḥ, 176, 178, 227n.1
Abū Tufayl, 236, 240n.107
'Ād (tribe), 72, 184n.17
Adam *(Ādam)*, 7, 87, 89, 90, 91, 100, 126, 129, 207n.43, 215n.41, 216n.50, 220n.29, 226n.39
Adisha, 206, 211n.17. *See also* 'Ā'isha
'Adnān, 72
Aḥmad b. Muḥammad, 163, 164, 166
'Ā'isha, 219n.16
'Alī b. Abī Ṭalib, 43, 80, 82, 135, 166, 167, 168, 171, 172, 195n.47, 212n.2
'Alī b. Ibrāhīm, 225n.3
Amalekites (tribe), 77, 210n.4
'Āmir, 174, 175, 176, 177
'Āmir b. Sa'd b. Abī al-Waqqās, 237n.62
'Amrū b. Nuḥayy, 89
Angels, v, 23, 52, 53, 54, 55, 56, 58, 61, 108, 109, 110, 144, 147, 199n.2, 202n.26, 207n.37, 215n.47, 220
Apocrypha, 4
'Arafa, 98, 148, 221n.35
Armenia, 68, 86, 87, 88, 165
al-Asmā'ī, 146
'Aṭā', 139 171, 173, 175, 176, 178
Atonement, 133, 134, 233n.39
Aws (tribe), 72
al-'Ayāshī, 225n.128
Ayefa, 211n.17. *See also* 'Ā'isha
Ayyisha, 211n.17. *See also* 'Ā'isha

B

Barīd b. Mu'āwiya al-'Ajalī, 146, 229n.23, 240n.113
Bayt al-maqdis, 140, 147, 187n.11, 229n.36, 239n.82. *See also* Jerusalem
al-Bayt al-muqaddas, 230n.42. *See also* Jerusalem
Beersheba, v, 23, 26, 48, 49, 50, 51, 61, 187n.8, 191n.25, 198n.8, 202n.27, 205n.17
Bishr b. 'Āṣim, 86
Black Stone, 83, 84, 85, 87, 88, 89 ,90, 91, 92, 130, 215, 216n.50
Brinner, 186n.36, 238n.64
al-Burāq, 69, 70, 78, 88, 117, 119, 138, 145, 146, 148, 205n.18, 208n.52, 211n.19
Burhān al-Dīn al-Fazārī, 169

C

Cain and Abel, story of, 129, 131
Circumambulation (in Pilgrimage ritual), 86, 89, 207n.43, 215n.40, 220n.29
Circumcision, 25, 55, 67, 93, 108, 200n.19, 201n.19, 206n.34
Cloud, magic, 68, 69, 83, 85, 86, 87, 88, 90, 91, 207n.45. *See also* Jinni

D

al-Daḥḥāk, 130, 175, 178, 203n.2
David (king), 45, 191, 231, 236
Dawha (tree), 81, 204n.10
Dāwūd b. 'Abd al-Raḥmān al-'Aṭṭār, 164
Day of Watering *(Yawm al-Tarwiya)*, 98, 99, 120, 121, 149
Devil *(iblīs)*, 32, 34, 35, 36, 98, 99, 100, 111, 112, 113 125, 132, 221n.44, 225n.34, 226n.46, 230n.43. *See also* Satan
al-Dhabīḥ (honorific name), 105, 108, 140, 223n.2
al-Dhimma, 42
Dhū al-Kifl, 45, 137, 196n.59, 197n.71, 234n.19
Dhū al-Qarnayn (Alexander), 90, 197n.71, 216n.62
Dhū Tuwwin, 90, 216n.59

E

Eliezer, 201n.19
Elijah *(Ilyās)*, 107, 231
Elisha *(al-Yasā')*, 45, 137
Esau, 3, 39

F

Fatima, 206n.25, 211n.17
Fitna, 43

G

Gabriel *(Jibrīl)*, 41, 56, 57, 64, 67, 68, 69, 70, 78, 83, 84, 86, 87, 90, 98, 99, 100, 101, 108, 109, 115, 117, 120, 121, 122, 123, 132, 149, 207n.39, 221n.36, 225n.35
Galilee, 154
Genealogy, Arab, 5, 25, 33, 37, 39, 61, 72, 73, 74, 140, 141, 151, 156, 163, 179n.1, 191n.32, 194n.39, 195n.52, 197n.62
Genealogy, Biblical, 3, 27, 29, 194n.39, 224n.20
Gerar, 37, 191n.25
Geshem, 3

H

Hagar *(Hājar)*, 23, 43, 51, 85, 92, 117, 118, 137, 138, 145, 147, 148, 149, 192n.37, 194n.32, 202n.31, 204n.10, 205nn.17, 20, 210n.4, 211n.17, 216n.53;

acquisition of, 32, 33, 34, 35, 36, 37, 39, 40, 41;
among the Jurhum in Mecca, 73, 74, 79;
and the Devil, 112;
as matriarch of Arab tribes, 32, 33, 37, 39, 40, 41, 42;
transfer to Mecca, 53, 55, 59, 61, 63, 64, 65, 66, 67, 68, 69, 70, 71, 84, 85, 122
al-Hajjāj, 142, 237n.49
Hāla bt. 'Umrān b. al-Hārith, 77
Hanbalite (school of Islamic law and practice), 163
Haran, 23, 25, 26, 28, 29, 187n.7, 188nn.17, 23, 189n.27, 202n.26
Harūn al-Rashīd, 168
al-Ḥasan al-Baṣrī, 43, 108, 131, 135, 146, 166, 167, 168, 172, 173, 174, 175, 176, 178, 224n.8
al-Ḥaṭīm, 220n.24
al-Hayfā' bt. Mudād al-Jurhumiyya, 77
al-Ḥijāz, 4, 6, 15, 16, 61, 63, 74, 136, 137, 154, 156, 205n.17, 215n.43, 230n.50
al-Ḥijr, 70, 86, 89, 97, 146, 214n.31, 220n.24
Himyar (tribe), 72
Hishām b. Muḥammad Abū al-Mundhir Ibn al-Kalbī, 163, 181n.21, 205n.20, 220n.28, 237n.55
Hit, 89
Holy spirit *(ruaḥ haqodesh)*, 189n.24, 193n.24
Hospitality, 25, 54, 55, 77
Hubal, 89, 224n.22
Ḥusayn, 172, 177
Ḥusayn b. 'Alī, 46, 47, 229n.39
al-Ḥusayn b. Numayr, 90, 237n.49

## I

Ibn 'Abbās, 9, 26, 27, 46, 57, 63, 64, 65, 66, 67, 68, 69, 70, 71, 72, 73, 75, 76, 79, 80, 81, 82, 85, 88, 91, 92, 93, 94, 95, 96, 97, 102, 103, 115, 129, 130, 131, 132, 135, 139, 141, 145, 146, 147, 150, 164, 170, 171, 172, 173, 174, 175, 176, 178, 188n.16, 203n.2, 204nn.4, 10, 211n.21, 212n.8, 213n.23, 218n.11, 219n.16, 223n.57, 232n.19, 236n.42, 238n.66, 241n.121
Ibn Abī al-Hudhayl, 140, 170, 172, 177
Ibn Abī Burka, 173, 177
Ibn Abī Ḥātim, 90, 176, 178
Ibn al-Zūbayr, 90, 142, 237n.49
Ibn Ḥumayd, 84
Ibn Isḥāq, 26, 27, 28, 41, 69, 88, 95, 110, 111, 113, 116, 117, 118, 119, 120, 123, 127, 142, 145, 146, 148, 164, 170, 174, 175, 178, 218n.6, 225n.30, 31, 36, 39, 226n.41, 240n.110
Ibn Jurayj, 86
Ibn Mas'ūd, 141, 170, 171, 173, 174, 177
Ibn Sābiṭ, 170, 171, 172, 173, 177
Ibn Shawdhab, 47
Ibn Taymiyya, 169
Ibn Yasār, 67
Idrīs, 45, 196n.59, 197n.71, 234
*al-Ifāḍa*, 99, 221n.39
'Ikrima, xv, 58, 95, 139, 170, 171, 172, 173, 174, 177, 203n.3, 218n.6, 220n.21
Īlyā, 140, 146, 197n.3, 238n.82. *See also* Jerusalem
Infallibility (of prophets, being *'isma*), 27, 188n.20, 189n.4
Iram (tribe), 72
Isaac *(Isḥāq)*, birth of, 52, 53, 54, 55, 57, 58; and Abimelekh, 50, 197n.4;
as the intended sacrifice, 105, 107, 108, 109, 110, 111, 113, 114, 115, 116, 117, 119, 120, 121, 123, 124, 125, 126, 128, 130, 132, 133, 134, 135, 136, 137, 138, 139, 140, 141, 142, 143, 144, 145, 146, 147, 149, 150, 151, 170, 171, 173, 177, 178, 223n.2, 1, 225n.39, 228n.17, 230n.47, 233n.35, 39, 236n.46, 237n.61, 238n.77, 241n.213;
in relation to Ishmael, 3, 39, 41, 42, 43, 44, 45, 67, 79, 196n.53, 202n.31;

Isāf, 143, 205n.20
Ishmael b. Ezekiel, 46, 47, 197nn.65, 69
*'Iṣma*, 27, 182, 188, 201
*Isnād*, xi, xv, 12, 13, 33, 48, 167, 173, 184n.12, 223
*Isrā'īliyyāt*, 13, 183n.5, 232n.19. *See also* Israelite Tales
Israel Levi, 134
Israelite Tales, 13, 14. *See also* Isrā'īliyyāt

J

Ja'far al-Ṣādiq, 41, 46, 69, 70, 73, 74, 95, 193n.21, 204n.10, 218n.6, 219n.12, 220n.30, 222n.50
al-Jabā'ī *(Shu'ayb)*, 144, 145, 171, 177, 238n.82
al-Jabal al-Aḥmar (Mt.), 91
Jacob *(Ya'qūb)*, 45, 52, 54, 55, 57, 108, 133, 135, 138, 140, 141, 201n.25, 236n.41
al-Jadā' bt. Sa'd al-'imlāqī, 78
Jam', 99, 100
Jamra (the three pillars of the lapidation), 98, 99, 115, 120, 121, 122, 123, 131, 148, 222. *See also* Lapidation
Jerusalem, xv, 3, 26, 48, 81, 124, 140, 144, 145, 146, 147, 168, 169, 187n.11, 196n.61, 208n.52, 213n.10, 226n.48, 237n.52, 238n.82
Jesus *('Īsā)*, 7, 45, 134, 156, 165, 216n.64, 226n.39, 229n.39
Jinni *(jinn)*, 70, 84, 214n.27, 226n.46
Job, 7, 45
Joktan *(Qaḥṭān)*, 3, 72
Jonah *(Yūnus)*, 45, 107, 199n.4
Josephus, 198n.8
al-Jūdī (Mt.), 91, 216n.64, 229n.39
Jurhum (tribe), 46, 72, 73, 74, 75, 210n.4
Jurhumite woman, 73, 76, 149

K

Ka'b al-Aḥbār, 15, 26, 28, 33, 37, 41, 111, 113, 124, 132, 134, 139, 143, 146, 170, 171, 172, 173, 174, 177, 180n.17, 184n.11, 191n.28, 196n.55, 225, 230n.47, 233n.38
Ka'ba, vi, 27, 30, 45, 59, 61, 68-74, 80-101, 103, 112, 120, 121, 122, 136, 141-150, 207n.43, 210n.9, 213n.20, 214, 215, 216, 218, 219, 220, 221, 224, 236, 237, 240, 242
Kahlān (tribe), 72
al-Kalbī, 57, 164, 175, 176, 178, 179, 211n.13
*Kalimāt*, 93, 108, 217n.81, 223n.4
al-Khalīl (honorific name of Abraham), 88, 169, 201n.25
Khazraj (tribe), 72
Kufa, 163, 197n.69
al-Kūlinī, 166
Kutha, 25, 26, 187n.2

L

Lapidation, 99, 100, 103, 115, 121, 123, 131, 132, 147, 148, 151, 221n.36, 44, 227n.53, 232n.25, 240n.108
Lebanon, 91, 186, 216n.64
Literature, oral, ix, 12-18, 15, 16, 17, 18, 50, 66, 139, 153, 154, 156, 157, 158, 165, 184n.15, 185nn.19, 20, 22, 28
Lot *(Lūṭ)*, 23, 27, 28, 30, 45, 52, 53, 54, 56, 57, 66, 107, 108, 109, 110, 124, 127, 142, 143, 147, 149, 188n.17, 192n.4;
  people of (Sodomites), 199n.1

M

Magic cloud, 71. *See also Sakīna*, Jinni
*Mahyam*, 32, 34, 35, 36
Makhūl, 172, 173, 177
*Manāsik*, 94, 95, 218n.8
al-Manḥar, 117, 131, 146, 148, 238n.71
Maqām Ibrāhīm, 77, 78, 81, 83, 84, 85, 87, 88, 97, 98, 210n.6, 212n.8, 213n.16, 23, 215n.46, 218n.10, 220n.24

al-Marwa, 64, 65, 66, 68, 69, 70, 71, 85, 98, 204, 221n.31
Mary *(Maryam)*, 7
al-Mash'ar, 99, 100, 115, 120, 121, 123, 149, 221n.45
Masrūq, 139, 170, 171, 172, 173, 177
al-Ma'zamayn, 99
Mecca, 5, 6, 23, 26, 27, 41, 53, 55, 61, 63, 65, 66, 67, 68, 69, 70, 71, 72, 73, 74, 76, 77, 78, 79, 80-90, 92, 94, 96, 97, 98, 101, 102, 103, 110, 117, 119, 121, 122, 123, 132, 135, 136, 138, 139, 140, 142, 144, 145, 146, 147, 148, 149, 150, 151, 157, 163, 164, 167, 186n.2, 194n.42, 205n.18, 208n.52, 210n.4, 211n.20, 216n.59, 221n.35, 237n.49
Medina, 4, 6, 10, 72, 82, 157, 186n.2, 225n.37
Melkizedeq, 191n.26. *See also* Zadok
Menstruation, 48, 58, 87, 203n.34, 205n.20
Michael *(Mikhā'īl)*, 56, 57
Minā, 98, 99, 100, 113, 115, 117, 120, 121, 122, 123, 131, 132, 145, 146, 148, 149, 151, 238n.69
Moses *(Mūsā)*, 7, 45, 107, 140, 141, 156, 187n.3, 193n.24, 203n.1, 214n.27, 216n.59, 229n.39, 236n.41
Mu'āwiya b. Abī Sufyān, 43, 142, 195n.48, 204n.3
Muḍāḍ b. 'Amrū, 210n.9
Muḥammad b. Ka'b al-Quraẓī, 141, 143, 174, 175, 176, 178, 236n.42
Mujāhid b. Jabr al-Makhzūmī, 58, 63, 67, 69, 70, 71, 86, 92, 94, 95, 96, 97, 102, 124, 130, 135, 172, 173, 174, 175, 176, 178, 203n.2, 204n.4, 213n.23
Muqātil, 46, 57, 139, 173, 174
Mūsā b. Hārūn, 56
Musaylima, 5, 242n.14
Muta'arriba Arabs, 72
al-Muzdalifa, 99, 100, 221n.45

N

Nā'ila, 143
Nahor, 3, 28, 188n.17
Nimrod *(Nimrūdh)*, 25, 33, 34, 93, 108
Noah *(Nūḥ)*, 3, 7, 45, 90, 107, 207n.43, 216nn.50, 64, 229n.39

O

Olives, Mt. of, 91, 216n.64

P

Paran *(Fārān)*, 65, 73, 78, 205n.17, 206n.25
Peleg, 3
Pharaoh *(Far'ūn)*, 33, 34, 35, 192n.10, 235n.39
Phicol, 197n.4
Poet, 126, 127, 208
Poetry, pre-Islamic, 15, 16, 126, 127, 167, 184n.15, 242n.12
Prophecy, regarding Isaac, 54
Prophecy, regarding Ishmael, 39, 41, 42, 43, 44, 66, 194n.35, 196n.53
Prophecy, Shi'ite view of, 193n.24

Q

Qaḥṭān, 3, 72
al-Qāsim b. Abī Barra, 171
al-Qāsim b. Abī Yarza, 172
Qatāda (b. Di'āma), 26, 27, 57, 98, 100, 139, 170, 171, 172, 173, 174, 177, 203n.2, 218n.7, 220n.30, 221n.31, 234n.6
Quraysh (tribe), 43, 61, 72, 75, 79, 89, 90, 114, 143, 149, 194n.42, 217n.76, 237n.25

## R

al-Rabī' b. Anās, 175, 176, 178
al-Rāfiḍa, 43
Ramle, 48
Razzāq, 168
al-Razzāq al-Qashānī, 168
Ri'la bt. Muḍāḍ b. 'Amr al-Jurhumī, 77
Ri 'la bt. Yashjub b. Ya'rub b. Lūzān b. Jurhum b. 'Āmir, 195n.52
al-Rukn, 84, 87, 89, 90, 92, 97, 215n.46

## S

al-Sa'i, 98, 122, 204n.12, 221n.31
Sa'īd, 80, 212
Sa'īd b. al-Musayyib, 175, 178
Sa'īd b. Jubayr, 73, 130, 135, 139, 171, 172, 172, 175, 176, 178, 203n.2, 218nn.6, 7, 220n.27
Sa'īd b. Sālim, 164
Sadūm, 198n.5
Sādūq, 33, 191n.26, 199n.15. *See also* Zadok
al-Ṣafā, 64, 65, 66, 68, 69, 70, 71, 85, 97, 98, 204n.12, 221n.31
Safya bt. Shayba, 142, 236n.47
Sahl b. 'Uqayl, 46, 47
*Sakīna*, 68, 69, 71, 83, 84, 85, 86, 87, 88, 89, 91, 207nn.42, 43, 213n.22, 214n.35, 215n.44. *See also Shekhina*
Sāma bt Mahlal b. Sa'd b. 'Awf b. Hayni b. Nabat, 77
Sama'el, 226n.42. *See also* Devil
Sāmarra (cave), 43, 195n.47
Sarah *(Sārah)*, 3, 23, 61, 70, 74, 76, 92, 202n.26, 240n.107;
  identity of, 27, 28, 29, 30, 188nn.17, 21, 24;
  and the Tyrant, 31-38
  and the angels, 54, 55, 56, 57, 58, 108, 109;
  relationship with Hagar, 40, 41, 42, 43, 51, 53, 63, 66, 67, 68, 206n.33, 227n.51;
  and the attempted sacrifice, 111, 113, 114, 116, 117, 121, 122, 123, 124, 125, 126, 136, 145, 148, 229n.37, 238n.82
Satan *(al-Shayṭān)*, 99, 110, 111, 112, 113, 114, 115, 123, 132, 147, 148, 225n.30, 226nn.42, 46, 227nn.52, 55, 229n.37, 232n.27. *See also* Devil
Schools, 21, 100, 222n.51
Seven, 48, 49, 50, 51, 64, 68, 70, 74, 98, 99, 115, 123, 124, 144, 145, 146, 148, 198n.6, 8, 13, 199n.15, 204n.12 209n.15
al-Sha'bī, 141, 145, 172, 173, 174, 175, 176, 178, 236n.437, 237n.62, 238n.82
Sharī'a, 9, 182n.42
*Shekhina*, 207n.42, 213n.22, 215n.44. *See also Sakīna*
Shem *(Sām)*, 3
"Shi'ite" version, 113, 114, 116, 120, 122, 123, 137, 240n.107
Shu'ayb. *See al-Jabā'ī*
Ṣiffīn, Battle of, 195n.48, 204n.3
Sodom *(al-mu'tafika)*, 53, 54, 145, 187n.4, 199n.1
Sodomites. *See* Lot, people of
Solomon, 7, 45
"Spider tradition", 68, 83, 85, 86, 87, 88, 207n.43
al-Suddī, 26, 27, 28, 33, 56, 57, 58, 67, 80, 82, 83, 91, 92, 96, 108, 109, 116, 117, 118, 119, 120, 123, 127, 130, 135, 139, 144, 145, 146, 147, 170, 171, 172, 173, 174, 176, 178, 203n.34, 212n.2, 217n.70, 220n.30, 227n.1
Sufyān al-Thawrī, 47, 236, 237
Sufyān b. 'Uyayna, 164
al-Sunābiḥī, 142, 143, 237n.51
Surad bird, 82

## T

*Taḥrīf*, 8, 140, 181n.30, 235n.30
*Talbiya*, 74, 97, 103, 180n.18, 209n.19, 219n.23, 220n.28

Tamīm (tribe), 72
Targum, xv, 32, 56, 119, 134, 190n.11, 202n.26, 223n.1, 233n.33
Ṭasm (tribe), 72
Tayma, 4, 154
Ṭayyi' (tribe), 72
Terah *(Āzar)*, 3, 29, 188n.17
Thabīr (Mt.), 91, 97, 118, 120, 121, 122, 130, 131, 145, 146, 149, 216n.64
Thamūd (tribe), 72, 184
Thaqīf, 72
Thighāma plant, 87
Torah *(tawrāh)*, 27 28, 29, 40, 65, 151, 170, 189n.25, 191n.32, 203n.2

U

'Ubayd b. 'Āmir, 218n.7
'Ubayd b. 'Umayr, 96, 140, 145, 170, 172, 173, 177, 219n.4, 235n.40
'Ubayy b. Ka'b, 26, 204n.4
'Umar b. 'Abd al-Azīz (Umayyad Caliph), 143, 144, 195n.45
'Umar b. al-Khaṭṭāb (second Caliph), 43, 74, 92, 171, 172, 177
'Umar b. Sa'd b. Abī Waqqāṣ, 197n.69
'Umayya b. Abī al-Ṣalt, 126, 127, 230n.50
'Uthmān (fourth Caliph), 43
'Uthmān b. Abī Hādir, 172, 173, 177
'Uthmān b. Ṭalḥa, 142

V

Vermes, 134

W

Wadi Saba'. *See* Beersheba
Wahb (b. Munabbih), 15, 26, 28, 29, 30, 33, 37, 40, 73, 90, 164, 184n.11, 188n.16, 191n.28, 205n.18
Well, magic, 23, 43, 48, 49, 50, 65, 66, 67, 68, 70, 81, 142, 197n.4, 198n.8, 10, 12, 204n.14, 205n.20, 231n.10

Y

Yaqūt *(Mu'jam)*, 65, 198n.8
Yazīd (Umayyad Caliph), 237n.49
Yūsuf b. Mihrān, 174, 175, 176, 178

Z

Zadok *(Ṣādūq)*, 33, 34, 37, 191n.26
al-Zanjī, 164
Zayb b. Aslam, 92, 172
Zayd b. 'Amr, 5
Zayd b. Jid'an, 173
Zaynab b. Qays, 212
al-Zuhrī, 139, 171, 172, 173, 177